52 Weeks of Cookies

To my wonderful kids, who have been not only my worry and my vulnerability but also my joy and my strength. My life would be so much less without you.

And to all who serve and the families who support them, especially the FHOTA, who kept my boy safe through two tours to Iraq.

Published by Familius LLC, www.familius.com

Familius books are available at special discounts for bulk purchases, whether for sales promotions or for family or corporate use. For more information, contact Familius Sales at 559-876-2170 or email orders@familius.com.

Library of Congress Cataloging-in-Publication Data
2015955949

Print ISBN 9781942934363
Ebook ISBN 9781942934936
Hardcover ISBN 9781942934943

Printed in the United States of America

Edited by Katharine Hale
Cover design by David Miles
Book design by Brooke Jorden

10 9 8 7 6 5 4 3 2 1

First E...

52 Weeks of Cookies

HOW ONE MOM REFUSED TO BE BEATEN BY HER SON'S DEPLOYMENT

MAGGIE McCREATH

Contents

Introduction

For as long as I can remember, hanging out in the kitchen has been one of my favorite recreational activities. What has become a general love of cooking (and an ever-expanding cookbook collection) began as a bowl-hugging, beater-licking, cookie-dough-stealing mania—a mania which I happily passed on to my own kids. Some of my earliest and fondest memories are of watching my mom in the kitchen sifting flour for a birthday cake, kneading bread dough on the countertop, or cutting out Christmas cookies from homemade, fresh-rolled cookie dough that I would eventually get to decorate. By the time I was six years old, Mom was allowing me my own (closely supervised) ventures into baking. I would carefully measure and calculate and stir as Mom instructed me on what I was supposed to be doing next, because I was not yet able to read.

By the time I was eight, I had graduated to taking over the kitchen for a couple of hours as I played Julia Child. (I guess that a young girl now would be playing Rachael Ray, but I cannot imagine it being nearly as much fun to mimic her voice!) I would roughly measure what was on the ingredient list, adding it to a large bowl where I would beat the collected ingredients and taste frequently to make sure the flavor was "spot on"—realizing, of course, that as long as it was still dough, it had a *great* flavor. Despite all of my mother's warnings about "getting worms" from too much cookie dough, I am here to tell you that I have never once been treated for worms, although I did have one uncomfortable evening doing the old curl-and-hurl because of an oatmeal-cookie-dough overdose.

Never being one to readily color inside the lines or play by anybody else's rules—including within recipes—I was soon using my kitchen time to experiment in a never-ending search for the ultimate chocolate chip cookie. My kitchen time became my release for all my bad days—my therapy. If I was sad, I baked! Mad, I baked! Bad grade at school, I baked! Just feeling lonely and neglected, I baked! Nothing could equal the release I felt through baking (until I discovered vacuuming, but that's a different story). The relationship between a bad day and baking was such a well-known fact that when, in later years, my mom would call and ask "What are you up to?" and my response was "Baking cookies," invariably, the next words out of my mother's mouth would be "What's bothering you?"

So, fast-forward about forty years from my wonderful childhood kitchen memories. It was January 2007, and my son, Buddy, an airborne soldier with the 82nd Division of the army, was traveling to Baghdad, Iraq, to be the tip of the Surge. I started baking cookies as if I were back in third grade, had just flunked a spelling test, and was rejected by the entire Kent Gardens Elementary School student body . . . and then scorned by the whole neighborhood gang. Somewhere along the way, the two worlds—grade-school geek and mother of a soldier—collided, and the result was fifty-two care packages over the course of the roughly fourteen and a half months that my son served in Iraq. Each care package would contain some attempt at a fresh-baked concoction to delight my son and his battle buddies living and fighting in a very precarious situation—essentially, fifty-two weeks of cookie inventions born of my son's service during the Surge.

For the most part, I would bake cookies every weekend and pack as many as would fit into care packages, which were then mailed to what was the Iraqi equivalent of the Western Front of World War II. What would not fit into the care packages was taken into work to be shared with my coworkers. I began receiving rave reviews, and with them came requests for recipes. I soon realized I did not want to just hand these recipes out for what I would characterize as frivolous enjoyment. In my mind and heart, these recipes came with a price. Figuratively speaking, of course, incorporated into each cookie were the blood, sweat, and tears shed by my son and his buddies, not to mention my unbelievable trepidation over having my son endure this amazingly hazardous duty station. It isn't that I thought that anyone else should understand that price firsthand, but I felt that to have these recipes meant to at least attempt to understand the unique realities of life for our troops and their families. But how?

I began sharing the requests for my recipes with my daughter, Haley, as well as my concerns regarding aimless—possibly unfocused—cookie baking. Haley reminded me that I was a "storyteller," a quality that more than once irritated my father as he would urge "Get to the point!" in the middle of one of my many soliloquies. To be fair, my father was not necessarily wrong in his appeal for brevity, given my penchant for providing five-minute answers to simple questions such as "Did you pass your spelling test?" However, being that the goal was to share our experiences as the family of a soldier, my ability to give my father five minutes of explicit details as to precisely why I, in actuality, *failed* that spelling test, seemed the perfect attribute for what was needed here.

So ultimately, these cookie recipes and the words that accompany them are my way of encouraging everyone to take the time to support our troops—in actions and not just words. (For reference, I support all of our "troops"—meaning all who serve in the military—but when I refer to our "soldiers," most of the time, I am referring to my son and those who deployed and continue to deploy with him.) It is also my way of reaching out to all the parents, spouses, and children out there who are facing this for the first time and are not sure what to expect. These are just my memories and reflections, but hopefully they will help you in the weeks and months ahead.

And now for my disclaimer, which comes in three parts. The first part addresses what I refer to as "my memories." Memories are funny things. They seem to be anchored in perception, and perception is anchored in personal experiences and self-views. That being said, it is not surprising that recollections of the same event tend to be different. This was keenly demonstrated by a college psychology experiment I heard about in a class I took once upon a time.

Basically, the experiment consisted of two men running into a classroom, shouting at each other. A struggle broke out, and one man appeared to stab the other man. The experiment demonstrated that an overwhelming majority of students who witnessed the event swore there was a knife involved, even though the "weapon" used was a banana. My disclaimer is this: If I saw a knife and everyone else saw a banana, it does not make my memories less genuine—only less accurate. This book is a collection of my memories regarding what it was like to have my son serve as a part of the Surge. The fact that my memories might not match the memories of someone else does not mean that this book is a work of fiction, but rather that my memories are unique to my own experiences.

The second part of my disclaimer involves names. All names have been adjusted to protect the innocent, shy, and otherwise unwilling to be associated with my memories and this journal. Not all involved with these stories wanted to be separated from my writings, but to protect all who are mentioned, it seemed only logical to change names and fudge identifications.

The third part of my disclaimer is a bit more difficult to define. It is directed at the sensitive and emotionally volatile aspect of my son's deployment. It addresses those facets of motherhood which compel a mother to pull no punches in defending and protecting her offspring in every way possible. Furthermore, I have discovered that when my ability to protect is restricted, my desire to defend is heightened. In other words, the tangible loss I felt by having my son in such intense physical danger was compensated for by an acute awareness of the intangible aspects—the perceived attitudes, the news reports and media hype, etc.—regarding this conflict, our troops, and their efforts.

As any mother will attest, it is at times difficult to know when to step in and when to step back as kids bumble and bump their way through childhood and adolescence on their way to becoming adults and beyond. As someone who believes whatever pops into my head has a right to fall out of my mouth, this difficulty has been intensified, not only with those whom I have "battled" on my kids' behalf, but with my kids as well. My son's deployment and this journal have certainly not been an exception— in fact, they are probably an example.

Basically, it is my assertion that this book is not about whether my perceptions or what I have written is right or wrong. Instead, it is simply about telling the story of what it took to survive physically, mentally, and emotionally while Buddy was deployed. The instances in this book where I voice my opinions regarding what I was experiencing were my sincere attempts to defend and support my son against all injustices, even if those injustices were simply me mishearing, misinterpreting, or misremembering an event (see part one of this disclaimer).

Pre-Cookie Weeks

Get ready . . . get set . . . no, wait; I'm not ready!

My son Buddy, who I have also been known to call "Bud-bear," or "Buddy-bear" when he was younger, is my only son. None, of course, are his real name, but they have been what I have called him—when he was not in trouble—almost since the day he was born.

It was his sister who ultimately gave him his nickname. The first day Buddy came home from the hospital, for all that the moment should have been calm, with quiet introductions to his sister and a bit of a respite for his mother—i.e., me—who was recovering from childbirth, my house was a madhouse. Filled to the brim with neighbors, friends, and family all gathered around the crib, *Ooh*ing and *Ahh*ing at the new baby, the house was anything but calm. Meanwhile, Buddy's sister, Haley—who was not quite three years old at the time—was trying to squeeze through the throng of people to see what all the fuss was about. After finally making her way to the bars of the crib and laying eyes on her brother for the first time, my only daughter was not impressed.

"What is it?" she asked me when she was finally able to wrangle a moment of my attention.

"Well, Sweetie, he's your new baby brother," I answered, attempting to ease her obvious concerns.

"Do we have to keep him?" Haley asked, apparently confused by the term *brother*.

In my pursuit of family harmony, I tried to ease the shock to my daughter that yes, we had to keep him. I struggled to paint the situation in a light that would entice Haley to welcome this new member of our family.

"Well, he is the baby bear," I claimed. "I am Mama-bear, you are Missy-bear, and Benjamin is Baby-bear, just like *Goldilocks and the Three Bears*."

To my surprise, Haley accepted it and immediately began calling him "Baby-bear." That was fine for an infant, but I saw it causing problems as he grew older. Over the next few weeks, "Baby-bear" was purposely morphed into "Buddy-bear" and eventually shortened to "Buddy." The rest, as they say, is history.

For as long as I can remember, all I wanted to be when I grew up was a wife and stay-at-home mom, just like my own mother. Despite an attempt or two at being a traditional family with a mommy and daddy and two kids and a dog, it simply was not meant to be. I was never able to be a stay-at-home mom either, but despite all this, the relationship I had with my kids remained close, and we did well, just the three of us. Still, at times, it felt like the kids and I had missed something special.

It was Haley who showed me how wrong I was. In response to an assignment for school, she wrote a paper on family. She began it by lamenting over the fact that we had never really been a "real" family and ended it with rejoicing over how wonderful our little family actually was. She explained that this was partly because we were unique but mostly because we had what every family should want: cohesiveness, love, support, and a whole slew of traditions that gave joy to life and made every occasion sparkle—especially Christmas.

Christmas had always been a wondrous time at our house. Take a modest dose of over-decoration, throw in a portion of anticipation like you might find in a house where the joys of childhood have refused to fade away, add some laughter and a generous amount of love, and then sprinkle the lot with the wholehearted belief in the magic of the season. That is Christmas at the "Bear Cave," the name I dubbed our home—wherever that might be—when I began to realize that my family's situation was special. With each of us having a different last name, I wanted to create a canopy under which we could all fit and be recognized as a single unit. Given my love for bears, the name "Bear Cave" seemed like the obvious choice.

The Christmas season was a jealously guarded time for my family. While we had welcomed all who wished to join us at the Bear Cave for our celebrations over the years, we had politely declined extended family's invitations to travel here or there for the holiday. I think part of the reason is the traditions that had developed as the kids grew up, like the Christmas Eve service followed by visits from the PJ Fairy, mimosas while watching age-old—and some new—Christmas movies (this tradition was only mine at first—the mimosas, not the movies!), and ingesting copious amounts of cookie dough while we prepared cookies for Santa, even though we were all well past childhood . . . at least age-wise!

Our traditions just did not seem to translate into other peoples' homes. Then again, maybe it was just our Peter Pan–like desire to never really grow up. Whatever the reasons, it was an unbelievable blow to have the army tell us that Buddy was not allowed to come home for Christmas this year. The only other time our family had been separated for the holidays was, once again, at the army's hands during Buddy's first deployment. All I could think was, *This will not do!*

For as long as I can remember, I never had any intentions of growing up, despite growing older, and I did not believe anyone could make me. So, not to be discouraged by this unwanted intrusion from the army—not to mention wanting to keep my son on an even keel despite his disappointment in not being allowed a trip home—and in keeping with the magic of the season, I immediately went to work to bring Christmas to Buddy. I carefully gathered all the fixings for a Bear Cave Christmas:

- ✓ The kids' ornaments that they have received every Christmas since their first
- ✓ A fully collapsible 6 1/2-foot Christmas tree
- ✓ Christmas stockings and stocking hangers to be placed on the TV, which would be playing a continuous recording of a fire burning in a fireplace
- ✓ A dozen or so CDs of Christmas music (which basically ends up being a dozen or so different arrangements of the same songs)
- ✓ A representative collection of Christmas movies (from the mystical to the maudlin)
- ✓ Christmas-scented candles
- ✓ Christmas Eve pajamas (compliments of the PJ Fairy)
- ✓ Appropriate Christmas foods (dinner, snacks, mimosa ingredients, and pre-made Christmas cookie dough)
- ✓ And last, but certainly not least, all the gifts that I had been collecting in preparation for the arrival of Santa Claus (I did mention the Peter Pan thing, right?)

I separated everything into two categories, the general holiday stuff and the surprises from Santa, which were carefully packed into cardboard boxes, taped shut, and "sealed" with self-adhesive Christmas tags which read in thick black marker SANTA SEAL! DO NOT BREAK!! (just to make sure there was no peeking until Christmas morning). On Christmas Eve, I piled it all into our car along with my nephew, Keith, and our 150-pound Bernese Mountain Dog, Whiskey (often called "the Whiskey-Dog" to avoid confusion with the beverage), to cart off to Buddy's army base 350 miles away from our home in Reston, Virginia. There was so much stuff collected for this adventure that Haley had to ride down in her own car, also filled to capacity with Christmas trappings.

By the time we arrived in Fayetteville, North Carolina, home of Fort Bragg and the 82nd Airborne, it was already well into the afternoon. We had a good deal to accomplish if we were to have everything ready for the following morning—not to mention that evening's activities. We dragged all the stuff we brought from home into the local Extended Stay hotel. In order to be able to set up our Christmas tree and the rest of our holiday paraphernalia, we needed two suites. Keith and Buddy took one suite, which essentially became our kitchen and dining room; all the food stuff, minus the cookie dough and mimosa fixings, went there. Everything else went with Haley and me into the other suite, which became our family room—and as such, the place where we would spend Christmas Eve and Christmas morning.

We got to work immediately to set up all our decorations, concentrating on Haley's and my suite. We hung some wreaths on the double doors to the bedroom, hung garland from the window, placed stocking hangers on the television, and uncollapsed our Christmas tree in the corner next to it. Even though it was pre-decorated, it was a mighty bare Christmas tree; I was glad I had brought along the extra decorations. We spent the rest of that afternoon hanging the decorations from the spiraling, holly and light–decorated wire that was our collapsible tree. By the time we were finished, we had created a uniquely decorated room, but we had also managed to generate an acceptable atmosphere in which to celebrate the day.

Room and tree decorating were followed by a Christmas Eve service and then a bite to eat. By 9:00 that evening, we were all back in our "family room" for some mimosas, a movie, and our surprises from the PJ Fairy. After returning from the service, we were joined by Buddy's barrack mate, Christian. Apparently, Christian was alone for Christmas Eve because his family was unable to make it up from Florida due to the short notice, but he assured me they would be there Christmas morning. I wished I had known beforehand, because I would have made sure that the PJ Fairy had something for him, as well as a stocking (at the minimum) from Santa. But even without that, Christian seemed happy to simply share our Christmas Eve activities with us.

We each sipped on our drinks as we attempted to watch the preselected Christmas movie—something with Muppets, though I am unable to remember which one. It would not have mattered anyway, because we did very little watching. Mostly, we talked and joked until about halfway through when we gave up on it altogether. Instead, we decided to play "Dictionary"—a traditional family game that requires writing utensils, paper, a simple dictionary, and a degree of cleverness. The game revolves around finding a word in the dictionary that no one else playing the game knows. While the person who is "it" (the one with the dictionary who found the word) writes down the real definition, the rest do their best to come up with a believable definition that would fool the other players into choosing theirs as the actual definition. Each player gets a turn with the dictionary, and points are then awarded depending on who picked false definitions and who identified the true one. I have seen store-bought games that were similar, but they were never the same. Besides, my family had been playing this game long before those ever hit the shelves—in fact, long before I had kids.

Being that it was my suggestion to play the game, I was first to take my turn with the dictionary. Though Buddy and Haley had been playing the game all their lives, it was the first time for Keith and Christian. However, by the end of my turn, they had a firm grasp of the concept. And just as it had been since the first time my family ever played over twenty years before, by the second player's turn with the dictionary, in this case Haley, everyone in the room was giggling as they wrote their definitions down, which turned into laughter as Haley tried to read them out loud.

By the end of the first round, the game had deteriorated into simply laughing. Haley was complaining because the dictionary we were using was too small and did not contain the word she wanted to use and we would not let her use any words that were not in the available dictionary. Christian did not like that he was not getting any points due to the fact that his definitions were obvious because they all involved descriptions of weaponry; Keith did not like the scoring, and Buddy just wanted another turn. I took a moment to evaluate. It might have been the mimosas or the fact that it had been a long and eventful day and the hour was late. It also might simply have been our inner children getting out of hand, but whatever the reason, it was time to open our pajama presents and call it a night, especially considering the fact that Santa had yet to arrive.

Christian stayed around long enough to experience the joy of the PJ Fairy's gifts but left shortly after because his family was due early on Christmas Day. After Christian left, we all donned our new pajamas and spent a few minutes taking pictures of ourselves in them. The minute the picture-taking was over, however, I shooed everyone off to their rooms, the Whiskey-Dog following the boys as they headed off to theirs. I immediately went to work setting things up for the next morning. With all of the presents arranged around the bottom of the tree and Christmas stockings stuffed to the brim and hanging from their holders on the TV, I performed my last tasks. I started the DVD of the burning fire in a fireplace on the TV to run all night and placed one of our Christmas CDs in the boom box for the following morning. I then took a moment to soak it all in. It might not have been home, but it was most definitely the next best thing!

My memories get a little fuzzy here. I do not remember who was the first to wake, but I do remember the surprise and delight on everyone's faces when they saw their Christmas morning. It made the whole effort worthwhile. The remainder of that morning was also a bit of a blur as we each took turns tearing into the sea of packages that awaited us under the tree. After opening presents, we began setting up for

Christmas dinner. Since most of that was prepackaged and premade, it did not take a great deal of preparation, leaving us time to simply take in the day.

By 3:00, my little family was sitting around the table in our "dining room" for Christmas dinner. The Whiskey-Dog had settled himself comfortably on the tile in the kitchen, just happy to be a part of it all. A forever tradition at the Bear Cave was to have grace at family dinners be a time to count blessings. This Christmas, Keith's blessing was that he was a part of a great family in a great country. Buddy's blessing was that he had a family that was willing to drop everything to bring Christmas to him. Haley's blessing was that she was a part of a family that not only could make anything work but could make it work well. Overwhelmed by what was in my heart, the only thing I could choke out was to thank God that I had such great kids and a great family!

Unfortunately, Christmas was not an extended holiday. The day after Christmas, we were all packing up to head back home. All of us, including Buddy, had work the next day. Haley headed out first, followed by Keith, the Whiskey-Dog, and me. For some reason, I felt it rather deeply when I had to say good-bye to my son, but I could not figure out why.

The day after I arrived back home—not even halfway to New Year's Day—I received *the* phone call from Buddy.

"Mom!" he said. "We ship to Iraq in five days! I need your help!"

All I could think was *Please, God! I can't do this again!* What I said was "I'm on my way!"

Pre-Cookie Week 2
28 December 2006–6 January 2007

I'm not crying; I just have something in my eye.

It felt like I barely had a chance to turn around twice and yet I was back on the road heading toward Fort Bragg. For this trip, I left the Whiskey-Dog at home to be looked after by a neighbor. Without any distractions, I had nothing but time and quiet reflection for the five-hour ride back down to North Carolina.

It was my son's second tour to Iraq, and I do not believe the two experiences could have been more dissimilar. Buddy's Military Occupational Specialty (MOS), the designation of what he was trained for, was 11 Bravo (11B), meaning he was trained to be an infantry-enlisted soldier—a ground troop. But Buddy was also airborne. To be a soldier was one thing, but to be airborne was special. Along with training in the normal duties of their MOS, airborne soldiers were also trained to jump out of perfectly good airplanes—on command.

Buddy's first duty station after his training was Fort Bragg, "Home of the Airborne and Special Operations Forces." He became a member of the 82nd Airborne Division of the army, the All-Americans. Buddy was assigned to the 504th, nicknamed the "Devils in Baggy Pants" or the "Devil Brigade." Specifically, he was a member of the first battalion of the 504th Parachute Infantry Regiment (1-504th PIR), also called the "Red Devils."

It was, in fact, the other side that christened the 504th during World War II because of their cunning, tenacity, and perseverance. As a member of the Devil Brigade, Buddy and his fellow soldiers were trained to deploy to anywhere in the world within eighteen hours and, once arrived, were primed to do whatever it took to fight and win. However, it was the "whatever it took" part that historically made these guys prone to be treated as the jacks-of-all-trades of the army.

For his first tour to Iraq, Buddy and his fellow paratroopers found themselves playing prison guards. Though to the soldiers of the Devil Brigade this felt like a demotion, in reality, they were deployed to be serious and professional soldiers, sent over to demonstrate to the "locals" (i.e., the Iraqi prison guards) exactly how it should be done. That being said, there were more differences in this second deployment than just Buddy's duties while deployed, and it began with deployment day.

First of all, there was over a month of lead-up to that first deployment. For all the expected tension, things were calm and organized on the day they shipped. Before I even showed up to see Buddy off, all the barracks were cleared and cleaned, with personal items already placed in storage or packed in trunks ready to be carted home. The length of the deployment was set for six months or less, and though Iraq was known to be a dangerous place even at that time, the danger seemed somehow removed from the deployment and our soldiers.

In contrast, the call that initiated my trip back to Fort Bragg for this deployment was abrupt and unexpected. The deteriorating situation in Iraq caused by insurgents trying to wrest control of the areas our troops were sent to protect required decisive action. Several strategies were discussed to counter the insurgents, one of which was to greatly increase the number of troops in and around Baghdad in a short amount of time, otherwise known as "surging" the troops. The thought was that if stability was achieved in Baghdad, stability would be achieved in Iraq. Though the Surge had been discussed by commentators on TV for the previous several weeks as a possible solution to the ever-growing danger to our troops and the indigenous population of Iraq, it was obvious that this short-notice deployment was pretty much unforeseen—especially by the soldiers themselves.

It was immediately apparent to me once I drove onto the base that I was not the only one who was surprised by "the phone call" the day before. The whole area in and around Buddy's barracks was abuzz with activity as family and friends helped their soldiers clean their barrack rooms in preparation for deployment. The stairs to the barracks were crowded with a constant flow of people carrying boxes, trunks, and other paraphernalia bound either for cars to be carted off for long-term storage or for the dumpsters. Yes, in addition to the constant flow of people hauling items down the stairs, there was a steady stream of people carrying clothes, bedding, mattresses, electronics, and other extraneous items to the dumpsters. These dumpsters were piled two stories high with the "junk" that, though a week before was important enough to keep around, now did not rate a second or even a third look for the storage unit.

It was no different for Buddy and me. Like all the other rooms in the barracks, Buddy's room was a train wreck! It seemed as though everything my son owned had been dumped into the middle of the room. As he sifted through the mayhem looking for the items on his checklist to be packed into his duffel bag, I stuffed storage containers, trunks, and anything else I could find with the leftovers. It was actually a little surreal. I was glad to be there to help my son prepare for deployment and to spend those last few days with him, but there were times that it was very difficult as well.

"Hey, Mom! I'm looking for another plate that looks like this one, only bigger. Have you seen it?" Buddy asked, holding what looked like a thin gray brick.

"Is this it?" I held up a very heavy rectangular thing which was several inches in length and width and about an inch thick. Buddy nodded yes, but I had to ask, "What is it?"

"It's the vest plate for my armor," he replied. I guess the look on my face showed a lack of understanding because he added, "You know—flak jacket? Bulletproof vest?"

I did indeed know—in fact, I was painfully aware. My facial expression, however, was contradicting that understanding by showing the uncertainty I was feeling about . . . well . . . everything. Even so, I was certain that what I held in my hand might very well be the difference between life and death. I wanted to kiss it, or pray over it, or *something* before handing it to Buddy to pack, but I refrained. I was equally certain that displaying my gut-wrenching doubt at that moment would not have been received well. Besides, I was afraid if I gave into the doubt—then or any time in the future—I would never rein it back in. And so we continued packing and cleaning, sometimes talking, sometimes complaining, sometimes joking, but often working in silence and left to our own unshared thoughts.

For all the insanity of those first couple of days as families helped their soldiers prepare to ship, deployment day was a different story. There was a somewhat bizarre combination of serenity and urgency that filled the air as families gathered to spend their last few hours together—serenity because for the soldiers and their families, this was the calm before the storm, and urgency born out of a desire to say everything that needed to be said before the soldiers boarded their plane for Iraq.

Haley had shown up that morning for the send-off. With all the packing and cleaning now complete, the morning was spent "relaxing" with breakfast at IHOP and a bit of a shopping spree at the local Best Buy for Buddy. Despite his eventual destination of Baghdad, he needed some games to amuse himself—or maybe as a distraction. But all too soon, it was time for Buddy to put on his uniform and meet the rest of his company for the final preparations before deployment. I was not ready.

The blacktop where the soldiers were gathering was crowded with a sea of people mingling about, trying to act normal with casual conversations and introductions between family members and best buddies. It was basically no different for Buddy, Haley, and me. Buddy spent some time hanging out with three soldiers he had become close to on his first tour, Christian being one of them, but mostly the families kept to themselves as they tried to verbalize all the emotions that were stirring in their hearts. All in all, the afternoon passed way too quickly. While Buddy went to in-process and weapon assignment, Haley and I went to find him something to eat. By the time we returned with the food, Buddy was finished with his official duties and all that was left was the wait.

In the dimming light of early evening, Haley and I sat on the hood of my car and watched as Buddy tried to cram a six-inch knife into an already-overstuffed assault pack. Despite its formidable name, an assault pack is nothing more than a backpack made from the material of a camouflage uniform. Sitting on the sidewalk with the backpack resting on the pavement between his outstretched legs, his newly assigned rifle leaning up against his knee, Buddy packed and repacked that bag trying to fit everything into it. In between bites of fast food—taco-whatever that Haley and I had picked up for him—Buddy would remove a couple of things from the pack, shift them around, and then put them back, only to find that there was still not enough room for the knife.

I looked down at my son from the hood of my car, my soul flooding with memories. I swear at one point he was chewing on his tongue, just like a young child would do while learning to cut with a pair of scissors. Despite his well-built, almost-six-foot frame, it was difficult not to see anything but the small, young, dark-haired, dark-eyed boy that I knew from what seemed like millennia ago. In fact, if I ignored my surroundings and overlooked the fact that the object he was attempting to stuff into that pack was lethal, what I saw was one of a thousand memories I have of my son trying to stuff his suitcase with his favorite dinosaur bones for an overnight stay at his Nana's house as he was growing up. My heart ached as I wondered what the next several months would bring. I positively was not ready for this.

It's a funny thing. As clear as my memory is of Buddy and that backpack, I cannot remember saying good-bye to him. I do not remember hugging him, though I know I did. I do not remember if I spoke any words, though I know I must have. I do not even remember if I told him I loved him, though I cannot imagine that I didn't. It seemed that all that I had left was the uncertainty of the wait and the memories of being the mother of a soldier for Buddy's first tour. And yet, there at the beginning of another deployment to Iraq, none of these thoughts seemed helpful.

The trip home was as long and as quiet as the trip down to Fort Bragg had been. The question of how to say good-bye, which often haunts the families of our troops, had already become a moot point. Buddy and his fellow soldiers were on their way to Iraq, and there was nothing anyone could do about it. I was so proud of him, but it was all becoming a bit overwhelming. My memories from the distant past had begun colliding with my memories from the recent past, and what remained was a conglomeration of thoughts and images that crossed the boundaries of space and time. I had this vision of my boy as he stood in full battle gear; only in my mind, he stood there as a six-year-old with that angelic cherub face he had when he was young beaming from underneath his helmet. It was mind boggling. I felt so tired. The road seemed to stretch endlessly before me, and the drive was exhausting. I decided that if I could just get home again, I would start to feel normal.

Despite my desire for the comforts of home, being home did not seem to soothe my soul. In fact, almost a week later, the house still seemed overly empty, even though Buddy had not lived at home for the past few years. In an attempt to occupy my energies, I began putting away his gear that now cluttered the front foyer, living room, and dining room. There were more questions this time and, obviously, more dangers. Buddy and his fellow soldiers had been sent to Iraq to be the Surge, and being the first group of soldiers to be sent, they had become its tip—the first strike. I wondered what it was going to be like for Buddy and prayed often that God would protect not only his body but also his soul, even as I wondered when I would see him again.

I grabbed Buddy's Class A uniform that was lying in a garment bag over the back of the couch and hung it up in his closet. I smoothed the bag down so that it hung straight on the rack to keep the uniform inside it looking sharp. My mind inadvertently wandered toward one of our last conversations. It was a chat that Buddy and I had had over dinner the evening before he shipped. He expressed his final wishes, including that if the worst should happen, he wanted to be buried in his Class A's— the army equivalent of a man's best suit—with all the ropes, ribbons, and medals. *How can any mother be expected to bear this?* I thought, staring at that nondescript bag. A knot formed in the pit of my stomach. I shook my head vigorously to clear my mind and vowed to never think along those lines again. Even so, I found that I was contemplating all meanings of the words "casualties of war" and reiterated to myself, *I simply cannot do this again!*

In the midst of my lament, the phone rang and Buddy was on the other end. It was the first time since he deployed that I had heard from him.

"Hey, Mom! What's up?" Buddy asked, undeniably upbeat and completely accepting of where he was and what was expected of him.

"Hey, Sweetie!" I replied, making sure that I was equally as positive and chipper. I silently chastised myself for letting my imagination and emotions run away with me before asking, "Whatcha doin'? Where are you guys now?"

"We're still in Kuwait, training," he answered. "I don't know how long we're gonna be here, but I'll keep you informed."

"Oh, OK . . . " My voice drifted off; I didn't know what else to say.

"Your voice sounds funny," Buddy said. "Have you been crying?"

I was amazingly happy to be able to honestly answer that question with a "No!"

Buddy was not convinced but let it go. "I really don't have much time, Mom," he said. "I just wanted to let you know what was going on."

I was equally as happy to be able to tell him, "I love you, Bud. Take care of yourself . . . and *be safe!*"

"I love you bunches, Mom" was his reply—a phrase used often by Buddy as he grew up. "And miss you, too!" And with those last words, he hung up.

My heart was full with a mother's love for her son and an incredible pride, even as I wrestled with a growing, nagging sadness. I placed the phone back on the hook and, for a moment, stood in silence with my thoughts. It was only then that I began to cry.

Pre-Cookie Week 3

7 January 2007–13 January 2007

Passing the time with Whiskey—the dog, not the bottle!

I t had been about two weeks since my son's unit shipped: two weeks of sporadically timed phone calls, two weeks of convincing myself that I could—no— had to do this, and two weeks of random, spontaneous cookie baking. I had no address to send the cookies to, but cookie baking had always been my therapy, and now creative cookie baking had become my equilibrium. Concentrating on what to throw into the bowl next to concoct whatever flavor and texture I was trying to achieve gave me a break from the constant barrage of unknowns that were otherwise flooding my thoughts.

For the most part, I was left to my own devices in imagining what my son was experiencing. The few phone calls I had received from Buddy were short and sweet without a great deal of information, but he did manage to let me know that their training in Kuwait had almost ended and they were getting ready to deploy to Iraq. Despite the chill those words sent down my spine, this news meant that soon I would have an address to send care packages to, and for that, at least, I was grateful.

I was not a stranger to supporting the troops through care packages and letters. I was, however, unfamiliar with having my son directly in harm's way. Though Buddy's first deployment was to Iraq, it was relatively removed from danger. This time, though, he was the tip of the spear—the front line. As a result, I spent many of my baking hours considering what I needed to do to make sure I remained the "supportive" mom. At the same time, I could not help but wonder just how much support—mental, emotional, and otherwise—I was going to require over the next year for myself. For the previous five years, my support and comfort had mostly come from a very large, hairy, slobbering, goofy dog—my Whiskey. The Whiskey-Dog was not the brightest bulb in the box, but he had been my constant companion since my father passed away.

The kids and had I moved to Vermont to take some time to sort out my marital difficulties, but we came back to Virginia after only a year because of my father's health. He had experienced a steep physical decline that left us a little unsure as to when it all would end. My father was an impressive man. Orphaned at fourteen years of age, a World War II vet, and stricken with polio at the age of thirty-one, my father was one of those people who always remained positive and never gave up. But after eighty-four years, he was just plain tired. This should not be mistaken for despair; my dad had an earnest belief in God and the afterlife, and until the day he collapsed, he was upbeat and lived every moment as best he could. The polio, however, having taken a physical toll on him from its onset, was literally wearing him out in his final years. I think it was explained best by my mom right after the funeral when she told us all—my two brothers, my sister, me, and all of our kids—that he was simply ready to move on. Mind you, that did not make it hurt any less. In fact, the bottom line is that the death of my father left me hollow.

The kids and I moved back in with my husband after we returned from Vermont. Though it was only a year later when my father died, my marriage had already deteriorated to the point it was before the kids and I left, if not worse. About two weeks after we buried my dad, Haley left for her freshman year of college; about a month after that was 9/11. I was reeling from life itself and wanted to find something to calm the spin. While living in Vermont, Buddy and I had begun the search for our next family dog and settled on the Bernese mountain dog—a large, gentle, congenial breed that seemed a perfect match for the Bear Cave. With all that was happening in our lives now, I felt it was time to resume the search.

I found an ad for Bernese puppies and called, but I was told all the puppies had been sold. But a week later, the breeder called and informed me that one of the buyers had backed out; the puppy was mine if I still wanted it. It was almost as if Whiskey was meant to be with us. Without discussing the matter with anybody else, my husband included, I said yes. Though I questioned my sanity at the time, once I had Whiskey home, I never again doubted my decision. Less than a year later, my husband and I split up, and the kids, Whiskey, and I moved into a home of our own.

Whiskey grew from a nine-pound puppy to a 150-pound dog in just over a year. Even though he was what some might call a *huge* dog, his personality remained gentle and puppy-like. He did not appreciate normal dog games like fetch or tug-of-war. In fact, if you tried to throw a dog biscuit for him to catch, you could count on it hitting him square between the eyes before it fell to the ground, where he would eventually find it to eat. Whiskey did, however, love car rides and walks. When I was in the kitchen cooking, he loved to wrap himself around my feet. When I would step away, he would stretch out to make sure his paws still touched me. When I sat at the couch, he had to sit right next to me. I am sure if I had let him, he would have sat *on* me—he tried to at least a half a dozen times a week!

Though he had difficulty getting onto my platform bed, he slept dutifully at its foot on the floor every night—until there was a thunderstorm. On those occasions, I'd wake up to his front half laid across my chest, and him whining and panting loudly until I could calm him down. I didn't mind, though, because the Whiskey-Dog took care of me, too.

The Whiskey-Dog was there for me every time I was happy, sad, scared, relieved, lonely, or just relaxing with a glass of wine and an old movie. I told him my secrets, and he slobbered on me in return; I discussed my concerns with him, and he wagged his tail; I shared my ideas, and Whiskey tried to crawl into my lap. And if I asked him where Buddy was, he would cock his head to the right, stare at me for a moment, then plant himself at the front door for a couple of hours, waiting for Buddy to come back home again. For all of my cares and concerns, Whiskey could always make me smile, not to mention be an inspiration to me. In the past, when I wrote to our troops or my son and contemplated how to keep things cheery and upbeat, there always seemed to be at least one good Whiskey story to tell.

That evening, I sat on the couch trying to watch some television—Whiskey's big old head resting in my lap. I thought about Buddy and what I needed to do to encourage him and give him a bit of a reprieve from his surroundings. I would guess there are as many ways a mother can offer support to her soldier son or daughter as there are mothers themselves. For me, I had always thought that if a son or daughter (or an unknown soldier from a support website) was in a situation where they were far from home—especially if that situation involved extreme danger—what they needed was something to help them forget where they were, if only momentarily.

Musing over that thought, I remembered being in a hardware store a few years earlier looking for a specific type of spring for the construction of what I referred to as a gunpowderless firecracker to send to the troops for the Fourth of July. I had only vague ideas of what I needed, but I was convinced that I needed springs. I found the appropriate aisle, located the rack containing a wide assortment of springs, and then stood there studying the display—all the different shapes, sizes and strengths—attempting to conceptualize what was required to create what was taking shape in my imagination. After witnessing my level of concentration, an employee of the store came over to ask if I needed assistance.

Now, I have never been one to ask for help (or directions, for that matter), but I thought, *This guy is a professional; maybe if I describe what I am trying to do, he can suggest something to help me.* I took a moment to convey to the man what I was trying to accomplish and why. While I did, I watched the expression on his face go from interest to irritation. Mildly confused by what I was seeing, I quickly finished my description and waited for what he could offer to help me complete my project. What I received instead was a stern lecture on the seriousness of war and how the troops did not need "some ditzy blonde making light of it all." Not one to engage in frivolous confrontations, I stood in silence as I was berated, then watched the employee stomp off in his perceived righteous indignation. I am sure he thought he gave me a much-needed education, but all I could think was, *Oh boy, do you ever have that wrong!*

Apparently, what had always seemed obvious to me was not as obvious to others. These guys—our troops, *my son*—were neck-deep in serious. They did not need anyone writing from home to explain to them the gravity of their situation—especially their moms. Instead, what they needed was a distraction now and again. That was the support I had provided to our troops in the past—silliness with a heaping portion of my undying gratitude for their service—and that was the support I intended to give to my son.

I smiled to myself at the thought of my gunpowderless firecracker that sprayed confetti when its fuse was given a good tug. "And I never even needed the springs," I spoke aloud to Whiskey while gently scratching him behind the ears—as if he could read my mind and knew exactly what I was talking about. However, clever crafts and ill-mannered store clerks aside, the current circumstances of the Surge continued to occupy my thoughts.

Despite all my misgivings and doubts, I realized that this deployment was a marathon, not a sprint. I knew that I needed to pace myself, but I also knew that it was time for me to put up or shut up. I had finally been given the opportunity to demonstrate the "supportive mom" role that I had alluded to so often—even if that "opportunity" was my son serving on the front lines. I understood that I needed to bury my concerns, at least when communicating with Buddy—and probably when I wasn't, as well. The last thing Buddy needed was to be worried about me worrying about him, and I knew that for sanity's sake, I needed to start looking ahead—at least to the immediate future when Buddy might have an address where I could start sending care packages. I certainly did not want to look so far ahead as to get bogged down by the "What if"s and "How can I bear it?"s. Along those lines, this was definitely a "one day at a time" tour. But even so, I felt I needed to at least begin pulling together Buddy's first care package so that when he finally got an address, I could begin sending him mail right away.

"Let's see," I began speaking aloud to Whiskey. "What do you think we need to be sending Buddy in his first care package? Cookies? Definitely, but what else? I probably need to take a trip to Toys'R'Us, and maybe one to Target or Best Buy. Maybe I should start a letter now."

The second I mentioned Buddy's name, Whiskey opened his eyes and listened intently as if he understood everything I was saying. "We really need to get started," I added. "That is the supportive-mom thing to do, you know."

As it turned out, the Whiskey-Dog agreed.

Pre-Cookie Week 4
14 January 2007–20 January 2007

When life gives you lemons, play "Pomp and Circumstance."

I t had been another long week. There was very little contact with Buddy and no information regarding where exactly he was or what precisely—or even generally—he was doing. The days were long and the nights even longer. Nights always have seemed to bring out the darkness in everything, well beyond that of the sun disappearing behind the horizon. In the quiet of the evening, it was difficult not to have my mind wander far outside the bounds that I wished it would stay in. Without distraction beyond the companionship of Whiskey (dog, not bottle), I was adrift in a sea of doubt and growing apprehension. I was hesitant to call any friends or family for fear I would be projecting the wrong impression of a soldier's mom suffering from a boatload of doubt—even if that perception was true. What I wanted was the ability to project pride in my son, strength, and conviction in his safe return, even though my actual feelings were belying it all.

Luckily for me—though not necessarily for her—I had a daughter to pour my energies into as well. Haley had sort of graduated from Virginia Commonwealth University last spring with a mass communications major and a music minor. I say "sort of" because although we had made all our preparations to attend her graduation—including Keith and me buying her a used Saturn as her graduation gift—at the last minute Haley found out she was not going to be able to walk with the rest of her class because she had not been able to arrange for the required internship in time. Needless to say, she was heartbroken, and I was perplexed as to what to do with her gift. Of course we were going to give it to her, but the question became how and when.

As Haley and I talked through her disappointment, a plan emerged to hold our very own graduation, exclusively for Haley, on the day the rest of her class held theirs. One of her best friends had managed to sleep through her own graduation the year before, so we offered her the opportunity to graduate with Haley. We set up in the courtyard of Haley's apartment with folding chairs and a podium made out of poster board which I colored different shades of brown to resemble wood in a very abstract way. Buddy was able to take some leave to participate in the ceremony and donned his Class A's to be the ceremony's emcee. Haley's friend was valedictorian due to her higher GPA, and Haley was salutatorian. I was the commencement speaker. "Pomp and Circumstance" was provided on violin by another of Haley's college friends to accompany us as we marched to our designated seats. And finally, one of Haley's longtime friends from high school, a bona fide kindergarten teacher in the state of Virginia, signed the "diplomas" which were announced by Buddy and handed out by me.

At the end of our little ceremony, Haley was given the keys and then led to her car in the adjacent parking lot. We had filled the car with balloons and topped it with a huge handmade purple bow that covered the hood of the car—just like the ones in TV commercials. Unfortunately, the wind that day played havoc with the bow, so by the time Haley saw it, it looked more like a giant had sneezed purple all over the car. Even so, the surprise on my daughter's face was genuine, and the family moment was priceless. As an aside, all ten or so "guests" that were in attendance, as well as the ceremony participants, agreed that it was the best graduation ever.

After the graduation, we turned our attention to Haley's internship. Being a typical mother and having all the confidence in the world in my daughter, I started pushing Haley to not just "get by" with her internship. A fan of several Washington DC news organizations, I noticed on their various web pages that almost all of them took interns, so I encouraged her to apply. To make a long story short (too late, I know!), last fall, Haley interned with one of the more prominent DC bureaus of a national news station. I was so very proud of her accomplishments, and the station seemed to like her as well! (Of course—how could they not?)

After Haley completed her internship, just days before Buddy deployed for the Surge, I began once again to encourage her to try to get a full-time job with the same news organization. She kept on telling me to be patient, but patience is not one of my virtues! In fact, at a time when I was beginning to be anxious twenty-four hours a day, asking me to be patient was like asking me to grow wings and fly! Much to Haley's dismay, roughly every conversation we'd had since our Fort Bragg Christmas began with "What have you done?" or "What have you heard?" This week, however, instead of the obligatory "Be patient!" response, Haley informed me that she was offered a position. It was a probationary position—more along the lines of a freelance, work-your-way-up position—but it was a first step and I was excited for her. I knew she was going to do well.

In addition to beginning her new career, Haley was now going to be moving back home. The Whiskey-Dog had always been a wonderful companion to me despite the fact that there were rocks in the backyard that intellectually challenged him. However, given the current situation, I had a feeling that over the next several months, I was going to need something a little more substantial than tail-wagging and doggy drool for comfort. It meant the world to me that Haley understood this and was willing to be my support system for the foreseeable future. It left me with the comforting realization that even if I had nothing else, I had everything I needed because I had *great* kids.

Pre-Cookie Week 5
21 January 2007–27 January 2007

Because sometimes you just want to throw something!

Over Christmas, Keith had asked me if I had ever considered learning how to "throw pots."

I realized that I was old enough to know better, but all I could think was *How could anybody who had been in the marriages I had been in not have learned to throw pots—or at least thought about it?* But I responded with "No! Why do you ask?" thinking that somehow I was going to end up involved in some sort of touchy-feely "How to Deal with Life" symposium. I had no idea that he was referring to making pottery!

"Oh! That could be fun!" I replied once I finally knew what we were talking about. So right after Christmas, Keith had enrolled us in the next beginners' class, which ran once a week from the end of January to May at the local shop.

This week was our first scheduled class. We toured the shop, purchased our tools and clay, reviewed the rules and regulations—always a problematic topic for me—and got an overview of the pottery wheel and how to make it spin as well as getting a brief demonstration on how to use it. We were then given our first opportunity to create something bowl-like. I understood that Keith and I were only beginners and were just getting the fundamentals of pot throwing; however, to me it seemed like a whole bunch of "spin the clay this way" and "steady your hands that way" only to screw something up and be forced to start all over again.

It was quite frustrating at times, but before we knew it, our class was almost over. We were told to move our newly thrown creation to the drying shelf and to clean up our stations. I sat for a moment to evaluate my work before turning it over to etch "Mama Bear" on its bottom so all would know it was mine. I honestly did not expect much from my first attempt at using a pottery wheel, but after all my work, this initial piece was a rather lopsided cup—or maybe bowl—that I swear I could have made better without all that spinning stuff. I truly hoped that the process would get easier (and the results better) as we got more practice. Even so, I was just a little excited about—and maybe even a little proud of—my asymmetrical bowl now drying on a shelf in the back room of the shop, waiting to be glazed and then fired in the kiln. The most impressive part was that once fired, I knew I would have a permanent keepsake of this first (failed?) attempt at throwing a pot.

As relatively quiet as the morning was, it did give me a marginal hiatus from the otherwise perpetual worrying that seemed to be consuming me. Originally, I had thought nothing of the timing of our pottery class, but on my way home from the shop, I started thinking more deeply about it. I could not help but wonder if Keith had some sort of inkling regarding what was in our future back during the Christmas break. By the time of this first class, the Surge had been announced, Buddy had already shipped, and the distraction of this Saturday pottery class was a welcome diversion. *You know,* I thought, *it would be just like Keith to have an inkling and say nothing.*

Keith is Buddy's first cousin but is not related to either Haley or me by blood. Even so, I consider him to be my nephew and would fight anyone who tried to say anything different. Keith was also a soldier. After a stint with the infantry (also airborne), he went back to school to study law. Keith was now a major working with the army's Judge Advocate General's (JAG) Corps. Because of his army background, Keith did periodically have insight into things that others might not. Not only did he at times know deployment schedules that were not necessarily public knowledge, but he was also great at explaining what things meant when the information coming in was scarce or nonexistent. Because of this and the seemingly perfect timing of our pot-throwing class, I could not help but wonder just how much he knew and when. However, all that aside, I was just grateful for the variation in my increasingly stagnant routine.

Normally, I had several hobbies that I loved to submerse myself in. There was walking, which the Whiskey-Dog loved to do with me; crocheting or knitting with Whiskey happily resting his big old head in my lap; baking, also joined by Whiskey; writing; playing guitar; crafting . . . and cleaning! No, really, I love to clean! In fact, nothing had ever been more cathartic in my life than vacuuming, during which time the Whiskey-Dog makes himself as scarce as possible.

I simply love a clean house. The fact that vacuuming helped keep my house that way—not to mention its usefulness in getting rid of all creepy-crawly things that bother me—made it one of my favorite activities. In addition, there had never been a problem (barring an unfortunate cricket incident once upon a time) not made better by vacuuming, except for maybe having my son in a war zone.

By the fifth week of deployment, I began to realize that many of my long-standing favorite activities, including vacuuming, had started to lose their luster. Though the mind was willing, the heart just wasn't in it. My writing, though often a satisfying outlet for me in the past, had been confined to an effort to pull together Buddy's first letter. I wanted to create something light and newsy without an overtone of worry or care, but it was proving to be a difficult task. Baking—specifically cookie baking, the quintessential activity in my life for stressful times—had replaced vacuuming as my absolute favorite thing to do. I told myself that this was because I wanted to be able to send home-baked cookies with each care package and not because the current situation had reduced me to a stressed-out, cookie-dough-munching basket case. Given my ever-shrinking list of recreational activities that I actually enjoyed, I was happy to add weekly attempts at pot throwing to my routine.

Cookie Weeks: Part I

Me first!

Buddy knew that I supported him and his service. Though he was fully aware that he was my first concern, Buddy also knew that I always looked for ways to share my support with his fellow soldiers. This tour of duty would be no different. It would neither surprise nor offend Buddy to know that I would be including something for the other soldiers in his platoon, particularly the "FHOTA" (pronounced *foh-tah*), when I assembled the care packages. What I had learned from my son's involvement with the army was that soldiers—all soldiers—truly were a "band of brothers." Even so, there were always a few that became a soldier's primary support. The FHOTA, for all intents and purposes, was exactly that for my son.

The FHOTA consisted of Buddy and the three soldiers that he had become friends with during their first deployment to Iraq. "FHOTA" is an acronym for the "Four Horsemen of the Apocalypse." I guess Buddy and his friends christened themselves with this name as a way of feeling more like infantry soldiers during a tour where they felt they were operating at a level that was less than what they were trained for. Personally, I always wanted to know which one of those clowns was considered Pestilence, but when I asked, the only answer I ever got was each of them pointing at someone else. However, they all claimed to be Death! Anyway, as I was composing my first letter to Buddy, I realized that spelling out "Four Horsemen of the Apocalypse" every time I needed to refer to these guys was space-consuming, if nothing else. So, knowing how much the military loves acronyms, I made one of my own—that is, FHOTA!

I had known these guys since they returned from that first tour, but to varying degrees. Toby was the one I knew the least; I'd had a couple of brief, casual conversations with him in the past, enough to know that he was a truly nice guy. Like the rest of these guys, he had a sharp wit and was just as able to be on the receiving end of a playful (or not-so-playful) gibe as he was to give one. I guess it's a soldier thing—or maybe just a guy thing—but it's pretty entertaining to be present when they dig at each other, trying to silence the others with their best wit and witticisms.

The clearest memory I had of Toby came from a couple days before the soldiers shipped. The mad rush to get all the barracks rooms cleaned in a short amount of time left everyone rather focused on their own concerns. Buddy's favorite complaint was "You know, if they only gave us twenty-four hours, all we would've had to do is shut our doors and lock them behind us." My silent response was a resounding *Oh heavens, no!* I cherished every extra moment I could get, even if it did result in the insanity of packing and cleaning barracks rooms. In fact, in an attempt to ease Buddy's angst and to finish the room as quickly as possible to give us at least a few hours to relax before he deployed, I would pack huge boxes and try to carry them to the car—my parents' "Haste makes waste!" platitude ringing in my ears, chastising me the whole time. I was trying to carry one of these large boxes down the steps when I met Toby coming back up. As we passed, Toby asked, "Can I give you a hand with that?"

Never wanting to be seen as weak, and knowing that Toby had things to do as well, I attempted a smile as I answered, "No, I got it. Thanks anyway," trying to keep the strain of carrying that box from showing in my voice.

Toby said "OK" and continued on; however, he only had taken a few more steps when I heard from behind me, "Oh, I can do better than this!" Toby came back down and passed me by a couple of steps. He then turned around, reached out, grabbed the box—as I sincerely did attempt to resist—and said, "You don't need to be carrying this. I'll take it to Buddy's truck!"

Heading back up the steps to grab the next box from Buddy's room, I acknowledged to myself that it was very nice of Toby to stop his own preparations to help me. As easily as he handled that box, it really was heavy!

The next member of the FHOTA was Christian. Christian had been Buddy's barrack mate since they returned from their first tour. Even so, up until this past Christmas, I do not believe I had ever met him. I was glad that we had the opportunity to get to know him, especially now, after they had deployed so quickly! I was totally impressed by his ability to so seamlessly fit into the Bear Cave atmosphere. Yes, he was charming and clever, but his ability to connect with us was more likely due to the fact that he was mischievous, prankish, and, at times, juvenile, as well.

Christian's mischievous streak had been known to get him into hot water, especially where the army was concerned. Originally, he was the RTO for Buddy's platoon. An RTO is the Radio Telephone Operator and works closely with the platoon's leader, or PL. Basically, an RTO carries communication equipment on his back and is charged with supporting the PL, specifically remaining by the PL's side during patrols to allow the PL to communicate with others in the command. In addition, an RTO is the PL's right-hand man off the battlefield, acting more or less as the PL's "enforcer" to the other soldiers in the platoon.

Surprisingly, being an RTO does not seem to be a sought-after, prestigious duty assignment. Instead, being tagged for this duty is the equivalent of ending up with the Old Maid card in the children's game. Christian was no exception, and his displeasure oozed into his official duties.

There are specific phrases that initiate and confirm communications. These are not complex statements—in fact, I guess at times they can feel irritatingly simple, which apparently got the best of Christian on his last day as the platoon's RTO. It was just about a month before they deployed when, well, let's just say that Christian's response lacked the appropriate decorum required of the position—in other words, if you left out the swear words and sarcasm, he did not say much else!—and he was subsequently relieved of that position. However, Christian's "boon" was Buddy's misery, as Buddy was the next soldier tagged with the platoon's RTO assignment.

Christian's mischievous streak not only could get him into trouble but could suck other people into it right along with him. Even though he was only with us a few hours over the Christmas holiday, he managed to get me in trouble with Buddy. Christian coaxed me into calling Buddy by his airborne nickname, "Princess." I thought it was kind of funny, but once I realized how much it bothered Buddy, I stopped. Unfortunately, it was not before Christian was able to claim the victory! I scolded Christian for successfully involving me in their apparently ongoing battle of wits, but even that he considered a badge of honor.

The last member of the FHOTA was Shelby, who I had known for a couple of years. We had decided long ago that he was also a good fit for the Bear Cave. I guess not everyone would consider that a good thing, but in response to us adopting him, he adopted us.

Shelby is unique. To begin with, Shelby is this soldier's last name. As far as the army is concerned, soldiers do not have first names. Buddy is always Rogers, Toby is always Dillon (which, for the longest time, I thought was his first name), and Christian is always Dunham. For the most part, when it came to friends and family, soldiers want to be called by their first names to delineate between the "I order you" relationship the soldiers have with the army and the softer "would you please" relationship they expect to have with everyone else, but not Shelby. It's not that his first name is embarrassing or unusual—in fact, it is the same as Buddy's given name. No, that's just the way Shelby is.

And then there's the tattoo he got over Christmas. At the urging of the other three on the day of deployment, Shelby lifted his uniform to bare his chest and his brand-new, huge Superman "S" tattoo to Haley and me. I was speechless! All that Haley could say was, "Oh wow, Shelby!" What we both were thinking was, *Oh, Shelby! No!* as visions of the torment that "S" might bring him filled our thoughts. I just hoped he didn't have to spend much time shirtless over the next several months of the deployment, let alone the remaining years of his life!

Leading up to this week, I had already initiated the care package building process despite not having an address yet. When I began to pull together this first care package for Buddy and the FHOTA, the stores had their racks full of Valentine's Day goodies. This seemed to me as good a place as any to start. So, along with my first letter to Buddy, I had packed several little boxes of Valentine's chocolates adorned with Teenage Mutant Ninja Turtles "Be My Valentine" cards. There was one for each of the FHOTA and a few extra for anyone else Buddy thought deserving. In addition, I had packed several bags of Buddy's favorite Valentine's candy and a proper card that let him know how much he was loved. I also included some little stuffed Valentine's critters and a couple of Valentine's toys (like PEZ dispensers and 3-D hearts that spun like tops) for good measure. By the end of last week, the only other thing I needed, besides an address for Buddy, was to whip up some of my homemade cookies—chocolate chip, Buddy's all-time favorite—and the care package would be complete. If I could have ever figured out a way to get the cookie dough to Buddy without it turning green, growing hair, and walking out of the box once it arrived, I would have sent that instead. But I knew that baked cookies would be appreciated almost as much!

In a "be careful what you wish for" scenario, this week I received not one but *three* addresses for Buddy—all different and all "permanent"! The first email announcing Buddy's new address arrived at the beginning of the week. It was while I was waiting for an address for Buddy during his first deployment that I made the misguided decision to not give Buddy's address to Nana until I had the chance to get a package put together and in the mail to him. I wanted whatever I was sending to be the first thing Buddy received. It was petty, I know, but the worst part was, it didn't even work! Even though my package was in the mail a full twenty-four hours before Nana's letter, her letter still managed to arrive first! Personally, I think it was because God has always looked out for Nana—probably that, and the fact God has never been very keen on pettiness.

This time around, the instant I received that address for Buddy, I called Nana right away to let her know. She said she did not have a pen or paper readily available at that moment but would call later after she had a minute to jot a letter to him and could write the address down. In the meantime, I would box up my pre-prepared package and send it off to Buddy so that he could start receiving mail right away.

The only thing the care package needed before being taped shut was a batch of fresh-baked chocolate chip cookies. Over the course of Buddy's life, I must have baked a few *thousand* batches of these cookies for him and Haley. I baked them for Christmas, for parties, for special school occasions, and simply because we wanted fresh-baked cookies—or cookie dough. I stood in the kitchen, ready to begin the ritual of combining the appropriate ingredients, but was frozen in my tracks. I believe that this was the first time since I was six years old that I was actually nervous about throwing together a batch of cookies—chocolate chip or otherwise. I needed them to be perfect, but after all this time, I was afraid that I would fail at my endeavors.

I started with the basics—shortening, sugars, and an egg. I beat them thoroughly before I taste-tested for the first time. Baking cookies is all about taste and texture. The taste needs to be established early on; the texture comes later, sometimes after a "test" batch of a couple of cookies. It did not take long before I forgot to be nervous and was focusing on the task at hand. After I stirred in the flour and leavening, however, doubt returned. I mixed in the final ingredient, the chocolate chips, and after one last taste-test for texture, I put two scoopfuls of dough on a cookie sheet and put them in the oven. I poured myself a glass of wine and waited for the results. The test cookies let me know that batch was a success, and before long, all cookies were baked and ready for shipping, my fears now alleviated.

So all I needed was to get an address (received), whip up some homemade cookies (completed), and get the whole thing in the mail (accomplished). It looked like we were off and running—or so I thought! By the time Nana called me back ready to confirm Buddy's address, the address had already been changed, then changed back to the original address, and then changed to a third address that the army insisted would be the *real* permanent address—all of which I passed along to Nana with all due haste. With each new address came the assurance that our packages would get to our soldiers . . . eventually. Petty though it was, as I read off Buddy's current "permanent" address to Nana, all I could think was *Nana's letter is going to get there first . . . AGAIN!*

Despite all the obvious downsides, I was uncharacteristically grateful for the countless bad days at school and work, the numerous disagreements with family and friends, and the general troubles, worries, and cares that sent me to the kitchen for the comfort I found in baking. Each baking session brought me a little closer to a chocolate chip cookie that would maintain its fresh-from-the-oven, gooey goodness for an extended period of time. I was confident that a batch of my cookies could at least arrive fresh to one permanent address without turning into a rock-like substance dense enough to bring down giants when flung from slingshots! The problem was, of course, the army's connotative definition of the word "permanent." Whether a batch of my cookies could last through three renditions of it was left to be seen.

Maggie's Chocolate Chip Cookies

1/2 cup shortening	1 teaspoon vanilla
1/2 cup margarine	1 egg
1 cup brown sugar	1 teaspoon baking soda
1/4 cup granulated sugar	1/2 teaspoon salt
1 tablespoon corn syrup	2 1/2 cups flour
3 teaspoons cornstarch	1 cup semisweet chocolate chips

1. Preheat oven to 350 degrees.
2. Cream together shortening, margarine, brown sugar, granulated sugar, corn syrup, cornstarch, vanilla, and egg with an electric mixer until light and fluffy, about 3 to 5 minutes.
3. Add baking soda and salt. Continue to beat with electric mixer for about a minute.
4. With a spoon, mix in flour until well blended. Stir in chocolate chips.
5. Drop dough by rounded tablespoons onto cookie sheets.
6. Bake for 10 to 12 minutes.

"'Tis folly to be wise" . . . or even to want to know

Keith and I continued our weekly pottery classes, and I reckoned we were coming along quite nicely for beginners! Keith was definitely better at throwing pots than I was. I simply could not master the all-important steadying-your-arm maneuver. You see, with your arm correctly braced and your elbow firmly in your hip (a little bit awkward, to say the least), you set your clay in preparation to begin your piece. With your clay properly set and your arm properly steadied, the sides of your bowl (or whatever you are making) are round and smooth. My bowls, although smooth, were oval at best.

The instructors informed me that part of my problem was that I was trying to throw pots left-handed on a right-handed wheel. Unfortunately, that was a familiar problem; I had never quite been able to properly distinguish between left-handed and right-handed activities, and for most of my life, I had done things with *both* hands. I tried to solve my problem by going right-handed on the right-handed wheel—and then left-handed on the left-handed wheel—but things went from bad to worse. After several attempts to correct the problem, my pottery station was littered with similar-looking lumps of misshapen clay that had reached various stages of bowl-hood before somehow getting severely screwed up. Eventually, the instructors took pity on me and told me to go back to my original way of doing things. It was not necessarily incorrect, but it was definitely more awkward for most—if not all—other people.

After class, Keith and I went to grab a bite to eat. I had brought the final "permanent" address for Buddy with me, and as we sat down at our table, I took the piece of paper out of my back pocket to show him. I am not quite sure what I expected from Keith, but I figured that since he had been over to Iraq twice, he just might recognize the address. I thought that maybe it would be nice to have a hint as to where Buddy was actually stationed, but I might have been a dash naïve. As Keith read through Buddy's address out loud, I began to feel those burdensome pangs of doubt indicating that knowing just might not be a good thing.

"SPC Rogers, Benjamin," Keith read.

Yeah, yeah, Specialist Rogers, I thought.

"C/1-504 PIR . . . C-Company, first of the 504th," Keith continued.

OK! OK! I know all that! What about the rest?

"2 BCT 82D ABN . . . Ah, Buddy is in the 2nd Battle Command Troop!"

*Battle? He said **battle**?!* I concentrated on keeping my face as expressionless as possible.

"FOB Loyalty. I believe that is in North Baghdad."

North Baghdad? Really? Isn't that where all the fighting is?!

I knew Buddy was in a war zone, but hearing the words "Battle Command" and "North Baghdad" was like having the wind knocked out of me. I could feel the blood drain from my extremities as everything inside of me silently proclaimed, *Oh, I can't do this!*

It was about this time that Keith noticed I was no longer listening to him and maybe even seemed a bit distracted. "Are you OK?" he asked.

Maybe it was all the color draining from my face that gave me away. As I looked back up from blankly staring at the table, the only words I could think to say were the only words that were echoing through my head: "I *can't* do this!"

My nephew seemed surprised by my revelation and mumbled something about Buddy being just fine and addresses meaning nothing. However, that just insulted my intelligence—I hated feeling that I was being coddled or, even worse, talked down to—so I pulled myself together. I smiled and informed Keith that I was OK and we continued to have a very enjoyable lunch.

A few hours later, though, in the quiet of my family room, I reflected on that moment. It occurred to me that there was a pattern forming where the people closest to me seemed surprised when I displayed signs of weakness. They did not seem to recognize the mushy, insecure, blob-ish inner core that I saw every time I looked in the mirror.

My kids have been introduced to this blob-ish inner core once or twice, and while Buddy always seemed surprised when he saw it, he also started taking great care to protect it. He once told me he would "break up" with me to save me the pain of deployment if he could. In addition, as we all stood around waiting for the soldiers to board the buses for the planes at the beginning of this deployment, Buddy told me that Shelby told his parents that he was going to Iraq to be a mail clerk in the Green Zone. Buddy then informed me that he considered doing the same thing and asked if it would have upset me. I answered simply that I would "kick your butt from here to Baghdad if you ever pulled that on me!" I understood that knowing was better than not knowing, but sometimes, I couldn't help but wonder if ignorance truly was bliss!

Sugar Cookies

1/2 cup shortening

1/2 cup margarine

1/4 cup brown sugar

1 cup powdered sugar

1/2 tablespoon cornstarch

1/2 teaspoon vanilla

1/4 teaspoon butternut flavoring

1 egg

1/4 teaspoon baking soda

1/4 teaspoon baking powder

1/4 teaspoon cream of tartar

1/2 teaspoon salt

2 3/4 cups flour

1. Preheat oven to 350 degrees.

2. Cream together shortening, margarine, brown sugar, powdered sugar, cornstarch, vanilla, butternut flavoring, and egg with an electric mixer until light and fluffy, about 3 to 5 minutes.

3. Add baking soda, baking powder, cream of tartar, and salt. Continue to beat with electric mixer for about a minute.

4. With a spoon, mix in flour. Refrigerate dough until firm.

5. Split dough into quarters. Roll out a quarter of the dough between two floured sheets of wax paper until approximately 1/8 to 1/4 inch thick. Use cookie cutters to cut dough into various shapes. Transfer cookies onto cookie sheets with a pancake turner. (Alternately, drop dough by rounded tablespoons onto cookie sheets and use a floured cookie stamp or a floured bottom of a glass to flatten the dough to 1/4-inch thickness.) Before baking, sprinkle with decorative sugars and candies.

6. Bake for 10 minutes or until cookies are lightly browned.

The elephant in the room

I had reached the point where I was consciously trying to avoid the news, yet every evening I was drawn to the television to see what was being reported on the Surge. I wanted to know enough of what was happening to keep me informed without hearing so much that I started to worry. In addition, I would have loved to see Buddy on television—like others had told me that they had; however, I did not want to see my son when they were showing some hellacious gun battle or catastrophic explosion. It would have been great to turn on the news and hear numerous reports on how successful and wonderful our troops had been—but alas, I just did not see that happening. Instead, day in and day out, I was hearing about the discussion on Capitol Hill on whether or not Congress was going to fund the Surge and its associated troops. It was the end of February; the Surge's troops had been deployed since January 2. Surely our government would not turn its back on our troops already in harm's way? It was scaring me almost as much as the danger Buddy was facing on the ground in Iraq.

From the standpoint of a soldier's mom whose son was already in a war zone, it was tough to hear reports that focused on the failures of the past years as they explained reluctance to fund the efforts that were already underway. The soldiers were busy, and I knew this to be the case. I was not hearing very much from Buddy, and when we did talk, it rarely involved anything about his day-to-day life, but I did hear enough to deduce that the soldiers themselves felt they were achieving at least some level of success. It was nothing specific, just an overall feeling that comes from knowing my son and his moods. My mom, Nana, has always told me that "No news is good news," but surely news channels reporting out of Iraq could have done a smidgen more to emphasize our soldiers' efforts and apparent successes, if only for the neurotic mom sitting at home waiting to hear something positive about her son, the soldiers, and the Surge.

It was my inferred knowledge of the soldiers' success juxtaposed against what I heard on television that lead me to believe that the news had been misreporting this thing from the beginning—always starting each report with some talking head explaining why the Surge was going to fail and then sliding downhill from there. I tried to ask Haley, my own personal "in" to the news world, why this was, even with her news station, which undeniably supported our troops, only to be told that I shouldn't be watching the news!

"You can't handle it, Mom!" she said. *Great!* All of a sudden I was a member of the cast of *A Few Good Men* being told, "*You* can't handle the truth!"

The problem was that none of this shed any light on why there seemed to be so many who were so eager to declare defeat when victory seemed to be in our grasp! I knew it seemed a waste of cognitive efforts, but I was spending a good deal of energy contemplating why there seemed to be such diverse perceptions when it came to our troops and the conflict that we were in. I could not help but be reminded of a Hindu parable my Dad would share now and again when he wanted to make a point about expanding our view of the world to allow for someone else's speculation or attitude. While I was growing up, this parable was generally thrown out there to get me to stop fighting with my brothers, but in the light of the war, it seemed to take on a whole new significance.

The parable is a poem about how six blind men are led to an elephant for the first time and then asked to describe it. Each blind man is led to a different part of the elephant, which means six different vantage points, creating six different mental images—one for each blind man. The blind man led to the trunk thought that an elephant was some kind of a serpent; the blind man led to the leg thought the elephant was a tree. The blind man led to the ear thought that an elephant was some kind of a flying beast with large, featherless wings, whereas the elephant's tusks evoked images of a huge, saber-toothed, flesh-eating monster—which would explain why that blind man went screaming from the room and hid in the broom closet yelling for everyone else to save themselves. (At least, that's what *I* would have done!) I imagine this behavior was quite confusing to the blind man who was led to the elephant's tail—a relatively small, leathery thing with a tuft of hair sprouting from the end of it, hanging from the center of a very large something else with very little distinct definition beyond its size. However, within this man's mind, there was probably a similar vision to the blind man who was led to the elephant's side and declared the beast was as large as a house! But since the elephant (who, at that point, was probably feeling a tad self-conscious and insisting it was just a glandular problem) was more than just a side, this man's vision was not exactly right either.

An argument ensued as the blind men attempted to impose their perception of the elephant on each other. Even the sighted man got involved, but to no avail. Where the blind men's perceptions were clouded by their lack of sight, the sighted man's perception was clouded by the whole elephant and not its parts—kind of similar to not being able to see the forest for the trees—and therein lay the problem.

To summarize: an elephant is *BIG*! Logically, if you were only exposed to a small area of elephant without the capability of visualizing the whole beast, you would obviously end up with some misconceptions as to what an elephant actually looked like. Well, that was exactly what we had with the Surge, and I had finally found the explanation I had been searching for. The war was an elephant—most likely with a glandular problem—and we were all blind men!

As if my dad were standing before me relaying that parable himself, I began wondering how much of all the different views of the war were tied to the reporting of the Surge and how much people's own general life experiences were clouding their perceptions when it came to the War on Terror and the current conflict. Of course, I also realized that I was one of those "clouded" individuals influenced by my own son's intimate involvement. Still, I could not help but feel that the news outlets could have been a little more positive when they reported on our soldiers and their efforts!

White Chocolate Macadamia Nut Cookies

2/3 cup shortening	1 egg
1/3 cup margarine	1 teaspoon baking soda
1 1/4 cups brown sugar	1/2 teaspoon salt
1/3 cup powdered sugar	2 cups flour
1/2 tablespoon corn syrup	1 cup white chocolate chips
1 tablespoon cornstarch	2/3 cup very coarsely chopped dry
1/2 teaspoon vanilla	roasted macadamia nuts
1/2 teaspoon butternut flavoring	

1. Preheat oven to 350 degrees.
2. Cream together shortening, margarine, brown sugar, powdered sugar, corn syrup, cornstarch, vanilla, butternut flavoring, and egg with an electric mixer until light and fluffy, about 3 to 5 minutes.

3. Add baking soda and salt. Continue to beat with electric mixer for about a minute.

4. With a spoon, mix in flour until well blended. Stir in chocolate chips and macadamia nuts.

5. Drop dough by rounded tablespoons onto cookie sheets.

6. Bake for 10 to 12 minutes.

Cookie Week 4

18 February 2007-24 February 2007

I don't like this game; can we play something else?

The initial shock of my son's abrupt departure was beginning to wear off. As a full range of emotions slowly stirred in me, so did the realization that no matter how I sliced it, this was my life for the next nine months or so. Buddy was off experiencing the ambiguous hospitality of Iraq and all its dubious accommodations, executing the Surge, and I was left to deal with it. There was no getting out of it; that was just the way it was, and I was having a hard time wrapping my head around it all.

My life had developed a dreamlike quality—maybe closer to nightmarish—since the beginning of the Surge. It seemed almost fantasy-like to me—a B-movie somewhere between make-believe and drama—as I worked my way through the current circumstances. My insides had been churning with a combination of a mother's pride, dread, and a weird feeling of excitement. I was determined to not only get through it all but to stay positive. I went through each day on autopilot pretending that soon everything would be returning to the way it was before this deployment began. I had almost convinced myself that nothing would, or could, change. And then the FRG leader sent out an email.

FRG is the acronym for the Family Readiness Group—a support organization for soldiers and their families born out of a soldier's unit. This organization provides a network of communications between families, their soldier's chain of command, and, in some ways, the soldiers themselves. For the family of a soldier, the people working in these organizations feel like a lifeline.

Normally, the FRG leader would be the spouse of the unit's commander. There was some sort of a personal "in" that was created by having your soldier's commander's spouse reporting on your soldier's unit's activities. And this was not stuff that you would hear on the evening news; this was an inside look at what your soldier was experiencing and very specific things that you, as the immediate family of a soldier, would need to know. For this email, our FRG leader was reaching out to touch base with all the families. In the email, she wrote:

I think we're finally hitting that part of the deployment where we start playing the waiting game. The guys are somewhat settled and working hard, so there's not much communication from the front, and the families back home have settled into a sort of routine.

As innocuous as this simple statement seemed, it was the kind of thing of which a mother's bad dreams are made—words like "the front" and "waiting game" against a backdrop of "working hard." Add to that the implication that anything could have been "routine" in my life, and I fell headfirst into a vortex of conflicting emotions and mental images. My thoughts about Buddy as a cherub-faced little boy sitting on the floor playing with his dinosaur bones contrasted against the image of him as a soldier—tall, strong, and resolute, but at the same time oh-so-fragile. I also considered the differences between a twenty-year-old who would strap a vest of explosives to his chest to blow up as many people as possible and a twenty-year-old who would readily put himself in harm's way to protect his family and his country, but most likely just to protect the soldier next to him—probably Pestilence! I then reflected on the contrast between a young soldier sent to a foreign land to play prison guard and a soldier sent to "the front" to "work hard." I had no misconceptions as to what the term "the front" meant and what "working hard" at "the front" implied.

Although I initially rejected the term, a quick review of my current life revealed a pattern that someone, for lack of a more descriptive word, just might have referred to as a "routine." It was a numbed—sometimes artificially numbed with wine—lethargic, predictable existence with well-defined limits and very few extracurricular activities outside those limits. Whether routine or simply void of energy for anything other than what I had deemed absolutely necessary, I certainly was not looking for any shake-ups to disrupt the unchanging venture in which I found myself.

In between work, weak attempts at general house upkeep, and throwing pots, I tried to focus my energy on my weekly care packages and home-baked cookies. To me, home-baked cookies were an essential component to any care package. Yet, with the army's use of the word "permanent" being such a fleeting term, I was left with only a couple recipes that I felt could withstand the journey from my house to his location in Iraq. I feared that unless I could create more durable recipes than those found in my collection of cookbooks, Buddy was going to find the weekly allotment of fresh-baked-when-sent chocolate chip cookies overly repetitive, monotonous, and maybe even just a pinch irritating.

I decided that weekly innovative cookie-baking sessions in my kitchen could be beneficial to all concerned. I would allow my anxiety to give way to my creative side in an attempt to concoct a variety of durable cookies to send to my son. Not only would Buddy get an assortment of homemade goodies, but I would get some relief as well—not to mention a weekly session of cookie dough overindulgence. For the first innovative batch, I thought I would regress to an earlier time when the kids were in grade school and all seemed right with the world. One Saturday afternoon, Buddy and I decided to try our hand at creative cookie baking. When he was just beginning to learn to spell, if you asked him to spell "Buddy," he would answer "B-U-R-S-N-U-T." It was a bit uncanny, but he would spell it that way every time. Buddy, of course, eventually learned to spell his name correctly, but the name "Bursnut" lingered. On that Saturday afternoon, Buddy and I invented the Bursnut cookie, and that was the cookie I was going to try to duplicate now.

As far as I could see, it was a win-win endeavor. Rather than something that could ever be labeled as simply "routine," these cookie-creating sessions would be exercises in emotional survival. Then again, it might just have been a difference in the connotative meanings of the word "routine."

Then there were the words "waiting game." As a long-standing female member of Peter Pan's Lost Boys, I had taken my vow to never grow up quite seriously. When I heard the word "game," I envisioned Kick-the-Can or Candy Land. If not those two, there were a plethora of other games that amused and entertained. All of the games that came to mind produced visions of raucous good times filled with laughter and all-around frivolity; there simply was nothing about them that resembled the "waiting game" I was reluctantly playing now.

If I were the FRG leader, rather than comparing the situation to a game, I might have been more tempted to compare it to a long car trip with my family when I was six. Even though Grandma's house and Disneyland were the ultimate destination, I asked my parents "Are we there yet?" every five minutes from the east cost to the west coast. And even though there were pleasant times as we stopped for a swim at a local watering hole and visited "Santa's Summer Home," the general feeling of the adventure along the way was one of endless torture.

Finally, there was the phrase "families back home." Whether a wife of one of our soldiers or a parent, this deployment had already proven to be worrisome and disruptive for all involved. Wives had to handle the chores their husbands would have gladly taken on if duty had not called them away. They were left to continue their roles as mother even as they did their best to represent their husband's role as father. On top of all that, there were the endless nights of sleeping alone. But it was no picnic for us parents, either—especially the parents of single soldiers. We, too, had the normalcy of our lives fractured as we adjusted to the lack of routine phone calls and the absence of our sons' frequent trips home for long weekends. There was an emptiness that enveloped us, as well, as we labored to get through each day without too many random thoughts that took our hearts and emotions to places they just did not want to be. We, too, worked very hard to put on a positive public face to conceal our internal fears and concerns in order to shine the best possible light on "our guys" and the work they were doing. But despite any differences in what wives and parents were experiencing, what I did know was that for all of us—wives, children, parents, grandparents, and siblings—this "waiting game" was going to feel like an eternity.

Bursnut Cookies

1/2 cup shortening
1/2 cup margarine
1/3 cup brown sugar
3/4 cup powdered sugar
1 teaspoon vanilla
1 teaspoon ground allspice
1/4 teaspoon cream of tartar

1/4 teaspoon baking soda
1/2 teaspoon salt
2 1/2 cups flour
1/3 cup coarsely chopped walnuts
1/3 cup coarsely chopped pecans
1/2 cup finely chopped walnuts
1/2 cup finely chopped pecans

1. Preheat oven to 350 degrees.
2. Cream together shortening, margarine, brown sugar, powdered sugar, and vanilla with an electric mixer until light and fluffy, about 3 to 5 minutes.
3. Add allspice, cream of tartar, baking soda, and salt. Continue to beat with electric mixer for about a minute.
4. With a spoon, mix in flour until well blended. Stir in coarsely chopped walnuts and pecans.
5. Shape dough into 2 long rounds, 2 inches in diameter.
6. In a separate bowl, mix together the finely chopped walnuts and pecans. Spread the mixture onto a flat surface.
7. Roll each long round of dough in the nut mixture to coat its outside. After coating with nuts, wrap the round first in wax paper then in aluminum foil. Refrigerate the dough overnight.
8. Remove the dough from the wax paper and foil. With a very sharp knife, slice the round in 1/8- to 1/4-inch slices and place on a cookie sheet.
9. Bake for 8 to 10 minutes until the edges are lightly browned.

Cookie Week 5

25 February 2007-3 March 2007

While we are on the subject, or maybe subject *lines* . . .

It had already been several days since I had heard anything from Buddy. After the previous week's email from the FRG leader, it was not all that surprising; but still, it did make for moments of wandering thoughts depicting intolerable mental images. Furthermore, I did not live close to Buddy's home base, so the only time I was privy to the rumor mill was when the FRG leader attempted to dispel the current rumors. Generally, this was a good thing, because a considerable amount of needless worry was alleviated that way, but it also made for a fascinating read as I perused emails intended to ease anxious hearts by quelling erroneous information that I did not know was an issue to begin with. That being said, sometimes these emails had the opposite effect on me.

I was at work and had just finished my lunch when an email from the FRG leader popped up in my inbox with the subject line *Casualties*. I stared at that subject line for several moments trying to work up the courage to open the email. All I could think was *Casualties? There were casualties?* After all, there had been nothing on the evening news, no word that anything was amiss. Besides that, our soldiers had only just begun their work over there. And yet, there it was—*Casualties*! "And so it begins," I mumbled to myself as I opened the email.

And so it begins. The words continued to resonate deep within my heart and soul. I had begun to read the email when a question bubbled up from somewhere deep in my subconscious: *OK, so it has begun . . . but how will it end?* I fought to push that question—and all that it could imply—back out of my consciousness and read what the FRG leader had to say.

According to the email, there were casualties taken by a unit in another battalion. When the word first trickled down to the wives of the soldiers in Buddy's unit, there were questions as to whether our guys were affected. Reading through the closing words of the email urging us all to continue to pray, I surmised that the soldiers of Buddy's unit and battalion, and hence the families of those soldiers, were indeed safe. However, instead of calming any fears, the email left me feeling more uneasy. *I can't do this!*

My office is a very large room, probably the size of a football field, divided into several different worker areas with what I like to refer to as "half-icles." A half-icle is like a cubicle, only the walls are just waist high, which made them half-icles in my mind. Now, the reason for this was apparently to allow for "open lines" of communication. This meant that someone was able to sit at their desk and yell across the football field (from here on to be referred to as the "bullpen") to someone on the other side of the room, thus alleviating the necessity for anything as inconvenient as walking. All worker areas were connected by a shared half wall or desk area. Privacy was not an issue in this office—it was simply nonexistent!

I stared at the laptop screen on my desk, trying to decide if my newly churning stomach was going to "release" the bowl of soup that I had just finished for lunch. My supervisor had just returned from lunch himself and walked up to his work area, which was adjacent to mine. I guess he noticed the somewhat dazed, deer-in-the-headlights look on my face and asked, "Are you OK, Maggie?"

Unable to speak because of the fear of what else besides words might fall out, I simply turned the laptop around so that he could read the email himself. My supervisor was aware of my son's precarious location, but I also knew that my supervisor was socially awkward at times—and that is putting it mildly. Even so, I must admit that I was not ready for his response. After taking a minute to read through the email, he looked me in the eyes and asked, "Don't you think it would be more appropriate for you to set aside five minutes in the morning or in the evening to handle this type of stuff?"

I was speechless. I honestly did not think I was capable of detaching myself from the part of me that is eternally connected to my kids—and with one of my kids in a war zone being shot at every day, I thought it absurd that someone would actually ask it of me. I was torn between professionalism and being the mother of a soldier. Apparently, the two are supposed to be mutually exclusive, but not in my world. What I did know was that, added to my often-asserted "I can't do this," I discovered a new sentiment: "What the heck am I doing here with these social idiots?"

Once I arrived at home, I shared the whole incident with Haley. I opened up my laptop to let her read through the email herself and waited for her reaction. She sat in front of my laptop for the longest time without saying a word. I knew that she was a much faster reader than that, so I could not understand her silence.

"Well?" I finally asked. "What do you think?"

"I think the FRG leader could have been a little nicer here," Haley responded.

"What? Nicer? What are you talking about?"

"Well," Haley paused a moment to gather her thoughts before continuing. "It seems to me that the most upsetting part of this email is the subject line. *Casualties!* Isn't that just a little harsh?"

"What? I mean, there *were* casualties," I replied. "What would you have her say instead?"

"I don't know; maybe something softer," Haley opined. She leaned back on the couch as she further contemplated that idea. "Something to ease you into the content of the email. You know?"

"Softer? Ease you into the email?! Like what?" I asked. "Maybe *Tinker Bell has a secret*? How would that help?"

Haley laughed at my suggestion. She was pleased with the ridiculous direction the conversation had just taken but did not want to have her idea dismissed so easily. "It helps because the subject line has not tied you up in knots before you even get to the email," she replied.

"So it's like delayed gratification, only we're talking about gut-wrenching anguish?" I inquired. "I'm just not sure that it helps. And besides," I continued, "at what point would *Tinker Bell has a secret* elicit the same gut-wrenching anxiety as *Casualties*?"

"Well, what if it wasn't always Tinker Bell with the secret? And what if sometimes the secret wasn't all bad news?" Haley asserted. "That would work, right?"

"We're bringing Mickey Mouse and Goofy into this insanity?" By now I was laughing, too. "And worse than that, you're changing it up so that every single email we get will cause the gut-wrenching anxiety because nothing distinguishes one from the other? Yeah, no, I don't think that helps!" I thought about it a moment before adding, "In fact, causing every email subject line to equate to bad news is probably worse than dealing with the subject line of *Casualties*, don't you think?"

Haley claimed the last word. "Maybe," she said, then quickly added, "but I still think *Casualties* is harsh and letting Tinker Bell have a secret would be better!"

I am not sure that the emotional upheaval that was associated with this email could have ever been lessened by softening the harshness of the email's subject line. Even if the subject line was changed, the content of the message would have remained the same. Maybe not the first time Tinker Bell's secret showed up in my inbox, but in the emails to come—and somehow I feared there would be more to come—seeing Tinker Bell on the subject line would become associated with bad news. Like Pavlov's dogs, the programmed response would soon become queasy butterflies in the stomach accompanied by a rapid heartbeat and not the initial "Aww, Tinker Bell has a secret! I wonder what it is?" that might have been present the first time.

Truth be told, even without the emails with questionable subject lines, to say I had been living at a higher state of anxiety since January would be a bit of an understatement. Since Buddy deployed, every waking moment was encompassed by an underlying sense of imminent catastrophe, and sleep—if I could actually fall asleep—was restless and often filled with haunting dreams. In some ways, defining the new level of anxiety brought on by this email was like trying to gauge the difference between a spilled gallon of milk and a spilled gallon plus a cup of milk. There is obviously a measurable difference in the puddle that would be expanding on the kitchen floor—I'm just not sure it would feel like much of a difference when it came to cleaning up the mess. Like the spilled milk, I figured I was a "cup" more stressed by this point, and I just was not sure that I could really feel the difference.

Cream Cheese Cookies

Cookie:

1/2 cup shortening	1/2 teaspoon vanilla
1/2 cup margarine	1 egg
1/4 cup brown sugar	1/2 teaspoon cream of tartar
2/3 cup granulated sugar	1/2 teaspoon salt
1/2 teaspoon ground cinnamon	2 1/4 cups flour

Filling:

1/2 cup margarine	2/3–3/4 cup powdered sugar
8 ounces cream cheese	

Topping:

1/4 cup chocolate chips	1 tablespoon milk (approx.)
1/8 cup margarine	

1. Preheat oven to 350 degrees.
2. Cream together shortening, margarine, brown sugar, granulated sugar, cinnamon, vanilla, and egg with an electric mixer until light and fluffy, about 3 to 5 minutes.

3. Add cream of tartar and salt. Continue to beat with electric mixer for about a minute.

4. With a spoon, mix in flour.

5. Drop by rounded tablespoons onto cookie sheets. With the bottom of a small glass (or the bottom of a standard spice container), flatten the dough to about 1/4 inch in the center. The edges of the dough should be slightly higher, creating a shallow bowl.

6. Bake for about 10 minutes until the edges of the cookie are slightly browned. Remove from the cookie sheet to cool completely.

7. To make the filling, melt together the margarine, cream cheese, and powdered sugar in a double boiler.

8. Stir the mixture until it thickens to a pudding-like consistency. While the mixture is still very warm, drop a dollop into the "bowl" of each of the baked cookies. Allow to set for several minutes; an hour or two would not be unusual.

9. When the cream cheese mixture is set, melt the chocolate chips, margarine, and milk in the double boiler to create a decorative topping. Use enough milk to make the chocolate mixture drizzle-able but not so much that it would not solidify when cooled.

10. Drizzle the chocolate mixture across the top of the cream cheese–filled cookies, making crisscross decorations on each. Allow the cookies to cool thoroughly before packing into a care package. Separate the layers of cookies with wax paper when packing to ship.

Happy New-Valen-Saint-Easter-
Hallow-Give-Mas Day

I had settled into full-on survival mode. Survival at work was centered on keeping to myself—more specifically, steering away from non–work related conversations with my supervisor. Survival at home was centered on participating in and taking full advantage of the few extracurricular activities in which I still engaged. Even so, pot throwing was coming along slowly. Though I had my first completed bowl—more oval than round and with only a minimally acceptable glaze applied—further bowl initiatives had been sluggish in developing, at best. I could spin the clay and form the bowls—marginally—but the act of glazing intimidated me.

As far as care packages for Buddy, besides creating a different variety of home-baked cookies built to survive the journey to Iraq, I decided awhile back that all holidays should be recognized by the troops and commemorated with whatever paraphernalia I could find. I was driven to help Buddy, the FHOTA, and the rest of the soldiers celebrate each holiday occasion to the fullest—or at least to the fullest they were able. Since it was March, I figured they should be celebrating Saint Patrick's Day and the luck of the Irish, which I prayed they were *all* blessed with, Irish or not!

So I asked myself, *How do you commemorate a day that is generally celebrated by wearing green and drinking excessive amounts of beer when you are not allowed to drink and wear green every day?* My answer came in the form of green suckers adorned with leprechauns, pressed four-leaf clovers laminated on cards containing traditional Irish prayers and toasts, and a half-dozen or so whiskey-flavored cigars (the alcohol, not the dog) that I had discovered at the local tobacco shop. I also found lovely green bands with "Kiss me, I'm Irish" buttons attached to them to include in the care packages, as well.

Once collected, I set the assortment out on the dining room table and eagerly waited for Haley to return home from work so that I could share my awesome finds with her. As soon as she walked through the front door, I called her into the dining room where I was assembling boxes. Haley perused it all, silently nodding in approval, until she came to the green bands. She picked one up to get a closer look. A frown flashed across her face as she held the package up.

"Why are you sending the FHOTA a bunch of garters?" she asked.

"Those aren't garters. They're arm bands!" I asserted.

"Mama, look at them! They're garters!" Haley shot back.

"Flip the package over and see what it says," I answered. "See? Look there. The package is clearly labeled ARM BAND! It's an arm band, not a garter!"

"Seriously?" Haley was still unconvinced.

"Yes!" I responded. "Mind you, the garters were identical, only they were in packages labeled GARTER instead of ARM BAND. So, yes, seriously!"

Quite honestly, I saw the whole care-package-for-Buddy-(and the FHOTA)-in-a-war-zone thing as an evolving process. I was always looking for ways to "enhance" their care package experience without breaking any of the army's many rules. It was not as easy as it might seem—at one point, even comic books were considered too risky for the troops' well-being. The way I saw it was that I would push up against all the rules without actually breaking them to support Buddy and the FHOTA in whatever way I could—including sending arm bands that might actually be garters.

Once Haley had given her seal of approval, I packed it all into boxes along with this week's freshly baked cookies, Shamrock Cookies. These cookies were simply a thin-rolled butter cookie dyed green with an overabundance of green food coloring (so the FHOTA would end up with a green tongue and lips if they ate too many) and then cut out using a shamrock-shaped cookie cutter. I also added short written notes for Christian, Toby, and Shelby reminding them to "be safe." Before I sealed the box up, I added a long letter to Buddy and then took the care packages to the local post office to be shipped off to Iraq. As always, no matter how early I was shipping, I could only hope that it would get to the guys in time to celebrate the day, but I figured as long as they received it before the next holiday, it was all good.

Toward the end of the week, after I had arrived at work, I logged onto my Hotmail account to see if there were any messages from Buddy or the FRG leader, as was my standard operating procedure. I know that it had been requested by my supervisor that I refrain from this activity while I was at work, but I felt that was an unreasonable, if not ludicrous, request. I checked my email regularly at home as well, but a work day is eight and a half hours long. Add to that two hours of commute time, and it was a quasi-lifetime to be disconnected from and unavailable to my son.

On this occasion, I was delighted to find an email from Christian. The subject line was simply *hiya* and the message was a thank-you note for the care package. In the message, he wrote that they had decided to pretty much ignore all holidays over the next year or so and instead were going to celebrate them all at once when they returned to the States with a huge "New-Valen-Saint-Easter-Hallow-Give-Mas-Day" party.

Awesome! I immediately wrote him back to say, "Count me in! You can even host it at my house!" It was always good to hear that Buddy and the rest of the guys were in high enough spirits to spend a few minutes joking around. In addition, the thought of throwing a party like this gave me something else to occupy my thoughts besides the constant worry of having my son in a war zone. The email exchange left me in a marvelously good mood for a change, and I could not wait to share it. I immediately called Haley, even though I knew she was at work and would not be able to talk long.

I felt exceptionally positive for the rest of the day. Every so often throughout the morning, I would allow my mind to wander to what a New-Valen-Saint-Easter-Hallow-Give-Mas-Day party might look like and how one might prepare for it. I was aware that every thought along these lines left a huge smile on my face. For the first time in a while, life felt normal—maybe even good! However, my good mood dissipated slightly when I pulled into my driveway that evening.

Though I had at least managed to get my Christmas lights turned off, they were still hung up with appropriately (or inappropriately, considering it was March!) festive garland all along the front of the house. Walking down the pathway to the front door, I noted my one battery-operated candle still burning in my kitchen window surrounded by Valentine's Day window stickers. The candle was one of several that previously adorned the front of my house for the Christmas holidays. I had managed to get the other candles down—though certainly not put away—but I had decided that this candle should remain burning from sundown to sunup until Buddy returned home.

Approaching the front door to my house, I was greeted by a St. Patrick's Day wreath which shifted back and forth on its hook as the front door swung open. I stepped into my front foyer only to get slapped in the face by some hall streamers that had been hung from the ceiling for a New Year's Eve celebration. My enthusiasm for the day was evaporating rapidly. I murmured something about it all being ridiculous—while at the same time realizing that, as ridiculous as it was, I still did not have the energy to do anything about it.

The Whiskey-Dog had bounded towards me the moment I walked through the front door—undoubtedly just trying to demonstrate that he was glad to see me. Even so, I scolded him to calm down. At the moment, I found his incredible enthusiasm regarding my arrival a pinch irritating. Haley had been in her room reading, but after hearing the ruckus at the front door just above the ceiling of her room, she decided to see what the commotion was about. Haley walked up the stairs and paused on the last step before the landing. She watched the melee a moment before commenting.

"Hey Mom! What's up? Having a bad day?" she asked.

I thought, *No, actually, I have had a* good *day*, but what I said was, "Look at this place! Christmas out front, Valentine's Day in the kitchen, New Year's in the front hall! This is just *nuts*!"

Haley took a moment to think before saying, "You know, Mom, if you really are planning to have the New-Valen-Saint-Easter-Hallow-Give-Mas-Day party here, you're actually behind on your decorations. It seems to me you have at least a half-dozen or so holidays that aren't accounted for yet. You'd better get a move on!"

I stared blankly at Haley for a moment as her words sunk in and my frustration dissolved—and then I began to laugh. I guess the situation boiled down to personal perceptions and perspectives—kind of a glass-half-full-or-half-empty thing. I could either spend my time focusing on all that was wrong, like a buildup of seasonal decorations that was spanning the seasons, or appreciate everything that was right, like a house already half-decorated for a New-Valen-Saint-Easter-Hallow-Give-Mas-Day party and a wonderful daughter who helped me see it.

Shamrock Cookies

1/2 cup shortening

1/2 cup margarine

1 cup powdered sugar

1/2 cup granulated sugar

1 tablespoon light corn syrup

1 teaspoon vanilla

1 egg

6–8 drops green food dye

1/4 teaspoon cream of tartar

3/4 teaspoon baking soda

1/2 teaspoon salt

2 1/2 cups flour

1. Preheat oven to 350 degrees.
2. Cream together shortening, margarine, powdered sugar, granulated sugar, corn syrup, vanilla, and egg with an electric mixer until light and fluffy, about 3 to 5 minutes.
3. Beat in green food dye.
4. Add cream of tartar, baking soda, and salt. Continue to beat with electric mixer for about a minute.
5. With a spoon, mix in flour.
6. Refrigerate dough until stiff. Roll out the dough by quarters between floured wax paper until the dough is about 1/8 inch thick. Use a cookie cutter to cut out shamrock shapes, then use a pancake turner to transfer the shamrocks to a cookie sheet. Optionally, sprinkle the cookies with green decorator's sugar before baking.
7. Bake for 8 to 10 minutes or until edges show a slight browning.

Passing the time with Nana—my mom, not the dog!

I received another email from the FRG leader this week. As if the recent emails regarding reported casualties hadn't been bad enough, this was an email explaining different issues concerning wounded soldiers and our options as family. Those issues and options were a reminder of the brutality and uncertainty of war that I did not—and hopefully would not—need, but as the Surge had heated up, the news from the front had contained increasingly more reports on its cost—and not just monetarily. Though it stood to reason that available help for families of soldiers could potentially be beneficial, it simply left me with a churning in my stomach and an ache in my heart that made me feel helpless.

Since the news had been reporting more on the Surge, I realized that Nana was hearing more of the details about our soldiers than I had intended. I had been trying to shield her from the more volatile aspects of having her grandson serving in combat, though I am not totally sure why. Nana is quite a remarkable woman and not given to overreaction or alarmist behavior. Like many others in her generation, she has often been required to be strong, and she has done so with resilience. For instance, in 1942, at just twenty-one years of age, Nana left her home in Seattle to travel to Washington, DC, to support the war effort. She did not know anyone in the area, nor did she have a place to stay, yet she boarded the train anyway. She had a train ticket, a small amount of money that her father had given her for the trip, and an address, date, and time for reporting to her new job. It was only through the kindness of a woman she met on the train that she acquired the name and address of someone who could help her with living arrangements. Other than that, she began her adventure totally on her own.

By current standards, Nana's journey to her new job—let alone accepting the job—does not seem like such an exceptional act. In those days, however, planes were for the war effort and Seattle was several days by train from Washington, DC; phones were more rare than common—the concept of cell phones nothing more than science fiction; and the letters sent between Nana and her family took a week or more to arrive at their destinations—once again, the concept of personal computers and email being something from a Jules Verne novel.

It took strength and character for her to leave her home and family to travel to the unfamiliar and unknown—and this was the woman I was trying to protect. I guess I just figured, *Why worry her needlessly?* So when I talked with my mom and she would ask for clarification as to where exactly Buddy was located, I would answer, "Nana, I really do not know *exactly* where he is!" and then quickly change the subject before she had a chance to press the issue. Since I was only aware of his general location, I felt I could tell Nana this without fear of recrimination for lying. Was this behavior correct on my part? Probably not, but I did give her copies of the monthly newsletters and tried to keep her current on all the information that would not keep her up at night worrying. I reckoned I was worrying enough for us all!

At the time of the Surge, Nana was eighty-six years old. Even so, she was still markedly independent and self-sufficient. She loved children—all children, not just her offspring—was an avid card player, created amazing counted cross-stitch artwork, doted on her Annie-dog—a middle-aged Cavalier King Charles Spaniel—and cherished her time with friends and family. She was a selfless and giving individual, donating her time to charities weekly and agreeing in her spare time to be the designated grocery shopper for those in the neighborhood who could not drive themselves to the store. Whether neighborhood driver or church deaconess, foster mother or babysitter, what Nana did, she did with an open and giving heart, without begrudging or complaint. Nana was simply amazing.

Though the first thing people noticed was Nana's heart, the second thing was her naïveté. For all of her basic street sense, Nana definitely missed a lesson or two on street talk and behavior, which was evidenced by a favorite Nana story from my youth. Nana would do her ironing in front of the television, and on this occasion there was a local breaking news story; a nearby prison had been taken over by the inmates. Nana had some questions.

"Did these guys go bad because they hated their mothers?" she asked, followed by "Do they bring the prisoners' families in—like their mothers—to try and talk the prisoners into giving up?"

We could not fathom what was on her mind.

"What are you really asking here?" my dad finally inquired.

"Well," Nana answered, "I was watching the news on the prison takeover this afternoon, and the prisoners kept on yelling through their bullhorns, 'We hate you *mothers* out there!' *Why* do they hate their mothers?"

Clearly, Nana had no idea that these prisoners were not talking about their mothers and in fact were only using half a word. Following our moment of understanding came several moments of uncomfortable explanation as we attempted to reveal to Nana what was being said without actually *saying* the words.

"They shouldn't be showing that on afternoon television!" came the classic Nana response when she finally understood what the prisoners were yelling. "Young children could be watching!"

"What difference should that make?" my brother quipped. "*You* didn't know what they were talking about!"

However, for all our ribbing, Nana was the one who realized that although she did not grasp what was being said at that prison, her teenage children did! So it would stand to reason that though she was unaware, young children who were watching just might be a little more astute. Like I said, wise but naïve, and spunky and energetic, too, with a tendency to draw the best out of people.

Like me, Nana tended to enjoy periodic random conversations with complete strangers on street corners and in store lines. Sometimes, though, these conversations raised great concern regarding Buddy. The difficulty was that Nana's honest, open heart left her susceptible to others' views, especially when those views immersed her in that which I spent my time trying to protect her from.

The outcome of these conversations were, more often than not, a perceived danger for her grandson. That translated into a problem she needed to solve, and the first step in that problem-solving process was to share her concerns with me. After one of these conversations with a random person, Nana was always on the phone warning me about what some stranger standing in line in front of her was kind enough to share. Mostly, I was more than happy to alleviate Nana's concerns by sharing with her what little I knew, but sometimes her concerns bordered on my own. When this happened, the combination of her concerns, my concerns, and current events would collide. I would not be able to relieve Nana's worry, and instead, she would heighten mine. With my emotions raw and my capacity to listen severely impaired by my emotions, I would fight with myself over my inabilities to remain strong, while poor Nana stood directly in the path of my emotional train wreck.

I was keenly aware that not all dangers Buddy faced were physical, so when Nana called to tell me about a conversation she had with some stranger regarding the problems her son was having since returning from Iraq, it was like rubbing salt in an open wound. The crux of the situation was that this woman's son had some injuries but was suffering more emotionally than physically. This was a tragic situation, and the thought of it twisted my soul into knots.

In a nutshell, what I heard Nana saying was that this woman felt that the military and government were not taking responsibility for her son's ailments. She said that she just wanted her son taken care of but in the same breath spoke of the "tens of thousands" in lawyers' fees she was paying to get the military and government to accept culpability. I was confused. Tens of thousands were going to lawyers, but was anything going to doctors?

"She doesn't think her son is going to live beyond the year!" Nana exclaimed.

"He's dying?" I asked, my stomach churning as I tried to make sense of what Nana was saying, the whole time envisioning Buddy as the victim, not some stranger's son.

"*No!*" Nana answered. "This woman says her son is going to kill himself!"

I could see why this conversation upset Nana. Heck, it was upsetting me! But for the life of me, I could not figure out why this woman was spending bundles on lawyers while her son was suffering, according to her, from a lack of treatment.

While Nana passionately tried to explain to me the horror of this woman's situation, I continued to try to determine what was actually being done to *help* this woman's son. Do I believe that the government and the military have a moral obligation to care for our troops and *all* their ailments? Absolutely! However, from what Nana was telling me, it seemed that this woman was spending more on lawyers for moral outrage than she was to help her emotionally distraught soldier son, and, though I was earnestly trying, I could not figure out why. Meanwhile, a soldier sat languishing somewhere without proper care while his mother fought the government. I was overwrought as I tried to make sense of it all.

Needless to say, the conversation went nowhere! After a few spirited minutes of verbal exchange, we each took a deep breath, and decided it was best to simply end the phone call.

I was sure I was no help in calming Nana's fears, let alone in easing my own anxieties. There were just too many unanswered questions regarding this woman and her son's situation. I likened it to parents in an ugly divorce using their children as pawns in an effort to hurt one another. Obviously, it is not their intention for the children to be collateral damage, but because they are so wrapped up in their own situation, they overlook the ultimate consequences of their actions. I could not help but feel that this was part of this woman and her poor soldier son's problem. Despite my feelings, though, I could not imagine how this woman felt, nor did I want to, because the whole situation scared me. As insensitive as it sounded, I needed to believe that, despite what this woman was telling Nana, it would be different for Buddy. *I* would be different for Buddy.

My own experience with the army and FRG leaders and their timely email messages regarding options for wounded soldiers led me to believe that the army was not only aware of but also on top of the issues that our boys could face when they arrived home. Beyond that, I wanted Nana to understand that even if the army, military, or government did not handle Buddy's issues appropriately upon his return, I would absolutely make sure that he received whatever help he needed, even if I had to pay for it myself.

Peanut Butter Buttons

1/2 cup shortening

1/2 cup margarine

1/3 cup peanut butter

2 1/3 cups powdered sugar

1/2 teaspoon vanilla

1 egg

1/4 teaspoon baking soda

1/4 teaspoon cream of tartar

1/2 teaspoon salt

2 cups flour

1. Preheat oven to 350 degrees.

2. Cream together shortening, margarine, peanut butter, powdered sugar, vanilla, and egg with an electric mixer until light and fluffy, about 3 to 5 minutes.

3. Add baking soda, cream of tartar, and salt. Continue to beat with electric mixer for about a minute.

4. With a spoon, mix in flour.

5. Drop dough by rounded teaspoons onto cookie sheets.

6. Bake for 8 to 10 minutes.

Cookie Week 8

18 March 2007–24 March 2007

"I'll get you, my pretty, and your little dog, too!"

I believe I could safely say that I was stressed. Maybe it was the fact that two months before Buddy deployed, I began a new job. Actually, it was more like a whole new career as an analyst, where I was paid to think about stuff—180 degrees from my first career as a computer scientist, where I was paid to make stuff work, which I had done for roughly twenty-five years. Or maybe it was simply the fact that Buddy had deployed, but whatever the reason, I knew that I was stressed. So, bright and early on Monday morning when I felt an intense pain on the right side of my back as I sat up in bed, I was sure it was just my body hitting me where I was the weakest. An active but klutzy life had left me with more than one back injury, which was why it was always the first body part to feel any random malady that came my way. I concluded my back was simply telling me to take an extra day for rest, so I called in sick and spent the day trying to relax.

By Tuesday morning when I arrived at work, I was operating at about eighty percent. I was walking a tad slower than normal because I was still feeling a twinge of pain now and again. After observing me hobble to my desk, one of my coworkers inquired if I was all right. I answered, "Sure. I just have a little twinge in my back— probably just stress!"

"It's your gallbladder!" was his diagnosis. "You'll need to have it removed!"

Huh?! Once again, I felt like I was in a movie—only this time the movie was *Kindergarten Cop* and I was telling a five-year-old "It's not a tumor!" However, accepting that this man was also just a tad socially awkward made it easier for me to just smile and move on. As the week progressed, however, I soon learned that the social ineptitude I had been experiencing was definitely more prevalent than I had originally thought.

One of the reasons I was feeling more stressed was the lack of communication I had been receiving from Buddy—in fact, it had been over a week since I'd heard from him. I did realize that the troops were quite busy, but on the occasions when conversations and correspondence with my son grew scarce, my mind would begin to wander as it imagined all possible reasons for the silence, beginning with the bad scenarios and moving right on through to the worst cases possible.

Luckily, at the beginning of the deployment, I discovered a little trick to ascertain my son's well-being. I realized that even if Buddy had not had the time to call or go online, he had often been shopping on base at the local military establishments. I had been given access to his accounts in case of emergency and discovered that I could log in and see where and when he was making purchases. I might not have been able to hear how he was doing, but I had a sort of confirmation that he was OK. Buddy had made a purchase of $5.78 at 10:36 that morning, which allowed me a small sigh of relief.

Unfortunately, the comfort of that small sigh lasted only until the afternoon. While in the ladies' room during a restroom break, a coworker was kind enough to inquire what I had heard from Buddy lately. It was always nice to have friends, family, and coworkers show genuine concern and interest in my son, but it was especially appreciated during the Surge. And though, at times, it could cause an emotional upheaval for me, I was always grateful for the regard and more than happy to share. On that afternoon, I dutifully explained that I had not heard from Buddy in a while, but I did see that he had been shopping earlier, so I was pretty sure that he was still OK.

"So I guess as long as Buddy continues to use his check card to spend his money, I can continue to see that he is OK!" I gave a small, half-hearted laugh in an attempt to give the impression that I was strong and all was well.

As my coworker and I chatted, there was another woman at the other end of the restroom staring in the mirror as if she were silently judging herself—or maybe just trying to look inconspicuous as she listened to our conversation. As my half-hearted laugh waned, this woman turned toward us and interjected herself into our conversation.

"At least you *think* it was your son using the card!" she said, and then I *swear* she cackled like a witch.

It felt like I had taken a solid punch to the solar plexus. Maybe my half-hearted laugh was way more convincing than I originally thought and this woman was only trying to "help" me face reality. Maybe she was just another example of "socially awkward" and simply did not know any better. Or maybe she really was evil and really did cackle! Whatever the case, I was stunned.

I am not sure how well my facial expressions and overall demeanor were able to hide the turmoil of emotions that she ignited. Just beneath the surface, I was a crumbling mess as my mind churned through all scenarios that would result in Buddy *not* being the one making purchases with his check card, again beginning with the bad and moving right on through to the worst. I immediately excused myself from the conversation. As I left the restroom, I gave this woman the widest possible berth, mostly to help me fight an unbelievable urge to deck her for her incredible callousness!

It seemed to me that these people had no concept of what was socially acceptable to say to a mom whose son was in a war zone. I'm not sure whether it was because they were unfamiliar with the cares, concerns, and issues that someone in my situation faced or if they were just *idiots*, but when I shared this story with Haley at the end of the day, I felt confident that I was not exaggerating when I made the assertion that this was the first time in my life I believed a group of people could have actually benefited from sensitivity training!

Chocolate Blasts

1/2 cup shortening	1 egg
1/2 cup margarine	1/3 cup powdered cocoa
1 cup brown sugar	1 teaspoon baking soda
1/4 cup granulated sugar	1/2 teaspoon salt
1/4 cup peanut butter	2 cups flour
1 teaspoon cornstarch	1 cup chocolate or peanut butter
1 teaspoon vanilla	chips

1. Preheat oven to 350 degrees.
2. Cream together shortening, margarine, brown sugar, granulated sugar, peanut butter, cornstarch, vanilla, and egg with an electric mixer until light and fluffy, about 3 to 5 minutes.
3. Beat in powdered cocoa on low speed.
4. Add baking soda and salt. Continue to beat with electric mixer for about a minute.
5. With a spoon, mix in flour until well blended. Stir in chips.
6. Drop dough by rounded teaspoons onto cookie sheets.
7. Bake for 12 minutes for cookie dough drops approximately the size of a walnut.

. . . But have you saved any orphans?

The word had come down; it was official. The deployment of the Devil Brigade had been extended to sixteen months. The rumor had been all over the news and echoed in the FRG email messages, so the extension was sort of expected, but *damn!* Buddy did not seem very happy about it, but I think that had more to do with him missing home than him being somehow disenchanted with his and the Devil Brigade's efforts in Iraq. In addition, this extension assured that he would not be home for the holidays again. Even as I gave Buddy the old "It won't be so bad! You guys are doing great! Cheerio, pip-pip, and all that rot," I also felt a little demoralized by the news and all that it implied. Though the extension was only for four months, that was four more months away from home—not to mention four more months of danger. To me, this seemed like a great deal to ask from our men and women in uniform—and their families. Once again, I was left contemplating—quite selfishly, I might add—"But what about *me*—my life, my feelings, my anxieties and fears?!"

As the news of the deployment extension slowly sank in, I headed to the kitchen for yet another therapeutic cookie-baking session; I figured something oatmeal related. I guess I could have vacuumed—the floors were suffering from my lack of energy for cleaning—but taste-testing the cookie dough was therapy unmatched by scrubbing floors—or anything else, for that matter. I formulated the recipe in my head; I decided that it would be useful to clear my cupboards of old ingredients so that I could start with fresh ideas for the next care package. I would call this current batch of cookies "Kitchen Sink" cookies because I would add everything but the kitchen sink to them! I measured the required ingredients into a bowl, allowing my mind to wander unfettered through a myriad of thoughts related to all things deployment, both past and present.

My mom and dad are card-carrying members of what has been deemed the "Greatest Generation"—the twenty-somethings of World War II, as defined by Tom Brokaw in his 1998 book of the same name. My dad was in the army, and Buddy has often mentioned that he joined the army because he wanted to honor his Grandpa. My dad would often recall how he was just "one month away from the end of my conscription"—that is, he had been drafted and only had a month left of his service—when Pearl Harbor was attacked and his remaining one month became four and a half years. Nana worked as a "bean counter" (her words) for the War Department. Nana's memories of World War II involved food and gas rationing, rubber and paper drives, and the sale of war bonds to support the cause. She described churches filled to capacity and communities working together to protect this country's shores. For Nana—and for my dad, for that matter—these memories were not recalled with bitterness or anger at the sacrifices, but rather with a sense of pride and accomplishment. I could not help but wonder how the Surge would be recalled in the years to come. Would people recall pride and sacrifice? Would they understand devotion to duty? I had no inkling, but I was concerned they would not.

I considered my own experiences as the mother of a soldier fighting in the current war while I beat the ingredients dumped into my cobalt blue mixing bowl with my electric mixer. There were and are many strong and diverse opinions regarding the Surge and our involvement in the Middle East, let alone in Iraq. Some people were able to find similarities between what happened in the years following 9/11 and what the Greatest Generation faced, and some found it more similar to the Vietnam era, but all seemed to think that theirs was the only correct assessment.

This, of course, was logical, considering most people will not hold to a truth they have decided to be inaccurate. Personally—and maybe ungenerously—I felt that the opinions that should have mattered most were from those individuals who were most closely involved with the conflict (i.e., the military and their families). However, there were also a plethora of opinions from this group, and once again, everyone thought that theirs was the only correct assessment. It was probably best to just put all comparisons aside.

I added a couple cups of flour and oatmeal to the concoction I was creating, but instead of mixing it into the dough with the large wooden spoon I had chosen for the task, I jabbed at the dough aimlessly as if I would find focus somewhere in the swirls of flour and cookie dough. It was useless to speculate on what others might or might not perceive to be true, but I did wonder what others saw when they looked at my son. What I saw was a resolute man who was determined to stand between his family and country and those who would seek to destroy them both, but I knew that not everyone would agree with me. I surmised it was similar to when my kids would paint pictures for me while they were in elementary school. I would proudly tape the pictures to the refrigerator, or maybe take them to work to display along with their other pieces on my wall there. Gazing upon those pictures, I would see brilliance—Van Gogh with a touch of Picasso or Dali—but I am not sure my evaluation was shared by others.

Then again, maybe a better analogy was something I remembered my sister, Evey, describing to me ages ago. Evey had taken her then-toddler son to the pediatrician for his regular checkup. My nephew was always a rather small child, but my sister was also adamant about limiting sugar intake. Whereas Nana always thought that little ones needed some "meat on their bones" in order to look healthy, my sister objected to the idea of her son becoming "fat." As she sat there in the waiting room with her thinnish son sitting on her lap, she glanced at the rather "healthy-sized" toddler sitting on his mother's lap across the room. As my sister noted his round, cherublike face and the rolls of baby fat that adorned the boy's arms and legs, Evey noticed the other mother eying my nephew with the same critical eye. It was at that moment my sister had a revelation. She imagined the event in comic strip format, the other mother and herself each eying the other's child with a single thought bubble above both their heads: "Oh, what a poor child! How could his mother do that to him?"

At first, I had no idea why I had managed to recall that random story that Evey had first shared with me roughly thirty years ago, but I began to realize that it might actually be applicable to the current circumstances. I mulled over that idea while I taste-tested the dough and dropped it by the spoonful onto a cookie sheet. The familiar, repetitive action of this task allowed my mind to drift freely along its current path. If Evey's son had been the "healthy" one and the other child the "thinnish" one, I have no doubt that the story would be the same—right down to the cartoon bubble above both their heads. It all stemmed from their personal experiences and perspectives, not to mention the fact that it was their flesh and blood sitting on their laps, which definitely tends to soften viewpoints.

The first batch of cookies now in the oven, I poured myself a glass of wine and went outside to my back deck to contemplate life—or at least life as it pertains to the mother of a soldier—for the twelve minutes the cookies needed to bake. I realized that was not enough time to embrace the magnitude of the subject, but it was enough time to brood over my take on my life and that of my soldier son.

It was a warm day in early March, and the bare branches of the trees in my backyard were just beginning to sprout the light green onset of new leaves. The flower bed in the middle of my backyard was also showing splashes of color from a collection of various spring flowers. It was a beautiful afternoon, but my heart was heavy. I was having such a difficult time balancing the amazing work that I knew my son and the rest of the soldiers were accomplishing against the weight and isolation of having my son be a soldier in the Surge.

I had recently been asked by a family member to define what I meant when I spoke of the great work that our soldiers were doing. "You say Buddy is doing great things, but, like, what?" I was asked. "Like, are they rescuing orphans from burning buildings?"

I was completely astounded by the question. While the sting of the inquiry lingered, my thoughts worked overtime to cultivate an answer, but somehow I was stuck on the question itself. *Oh, come on*, I thought. *Is that even a reasonable question? If my son were a doctor and I told you he was doing great things, would you then respond with, "Great things? Well, just how many lives has he saved?" Or, if my son were an airline pilot, would you gauge how good of a pilot he was solely by how many emergency landings he successfully executed? Better yet, if I had said my son the fireman was doing great things, would you have responded with, "Well, has he rescued any orphans from burning buildings?"* I guess I could have simply walked away without responding at all, but I really wanted to be able to answer—I just did not know how.

Once again, I thought of my dad. Dad contracted polio when he was thirty-one years old; he and my mom had only been married for a few years, and Evey, my oldest sibling, was just a toddler. The polio was severe enough to keep my dad in an iron lung for several months, and his recuperation after that was long and hard. It was questionable what degree of recovery Dad would be able to achieve and whether he would even be able to walk again. Many who faced what my dad faced might have given up, but Dad was a special man. The effort to regain his legs was hard, with many setbacks and a great deal of falling down, but Dad persevered. Eventually he did walk again, although for the rest of his life, he walked with a limp.

So how do you explain the heroic significance of a simple limp? That question seemed to have some relevance to what I was facing. Some might immediately have seen my dad's efforts as extraordinary, while others might have viewed it all with disappointment because his actions were not flashy enough. But for those of us who had the privilege to know my dad, it personified the courage and the selfless effort of an exceptional man—an example for others to follow. It all seemed to be a matter of perspective, Evey's comic strip revelation once again coming to mind.

The bottom line was that some heroics were more obvious than others, like— heaven help me—rescuing orphans from burning buildings. Other actions, though no less heroic, were a little subtler and seemed to be evaluated through individual attitudes and judgments. Those who knew my dad did not question his unbelievable valor and spirit. However, if you pointed his slight frame out to a stranger and tried to explain his strength and bravery, they might not understand the references.

With the cookie baking now completed and the cookies cooling on a rack, I headed back out to the deck to finish my thoughts—and my wine. When I thought of Buddy and all the rest of our troops, what came to my mind was an incredible group of heroes. Maybe this was due to the many troops I had known and worked with in the past, and maybe it was simply that I knew my son and his heart. But I also knew that the willingness of our military to voluntarily put their lives on the line to defend others, in my opinion, allowed them to stand proud and tall, alongside and equal to the Greatest Generation. It was my opinion that our troops' actions were equal to that of saving orphans from burning buildings, even if I was not able to successfully articulate how.

I finished my last sip of wine and stood a moment in the fading light of dusk. I guess it did not matter how others viewed my son and our soldiers. What did matter was that I knew I would be there to fully support them and their efforts as long as they served overseas—which I now knew would be for an additional four months.

Kitchen Sinks

2/3 cup shortening	1 egg
2/3 cup margarine	1 teaspoon baking soda
3/4 cup brown sugar	1/2 teaspoon salt
1/3 cup powdered sugar	1 2/3 cups flour
1/2 tablespoon light corn syrup	2/3 cup old-fashioned oats,
1/2 teaspoon vanilla	coarsely chopped

Additionally, any of the following or similar left-overs in quantities of 1/2 cup each:

Coarsely chopped nuts	Peanut butter or butterscotch
Chocolate chips	chips

1. Preheat oven to 350 degrees.
2. Cream together shortening, margarine, brown sugar, powdered sugar, corn syrup, vanilla, and egg with an electric mixer until light and fluffy, about 3 to 5 minutes.
3. Add baking soda and salt. Continue to beat with electric mixer for about a minute.
4. With a spoon, mix in flour and oats until well blended. Stir in any leftovers.
5. Drop dough by rounded teaspoons onto cookie sheets.
6. Bake for 10 to 12 minutes.

Let the games begin!

I had always looked for ways to show our troops that most of us were unabashedly grateful for their service, their sacrifice, and the job they had currently undertaken in Iraq and Afghanistan. Despite what was being reported on the evening news, I did believe the lion's share of Americans supported our military and their efforts, but that did not blunt the distress caused by the lack of support coming out of our own Congress—like the House's resolution of nonsupport in February and Senator Reid's infamous declaration that the war "is lost." I was astounded that with "our boys" in harm's way, anyone—let alone Congress—would disparage them so publicly. I, however, was more than happy to try to prove to everyone overseas that Congress was misinformed. To me, after all, the words "I support the troops" denoted action.

Before Buddy deployed, I would "adopt" troops through different Internet sites such as AnySoldier.com and send them my home-baked cookies and whatever else I could think of to provide them with appropriate distractions, even if the distractions were only momentary. But since January 2nd, my sole focus had been on the 504th Brigade of the 82nd Airborne Division, specifically the 1st Battalion, C-Company—Buddy's group—and B-Company. My choice of B-Company was not random. During Buddy's first tour to Iraq, I became acquainted through email with his first sergeant. It all began with me simply trying to get information so that I could be kept abreast of the battalion's efforts, as all military families are entitled to be.

As the result of my initial inquiry, I was given the name of 1st Sergeant Ramirez as the "go-to" guy for basically all things concerning Buddy's deployment. In the army, the first sergeant (1st Sgt.) is the non-commissioned officer who is responsible for a company of soldiers—in this case, Buddy's company. What started as a few emails regarding the various questions of a concerned mother slowly degraded into innocuous idiocy as my "questions" became the prattle of a concerned mother with a mildly warped sense of humor, which 1st Sgt. Ramirez seemed to appreciate! We remained "pen pals" throughout that deployment; however, sometime after the 504th's redeployment to the States at the end of that first tour to Iraq, 1st Sgt. Ramirez was moved to B-Company and our pen pal acquaintance kind of fizzled out.

At the beginning of the Surge, my thoughts wandered back to 1st Sgt. Ramirez. Since he was with Buddy in a war zone, albeit in a different company, I thought it was time to strike up our pen pal–ship again. It began with an email from me sporting the following intro: "Just because you are no longer in Benjamin's chain of command does not mean that you won't be getting harassed by me on a regular basis!" (I try to use Buddy's given name when speaking to his army mates.) His response back to me was basically "Bring it on."

I had taken 1st Sgt. Ramirez at his word and done my best to provide him the same level of distraction that I had been providing to Buddy. It was during the previous week when I contemplated what theme I would use for the next round of care packages (post-winter and pre-summer/Fourth of July) that 1st Sgt. Ramirez and his B-Company popped up in my mind.

It was a beautiful spring Saturday, and I was walking the Whiskey-Dog through the neighborhood on our way to the lake. Breathing in the clear, fresh air, still laced with a hint of the rain shower from earlier that morning, I discovered that I was actually beginning to relax a bit. I could feel the weight of the deployment ease with every step, even if it was only a little. It was invigorating, and I quickened my pace to take advantage of my newfound energies.

I was cutting across the park to head for the woods when I noticed a T-ball game was underway on the local baseball diamond. Even though the warm spring day felt wonderfully pleasant to me, I could see that it might have been less so for Whiskey, given his thick black fur, and though I had experienced a burst of vitality born out of my temporary delivery from stress, Whiskey did not seem to share my revival. I decided to take a break to give him a rest and to watch the game for a few minutes. I found a spot beside the bleachers at the edge of the field with a clear view of all the players and their parents. The Whiskey-Dog immediately lay down on my feet. Standing there under the clear blue sky, soaking up the sunshine, Whiskey-Dog panting away as if he were going to succumb to heat stroke, things almost felt "normal" again.

Meanwhile, on the baseball field, several T-ballers took their turn at swinging at the stationary ball in front of them before a batter finally connected. Amazingly, the ball went flying into the "outfield," which was the infield for regular ball players, where the T-ball outfielders had gathered to examine a bug that was crawling across the grass. As the parents excitedly urged the young slugger to "Run!," the coaches were urging the young outfielders to "Leave the bug alone and get the ball!"

Unfortunately, by that point, the outfielders had no idea where the ball was to go get it, but it did not matter, because the runner was not really clear on the concept of "run" either. *This has to be their first game!* I thought; but then again, remembering how Buddy was at that age, maybe not.

Standing there reminiscing about Buddy's ball-playing years, I was struck with inspiration that took advantage of the fact that Buddy and 1st Sgt. Ramirez were now in different companies—"rival" companies, so to speak. It occurred to me that Buddy and 1st Sgt. Ramirez (et al.) were immersed in a perpetual mortal combat–type situation. I figured what they could probably use at that point was a little friendly intramural competition to take the edge off of their environment. In my mind, there could be no better way to do that than with a friendly game of America's favorite pastime: baseball!

In my attempt to invent the perfect, "friendly," in-a-war-zone competition, I began to collect all the necessary items for a proper match-up. I figured since regular baseballs and bats were heavy and therefore expensive to ship, Wiffle products were outstanding alternatives. Since there were two companies, there were two color schemes. For Buddy and C-Company, it was blue. I filled a box with blue Wiffle bats, an assortment of blue Wiffle balls, and blue T-shirts with a big red "C" ironed onto the front of them. The box that was meant for 1st Sgt. Ramirez and B-Company was the same, but with a red theme and red T-shirts with a big blue "B" ironed onto them. As a final touch, included in each of the boxes was a letter explaining my ingenious plan, just in case the T-shirts, bats, and balls were not enough of a hint and left them confused. I also included a batch of what I called "Chocolate Snowflakes"—sort of a chocolate brownie in cookie form—mainly because Leo, Haley's boyfriend, was begging for me to invent something chocolate like his mother used to make.

I must admit that I was not sure how well this idea of setting B-Company against C-Company would be accepted or if it would even be able to happen once those boxes reached their destination. I hoped that the soldiers of the 1-504th would find the concept appealing, though, because in my mind, the best part about all this was the endless sea of possibilities for variations on the theme. Those T-shirts could not only serve for Wiffle ball but also for a friendly game of Nerf football or maybe a competitive game of Kick the Can—I could send them appropriate cans later—or even championship Tiddlywinks! The tournament potential seemed endless, and I was undeniably excited to hear what the guys thought of my concept of intramural competitions. However, when it came right down to it, even if nothing else came of it all, I just hoped my idea gave them an opportunity to think about something other than their daily grind—if only for a short while.

Chocolate Snowflakes

1/3 cup shortening

3/4 cup margarine

1 1/2 cups granulated sugar

1/2 teaspoon vanilla

1 egg

1/2 cup powdered cocoa

1/2 teaspoon baking powder

1/4 teaspoon cream of tartar

1/2 teaspoon salt

2 cups flour

1/4 cup powdered sugar

1. Preheat oven to 350 degrees.
2. Cream together shortening, margarine, granulated sugar, vanilla, and egg with an electric mixer until light and fluffy, about 3 to 5 minutes.
3. Beat in powdered cocoa on low speed.
4. Add baking powder, cream of tartar, and salt. Continue to beat with electric mixer for about a minute.
5. With a spoon, mix in flour.
6. Put powdered sugar in a round-bottomed bowl. Drop a rounded teaspoonful of dough into the sugar and roll the dough around in the bowl until coated. Place the coated dough on a cookie sheet.
7. Bake for 10 minutes.
8. While cookies are still warm, sprinkle with a little more powdered sugar to freshen the sugar coating.

Here comes Peter Cottontail . . .

I t was Easter and, as such, it was the first "major" holiday of the deployment that Buddy was not home to celebrate. Though I realized "major holiday" could be rather subjective, for my little family, Easter time equaled family time and, generally speaking, family time equaled good times. So having my son deployed and so far away for the occasion felt strange and contrary to the general immaturity which I liked to apply to most holidays, special occasions, parties, picnics—generally those days that end in "Y." The potential of Buddy's deployment creating a dampening effect on the Easter festivities was definitely apparent to me, but I also realized that I could not cease to exist just because my son was where he was. I refused to allow that to happen—or I at least attempted to refuse.

I also wanted to make sure that Buddy was OK with being deployed for this first significant holiday—or at least as OK as he could be, considering where he was. That being said, as I prepared his Easter care package, I kept in mind the exuberance with which we at the Bear Cave approached these things. I knew that sending eggs for dyeing, dyed eggs, or anything else like that was a less-than-stellar idea. However, there were several plastic alternatives that easily provided the obligatory Easter eggs in a basket, and though these plastic eggs did not provide for the fun of egg dyeing— which might not have worked in a war zone anyway—the "surprise inside" was much more agreeable than the ripe sulfur smell that hides beneath the shell of a beautifully decorated but non-fresh hard-boiled chicken egg!

At one point, I even debated buying a half dozen or so premade Easter baskets from the local grocery store—making sure that the FHOTA, at least, had been pro- vided for—but I realized that would not have been me. I knew that Buddy would have noticed the lack of "me" in those baskets as well—which would have defeated my purpose in sending the care package at all. Besides, it did not take a rocket scientist to create a properly adorned Easter basket that would radiate my personal touch and give Buddy that little taste of home that I was bound and determined to create.

To begin with, there were basic requirements for creating the perfect Easter basket, such as marshmallow Peeps, malted milk Robin Eggs, Easter Bunny PEZ dispensers, and Cadbury Creme Eggs—Buddy's favorite. But equally as important to every Easter basket were the toys that I firmly believed *no one*—not even soldiers in a war zone—should ever outgrow. In fact, I was quite pleased with myself regarding my airborne-themed Easter basket toys that included rubber-band-launched jets; various Easter animals in self-propelled vehicles such as tanks, ATVs, and planes; "Egg of Bunnies" games—like the age-old "Barrel of Monkeys" with little pastel bunnies inside of an egg instead of monkeys in a barrel; and my favorite: paratrooping bunnies, ducks, and chicks. I also included a batch of what I called "M&M Yummies." The bright colors of the M&M's in the cookies seemed perfect for celebrating spring and Easter.

Despite Buddy's current location, I was also expected to provide for our Easter celebrations on the home front in a way that was appropriate and reminiscent of our Easters past. Once again, this was not rocket science; it simply took a childlike heart and a willingness to ignore the fact that my kids were no longer ten years old. I know this might sound a little creepy in the mothers-who-refuse-to-let-their-children-grow-up department, but understand that it was more of a mutual mindset than anything else. While we were filling the plastic eggs that went into the care packages, Haley commented that in addition to the standard egg dyeing on the eve of Easter, she—the twenty-four-year-old—*really* thought that we should have an Easter egg hunt on Easter morning, just like we used to!

Joining us over Easter weekend was Haley's boyfriend, Leo, and his new puppy, Marjorie. Several months before Haley moved in with me, she had met this young man as she played her guitar on her apartment's balcony. Leo was across the street on his balcony, also playing his guitar. Apparently, he appreciated her musical talent in her rendition of "Drain You" by Nirvana and applauded her. He then responded by playing "Just Like Heaven" by The Cure. By their own telling, even though both of them had basically sworn off relationships at the time, they still ended up falling for each other hook, line, and sinker.

The first time we ever met Leo was last October when he joined Haley, Buddy, and me for our annual trip to the local Renaissance Festival. This is another one of those activities that demonstrates whether an individual is going to "fit in" with our little family. We do not dress up, but we do enjoy interacting with those who do and participating in the different activities. We met at the Bear Cave for introductions. Introductions were immediately followed by Buddy threatening Leo with bodily harm if he ever hurt Haley in any way! At least Buddy did the threatening with a smile on his face, even if there was sincerity in his heart. Despite the trip's beginning, by the time we were heading home, Leo and Buddy had bonded and we had become one big, happy family. From that day forward, Leo has demonstrated often that he "belongs"—poor guy—and has been welcomed at all family activities, like Easter egg hunts on Easter morning.

As planned, Easter Eve found Haley, Leo, and me in the kitchen with two beers, a glass of wine, a box of Paas dye, and a couple dozen hard-boiled eggs. We sat at the kitchen table trying all kinds of techniques: double-dipping the eggs, creating designs on them with noncolored crayons only to find after dyeing that the design was nowhere near what we imagined, applying various Easter stickers to the brightly colored eggs, and competing over who had done the best decorating job, with both Whiskey and Marjorie looking on from a safe distance. I could not help but marvel, once again, at how well Leo fit into the Bear Cave. Even after the egg dyeing was finished, Leo was the first to suggest we see what colors we could produce by mixing the dyes together, just like all "children" love to do.

Later that night, after Haley and Leo had gone to bed, I set out four Easter Plops on the dining room table—one for me, Haley, Leo, and Keith, who would be joining us Easter morning. An Easter Plop is something I came up with when the kids and I were in Vermont. We did not have Easter baskets that year, so I simply placed our Easter goodies in little piles on the table and gave them the name "Easter Plops." The way I figured it, something mildly pathetic became acceptable once you gave it a clever name—and I was right.

After the Easter Plops were set out, I went to work on the Easter egg hunt. I filled about three dozen plastic eggs with various candies and hid them around the living room, stairwell, and family room. As any Easter Bunny knows, a successful Easter egg hunt begins with hiding places where the eggs are visible but not obvious. The trick was to keep the hiding places age-appropriate to the participants. The Bear Cave is not a large house, so trying to find acceptable and unique hiding places for several dozen eggs that would challenge the participants of this particular Easter egg hunt was not as easy as it might sound. Eventually, all the eggs were hidden, but some of the hiding places were rather obvious.

Keith showed up bright and early on Easter morning. I offered him a mimosa, the drink of the day, and as I walked down the stairs to wake up Haley and Leo, I admonished him to keep his eyes to himself so as not to give him an unfair advantage over the others. When I woke Haley and Leo, I gave them the same warning. A few minutes later, armed with Easter baskets in one hand and mimosas in the other, the hunt began for the three "kids." Watching them wander through the rooms searching for the hidden eggs was amusing, to say the least. If it were not for their decidedly adult features, it would have been difficult not to see them as three small children gleefully filling their baskets with the various treasures they were finding. Surprisingly enough, some of the eggs were hidden better than I had realized. Though the obvious ones were found rather quickly, some of the others took a little bit longer to locate. In fact, a couple of the eggs actually needed the old "You're getting hotter! Nope, now you're getting colder!" in order to reveal their hiding places.

Eventually, all the eggs were found and we gathered in the living room so Haley, Leo, and Keith could evaluate their newly acquired haul. Keith and Haley sat on the couch, placing their baskets full of eggs on the coffee table and sorting through their collections one egg at a time. Leo, however, plopped himself down on the floor and dumped the eggs in his basket out in front of him. With Marjorie looking on with longing, he opened each egg and sorted all the candy by type, eating every third piece or so. It was hard not to notice just how well he fit in.

It was a great morning and a wonderful day, but it did leave me feeling a tad conflicted. Sitting there in the living room sipping our mimosas and enjoying each other's company, I was struck by the incomplete completeness of the day. I figured it had to do with the duality of my current life.

Since the beginning of the Surge, I woke up each morning with an onslaught of emotions regarding Buddy's deployment that I was unable to turn off. Basically, I just pretended that my emotions and my life were in check, even when I knew they were not. I struggled to project strength and confidence as I moved through my days, even though I was aware that I possessed neither of those attributes. I attempted to show my faith and that I was secure in my beliefs, even though at times I felt broken and abandoned. However, it was those times when I felt that I had actually achieved some level of normalcy—like family time during Easter morning egg hunts—that I was most keenly aware that things would never be normal as long as Buddy was where he was. On Easter morning, my family felt complete, even though I knew it could never be until my son came home.

M&M Yummies

1/2 cup shortening

1/2 cup margarine

2/3 cup brown sugar

2/3 cup powdered sugar

1 tablespoon cornstarch

1 teaspoon corn syrup

1 teaspoon butternut flavoring

1 egg

1 teaspoon baking soda

1/2 teaspoon salt

2 1/4 cups flour

1 cup M&M's

1. Preheat oven to 375 degrees.
2. Cream together shortening, margarine, brown sugar, powdered sugar, cornstarch, corn syrup, butternut flavoring, and egg with an electric mixer until light and fluffy, about 3 to 5 minutes.
3. Add baking soda and salt. Continue to beat with electric mixer for about a minute.
4. With a spoon, mix in flour until well blended. Stir in M&M's.
5. Drop dough by rounded tablespoons onto cookie sheets.
6. Bake for 10 to 12 minutes.

To be a soldier's mom

T he day began like any other. Up hours before the crack of dawn, I was on the road heading toward the train station for my ride into work. I was only about five minutes from home when the news came on the radio, and hearing the news at that point meant I was about fifteen minutes behind schedule. I began silently chastising myself for being late, but my exasperation soon gave way to a multitude of colliding emotions as the opening story came over the airwaves: "Today in northern Baghdad, nine soldiers out of the 504th Brigade, 82nd Airborne Division, were killed and several wounded . . . "

I could not say what the rest of the report was because I had stopped listening. My throat tightened as my heart pounded in my chest, and my mind began to race. *Oh God, help me! What do I do now? Go home and wait for the doorbell to ring? I couldn't imagine anything worse! Go to work like normal? NORMAL?! How could anything be normal now? I don't know what to do! I* don't *know what to do!* Tears filled my eyes, and then I remembered, *Oh please, God! I didn't get a chance to tell him I loved him the last time we spoke!*

I decided that continuing on into work might actually be my best option. I figured I could pretend to think as I pretended to work, but at least I wouldn't be home waiting for the doorbell to ring. It also seemed reasonable to me that all the pretending might just be enough to keep my mind off of other things until I knew all the facts. So I continued into work, even as I silently vowed to *never* listen to the news again.

For the rest of the way into work, thoughts screamed through my head. My mind was filled with the "what if"s, the memories, the so very many times that I fell short when it came to my kids and others, but mostly my kids. And then there were the prayers—lots and lots of prayers—all reminding me that today was going to be anything but a normal day.

Somewhere on the metro train, I became conscious of an overwhelming desire to share my emotional upheaval. Somehow I thought that putting all my feelings into words would ease my doubt and concern. Through my previous experiences, I had learned that it was much better to speak with an individual who genuinely understood the situation. Needless to say, since Buddy first shipped, I had come to realize that many of my coworkers had a difficult time empathizing with what it was like to have a piece of your heart sitting precariously in a war zone. Though most of the time I could look beyond their lack of comprehension, I understood it would not be quite as easy when my emotions were running so very raw. Consequently, I phoned Haley the moment I arrived at work. Not surprisingly, rather than easing my own anxiety, the only thing I managed to do was screw up her day as well.

Once I settled into my routine, I actually did find solace in working through the mechanics of my job. I am paid to think, but before the thinking part of my work, there is a whole slew of cut-and-pasting and collating of various types of information that thankfully requires little to no thought. I had logged onto my Hotmail account right after talking with Haley, and every so often I would interrupt my cutting and pasting to check my email for any word from the FRG leader. Time passed slowly, the minutes dragging into hours without hearing anything from anyone. At times, I was actually happy to have heard nothing, because as long as I heard nothing, my life remained unchanged, but every so often, I was overwhelmed with the untenable fragility of the current circumstances.

It was just after 2:00 p.m. when I checked my email again. In my mind, it had been an eternity since I had last checked; in reality, I had no idea what the time frame was, but I must have looked at my email account at least a hundred times. Each and every time I checked, there were no new messages—no news. And each and every time, my anxiety grew a little bit more, even as I gave a small sigh of relief. However, this time there was an email, subject line: *Monday's Casualties.* There it was again— *Causalities*—only this time it was worse because I already knew that it applied to our guys. I checked the time stamp and realized it had only just arrived. *Casualties? Oh no!* I found that I was having trouble getting up enough nerve to open the email. Even Tinker Bell couldn't help now, because I already knew there were causalities.

I was frozen with apprehension and downright fear. I sat there in my little half-icle, in a room the size of a football field with people all around, yet at that moment, I felt like I was all alone. I also realized that I could not do this alone. Immediately, I called Haley.

"What have you heard?" she asked me as soon as she answered the phone.

"I have an email from the FRG leader," I replied.

"What does it say?"

"Haley, I can't do it—I can't open it! Would you please do it for me? I just can't. I—I just can't!"

Haley has been an incredible gem. For the life of me, I cannot figure out how I was lucky enough to end up with a daughter like her. Though we both can be soft mushy blobs when it comes to our emotions, she has always been there when I have needed to lean on someone. I know it seems strange for a mom to be saying that about their child, but I guess that's why I feel so blessed.

"Sure, Mom; hold on."

There was a moment of silence as Haley logged into my account, opened the email, and read it to herself before reading it to me, as I knew she would. It felt like an hour; my heart was pounding so hard in my chest I could feel it in my throat.

"What does it say? Tell me, what does it say?!" I asked.

"Hold on a minute!" she answered with a dash of impatience. "Give me a minute to read!"

Again, I waited for what seemed like an eternity, and after what was surely only a few seconds, Haley began to read.

We have received no official word yet on which battalion was affected or the actual number of casualties. I would further caution you on how much credence you give the media. I'm sure the army is in the midst of performing notifications. As soon as all the families are notified, an official statement will be released. Hang in there! Keep praying!

Once upon a time, my minister explained to me that anger was a second emotion; there is always some other emotion that comes first. If you make this statement to a room full of people, it becomes like a party game as everyone tries to invent the ultimate situation where anger was the *first* emotion. "You are in traffic as someone cuts you off, just as you receive a phone call that your child was injured by someone else's negligence, right after a call informing you that your spouse has run off with your best friend," someone will suggest. Yet basic analysis of the presented scenarios would show that if someone cut you off in traffic the first emotion is most likely fear; with the injured child, helplessness—and fear; with the disaffected spouse, rejection, abandonment—and probably also fear. No, anger is at least the second emotion.

Hence, after I felt the anxiety of still not knowing, I felt the fear that my life would be unalterably diminished and the longing to see my son just one more time, and *then* came the anger.

"I can't do this! I just can't do this anymore! How am I supposed to live like this? How can *anyone* live like this? I just can't *do* this! How can—my *heavens*, how is any—"

"Hold on Mom—hold on! There's a second email," Haley interrupted.

"Second email? What email? There was only one before!"

"Well, there's a second one now! Just hold on and let me get it opened!"

Once again, my heart pounded as I sat—quietly, this time—repeating over and over again to myself what has become my mantra over the past few months: *I can't do this. I just can't do this . . .*

And then my daughter read, "The casualties reported on the news were NOT from our company. All our men are safe!"

Buddy was safe! *Buddy was safe!* All my anxiety, my fear, my frustration, and my anger gave way to unbelievable relief—and absolutely uncontrollable tears. This time I repeated my mantra out loud, "I can't do this anymore! I just *can't* do this!" as I openly sobbed at my desk—not really caring whether anyone saw me. Eventually, though, as the tears started to subside, I added, "I gotta get outta here!"

Haley, who had, except for the occasional "Are you OK, Mom?" mostly remained quiet throughout my breakdown, finally spoke. "Wow, Mom! You took the good news harder than you took the bad!"

I guess it might have seemed that way from the outside, but from the inside, I knew that until I was sure that my world had remained unchanged, I had to keep my emotions in check. I might have been neurotic at points, angry, and maybe even petulant, but I refused to give into my emotions until I knew that Buddy was OK.

I hung up with my daughter, logged off my computers, cleaned up my desk, and left for the day. I had plenty of time to think on the forty or so–minute commute back home.

If I live another thousand years, I do not believe I could ever forget this day. It was just one day, but the events, the emotions—the essence—of the day changed the overall dynamics of my world, quite possibly forever. Thankfully, those dynamics were not changed as severely as they could have been; however, this day was the day that the deployment became real to me.

The offending incident was probably less than ten seconds, but in its aftermath, I was left with the stark realization that my world was a volatile mess. I was just one news report, one phone call, one knock on the door away from a gut-wrenching anxiety that I had not felt since the kids were small and Haley walked away from our blanket to the ocean's edge for a bucket of water on a crowded beach and managed to get lost. What I remember most from that incident was the horrible feeling that encompassed me for the five minutes that I had no idea where she was or what had happened to her. Twenty years later, not knowing was still the problem. As I struggled to regain composure and put my emotions in check—anxiety and helplessness, but also relief and elation—I was struck by a single, heart-wrenching thought: some-where, there were nine families whose lives were unalterably diminished and forever changed.

Comfort Cookies

3/4 cup margarine

3/4 cup granulated sugar

1 tablespoon corn syrup

1/2 teaspoon vanilla

2 eggs

1/4 teaspoon cream of tartar

1 teaspoon baking powder

1/2 teaspoon salt

2 1/3 cups flour

Any brand of frosting (I like to use Duncan Hines Creamy Home-Style Chocolate Buttercream)

1. Preheat oven to 350 degrees.
2. Cream together margarine, granulated sugar, corn syrup, vanilla, and eggs with an electric mixer until light and fluffy, about 3 to 5 minutes.
3. Add cream of tartar, baking powder, and salt. Continue to beat with electric mixer for about a minute.
4. With a spoon, mix in flour.
5. Refrigerate dough for about an hour until firm.
6. Drop dough by rounded teaspoons or tablespoons onto cookie sheets.
7. Bake for 8 minutes for rounded teaspoonfuls and 10 minutes for rounded tablespoonfuls.
8. Remove the cookies from the cookie sheet to cool. After they have cooled, frost generously. Top with decorative sprinkles, if desired.

There are no words.

I t was another difficult week. This time, it began with a phone call rather than a news report.

"Hey, Mom . . . what's up?"

I knew in an instant that something was not right. I could tell Buddy was trying to sound normal, but his voice was tight and very controlled.

"Hey, Sweetie. What's wrong?" I asked immediately. Once again, my heart pounded as I braced myself for the answer. A dozen questions filled my brain. *Buddy is obviously safe, but why does he sound so bad? Has he been wounded? Has someone else been wounded? Is it the FHOTA? Who was hurt? Or is it all worse than that?!* Haley and I had recently been discussing how, though Buddy was our primary concern, there were the others—Buddy's comrades-in-arms, the FHOTA and such—that also left our hearts so exposed to the dangers of this deployment. *This is* absolutely *intolerable,* I thought. *How is anybody supposed to live with all this vulnerability and uncertainty? I dread everything now—news reports, knocks on the door, even phone calls! It's like being in a constant state of anticipation as I wait for the other shoe to drop—always expecting the worst but trying to pretend that all is normal. Normal! What is normal? I don't even know normal anymore!* But at that moment, my son was on the other end of the phone and something was not right. I put my thoughts aside and listened for Buddy to say something, but I heard nothing.

"Hello?" I asked. It was always hard to tell whether I was dealing with a pause in the conversation, a satellite bounce, or a dropped call. Sometimes it required a bit of patience to find out, but even in the best of times, I do not do patience very well, and these days, it was the one virtue that I had in the shortest supply!

"Hello?" I repeated. "Are you still there?" I tried desperately to hide my anxiety and fear of what I was about to hear.

This time, I got a response. "Yeah, Mom, I'm still here." There was another short pause, and then Buddy continued. "Have you heard? Raybon is dead!"

Once again, my mind raced. *Raybon . . . Raybon . . . do I know that name? Raybon who?*

"Who, Sweetie?" I inquired.

"Sgt. Brad Raybon!" Buddy replied. "You know. I went through boot camp with him. He's the one who replaced me as RTO when I was moved back to SAW gunner."

Wait . . . what? My mind raced again, this time back to a phone call from Buddy a few weeks before. He told me how he had gotten out of being the RTO. He was quite happy about it, but that was all I could remember of the conversation. I knew that he was unhappy about having to give up SAW (Squad Automatic Weapon) gunner when he was first appointed RTO and did not appreciate all the extra work being an RTO created for him, especially in the five days leading up to their deployment. He often joked that being an RTO meant running around with a big target on your back—radios and huge antennas—and without proper weaponry to defend yourself. An RTO carries a gun, just not a big one. As a SAW gunner, Buddy had a big gun, and it was his job to use that gun to lay down fire, giving the rest of the team the opportunity to get to the bad guys before the bad guys got them.

I felt sick to my stomach. The words "the one who replaced me" reverberated down to the depths of my soul, a multitude of "what if"s flooding my thoughts as I struggled to regain some sort of control. *This is the worst! I can't do this!* I silently screamed to the universe. But I knew that what Buddy needed at this point was a strong mother to listen to him.

While I reined in my random thoughts and emotions, I searched my memory for any recollection of Sgt. Raybon without results. I returned my full attention to Buddy.

"I'm so sorry, Sweetie. Are you OK?"

As a mom, it's hard not to ask that question, even though I have long since come to the conclusion that being "OK" is a relative thing.

"Yeah, I'm OK," was his reply. "It is just hard to accept he's dead, that's all."

We continued to chat for a few minutes as Buddy started describing the service they conducted for the sergeant in Iraq. The body had already begun its journey back to the States, so for their service, a memorial to Sgt. Raybon was created out of items that were left behind. His weapon, which was some kind of rifle, was placed barrel down in a position of honor at the front of the assembled troops of C-Company, 1st Battalion, 504th Parachute Infantry Regiment. His boots were placed in front of it, his helmet was placed on the butt of the weapon, and one of his dog tags was hung from its grip.

As Buddy detailed the ceremony, images formed in my mind. They vividly played out as if watching a movie, leaving my heart aching for Buddy, for the rest of C-Company, and for Sgt. Raybon's family—now going through what must be the worst days of their lives. Buddy continued to talk, and though I wanted to hear what he was saying, I could not stop my mind from wandering. Among his words describing how much Sgt. Raybon meant to all of them and how difficult it was to say good-bye, I was continually drawn back to the words "the one who replaced me" and its endless implications. I wondered whether Sgt. Raybon's comrades-in-arms felt that they had failed him, something I had learned could happen from the Vietnam vets I worked with for the dozen or so years I worked at the Pentagon. More than that, I wondered if, because of the circumstances, this feeling was even more pronounced for Buddy, but I dared not ask. I also began to wonder how much more of this was in our future—and just how much more of it I could take. Realizing that I was becoming entrenched in my own self-pity, I refocused on Buddy and what he was telling me.

Buddy continued to talk for a few minutes about his thoughts and his memories. When he had finished, I could not help but to again ask, "But are you guys doing OK?"

"Yeah, Mom. I'm OK, and we're OK," Buddy replied. "Besides, we're all confident that Sgt. Raybon is in a much better place now."

I knew it was my turn to talk at this point, but I was finding it difficult to think of anything to say. I wanted to be able to continue to converse with my son in some meaningful manner, but my thoughts kept on getting tripped up on the subtle implications of this phone call and the events that led to it. Instead, I pretty much ended the conversation by letting Buddy know that I would send flowers to the family once that information was forwarded to me. Before we hung up, I made sure I told Buddy just how much I loved him.

"Yeah, I know," he said.

Maybe so, I thought, *but that does not affect my need to say the words!*

It was not long after this phone call that the FRG leader sent an email telling of the incident and providing an address for cards and flowers. The address actually jogged my memory a bit. As I perused a florist's website looking for an appropriate arrangement, I recalled Buddy introducing me to a fellow soldier as we waited for the buses the day the boys deployed. If I recall correctly, the soldier was a sergeant, and I remember a conversation I had with his father. The man explained that when his son called to inform him of the deployment, he immediately left work and drove the several hundred miles to the base so he would have the opportunity to see his son, tell him he loved him, and say good-bye. His words were haunting me now. Was that Sgt. Raybon and his father I met? If so, was his father motivated by a premonition? Did he have some feeling that let him know he needed to see his son one more time? Did Sgt. Raybon know? Are the feelings *I* have premonitions?

The uncertainty of it all, as well as the pain I was feeling for this family, was over-whelming and made it difficult to accomplish the task at hand. Eventually, though, I was able to pick out an arrangement. However, because I wanted to make sure that only red, white, and blue flowers were used, I could not place the order online. As I dialed the florist's phone number, I took a deep breath and cleared my throat in an attempt to steady myself for the conversation—which did not work! As I began to explain what I wanted, tears filled my eyes. As I worked through the details, my voice cracked. By the time the florist asked what I wanted the accompanying card to say, I could no longer speak. Of course, it did not help that the florist was also crying. She explained that orders for flowers were coming in by the dozens and the phone calls were all very emotional. She told me it was one of the hardest funerals she ever served. I just could not imagine.

I could not imagine being in Sgt. Raybon's family and going through what they must have been experiencing—I could not even imagine having to be the florist! Heck, it was hard enough just being the mother of a fellow soldier! In fact, the whole incident seemed to exemplify every worst possible outcome. As I hung up the phone with the florist, I realized it was exactly the right time for selfish platitudes, and all I could think was *God give me strength! I just can't do this anymore!*

Oaties

3/4 cup shortening
1/4 cup margarine
1 tablespoon peanut butter
1 1/4 cups brown sugar
1 tablespoon light corn syrup
1 teaspoon vanilla
1 egg
1 teaspoon ground cinnamon

1 teaspoon baking soda
1/2 teaspoon salt
2 cups flour
3/4–1 cup old-fashioned oats,
   coarsely chopped
3/4 cup walnuts, chopped
1 cup chocolate or peanut butter
   chips

1. Preheat oven to 350 degrees.
2. Cream together shortening, margarine, peanut butter, brown sugar, corn syrup, vanilla, and egg with an electric mixer until light and fluffy, about 3 to 5 minutes.
3. Add cinnamon, baking soda, and salt. Continue to beat with electric mixer for about a minute.
4. With a spoon, mix in flour and oats until well blended. Stir in walnuts and chips.
5. Drop dough by rounded teaspoons onto cookie sheets.
6. Bake for 10 minutes or until lightly browned.

"The heel bone's connected to the foot bone / Now hear the word of the Lord!"

I had often heard it said that there are "no atheists on the battlefield," sometimes worded "no atheists in foxholes." I had yet to determine who originally said these words, but I had seen them attributed to everyone from priests to presidents. I also had no idea how accurate the statement was as far as our troops were concerned, but what I did know was that for me, the mother of a soldier, these words, slightly tweaked, spoke the ultimate truth: there are no mothers of soldiers who are atheists—at least, that's the way it felt to me.

Beginning in January, I had been praying every waking moment of every day. The second my eyes opened, my first thoughts were prayers that our troops remained safe, especially my son. I prayed that they were protected, not only from physical harm, but mental and emotional harm as well. I then prayed for the families of our troops, especially for those Gold Star families who have lost their soldiers in battle, while at the same time praying that I *never* had to know their pain. I continued to pray as the news played on the radio; I continued to pray as I fought the crowds on the subway; I continued to pray as I made my way through the day. And at the very end of every day, I fell asleep thanking God for the opportunity of tomorrow, even as I once again asked his help in protecting our troops, especially my son.

I stumbled across Buddy's extra dog tags while I was putting away his "stuff" after he deployed. I took one and put it on a silver chain along with a pair of silver crossed rifles, the insignia for infantry, which Buddy had given me the Christmas after he graduated boot camp. From the day I found those dog tags and forward, if I was not in my pajamas, I was wearing that chain. It was my constant reminder to pray for my son—and the rest of the troops, of course. But it had also become a conversation starter as I plodded along through my days.

"Whose dog tag is that?" some stranger would ask.

At this point, I would involuntarily reach for the dog tag and crossed rifles as if touching them somehow brought me closer to Buddy.

"It's my son's!" I would respond with great pride. "He is airborne, the tip of the Surge."

From this point, it was pretty much a crapshoot as to what the stranger's response would be, though it would usually be positive and very supportive. In fact, at times people were so supportive they almost startled me. At those times, I was left feeling not only surprised but also grateful. I was grateful because their blatant appreciation assured me that the impression that our soldiers were not supported by most Americans was very much wrong, which somehow gave me peace.

It was after a full day's work followed by an ugly commute on one particular evening that by the time I had reached the grocery store, I was harried and distracted. Never one for writing down grocery lists, as the day progressed, I simply made mental notes of what I needed to pick up on the way home. Every time I thought of something new, I would add it to my imaginary checklist and then silently repeat the ever-growing manifest over and over again in an effort to imprint it on my brain so that nothing would be forgotten.

It was like the game my family would play on long road trips when I was young. Being the youngest, I would start: "I am going on a trip, and on my trip, I will take an apple." This initial statement would be followed by my brother, the next youngest, who would continue the game with the next letter of the alphabet: "I am going on trip, and on my trip, I will take an apple and a banana." The collection of what we were taking on the trip would grow as each family member took turns moving through the alphabet, but only after they were able to recite *everything* that was mentioned before. Besides taking hours to get through the alphabet this way, let alone being infinitely more stimulating than simply singing "Ninety-Nine Bottles of Beer on the Wall" to its ultimate conclusion, the game did tend to sharpen one's cognitive abilities. The trick was to be able to create some sort of a pattern or rhythm to everything that was being listed—a talent at which I eventually excelled.

As I waited in line to check out, I reviewed my mental list. Having certified that all previously-committed-to-memory articles were in my basket, I was free to occupy my mind with other endeavors—specifically, checking out all those sleazy magazine covers that I would not actually buy in a million years.

Reading through all the various headlines, I could not help but make comments to myself—except this time, I must have said it out loud, because the gentleman standing in front of me in line turned around. I looked to meet the man's gaze and smiled sheepishly, feeling a bit stupid. Instead of the expected smile and nod, the man asked, "When were you there?"

"Pardon?" I asked.

The gentleman then pointed to my chest and repeated, "When did you serve? Were you over there?"

I looked down and realized that Buddy's dog tag was resting on my Virginia Military Institute sweatshirt. "Oh!" I responded. "My nephew is the one who attended VMI, and the dog tag is my son's. Right now, he is serving in Iraq as a part of the Surge."

I did not even have the time to ponder what his response would be before the man began praising my son, my family, and me! At the end of every sentence, he would say "God bless them!" or "God bless you!"

The man wanted me to understand the depth of his gratitude for Buddy's service and our collective sacrifice. He explained to me that if he were to see a soldier or any of our troops walking through an airport terminal or down the street, he would walk up to them and give them the "biggest ol' bear hug" that they'd ever had. He further explained that it was all about his undying gratitude—not just his own gratitude, but that of all the people he worked with as well. As he finished checking out and walked away, he turned back to me and asked if I would not mind passing along his gratitude to the "rest of your family."

I was overwhelmed with emotion by this man's support. I felt as though my heart would explode. "Absolutely!" was my barely discernible response. And then came his final words to me:

"I will be praying for your son and for your family!" he called back to me from the door to the grocery store.

It took several moments before I regained any sort of composure. What was rather interesting to me, though, was that following each of these types of chance encounters, the final comment to me an overwhelming majority of the time was "God bless you and your son. I will be praying for him!"

The first time I ever heard that, I was amazed to find out that the words were directly connected to my tear ducts! No matter how "strong" I was feeling at the time, the instant I heard any such phrase, my eyes would get all watery and a huge lump would form in my throat. I had come to understand that the only response I was capable of at that moment was a smile and nod at best, but I was sure it was always understood. I also knew that even if they forgot that night when they said their prayers—or, for that matter, the moment they walked away—the fact that the phrase was spoken at all sent those words out into the universe—and, in my opinion, out for the Almighty to hear.

In my lifetime, I have heard many people assert that religion is nothing more than a crutch for the weak—and they would say this like it was a bad thing! But the beauty of having that old reliable crutch was that it allowed me to take comfort in the fact that not only were prayers being said, but they were also being heard. The bottom line was, I could not imagine being a mother, let alone the mother of a soldier serving during a war, without that crutch to lean on.

Snicker Button Cookies

Cookie:

1/2 cup shortening

1/2 cup margarine

1/2 cup powdered sugar

1/2 cup granulated sugar

1 tablespoon corn syrup

1 tablespoon cornstarch

1 egg

1/2 teaspoon cream of tartar

1/4 teaspoon baking soda

1/4 teaspoon salt

2 1/4 cups flour

Coating:

2 tablespoons granulated sugar

2 teaspoons cinnamon

1. Preheat oven to 350 degrees.
2. Cream together shortening, margarine, powdered sugar, granulated sugar, corn syrup, cornstarch, and egg with an electric mixer until light and fluffy, about 3 to 5 minutes.
3. Add cream of tartar, baking soda, and salt. Continue to beat with electric mixer for about a minute.
4. With a spoon, mix in flour.
5. To make the coating, in a round-bottomed bowl, mix together granulated sugar and cinnamon.
6. Drop dough by rounded teaspoons into the sugar-and-cinnamon mixture and roll until coated. Place the coated dough on a cookie sheet.
7. Bake for 8 to 10 minutes.

My dad always said, "If you can't say anything nice . . ." Why didn't I listen?

With all the events of the past few weeks, I had been feeling overwhelmed—to say the very least. At times, it seemed as though I had only just caught my breath from one incident before another popped up in my inbox, or on the news, or in my sleep! It was emotionally draining to simply exist, and I found myself marveling at generations past.

"How did you do it, Nana?" I asked my mom one day. "How did you get through each day during World War II when basically the whole world was deployed?"

"We just persevered," she answered. "Just like we need to do now."

Those were easy words to say but not always as easy to execute. There were days when "persevering" seemed more like torture. Even so, when Buddy called, I made sure our conversations were all about happy thoughts, good times, and every idiotic idea that popped into my head. However, there were times when I heard his voice that all my thought processes ceased. Basically, I was overcome by the simple truth that the sound of his voice indicated—even if only for the moment—that all was well, especially when he sounded positive and strong. Sometimes it was me carrying on both sides of the conversation as Buddy just listened in his crushing desire for a piece of home; then there were the times when all the pieces just fell into place and we were chatting as if Buddy was just down the road and calling home on a Sunday morning to see what his mom was up to. One of those happy calls came today. The phone call started like any of the others, with Buddy sounding upbeat and chipper.

"Hey, Mom! What's up?"

"Sweetie!" I responded without hesitation. "How the heck are you?!"

"I'm OK," he answered. "What's going on there? How's my Whiskey-Dog?"

I began to tell him all the recent Whiskey stories followed by a quick summary of who was doing what to whom—also known as the local gossip. As I rattled off all the stories, embellishing for effect wherever I could, a thought occurred to me. "Hey,

Buddy! Did you ever receive the Wiffle balls?" I asked. "Did you and 1st Sgt. Ramirez ever get together for a game?" I continued. And then, without waiting for a reply, I added, "Who won?"

"Yeah, we got them," he said. "But we never got to play, and now all the balls are gone!"

"What?" I asked.

Buddy's response took me by surprise as he described shooting the Wiffle balls from tank turrets and using the C-Company T-shirts I sent for cleaning rags for their weapons. To complete his description of their Wiffle activities—which did not include a ball game with B-Company—he added, "We use the bats for Toby training!"

"Huh?"

"Yep!" he answered. "Basically, every time Toby starts to act like Toby, we smack him with one of the Wiffle bats! They make a really great noise when they hit him, but they aren't hard enough to actually hurt him. So they're perfect for keeping Toby in line but not very functional for playing ball any more 'cause they're kind of bent up now!"

"Oh." I was a little disappointed by the final disposition of my brilliant Wiffle ball idea, my thoughts drying up as I processed the information. I simply did not know how to respond or what to say next. Buddy's response, however, shook my brain loose.

"I'm sorry, Mom." His voice sounded sullen and subdued for the first time this conversation.

"Oh, Buddy! It's all OK!" I quickly told him. "Everything is fine. I—I guess I'm just a little disappointed, you know?"

All I heard on the other end of the phone was silence.

Idiot! I silently chided myself, but I tried to explain. "I didn't mean that I'm disappointed in you! No, I—I'm just a little disappointed . . ." I paused briefly as I tried to gather my thoughts. "I mean, I was just looking forward to hearing all about a Wiffle ball game, not Toby discipline," I added, then I realized I probably should have stopped after the "I'm not disappointed in you" part.

I paused again, waiting for a reply, but still heard nothing, so I continued. "I mean, it's just that I worked so hard on the Wiffle ball idea—" *STOP TALKING!* I silently screamed to myself, but it was too late.

"I'm really sorry, Mom," Buddy repeated.

Idiot! I silently chastised myself again as I tried to figure out a way to undo my words. *This shouldn't be about a* stupid *game*, I continued silently scolding myself. *Damn it! What now?*

But there was no time for me to do anything. The next words I heard were "I gotta go now, Mom. I really love you." He was now sounding a good deal less happy than when the conversation started.

"I love you too, Sweetie, with *all* my heart." I continued to try to figure out a way to defuse the situation, but, coming up with nothing, I simply added, "Take care of yourself, and BE SAFE!" With that, our conversation ended, and my stomach twisted into a knot yet again as I worried about my son's well-being—the current blow to it coming directly from me. "Idiot!" (This time I said it out loud.)

Haley was now awake and had walked upstairs to see what was going on. She took one look at the expression on my face and immediately asked, "Who was that? What's wrong?"

"I simply *cannot* do this!" I answered, the echoes of Buddy's and my conversation still ringing in my ears. I then proceeded to describe to Haley the adventures of Wiffle balls in airborne-land. Haley started laughing somewhere around the shooting-Wiffle-balls-from-tank-turrets part and did not stop until the description was complete.

Haley then asked the million-dollar question: "So what's the problem?"

"Nothing!" I replied. "It's just that now Buddy doesn't *know* there's no problem!"

"What?"

I found it unbelievably difficult to describe how I had failed at my primary objective—keeping Buddy's spirits up. It was even more difficult to explain that the care packages were doing the trick; it was just my spoken words that were lacking! "I just don't understand it," I lamented. "I keep reviewing my phone call with Buddy over and over again in my head, and each time I find myself confused by my own responses."

Haley nodded in agreement. She was also perplexed by my apparent overreaction to what was most likely nothing more than a bonding-in-a-war-zone, band-of-brothers thing. She has often seen me celebrate insanity on a much greater scale, but just the same, she patiently listened to my analysis.

"The reality of it is, I could have seamlessly stopped the discussion at any time and maneuvered the conversation to some other topic to keep it all light and carefree. I am a mom, and moms are expert at that kind of thing."

Haley rolled her eyes but again nodded in agreement, once again asking a simple but very important question: "So why didn't you?"

Unfortunately, I didn't have an answer for her. I shook my head as I picked up my now-empty mug and headed to the kitchen to heat the kettle for another cup of tea. Haley followed me and sat down at the kitchen table as I leaned up against the countertop. I stared at my bare feet against the kitchen floor, searching for an answer to her question, but nothing came to mind. My gaze shifted to a fluff of Whiskey hair gently wafting across the floor until it came to rest at the door that leads to the garage.

"I really do need to get back to my cleaning routine!" I reflected. "I mean, when was the last time I put lines in the carpet? I always feel so much better when the house is clean, you know?"

"Mom!" Haley scolded. "You're trying to change the subject!"

Yes, I was! Without even being totally aware of it, I attempted to end the conversation by starting a new one—so why didn't I do the same thing with Buddy?

"I was, wasn't I?" I said, a little chagrined that Haley had called me out. I paused a moment before adding, "But I'm not sure if any reason I might come up with would justify the ultimate outcome of Buddy's and my conversation. I mean, what—?"

"So forget the reasons why," Haley interrupted. "How do we fix it?"

The tea kettle was now whistling. I turned my back to my daughter so that I could pour the hot water into my mug. I was grateful for the extra couple of seconds to think, but they did not help. "I've got nothing!" I replied as I turned back around and leaned back up against the counter. "All I wanted to do was to let Buddy know I felt his actions were not suitable for proper societal circles—like I know anything about proper societal circles! However, all I am left with is this uneasy, nagging feeling that it was *my* response that was not suitable, and all over stupid Wiffle balls!"

"And I would agree with that," Haley responded.

"So how do I fix it?" I asked. "I can't just call Buddy back and discuss what just transpired, and writing a letter leaves too much to chance because of the unintentional 'between the lines' thing. This all just stinks, but what can I do?"

"Well," started Haley, "for one thing, you can let it all go and pretend that nothing is wrong, then, to *prove* that you are OK with everything, send him a bunch more Wiffle balls for his tank turret enjoyment. Like you always told me, actions speak louder than words!"

My daughter, the genius! She was right, of course. What I needed to do was to show Buddy that I really was OK with his behavior so far—at least most of it. I could continue to bake cookies and send toys and write letters and do whatever it took to help sustain my son, the FHOTA, and any of the other troops that enjoyed my care packages. I could continue to support their need to "let go" every once in a while by continuing to give them reasons to play, however they chose to do so. But, most of all, when I actually managed to supply a respite from their everyday stress, I could keep my own inappropriate behaviors in check, at least for the time being. Basically, until Buddy was back in proper societal circles, I could persevere!

Oh, NUTS!!!

1 cup margarine

1 1/2 cups powdered sugar

1/3 cup granulated sugar

1 teaspoon vanilla

3 egg yolks or 1 whole egg

1/2 teaspoon cream of tartar

1/2 teaspoon salt

2 1/2 cups flour

1 cup chopped nuts (preferably walnuts)

Extra powdered sugar for coating

1. Preheat oven to 350 degrees.
2. Cream together margarine, powdered sugar, granulated sugar, vanilla, and egg with an electric mixer until light and fluffy, about 3 to 5 minutes.
3. Add cream of tartar and salt. Continue to beat with electric mixer for about a minute.
4. With a spoon, mix in flour until well blended. Stir in nuts.
5. Roll dough into balls about the size of walnuts.
6. Coat the dough balls in powdered sugar and place on a cookie sheet.
7. Bake for 8 to 10 minutes until cookies are slightly flattened and set; they should not turn brown.

When is a mother not a mother?

I was glad to hear Buddy's voice again this week. It wasn't that I was ever *not* elated to get his phone calls; it was just that after last week's conversation, I was especially happy to be able to clarify my thoughts and feelings. And since 1st Sgt. Ramirez had started harassing Buddy regarding Wiffle ball games and intramural battalion competitions, he was equally happy—though a smidge contrite—to be able to request more T-shirts and Wiffle balls from me. After some discussion, Buddy assessed that the bats they had were functional enough, even after several Toby-training sessions.

It was a bit of a difficult conversation as we each tried to apologize for our own perceived "bad" behavior. After all was said and done, however, the painful reality was that life was too short—*way* too short—to sweat the small stuff. Besides, the idea of those idiots shooting Wiffle balls out of tank turrets *was* funny! But the whole situation had highlighted an underlying issue that had actually been there from the beginning of the deployment: what role should I play as the mother of a soldier?

Since the day we saw Buddy off and every day since, I found it more and more difficult to strike the appropriate balance between the role of "mother of soldier" and the role of just plain "mother." It seemed like they should have been the same, but subtle differences were surfacing. For example, as the mother of a young man, one is expected to ensure that the young man has learned the finer points of good hygiene, acceptable table manners, social civility, and the like. The mother of a soldier, however, understands that these attributes are next to useless for her son who is currently serving in a war zone, but she also understands that, one day, they will again be important. What's more, the mother of a soldier realizes that in any given situation, she might be called upon to instantaneously switch from her role as a mother of a soldier (overlooking rough behavior) back to being simply "Mom" (chastising that behavior)—and often without warning or preparation. I was learning that navigating between the two roles was definitely challenging.

The one constant I saw between this conflict and Desert Storm, Vietnam, North Korea, World War II, World War I, and every other war was the wear and tear on those fighting—not to mention the wear and tear on the *families* of those fighting. I am not just talking about the physical dangers and stresses—the emotional attacks on the souls of both groups were immense. I knew that on some level we were all aware of this, but I began to wonder if there was a single moment where the wear and tear went from a nuisance to a harmful side effect. Was there a single point in time at which unexpected behavior was no longer a sign of natural, youthful exuberance among young men thrown together in an unnatural situation that we could all feel free to laugh at, but was instead an indication that things were becoming more sinister, like a young man beginning to lose himself in that unnatural situation? I did not know the answer to this question, but what I did know was if that moment existed, it would be most readily recognized by those closest to the ones fighting, like a spouse, or a sibling, or a *mother*. The way I saw it, at that point, it would be the mother-of-a-soldier's duty to return to the role of simply "mother" and attack that moment to defeat its effects.

The previous week's issues arose because I heard things that were the antithesis of what I expected to hear but that my son was telling me with great enthusiasm. What I heard, I heard as Buddy's mother, and I handled the situation like all the other times throughout my son's life that I have found his behavior unsatisfactory: with grace comparable to a bull in a china shop! But I should have been listening with more of a mother-of-a-soldier's ear. I began the conversation that way, but at some point, I shifted back to just plain "mother," and there was no conscious thought process that prefaced that shift—perhaps there should have been. I understood that I handled the situation poorly when I attempted to hold Buddy to the social norms of Anywhere, USA, while he was still serving in a war zone. Not only was it a waste of effort to do so, but it ran the risk of shutting down a line of communication that I believed would be essential to Buddy's readjustment once he redeployed back to the United States.

Because of my background with the military, I believed I had a good idea of what Buddy might be facing. But also because of that background, I realized that my "good ideas" most likely did not hold a candle to the realities of war. Though the reports regarding the emotional problems of our returning troops weighed heavily on my heart, I also felt that being too proactive in trying to counter those issues could increase their ill effects. My response to this catch-22 situation was simple: for the time being, I vowed to be the mother of a soldier first.

Blueberry Shortbread

1/2 cup shortening

1/2 cup margarine

1/2 cup powdered sugar

2/3 cup granulated sugar

1/2 teaspoon vanilla

1/2 teaspoon salt

1/2 cup dried blueberries

1/2 cup chopped pecans

2 cups flour

1. Preheat oven to 350 degrees.

2. Cream together shortening, margarine, powdered sugar, granulated sugar, vanilla, and salt with an electric mixer until light and fluffy, about 3 to 5 minutes.

3. With a wooden spoon, mix in blueberries and pecans. Once well dispersed, stir in flour.

4. Roll out dough until it is 3/8 inch thick and cut with a 2-inch round cookie cutter. Arrange cookies on a cookie sheet.

5. Bake for 15 minutes.

Curiosity killed the cat, and it hasn't been much better for me!

O nce again, work provided yet another degree of anxiety to my already-anxious life—and, once again, it came at the hands of someone who was not necessarily trying to cause me grief. In fact, I think he was actually trying to be helpful as he offered up his own perspective—at my request, no less!

I worked with two army reservists who, since I had begun work for my office, had been deployed to Iraq. From what I could gather, they were not infantry nor were they "front lines" types of soldiers. Instead, I was under the impression that they spent their time in Iraq working from the Green Zone—the protected four-square-mile area in Baghdad which was the governmental center for the Coalition Provisional Authority. Nonetheless, they were army, and they had been in the same vicinity—at least the same country—as Buddy. Needless to say, I felt a very strong kinship to them, though I actually had no idea who they were.

They had both recently returned to the States and had started back to work. I actually attended their "Welcome Home" party, which was held there in the bullpen. It would have been hard to avoid the party even if I wanted to, since it occurred practically on top of my half-icle. Besides, I had baked cookies for the celebration. Even though the party was held right there at my desk, with all the other random people showing up to welcome them back, I was sure I would not be able to pick these guys out of a group of three. However, given my last few weeks, I felt the need to seek them out—to be able to "commune" with someone who could possibly give me some first-hand insight as to what my son was facing day in and day out.

Shortly after the "Welcome Home" party, I sought out these gentlemen. After having someone point them out to me, I went to speak with Reservist #1. He listened quietly as I explained who I was and my current interest in seeking him out. I asked for anything he could tell me about Iraq, Baghdad, or whatever else was affecting my son's life at the time. As best I could, I described where Buddy was: North Baghdad, Forward Operating Base (FOB), and such. I then waited for anything he had to say— which turned out to be nothing. He had been in the Green Zone, and his job did not take him anywhere near where Buddy was deployed. However, he did suggest that I speak with the other reservist; though Reservist #1 was not exactly sure what Reservist #2 did, he did know that Reservist #2 was involved with a "different area."

Reservist #1 was kind enough to walk me over to Reservist #2 and introduce me. During the introduction, Reservist #2 was provided all the background information and my general area of interest. Upon hearing my son's job and where he was located, the expression on Reservist #2's face went from a pleasant "Pleased to meet you" to what I could only describe as "Oh, shit!" As the knot which had been residing rent-free in my stomach since January twisted tighter, he uttered the words, "Oh, wow! That's a rough place!"

Well! That encounter did not help me at all! I mean, I knew Buddy was in a bad area; I knew why Buddy and the 504th were sent over to be the Surge. But somehow, seeing the reflective response of someone who had been there—someone who *knew*— put an exclamation point on what I already knew to be the truth. Once again, I felt all the blood drain from my extremities. I had no idea where my blood went, but when my fingers began to tingle and my knees got weak, I knew it was no longer where it belonged. I tried to think of some clever comeback to demonstrate my strength, resolve, and support, though I would have settled for something coherent. Nothing came to mind, and I was left standing there with what was probably a look of panic on my face. Whatever the look was, Reservist #2 did try to ease it by adding, "But they are doing good stuff there! Those guys really know what they're doing!"

I was grateful for his words of support, but I was also a little sorry I had sought him out in the first place. I definitely experienced more than I really needed to. Having decided there were no other questions I wanted to ask, let alone have answered, I thanked him for his time and headed back to my desk. I worked very hard to un-ex-perience the last interaction as I walked across the bullpen, which I thought would be easier than forgetting it. I just could not believe that I had so totally sabotaged my pretend ignorance and make-believe state of well-being. What was I thinking?!

Acknowledging to myself that I had failed in my attempts to un-experience the last fifteen minutes, I dejectedly sat down at my desk. My mind was wandering more than usual, skipping through a variety of ugly scenarios—none of which I relished for long-term storage. Staring at the pile of new documents to review on my desk, I pondered my current predicament. *So how do I move forward with no lingering effects from an ill-spent morning delving into areas that I had no business knowing anything about?*

With seemingly no chance of salvaging the day, I attempted to refocus my thoughts by concentrating on something positive, like reviewing my life's major lessons. There have not been many, but there have been a few significant ones. I learned that not everyone is trustworthy, but if you want to be given trust, then you need to be able to trust. I learned long ago to cherish time spent with loved ones. Along those lines, I learned to never pass up the opportunity to tell the people I am closest to just how much they are loved. I learned that I feel stronger when I am with my kids and am strongest of all when I'm defending them. But, being the compulsive worrier and self-professed hypochondriac that I am, one of the most important lessons I have learned is: if you can't handle the answer, *don't ask the question!*

Memorial Melts

1 cup margarine	1/2 teaspoon salt
1 1/2 cups brown sugar	2 1/2 cups flour
1 teaspoon vanilla	2 flavors of ice cream topping,
1 egg	preferably the kind that comes
1 1/2 teaspoons baking soda	in a squeeze bottle

1. Preheat oven to 350 degrees. Grease a 7x11–inch baking dish.
2. Cream together margarine, brown sugar, vanilla, and egg with an electric mixer until light and fluffy, about 3 to 5 minutes.
3. Add baking soda and salt. Continue to beat with electric mixer for about a minute.
4. With a spoon, mix in flour.
5. Spread half of the dough in the bottom of the prepared baking dish.
6. Using the ice cream toppings (I used caramel and dark chocolate), squeeze alternate lines of topping across dough in baking dish.
7. Cover the toppings with the remaining dough sandwiching the toppings in between the two layers of dough. Use a knife to swirl the toppings into the dough. (The goal is to distribute flavors rather than create a design.)
8. Bake for 30 minutes. Wait until fully cooled before attempting to slice into bars.

Cookie Week 18

27 May 2007-2 June 2007

Real men use duct tape, as do the mothers of soldiers!

A t the beginning of this deployment, the FRG sent me a 112-slide PowerPoint presentation—the army just *loves* PowerPoint—covering every possible scenario and thing that a family member would want to know about the deployment of a loved one, from the day they left to the day they redeployed and everything in between. Though Haley and I seriously tried to make our way through *all* 112 slides, there were some (like what is available if your soldier is injured—or worse—and how to recognize posttraumatic stress disorder) that we just did not have the heart to read, and others (like those addressed to children of the deployed) that simply did not apply. Still others contained the things we might have read but *definitely* chose to ignore, like the slide that contained the words "Do not send chocolate!" This was inconceivable to us, and the reality of it was that they chose not to give a reason; they just made the assertion.

All in all, the slides did offer some good information and some good suggestions for things like packing a care package—minus the chocolate fiasco, of course! One of the suggestions offered was regarding the use of shoe boxes for sending care packages. They are compact, ship well, and can contain an admirable amount of goodies. At the beginning of the Surge, this seemed like a great idea. Soon, however, I ran out of suitable shoe boxes—no problem there . . . just buy more shoes—but eventually, the shoe box just did not provide enough room.

The past few months had seen me graduating to bigger and bigger boxes, but this week seemed to be the exception. My stash of care package toys had been running low, and I had been unable to find irrelevant and irreverent-yet-appropriate replacements. I had collected the applicable items from my rotation of soaps, cigars, and baby wipes along with the cheese, crackers, and tuna fish that I included with each week's care package, and, inspired by the warmer weather of upcoming summer, I had created a batch of Lemon Zinger cookies. Barring the few "test" cookies enjoyed by Haley, Leo, and myself, I had packed up the whole batch for shipping. Even so, I just did not seem to have anything big to send off to Buddy. Enter the shoe box, once again.

Unfortunately, the only shoe box available was slightly dilapidated and a solid, shiny black color to boot! I was not concerned about addressing the box; however, I was a little concerned about how well an already-dilapidated box would fare in its journey halfway around the world. Enter the duct tape—good old duct tape! The way I had it figured, with enough duct tape, we could turn that slightly dilapidated shoe box into a veritable fortress. So Haley and I went to work. First we wrapped the box lengthwise a couple of times, then we wrapped it widthwise a couple of times . . . and then we got stupid!

It began with noting that a perforation in the side of the shoe box had escaped our attempt to cover all tears and holes with our carefully placed duct tape. As we placed a duct tape bandage on the noted ding, we noticed that on the other side of the box, there was an unsightly crease mark on the box's shiny black surface. Not to worry; we had plenty of duct tape, and we figured that *anything* was better than the identified imperfection. Of course, then there were the various words printed on the box—shoe size, brand name, model, etc.—that we decided needed to go. And, finally, we decided that we did not like the shiny black color either! By the time we were done, there were only a few very small patches of the shiny black of the shoe box exposed. Every other part of the box had up to about a sixteenth of an inch of duct tape covering it. We addressed the box with a black Magic Marker then took a step back to admire our handiwork.

"Impressive!" I said.

"Yeah!" Haley responded, and then added, "Good thing there are no wires hanging out of it!"

"Huh?" I asked, just as a dozen images of homemade bombs that I had seen on the Internet and TV flashed through my head—all of them sporting the unmistakable footprint of duct tape! "Oops!" I acknowledged.

Realizing that labeling our now fully duct-taped box with something like "This is not a bomb!" would be a little self-defeating, we examined our options. Eventually, we decided to slap some stickers on the box—a couple of "Support Our Troops" and a few Pokémon stickers I found—in an attempt to make it look as harmless as possible. We then took it to the post office to ship it off in all its duct-taped glory.

Although the post office did not seem to have a problem with our little care package, we had no idea if it was actually going to reach Buddy. We kind of envisioned it being identified as a suspicious package somewhere along the line and then being rendered harmless by blowing it up, raining bits of homemade cookies and baby wipes all over everything. Equally, we envisioned Buddy resorting to blowing the package up just to get into the veritable fortress that Haley and I had created. Despite all the random scenarios we could come up with, we were having great difficulty in finding it all anything but hilarious.

Lemon Zingers

2/3 cup shortening	1 egg
1/2 cup margarine	1/4 teaspoon cream of tartar
2 cups powdered sugar	1/2 teaspoon baking powder
1 tablespoon corn syrup	1/2 teaspoon salt
1 tablespoon cornstarch	4 cups flour
1 tablespoon lemon zest	Lemon frosting
1 teaspoon lemon flavoring	

1. Preheat oven to 350 degrees.
2. Cream together shortening, margarine, powdered sugar, corn syrup, cornstarch, lemon zest, lemon flavoring, and egg with an electric mixer until light and fluffy, about 3 to 5 minutes.
3. Add cream of tartar, baking powder, and salt. Continue to beat with electric mixer for about a minute.
4. With a spoon, mix in flour.
5. Refrigerate dough for about an hour until thoroughly chilled.
6. Divide dough into quarters. Roll each quarter out between floured wax paper until thin. Cut dough into rounds (or whatever shape is desired). Move to cookie sheet with a pancake turner. (Alternately, drop cookies by rounded teaspoons onto cookie sheets and use a floured cookie stamp or a floured bottom of a glass to flatten the dough to the appropriate thickness.)
7. Bake for 10 to 15 minutes.
8. After cookies are baked, allow to cool. Once cool, squish a heaping teaspoonful of lemon frosting between two cookies.

"Happy birthday to you, happy birthday to you . . ."

My nephew George's birthday was this week. I guess in the big scheme of things, my extended family is rather small when compared with other families. I have three siblings, but none of us were fruitful in our "multiplication," so I only have three nieces and three nephews. It would be difficult to choose a favorite, but because George was born and raised locally, I have become rather close to him. Despite the fact that when the whole extended family gets together I am never quite sure where I belong, George and my kids have always accepted me as part of "the younger crowd" at our local family get-togethers. This, thankfully, relieves me of having to pretend that I managed to grow up somewhere along the line. And even though I think George sometimes uses this as a friendly dig, I have always been grateful for the categorization.

For the past several weeks, news from Iraq had been a little rough, to say the very least. As it had been since the beginning of time, my way of handling the stress of the situation was to withdraw into myself and bake cookies. Unhealthy? Maybe, yes. But in an environment where I was never quite sure of the opinions of others, it was sometimes difficult to take the risk of social interaction, especially considering that my own emotions and sentiments were rather fragile. So when my brother Albert called to invite me to a birthday dinner with both of George's families (my brother and George's mother are divorced and both remarried), I was a little hesitant.

There were actually two reasons for my hesitation. The first was connected to a fear of finding myself in a situation where I had to defend my opinions (and, indirectly, my son) against perceived verbal injustices. The second reason had to do with Buddy. As he served in Iraq, I often felt conflicted as to whether I should tell him all about our family gatherings and outings or whether I should play it all down so that he felt less isolated and left out. It was a difficult decision that was made moot by simply doing nothing. However, I do love George and would do just about anything to show him my support, so though I initially put off my RSVP, I eventually decided to attend the party.

There were ten people at the party, all seated at a single, huge, round table at a local Chinese restaurant. The seating arrangement at the table had me sitting next to George's mom, Karen, two seats away from George. This meant that I was pretending to be an adult for the evening, and for the most part, I was OK with that arrangement. I have always liked Karen, and we have always seemed to connect well, even when I was failing at attempts to be adult! This could be attributed to the fact that Karen has a penchant for moments of less-than-adult behavior, as well, like at Thanksgiving many years ago when all of our kids were under ten.

The two of us were in the process of clearing the dinner dishes and serving dessert, when Karen engaged me in a massive whipped cream fight in Nana's kitchen. Despite our shrieks and laughter no one witnessed the actual event, but a very young George saw what his mother and aunt were capable of as we tried to clean the evidence of our indiscretion, laughing so hard during it all that we could barely breathe.

Many years after the whipped cream incident, George still seemed a little concerned about what the two of us might be discussing so intently the night of his birthday. Because of the size of the table and the distance between him and us, he was not able to hear any of our conversation, and I certainly was not going to share. Though we were not saying anything about him, it was simply a great way to torment him, in a loving-aunt kind of a way.

In fact, most of the conversation revolved around Buddy and how I was handling it all. The one thing I had craved since the deployment began was someone who would simply listen—basically, a sounding board. I leaned so heavily on Haley, but because she was my daughter, I sometimes felt as though I was doing her an injustice. After all, I was the mom, and moms are supposed to be strong. Yet I also felt a tad guilty trying to lean on my *own* eighty-six-year-old mom! So I looked for people to dump on, and sometimes it took only an innocent "How are you doing, Maggie?" to release the floodgates. This was especially true when the words came from a trusted friend that I had known for years, even if I only saw her infrequently.

I talked about the last few weeks, the emotional stress, and the sleepless nights. I described my worries about Buddy's emotional health, even as I sometimes question my own. I told her about Haley, Leo, and my evenings of wine and commiseration and then spoke of our hesitation to even hope.

When I finally paused for a breath, Karen spoke. "George is always telling me that you are confident and strong and completely OK with Buddy being in Iraq, but I knew that was not completely right!"

I sat there dumbfounded for a moment while I slowly digested her words. *What does she mean, implying I'm not confident and strong?* I thought. *I am confident; I am strong; I support my son and all that he and the rest of the 504th are trying to do! I can't help it if sometimes I tend to whine!* I was desperately trying to think of a comeback for her assertion but was overwhelmed with the thought that what she said might actually be the unvarnished truth. I was at a complete loss for words and secretly wished that someone would somehow interrupt our conversation—like by spilling a glass of red wine or demanding more wontons—so that I would have the excuse to dump this train of thought and move on to a more pleasant topic of conversation, like maybe root canals!

On an intellectual level, I knew that Karen was showing me unqualified support. The bottom line is, there are certain facts that give her latitude where others would not rate. For one, we have great history. But more than that, when George was only four years old, his older sister was taken from us quite suddenly. To this day, we all bear the scars, but no one more than Karen. I knew that her words came from a place that knew the pain of loss, but nonetheless, I was stung by her comment, though she surely had not intended to sting. I was left grasping for some sense of fortitude and determination—something that would shine solidly so that no one could question my resolve in my undying support for my son and his mission.

I have often been cautioned against ever thinking I could play poker successfully. In fact, I have been told that I wear my emotions on my face to such a degree that my ability to bluff would be nonexistent. Apparently, this inability to hide my emotions was even more pronounced now, so Karen had a front row seat for whatever was playing across my face. Whatever it was—anxiety, uncertainty, exhaustion—Karen did her best to let me know that she meant no offense with her words.

"Oh, Maggie!" she began. "It's OK that you feel this way. In fact, it's very understandable! I'm not judging you—I support you! I'm here for you whenever you need me."

It was clear that Karen was trying to show me absolute support, but all I could hear was "See? This mother of a soldier doesn't agree with the war! See? There is no hope! See? Our troops will fail!" This obviously was not what she said nor what she meant. But, nonetheless, all I could think was that by whining, I had just created another naysayer when it came to the war. I tried to back away from my earlier words. "No!" I said. "Maybe . . . maybe I have been a little overdramatic. I am doing OK. I'm—I am very proud of Buddy and all that they are accomplishing. Yes, I'm OK; I—I will be just fine!"

"Maggie," Karen countered, "don't think you are fooling me! I know better. I also think Buddy's service is wonderful; I am just worried about you! If you need a break, if you just need someone to listen, I am here for you."

I had become so oversensitized to the perceived lack of support for the war and, by extension, our troops that I just could not outwardly accept her words. This was the reality even though I understood that outside of my immediate family, there was probably no one more supportive of me and my concerns than Karen. I think my biggest problem was that I hated appearing weak even more than I needed someone to listen. In addition, I felt that even the slightest impression that I was wavering in support of my son or the troops was unacceptable. Though I knew it was illogical, it felt as though my brief moment of absolute honesty with Karen had yanked a rug out from under our troops and left them all in great peril. Even more than that, however, I think my greatest anguish was that I felt I had let George down by not being that strong, confident mother of a soldier that he had portrayed me to be.

Cake Batter Cookies

Cookie:

1/3 cup shortening	1 egg
1/3 cup margarine	1/4 teaspoon salt
1 tablespoon brown sugar	1 1/2 cups flour
1/2 cup powdered sugar	1 1/2 cups cake mix

Filling:

"Fluffy" white frosting	Water
Cake mix	

1. Preheat oven to 350 degrees.
2. Cream together shortening, margarine, brown sugar, powdered sugar, and egg with an electric mixer until light and fluffy, about 3 to 5 minutes.
3. Add salt. Continue to beat with electric mixer for about a minute.
4. With a spoon, mix in flour and cake mix.
5. Split dough into quarters. Roll out a quarter of the dough between two floured sheets of wax paper until about 1/16 inch thick. Use

cookie cutters to cut dough into rounds. Transfer cookies onto cookie sheets with a pancake turner. (Alternately, drop cookies by rounded teaspoons onto cookie sheets and use a floured cookie stamp or a floured bottom of a glass to flatten the dough to the appropriate thickness.)

6. Bake for 8 to 10 minutes.

7. To make the filling, mix equal parts frosting and cake mix with enough water to make the filling creamy. Taste-test and adjust if necessary.

8. After cookies are cooled, squish a heaping teaspoonful of filling between two cookies.

Always in my heart!

After the army extended the 504th to a sixteen-month deployment, they also announced that one of the "perks" of an extended deployment was an extended midtour R&R—a break in a soldier's tour of duty for rest and relaxation. Even though the break was only extended from fourteen to eighteen days, that was still four extra days Buddy could be home. Buddy and I had been discussing his R&R for a while, when he hoped to take it, and what he wanted to do with his time. He wanted his R&R to coincide with his twenty-first birthday at the end of August. Of course, the army would have the final say, but in the meantime, I had a time span to focus on without actually *dwelling* on it.

As always, I headed to the comfort of my kitchen to unravel a multitude of memories and thoughts related to all things R&R. This time, though, I had no idea what to create. I opened the cupboards and stared at the various ingredients stored there, but nothing came to mind. After a few minutes of contemplating all the various-shaped boxes and packages containing all things baking related, I decided a glass of wine might be more productive. I poured a rather robust glass and returned to the cupboards to come up with a cookie creation for Buddy's next care package.

As I have mentioned before, arbitrary memories are the cornerstone of any and all of my introspection. It was no wonder that I sometimes had trouble focusing with the parade of various images that constantly flooded my thoughts. It did not seem to matter what the task was; somehow, there was always a corresponding memory to distract me. For instance, preparing for church on Sunday mornings tended to generate some of my most comforting recollections, like sitting on my dad's lap on a Sunday afternoon as he read the Sunday comics to me. The most vivid part of that memory was the feeling of my father's baritone voice reverberating through me as I leaned my back against his chest and listened to him read.

Kitchen time tended to generate memories of my kids. Even today, I remember the moment of each of my children's births. I remember the first day they walked and their first day of school just as vividly as I remember the day they graduated. In between these moments, I cherished a million memories more—many of them significant but many more just as unpredictable and indiscriminate as those I have from my own childhood. There were times these random memories were trouble-some, but at other times, the memories comforted me and even gave me strength. This had been the case since the beginning of the Surge.

I tried to refocus my thoughts to the task at hand. I was a tad disappointed with my cookie-baking efforts. Nothing seemed to be formulating in regards to cookie recipes, and seconds later, my mind was wandering again. As the days and weeks of the deployment had worn on, my memories not only sustained me but also, at times, haunted me. It was not that anything specific had to happen to trigger them. In fact, it was during the quiet times that my mind wandered the most, and this had certainly been a quiet week. Instead of it being an unequivocal blessing, I had the constant feel-ing that I was basically living in limbo as I worked to get through every day without any real focus, not on memories that I feared might end up being the last memories I have of my son and especially not on the future! This was becoming a difficult task considering that the date of Buddy's R&R was approaching. We were heading into the end of June, and it felt as though Buddy's homecoming was just around the corner. I could not help but think about him being home again, even though at the very same time, I refused to consider the prospect.

In the meantime, a suitable cookie recipe was proving to be elusive. Nothing in my cupboards sparked even the remotest inkling of what might be considered a rea-sonable cookie. I let my thoughts wander, hoping they would produce a memory that I could turn into a cookie. Almost immediately, a recollection from a summer long past sprang to mind.

It was in the beginning weeks of summer, and I was waiting for Buddy to come home—only then, Buddy was returning from Boy Scout summer camp. Anyone who has ever dealt with boys—particularly the kind that are akin to the likes of Tom Sawyer or Dennis the Menace and see a career of jumping out of airplanes as a viable option—knows the level of mischief they are capable of, especially when they are gathered together in large numbers. Similar to the current situation, I was confident in the Scout leaders and in the Scout camp. However, knowing my son as I did, I was never quite sure what trouble he was going to find—or, more importantly, what trouble was going to find him. History had taught me that one or the other was bound to happen.

Buddy always meant well and always had a desire to do what was right, but he was, as he is now, "all boy." It meant that Buddy's favorite things while growing up were running and jumping and doing backflips into piles of leaves as opposed to sitting quietly and reading a book. It meant that he would spend his last penny of allowance to buy a corsage for his mom, even though now he would spend the last dollar of his paycheck to add some new racing part to his truck. Being "all boy" meant the same boy who for years tried to assert himself as "the man of the house" would now, as a man, proudly assert that he was a mama's boy. It meant that the same boy who would have done anything to protect his mother and his sister would, as a man, choose to fight for his country—even when it took him halfway around the world to a war that some said was not winnable. That is just who my son is.

So, as in the current situation, during that week a decade ago while Buddy was in Scout camp, I lived from anxious moment to anxious moment, dreading phone calls and knocks on the door as I waited for him to come back home. Eventually, the day did arrive, and I headed to the parking lot of a local church to greet my son. In all the commotion of parents finding their boys and vice-versa, Buddy seemed to make a beeline for me. Apparently, he was not so much excited to see me as he was to ensure that he was not already in trouble.

The trouble this time had to do with putting out a campfire without using water. It was supposed to be a teaching moment that encouraged the Scouts to think of smothering the fire with dirt. However, it quite literally became a "pissing contest"— one started by my son! Even though it took everything inside of me *not* to laugh as Buddy related the story, I could see he was horrified at the possibility that what he did was damnable. I did my best to ease his mind and let him know he was OK and then suggested we do something special to celebrate his homecoming. At his request, we went to see the new Disney movie *Tarzan*. As a mother, it was hard to imagine how anyone could watch that movie and not be moved. It was equally hard to hear the song "You'll Be in My Heart," even for that first time, and not be reminded of how very blessed I was to have my son. Tears filled my eyes that day as I recognized how very much Buddy was, and always would be, in my heart. And, all these many years later, that fact remained unchanged.

Just like when Buddy was returning from Scout camp, I left the door open to whatever he desired for his R&R. I told him early on that there was not a whole lot that he could ask for that I would not do for him if it was at all in my power to accomplish. It was no big surprise to me that his heart's desire was just to be home. He simply wanted to get everyone together for his birthday and spend some quality time with them—and then he added "in a hot tub!" The kids and I had had a hot tub before, and we really enjoyed it. To be honest, I had been planning to install one for quite some time. In fact, I had already had the deck installed where I wanted the tub placed and the electricity run to it, so Buddy's request was slightly less of a shock than it might have originally appeared. Rather than initiating a full project, Buddy's request simply nudged the project to completion.

Frustrated with my cookie-baking efforts, I shut the cupboards, grabbed my glass of wine, and went to the back deck for a few minutes of fresh air. I stood in the bright sunshine, sipping on my wine, and watched the Whiskey-Dog lumber across the backyard, stopping every so often to sniff at a clump of grass. I was trying hard not to imagine my deck filled with people celebrating Buddy's birthday, but it was difficult. As the weather warmed from spring to summer, it had become easier to imagine the dog days of August when Buddy was due to be home once again. With reporting out of Iraq becoming more and more scarce, it was becoming more and more challenging to find the balance between restraint and anticipation. I longed to have my family together again, and I would have loved to start doing some preliminary planning for Buddy's party to help pass the time, but I was afraid that to do so might jinx everything. I would have loved to have felt free to wish the time away to bring August around faster, but I was afraid of what I might lose in the process. I would have loved to have found a distraction that would free my heart, if only for a few hours, but I feared that to do so would be taking my eyes off the ball, and that just seemed dangerous.

"It's too pretty a day to be inside baking," I said to Whiskey, who had now joined me on the deck. I sat down in one of my Adirondack chairs and leaned back into it as Whiskey sat down next to me. I sipped on the last of my wine while continuing to ponder cookie recipes.

"Maybe instead of something new, I should go with one of the old recipes," I opined to Whiskey. "I will make some old-fashioned oatmeal cookies tomorrow. Buddy should like that, since he used to help me bake them."

At the sound of Buddy's name, Whiskey wagged his tail and looked to the sliding glass doors as if he expected Buddy to walk through them any second. I scratched him behind the ears to comfort him but could not seem to ease my own heart. I could not shake the feeling of being in limbo nor the memory of sitting in the movie theater watching *Tarzan* with my son all those many years before. My eyes filled with tears as the song "You'll Be in My Heart" played over and over again in my head like some maniacal ditty that you hear once and are stuck with forever—but unlike one of those ditties, I did not necessarily want this song to end. It did remind me of my son, and that was a comfort. Nonetheless, here in June, a full two months before Buddy was due home, I was definitely left feeling the weight of the wait.

Plain Old Oatmeal Cookies

1/2 cup shortening

1/2 cup margarine

3/4 cup brown sugar

1/4 cup granulated sugar

1/2 tablespoon corn syrup

1 teaspoon vanilla

1 egg

1 teaspoon baking soda

1/2 teaspoon salt

1 teaspoon ground cinnamon

1 1/2 cups flour

1 1/4 cups old-fashioned oats

1/2–1 cup raisins or chocolate chips, optional

1. Preheat oven to 350 degrees.

2. Cream together shortening, margarine, brown sugar, granulated sugar, corn syrup, vanilla, and egg with an electric mixer until light and fluffy, about 3 to 5 minutes.

3. Add baking soda, salt, and cinnamon. Continue to beat with electric mixer for about a minute.

4. With a spoon, mix in flour until well blended. Stir in oats and raisins or chocolate chips (if using).

5. Drop dough by rounded tablespoons onto cookie sheets.

6. Bake for 12 to 15 minutes or until cookie edges are lightly browned and centers are set.

The more the merrier, right?

A few months back, Haley and I were discussing and planning for Leo, his dog (Marjorie), and his cat (Shesha) to move into the Bear Cave. During this conversation, Haley looked me square in the eyes and asked, "Are you *sure* you're OK with all this? I mean, have you actually considered that you will be going from just you and the Whiskey-Dog to a full house?"

When I answered my daughter, I spoke with conviction and straight from the heart. "I am positive! It will be great to have the house full once again!"

Most of the time, allowing my heart to make the decisions regarding my life choices does not present problems, but every once in a while, my head catches up with those decisions—and when it does, it generally means trouble. But as I considered Haley's question, I had to ask myself how any of what we were discussing could have an ill effect on either me or the Whiskey-Dog. After all, the Whiskey-Dog himself was a decision of the heart.

When I brought home the Whiskey-Dog as a puppy, my life was in shambles and my heart was broken. I wanted to believe that he was going to help heal everything for me and for my kids. Five years later, the Whiskey-Dog had lived up to all expectations! He was my great, lumbering, gentle giant—with the IQ of a mound of dirt—but we loved him to death anyway. He could melt my heart when he saddled up close to me, laid his big old head in my lap, and looked up at me with his huge brown eyes. Not only was he my sitting companion, but he was my walking companion, too. Whiskey was also my protector, though anyone who knew him knew that he was nothing but a big baby. However, the reality was he did not have to be anything but *big*—anyone who took one look at "big" had no desire to test disposition. Up until January, the Whiskey-Dog seemed plenty enough as far as housemates were concerned. However, when Buddy left to fight in the Surge, I felt as though I needed something more than my dog—loveable though he was.

When Haley first asked about Leo moving in, I did consider my Whiskey-Dog and the implications of going from a one-dog house to a two-dogs-and-one-cat house. After all, Whiskey was used to being an "only child." Whiskey had never been around cats before, but since he couldn't care less about the squirrels in the backyard, I doubted a cat in the house would make a difference. I couldn't see a problem with a second dog in the house, either. Though this huge, *un-neutered* male dog had never shown a lick of interest in other dogs, let alone dogs of the female persuasion, when it came to puppies, the Whiskey-Dog literally drooled with excitement. He just *loved* to clean them and take care of them. And now, one of those puppies—the now-grown Marjorie—was potentially going to be living with us 24/7. I just could not see any of it being a problem, leaving my heart free to make the decision.

As important as the Whiskey-Dog was to me, though, the animals were only half the equation; the human half was also something to consider. But try as I might, I could not see a problem with Leo coming to live at the Bear Cave, either. His exuberant participation in our family's Easter activities made him a shoo-in for our home. No, I could see nothing but good things coming from inviting Leo into the Bear Cave, so at the beginning of the week, Leo moved in, bag and baggage.

Following the hustle and bustle of moving day, we were all exhausted, but I still had work to do. Fourth of July care packages for Buddy, the FHOTA, and 1st Sgt. Ramirez needed to be completed for shipping.

Most of our care packages that included celebratory paraphernalia had some sort of homemade something that was crafted specially for the occasion, and these care packages were no exception. Along with the gunpowderless firecrackers that I had sent to overseas troops before, these packages included "Victory Dances." The whole idea of the Victory Dance came from the movie *Independence Day*, which seemed amazingly appropriate. The fighter pilots in the movie would not start a mission unless they were in possession of their Victory Dance—a cigar. I had watched the movie a few weeks before, and as they handed out the Victory Dances in the movie, I thought, *Perfect! That is just what I need to be sending now!* I bought a dozen or so fine cigars, but was worried that the guys would not understand their full meaning, that they were meant for that celebratory moment when they were once again safe. Rather than just write it out in a letter, I decided that a homemade, decorated wooden box to hold the cigars would be a much better option. I spent one evening making up the boxes, each box just big enough for one cigar, and then set the boxes aside for painting.

Both the gunpowderless firecrackers and the cigar boxes needed finishing touches before they were sent. In my mind, both needed some sort of personalizing. I wanted all the receiving troops to know that they were specifically intended as the recipient of our endeavors. I covered my coffee table with newspaper and sat down at the table with my red, white, and blue foam decorating sheets, paints, and a glass of wine. Before I had even found something decent to watch on TV as I worked, Haley and Leo had grabbed libations of their own and joined me at the coffee table for an evening of crafting.

Like me, they both put their hearts into their work. We sat there for hours painting the cigar boxes and then shifted to cutting and pasting different shapes for the gunpowderless firecrackers. In addition, we each put in our two cents as we named each of the firecrackers after their recipients. After our work was completed and we were deciding who was to receive which Victory Dance, Leo let me know that he wanted a specific box that he decorated to go to Buddy. Leo warmed my heart as he informed me that he wanted Buddy to know that it was his work! Yes, Leo seemed to be an excellent fit for the Bear Cave.

The last thing to do was to bake this week's cookie creation. I was thinking in celebration of the Fourth of July, the cookie should be something all-American—something like Apple Pie Cookies. As I worked away in the kitchen, Haley sat at the kitchen table to keep me company and Leo helped pretty much the way Buddy would have helped—by taste-testing everything, especially before it was baked. It was a great time.

I felt truly blessed by the new living arrangements, but the reality of it was I had not fully thought about all the ins and outs of the situation, which became apparent in this first week. There were the issues of cat boxes and extra poop to clean up in the backyard, not to mention the extra muss, fuss, and general untidiness of having three extra living things hanging out in the house. In the long run, though, none of it seemed to matter. My home felt full again, even if not complete because Buddy was where he was. *How could this be anything but wonderful?* I asked myself.

A week after Leo moved in, I came home from work to find my quiet home erupting into chaos. Haley was engaged in a rousing round of Poke the Kitty, a "game" where she poked Shesha in her side as she said "Poke the kitty!" and waited for Shesha to explode into a true hissy fit, generally because it was funny. The Whiskey-Dog—having (sort of) discovered his manhood since Marjorie had moved in—was *attempting* to hump the *spayed* Marjorie-Dog—"attempting" because he had yet to figure out that he was *not* supposed to be facing her. As Haley laughed uncontrollably and Leo yelled at the Whiskey-Dog for attempting (very unsuccessfully) to violate his dog, I surveyed the chaos a moment. *Yep! Anything* but *wonderful!*

Apple Pie Cookies

Cookie:

1/3 cup shortening
1/3 cup margarine
3 ounces cream cheese
1 cup powdered sugar
1 tablespoon cornstarch

1 teaspoon vanilla
1 egg
1/2 teaspoon cream of tartar
1/2 teaspoon salt
2 cups flour

Filling:

1/4 cup margarine
1 cup chunky applesauce (choose brand that does not require refrigeration after opening)

1 1/2 teaspoons apple pie spice
1 1/2 cups powdered sugar
1/3 cup finely chopped walnuts

1. Preheat oven to 350 degrees.
2. Cream together shortening, margarine, cream cheese, powdered sugar, cornstarch, vanilla, and egg with an electric mixer until light and fluffy, about 3 to 5 minutes.
3. Add cream of tartar and salt. Continue to beat with electric mixer for about a minute.
4. With a spoon, mix in flour.
5. Refrigerate dough until firm.
6. Split dough into quarters. Roll out a quarter of the dough between two floured sheets of wax paper until approximately 1/8 inch thick. Use cookie cutters to cut dough into rounds. For half the rounds, use a smaller cutter (1/4 to 1/2 inch in diameter) to cut a piece out of the center of the round. Transfer cookies onto cookie sheets with a pancake turner.
7. Bake for 8 minutes until the edges are lightly browned.

8. To make the filling, beat together margarine, applesauce, and apple pie spice. Gradually add powdered sugar until the mixture has the consistency of frosting. Stir in the walnuts.

9. After cookies are cooled, squish a heaping teaspoonful of frosting mixture between two cookies, making sure one of the cookies has its center removed.

Limp latex and cold spit!

Last night, I sat down to write out my weekly, meandering account of what my life had been like since Buddy deployed and realized I had *nothing* to say! It was not simply that I could not figure out what to write, like writer's block. No, for the first time in my life, my mind was *completely* still! Imagine! *Me!* I am normally one of those people who has a thousand ideas screaming through her head at any given moment. Even when I was six or seven years old, I would have so many thoughts running through my teeny, tiny brain at night that I would not be able to fall asleep. I had an attention deficit before it was defined as a disorder, and yet I was unable to conjure up a single reflection to enter into my little Eeyore notebook for posterity. I sat there for what seemed like an eternity, staring at the lined, purple pages with a different sketch of Eeyore in each corner, waiting for a thought—*any* thought—to fall out of the gray matter between my ears and onto the blank page beneath my pen. But, alas, it was not to be.

This morning, I was getting dressed for work—and trying very hard to ignore the news broadcasting from the clock radio that sits at the head of my bed—when a thought finally emerged. The very fact that it took a full day to produce the most basic of thoughts, in this instance, simply the musings of how I was feeling that week, spoke volumes. My once dynamic and extremely active mind had become constipated, for lack of a better word. Unfortunately, this was a substantial indication as to the state of affairs of my so-called life. Slowly over the past several months, all those things that gave life a little pizazz had been slipping away. As the days had turned into weeks and the weeks into months, I had continued to further restrict that which I allowed myself to "get lost" in to the point where I found myself getting lost in nothing. It was not a deliberate or intentional thing—it just sort of happened.

I used to believe that when the going gets tough, the tough get going, and the dazed and confused (that would be me) put lines in their carpet (vacuum!), but even that was not working anymore. I just did not seem to have the energy for physical activity, nor did I have the mental capacity for extending my thoughts beyond the here and now. Recently, I had begun to feel that if my mind were to wander at all, it would end up in places that I just did not need it to be. Even the last few weeks of my pot throwing class had become a chore. It was not that I had stopped enjoying the creativity; it was just that the exertion of energy to wake up, get to the class, set up for the class, create the pots, clean up after class, and then get back home again felt somehow overwhelming—and frivolous!

On one of those Saturdays, I actually called Nana for permission to stay home from "school" that morning. To my surprise, my mom, who was normally a zealous advocate of me not pushing myself too hard, basically told me I should suck it up and go anyway. She then added by way of an explanation, "All your energy is being sent overseas right now. You need to take care to not lose yourself in this current situation—to do so will be of no benefit to Buddy."

Wow! These were incredibly wise words from an often-wise woman. I did go to "school" that Saturday and every Saturday since, because I knew what she said was true. Even so, listening to my mom in this instance didn't actually stop the progression or change the path that lead me to the mental and emotional state that now consumed me.

So many times since the deployment began, I had felt as though my whole existence was like a huge, beautiful balloon. It sounds quite lovely, but it does have a dark and disturbing side. Basically, no matter how hard one tries, the air just cannot be stopped from eventually escaping that balloon. What is left is a delightful memory, but the only physical evidence of that once-beautiful balloon is a piece of limp latex filled with cold spit! And that had definitely become my life—beautiful, as all life is; however, somewhere about twenty-eight weeks earlier, my life developed a slow leak through which all things light and interesting seeped.

If this was my life now, what was it going to be like in ten months? Or twelve months? Even as I guardedly considered welcoming my son home again, I wondered who I was going to be as I greeted him. I wondered how much of myself was going to be lost through the emotional stress of the deployment, let alone who my son will have become. Worse yet, even though I was able to identify the presumed cause of the problem—the stress of deployment on both the troops and their families—I had no idea how to counter, let alone reverse, its ill effects. It was like I was a single leaf being whipped about by a tornado.

I really had no idea how to proceed—on any level—but at least now I had figured out what I was going to be writing in my little Eeyore notebook. It might not help refill my balloon, but at least it would get my thought processes moving again.

Chocolate Pockets

1/3 cup shortening
1/3 cup margarine
1/3 cup brown sugar
1/3 cup granulated sugar
1/2 teaspoon vanilla
1 egg

3/4 teaspoon baking soda
1/2 teaspoon salt
2 1/4 cups flour
Chocolate, butterscotch, peanut
 butter, or white chocolate chips
 (2–3 for each cookie)

1. Preheat oven to 350 degrees.
2. Cream together shortening, margarine, brown sugar, granulated sugar, vanilla, and egg with an electric mixer until light and fluffy, about 3 to 5 minutes.
3. Add baking soda and salt. Continue to beat with electric mixer for about a minute.
4. With a spoon, mix in flour.
5. Refrigerate dough until firm (a few hours or overnight).
6. Roll dough out until 1/16 to 1/8 inch thick and cut into 2- to 3-inch rounds. Move the rounds to a cookie sheet. Drop 2 to 3 chips onto the center of each round. Fold the cookie round in half over the chips and seal the edges by pressing with the tines of a fork.
7. Bake for 10 to 12 minutes until edges are lightly browned.

"O thus be it ever when free men shall stand / Between their lov'd home and the war's desolation!"

Today was the Fourth of July. For all the different parties and picnics that we have had or attended in the past to celebrate this holiday, it was amazingly subdued this year. Leo had to work in the morning, and Haley had to work in the evening, so I spent the day just hanging out on my back deck. By the time Leo returned home, Haley had already left, so at the appropriate time, Leo and I grabbed a drink and a blanket and joined the throng of people from the neighborhood walking down to the local lake for a fireworks display. As uneventful as the day and evening were, it still stirred a flood of memories.

My little family has lived in this town for over ten years. Since we moved here, no matter what the earlier festivities, the evening always found us joining the neighbors at the lake for what is a decent display, without having to worry about traffic jams and parking. I remember one year, Buddy and I had just set out for the lake when it started pouring rain. Though we had only made it to the end of the cul-de-sac, by the time we had run back home, we were soaked! Another year, Haley's friends joined us at the lake. After the first couple of fireworks exploded in the sky (accompanied by the appropriate *Oohs* and *Ahhs*), one of Haley's friends commented that it would all be much nicer with music. Haley and I obliged with a patriotic a cappella song—probably "The Star-Spangled Banner." Haley and I totally ignored the fact that we were surrounded by thousands of people as we were singing but were abruptly reminded of it by the applause we received when we finished. It was a smidge embarrassing but a great deal of fun.

But the Fourth of July memory that had stood out the most this day was from the summer Buddy graduated from high school. It was on an evening much like this one; I was relaxing in bed, reading, when my son came in and lay across the foot of it. As I looked up from my book, Buddy leaned over and pulled the Whiskey-Dog onto the end of the bed with him. As he rested his head on the now-reclining Whiskey-Dog, he turned to me with a mildly perplexed look on his face.

"Yes?" I inquired.

"It's all your fault, you know," he replied.

"Excuse me?"

"Me joining the army. You did it to me!"

I looked down at that beautiful face of his. His father was part Cherokee, and Buddy's dark eyes and dark features so distinctly reflected that Native American heritage. As I looked at him, I could almost see the little boy who used to crawl into my bed on a cold winter's evening for warmth. Walking at seven months, he learned shortly after to flip himself over the rails of his crib to escape its confines. By the time Buddy was nine months old, he was already sleeping in a "real" bed. I remember how small he looked that first night I tucked him in it. *But not so small anymore*, I silently acknowledged as I glanced at his feet hanging over the side of my queen-size bed.

I said the first thing that popped into my head. "Bite me!" Then I smiled, my heart filled with a mother's love and pride.

"No, really!" he continued. "Think about it! I was basically raised at the Pentagon; all the people you hang out with are either current or former military! What choice did I have?!"

At the time, I dismissed the whole conversation by blowing a raspberry at him and reminding him that I had *never* been able to talk him into anything he did not already want to do. However, with Buddy serving overseas, his words haunted me and weighed heavily on my heart.

Haley has explained to me before that she and Buddy are so afraid of disappointing me, all I have to do is casually suggest something and they will do everything they can to make it happen.

"You need to be careful, Mom," she says. "You've got some power here!"

I felt amazingly blessed to have my kids think so highly of me, but sometimes it seemed like a double-edged sword. I remembered how much my own parents' opinions would sway my decisions and choices. It is an amazing concept to me that I have the same sway over my own kids but with only half the capacity for adult-type reflection and behavior. But it is a scary thought, as well. Haley claims that her current situation with the local news station was anchored in my insistence that she apply. Though I am a tad conflicted on how I feel about this (i.e., her success at her job balanced against whether it is where she initially wanted to be), I also know that her time at that station has not put her in danger or caused her harm. However, I am unable to say the same thing about Buddy.

I am very proud of the man my son has become and of his service to this country. It fills my heart even as it consumes me with apprehension and a strange sense of premonition, though I cannot determine whether it is a glimpse of the future or simply fear. Haley is right when she claims that I encouraged Buddy to join up but wrong in her suggestion that I somehow was the *force* behind his decision—I think. From a very young age, Buddy demonstrated a desire to be a part of the military. Of course, I am unsure how much my military connections played into that, and therein lies the rub!

The truth is, I would be proud of Buddy no matter what occupation he chose. However, I do believe that his service has made him a better man. I also believe that Buddy is more than satisfied with his career choice, though at times, I can hear in his voice how difficult things can be for him. Even so, the challenge of his life as an infantry soldier does not necessarily equate to discontent on his part, but it does stir doubt in my own heart. I know Buddy's accusation was born of a fear of the unknown. He had yet to begin boot camp and was a bit uneasy regarding what he was about to embark upon. I believe this doubt would have been there no matter what challenge he chose to undertake there at the beginning of his adult life. Now, if I could only be sure that what I have given my son in the past was simply encouragement and not some sort of an ultimatum for my approval, I would be set.

Shippable S'mores

4 cups graham cracker cereal (I
used Golden Grahams)
2 1/2 cups mini marshmallows
1 1/2 cups milk chocolate chips

1 bag (10 ounces) marshmallows
3 tablespoons margarine
1–1 1/2 teaspoons liquid smoke
(for added authenticity)

1. Line a 9x13-inch pan with parchment or wax paper.
2. Use a wooden spoon to combine cereal, mini marshmallows, and chocolate chips.
3. In a medium saucepan, melt together marshmallows, margarine, and liquid smoke. Combine with dry ingredients until mixed.
4. Spread mixture into pan. Use remaining chocolate chips, a handful of mini marshmallows, and a handful of cereal to decorate the top before the mixture sets.
5. Allow to set and then cut into squares.

Cookie Week 24

8 July 2007–14 July 2007

But if you *really* believe it, does it make it true?

Have you ever had a bad dream about a loved one—a bad dream that, though it might have been fuzzy around the edges, was crystal clear when it came to the harm that befell someone especially close to your heart? If it is about your spouse, you might roll over and check to ensure they are still breathing or even spend a few minutes spooning. If the subject of your dream is your small child, you might go to their bedroom and check on them as they sleep. If it is your brother or sister, you might call them long distance just to verify that they are safe. But if it is your child that is serving in a war zone, it is an incapacitating experience because there are no immediate channels to relieve your fears.

I had one of those dreams tonight. It made no difference that things seemed so much calmer in Iraq. Buddy was still going on patrol, still standing guard, and still getting in firefights, and that weighed heavily on me. When it was not tormenting my conscious, waking moments, it seemed to be festering in my subconscious. It was as if I were outwardly saying "Not going to listen to it, not going to watch it, not going to think about it!" and yet, somewhere in the depths of my being, I was responding with "Oh yeah? Check it out!" Simply put, I did not want to dwell on the "what if"s or the "what's happening now"s; I simply wanted to survive it all, along with my son, safe, sound, and sane! It was what I prayed for every minute of every day.

Once the nightmare had entered my conscious thought, though, there was no dismissing it. I laid there in the dark with my heart pounding and tears streaming down my face as I tried to think of something else, but to no avail. The images in my mind were vivid—Buddy bloodied and broken and lying in the dirt alone in some desert—and the outcome of the images unmistakable. I could not keep from wondering whether they were the result of trepidation or premonition. I tried to will the phone to ring but then stopped; I was not confident that I would want to hear that phone call if it was not Buddy on the other end. So I continued to try to think of something else—*anything else*—even as I started to drift off to sleep again.

Now, the thing about nightmares is that if you do not displace the bad thought that gave you the bad dream, you are doomed to repeat the nightmare. Having fallen back to sleep without successfully replacing the bad thought that was haunting me, the bad dream just started all over again. This time, however, I managed to wake myself before the dream reached its immensely unpleasant conclusion. Realizing that I was *not* going to be sleeping for a while, I got up for a cup of tea and a quiet sit on my back deck under the stars. It was a cool midsummer evening, a little unusual for this area. A slight breeze rustled through the trees as I leaned back in my Adirondack chair and stared at the moon just peeking through the gently swaying leaves. It was a peaceful repose, and I was grateful for the stillness of the night that allowed my soul to recover from unwanted dreams.

At least I can say that most of my dreams have not been nightmares. But that certainly did not mean they did not have the ability to affect me. Some of the dreams were so very everyday and lifelike that they disturbed me on a whole different level. In particular, I recalled one dream a couple of months earlier where I was sitting on a canister drum across from Buddy, who was sitting on a similar canister drum. Between us was a makeshift table of a nondescript flat surface on some other canister. A T-shirted Buddy—no body armor, hence, no danger—was shuffling a deck of cards on the "table" as we chatted about how things were going and life in general. He was telling me about his life in Iraq, asking me a couple of opinions, and listening to how things were going with me. It was just like a thousand conversations we'd had before, only different. The uniqueness of the conversation is what made the feeling of déjà vu so confusing. It *really* felt as though I had spent at least a portion of that night chatting with my son. *But it was only a dream . . . right?!*

I took a sip of tea and rested my head on the chair back as I closed my eyes for a moment. I let my mind wander back to when I had that dream. It was just after we had learned of the deployment extension and Buddy and I had discussed ideas for his upcoming R&R, including the purchase of the hot tub. At the time, his home-coming seemed as if it were decades away, but it was good to at least have something that had to be done in preparation. Somehow, shopping for the hot tub brought the end of August just a teensy bit closer, even though that feeling disappeared once the purchase was made.

I remembered speaking with the hot tub salesperson about that dream, never being one to shirk the opportunity to share my thoughts on anything with anyone. I explained how it seemed so real that it was as if I were actually chatting with Buddy over a game of cards. She was a bit of a hippie-type flower child who was heavily into the mystical side of life, and she explained to me that those with Native American blood, specifically Cherokee blood, have the ability to connect on a spiritual plane. Well, as near as my limited ability in basic arithmetic allowed me, I calculated that Buddy was at least 1/16 Cherokee, possibly 1/8. It started me wondering if my amazingly lifelike dreams were actually a connection to my son on some other plane.

As silly as it seemed to me now, sitting in the dark on my deck these many weeks later, at the time, I decided I had to know. It was only a few days after my chat with the hot tub saleswoman that Buddy called again. I could not stop myself from laughing out loud as I recalled that conversation with my son—well, at least the beginning of it. I was so excited about the idea of this spiritual connection with Buddy that the first words out of my mouth after we said our hellos were "Hey, Buddy! Have you been dreaming about me?"

His response was unambiguous. "Oh, Mom, that's *nasty*!"

So much for meeting on some other plane! Having realized at that point that it was totally useless to try to explain my question, I just let it go and changed the subject.

I sat up in my chair and slowly shook my head as I laughed again at my ridiculous behavior. I realized that it was rooted in my very real and honest desire just to see my boy again, but still I had to wonder: if my kids and I *were* connected on some mystical, celestial plane—which, admittedly, I sometimes felt we were—then have I actually been seeing my son at times? I gathered up my teacup and stood up to walk back into the house. I opened the sliding glass doors and headed for the kitchen. *And if I am seeing my son, what does that say about the nightmare that sent me to the back deck to begin with?* Clearly, the cool night air and hot tea did not do their job in freeing my mind from undesirable thoughts. I resigned myself to the fact that the nightmare would be with me awhile—at least until the next time Buddy called and I was able to hear for myself that he was OK. I headed back to bed, though I had my doubts that I was actually going to be able to sleep. Thank goodness it was almost time for me to get up anyway!

Banana Nut Dream Cookies

1/3 cup shortening
1/3 cup margarine
1/4 cup brown sugar
2/3 cup granulated sugar
1 teaspoon vanilla
1 egg
1/4 cup buttermilk
1 ripe banana

1 teaspoon baking powder
1/2 teaspoon salt
1 teaspoon ground cinnamon
1/4 teaspoon ground cloves
1/4 teaspoon ground nutmeg
2 1/3 cups flour
1 cup chopped walnuts

1. Preheat oven to 350 degrees.
2. Cream together shortening, margarine, brown sugar, granulated sugar, vanilla, and egg with an electric mixer until light and fluffy, about 3 to 5 minutes.
3. Add buttermilk and banana. Continue to beat with electric mixer until well blended.
4. Add baking powder, salt, cinnamon, cloves, and nutmeg. Continue to beat with electric mixer for about a minute.
5. With a spoon, mix in flour until well blended. Stir in walnuts.
6. Drop dough by rounded teaspoons onto cookie sheets.
7. Bake for 11 to 12 minutes.

Sometimes you just need to speak your mind!

I could not help but worry about our troops in Iraq. I am not talking about the obvious reasons for concern but about a more subtle uneasiness I had been experiencing surrounding the question of whether they realized just how much they were appreciated. Maybe it had to do with all the Vietnam vets I had known and worked with in the past, but when I watched the news and read various editorials, I got the impression that there were many who thought Iraq was a bust on about six different levels. Maybe it was just my past shaping my current observations, but the way I saw it, we as a nation—or maybe just the media—could have been doing a whole lot better in showing support to our brave troops who had dedicated them-selves to protecting our way of life, wherever that took them.

In my opinion, the problem with what I was seeing when I got up the nerve to actually watch the news had everything to do with perspective and perceptions—partly mine and partly what the media was projecting. I was aware that what I was experiencing might be that Hindu-elephant-parable thing again, since much of what I felt was directly connected to our soldiers serving on the front lines. I knew that when I heard from Buddy or one of the other soldiers, I was hearing things only from their perspective and not necessarily the "big picture." And, of course, I did realize that *they* all realized I was the mother of one of their band of brothers, so I would surmise that their words to me may have been guarded. But nonetheless, from what I heard, there were positive accomplishments taking place in Iraq. So where were *those* reports on the evening news?

Everyone understood that war could be ugly—I believe the phrase is "War is hell!" But why was the "hell" the only thing the news focused on? When I questioned Haley about it, I found no satisfaction in her answers. Having long ago given up on counseling me against watching the news, she basically just avoided the conversations altogether.

"Haley, did you see that report?" I would fume at her. "What the hell is wrong with the news?! Why can't the news talk about . . . ? Why can't they . . . ?"

"*Stupid* news people!" Haley would respond, her words dripping with sarcasm. "You can't trust *any* of them! They are *all* horrible!"

Yeah, yeah, Haley; you made your point, I would think. *No broad strokes when discussing the news media—that is, until next time.* But the question still remained. In deference to Haley and her position as a news professional, *generally* speaking, why was it that the media seemed unable to see the positive things that were happening concerning our soldiers in Iraq?

To be honest, I think one of my biggest problems stemmed from the quickness of the deployment. It seemed as though I had barely had time to catch my breath during the five days from when I was first informed of the deployment to the day Buddy boarded the plane for Iraq. It felt as though I had spent every moment since simply trying to regain some sort of equilibrium. Since that day, I had felt emotionally unbalanced, and just about any little thing could set me off. Add to that the media's constant ragging on Iraq and possible mistakes made without acknowledging the successes—and there were many successes—and it all began to feel like a personal affront.

The media seemed to gleefully report on the drama of it all without taking into account that most of our troops were good people, dedicated to the mission, who left their families to suffer through a multitude of uncertainties regarding the deployment. I knew that I must have said an appropriate goodbye to Buddy, but I just could not remember it, and that haunted me. Since January 2nd, I must have told my son I loved him a thousand times, but it just did not seem enough. I tried with every fiber of my being to support my son and his fellow soldiers, to let them know that their efforts were appreciated, but somehow all my efforts felt empty. It was so close to Buddy's R&R, and yet the next few weeks felt like an eternity. There was too much water under the bridge—too much had happened in the past seven months that let me know how fragile the situation was.

However, my son's no-notice deployment was only part of my irritation with all things media generated. The other part of my hypersensitivity toward the reporting out of Iraq was directed at the media's unrelenting focus on not just the overall mistakes of the deployment but specifically the mistakes made by our troops. My uneasiness stemmed from my son's penchant for mischievous and rather impish behavior. It was something Buddy had wrestled with throughout his life, from his first day of kindergarten to the day he graduated high school. It accounted for an endless stream of teachers' notes and what I have always referred to as "inquisitions" due to inappropriate classroom behavior. I am not talking about some evil behavior that signified some sort of juvenile delinquency, just a precocious love of life that always seemed to leave Buddy on the wrong side of his teachers. I just did not want to see it leave him on the wrong side of the army—or the media!

Given his past with schoolteachers, Buddy has always done amazingly well within the structured environment of the army. I have actually been a little stunned by the words of praise regarding Buddy that have come from his chain of command. It was during Buddy's first tour to Iraq when 1st Sgt. Ramirez wrote to me:

> . . . [The] other soldiers look up to [Buddy] for guidance and advice. As a thirty-one-year-old father of two little boys, I can only hope that someday my children can grow to become what you have done with your son. He challenges me every day to continue to motivate and train him, which brings nothing more than pride and honor to serve with him.

I realized that when anyone in a soldier's chain of command speaks with that soldier's mother, they are supposed to be respectful and—if at all possible—flattering, but the various emails and communications I received seemed over the top. I questioned Keith for his insider's opinion. Keith—who can be *painfully* honest—let me know in no uncertain terms that what was relayed to me was not the standard "your boy is a good soldier" stuff. Considering the years I fought against the perception that my son would never be anything but a goof-up, this praise not only shocked me a little but also left me filled with pride—and a touch of vindication as well.

I knew my son, and whether I was talking about his school years or the army, I understood his personality. I did try to work with his schoolteachers in correcting his classroom decorum and basic social graces; however, I drew the line when Buddy's teachers would dismiss Buddy's honest efforts at improving as inconsequential. It was as if his efforts were not considered meaningful or somehow not grand enough for them to accept. For some reason, these teachers could not see how their own attitudes affected my son's attitude. Not only could I see how much they hurt Buddy's young feelings, but it also hurt my heart to see him so discouraged and belittled. It was at those moments that those teachers would see the Mama Bear come out to protect her young, and I guess that Mama Bear was still trying to defend her son.

I bristled at any indication that our boys fighting in Iraq might be getting the wrong information on how much they were respected, supported, and very much missed. Even though there were positive enterprises that I had seen involving people simply trying to show support, I could not understand why the only things shown in the media were the war protesters. Of course, the gestures of support were not necessarily grandiose; it could be the simplest things that could mean the most, like a woman from Fayetteville who made an effort to supply every soldier who deployed from Fort Bragg with a bandana imprinted with Psalm 91, the "soldier's psalm."

The undertaking of this woman, as well as other demonstrations of support for our troops, were simple yet positive—and were largely ignored by the news media. It was as if the efforts of average people to provide encouragement to and show faith in our troops—let alone their achievements—were not considered as meaningful as the efforts of those who spoke out against the war and the Surge. The ultimate effect of the media's one-sided reporting was experienced when talking to average Americans; "I support the troops!" became "I support the troops, *but* . . . " It felt as though Buddy were back in grade school and I were attempting to defend him against a presumed trivialization of his efforts.

The fact that the media seemed so one sided in its reporting made me extra grateful for the people—family, friends, and anyone like this woman in Fayetteville—who just simply understood. They were the people who took it upon themselves to show unfettered support for our troops—*my* boy. For these individuals, there was no "but," and for the families of those serving, these people ranked right up there with their heroes. More importantly for our troops, these people helped give meaning to their hardships. But still, I had to wonder if those serving realized that these Americans were in the majority, despite what they might be hearing on the evening news—with, of course, all due respect to Haley and her position as a news professional.

Eight-Layer Cookies

1 1/2–2 cups chocolate Teddy
  Grahams

1 stick margarine, melted

1 1/2 cups old-fashioned oats,
  coarsely chopped

1 cup semisweet chocolate chips

1 cup peanut butter chips

1 cup coarsely chopped walnuts

1 can (14 ounces) sweetened condensed milk

Chocolate frosting

Handful of Reese's Pieces
  (optional)

1. Preheat oven to 325 degrees.
2. Grease the bottom and sides of an 8x12–inch pan.
3. Spread Teddy Grahams across the bottom of the pan.
4. Drizzle melted margarine over Teddy Grahams.
5. Sprinkle oats evenly over margarine.
6. Spread chocolate chips over oats, then peanut butter chips over chocolate chips, then walnuts over peanut butter chips.
7. Drizzle sweetened condensed milk over the lot.
8. Bake for approximately 20 minutes or until all the ingredients are melted or fused together.
9. Remove from the oven and cool. Once cooled, cover with chocolate frosting.
10. As an optional layer 8 1/2, sprinkle lightly with Reese's Pieces, mostly for color.

"Do wah diddy diddy dum diddy do!"

I figured by this point, we were just about at the halfway mark of the deployment. It felt as though it should have registered as some sort of noteworthy accomplishment to have made it this far without going completely nuts, but I was not so sure that I was ready to celebrate yet. It seemed to me that even a small sigh of relief might be just enough to agitate the Fates and make things difficult again. I was aware that this was not necessarily projecting the appropriate faith that I needed to survive—in fact, one might even call it superstitious.

Actually, it had become a little easier to breathe. News reports out of Iraq had become noticeably scarce, and as Nana, my dad, the FRG leader, and so many others had always said, "No news is good news!" I was not positive that this adage was always accurate, but this was one time that I believed it was exactly right. Basically, massive death and destruction are considered big news while calm and harmony are not. I knew this could all change in an instant; however, for the first time in months, it almost felt as though I could relax, if only a tiny bit and for only a minimal period of time.

The break in hostilities in Iraq did give me the opportunity to be much more reflective and much less reactive to the world around me. I was able to wonder how Buddy *really* was without referring to just his physical survival. Since my son was young, I had always gauged how he might be doing, both mentally and emotionally, by talking with him. However, as it had been since the beginning of the Surge, communication from Buddy had been sparse, with conversations few and far between. I knew this was simply because my son and the rest of the guys were just a little busy, but with no means of interaction with my son presenting itself, I had no idea where to focus my wandering thoughts. I tried to look ahead to his upcoming R&R, but that only left me feeling anxious and a little uneasy. Deep down, I knew that the world— and the Fates—still most definitely held the reins to my life.

It was not just me who discerned the easing of hostilities in Iraq. Despite what the general population might have been hearing, those who were in contact with the troops saw that the spirits of those deployed for the Surge were generally high, and according to them, the prognosis for Iraq was good. One of the greatest indications of this was a decided absence of "excitement" in the troops' current situation. It would, at times, leave them sounding restless—maybe even bored. They seemed to suffer from feeling a distinct lack of purpose, even though that feeling was far more of an imagined thing than reality based—mainly because they still had their patrols and their duties and the bad guys still had a desire to do damage.

It was no different for Buddy, but I knew that Iraq was still a dangerous place. Even though the dangers were subsiding, a whole new set of concerns developed for us mothers of soldiers. There was a sense of relaxedness—almost a complacency—when it came to the attitudes of the troops regarding the remaining hazards. As any mother of a soldier could explain, any lapse of vigilance on the part of a soldier—in this case, my son—clearly was an invitation for something disastrous to happen.

I was concerned about how Buddy was handling it all since things had calmed down overseas. With our lack of communication, I was left trying to piece together his level of well-being from snippets of past conversations and emails—mentally comparing the "then"s to the "now"s—but getting nowhere with the effort. I was grateful when the phone finally rang and I heard Buddy's voice on the other end of the receiver. I immediately went into my mother-diagnosis mode. I listened to his tone and inflection, not just what he was saying. I attempted to read between the lines as I gauged his psychological health. A good call would help me sleep that much better, and a bad call would ratchet up the knot in my stomach by a degree or two. However, this call left me perplexed.

The phone call started normally, with the customary salutations.

"Hey, Mom! What's up?" Buddy asked.

"Buddy! How are you, Sweetie?"

It was what came afterwards that left me questioning my son's thought processes as well as his emotional well-being—well, sort of. On the occasion of this phone call, Buddy proceeded to explain to me that he had changed his mode of operation for his regular patrols through the markets—the very same markets that were the sites of all sorts of mayhem during the earlier months of the deployment. There were still incidents being reported, but not nearly as often or as calamitous.

"So I've been practicing my vocals," Buddy began.

"Your vocals?" I inquired.

"My routine!"

"Your routine?"

"Yeah! My moves!"

"Huh?"

Buddy proceeded to explain to me that he had taken to singing—apparently quite loudly, and accompanied with a few signature dance moves—on his patrols through the markets. As a mother, it was difficult to hear these words and not desire some sort of clarification for the purpose of evaluating mental stability.

"Huh?" I asked again, wondering if I was going to be on the phone with the Red Cross requesting the removal of my son after our conversation ended.

"You know the song," he replied. "As I walk through the market streets, I sing, 'There he was just a-walking down the street / Singing "Do wah diddy diddy dum diddy do."' I then throw in a couple of dance moves, just for effect!"

In my mind's eye, I could see Buddy doing *exactly* what he described, and it concerned me just a tad. "Um, Buddy? If you are on patrol, shouldn't you be a little quieter?" I inquired.

"The way I figure it," he responded, "it will be harder for them to shoot me if they are laughing at me!"

My boy had a point! He further explained that he had even developed a small repertoire of songs. He understood that just one song might have gotten old, which might have stopped the bad guys laughing, which might then have led them to, once again, take potshots at him. I only hoped and prayed that his cavalier attitude did not catch up to him by tempting the Fates to instigate some unforeseen and undesirable consequence to his actions. However, despite this concern, his actions did let me know that my son was *still* my son, and for that, I was grateful.

Bacon Biscuits

Cookie:

8 slices of bacon

1/2 cup shortening

1/2 cup margarine

1 cup powdered sugar

1/3 cup granulated sugar

1 tablespoon maple syrup

1 teaspoon vanilla

1 egg

1 teaspoon baking soda

1/2 teaspoon salt

2 1/2 cups flour

Frosting:

1 tub buttercream frosting

1/4 cup maple syrup

1. Preheat oven to 350 degrees.

2. Dice bacon and cook until crispy. Remove from heat and drain well. Set aside.

3. Cream together shortening, margarine, powdered sugar, granulated sugar, maple syrup, vanilla, and egg with an electric mixer until light and fluffy, about 3 to 5 minutes.

4. Add baking soda and salt. Continue to beat with electric mixer for about a minute.

5. With a spoon, mix in flour until well blended. Stir in bacon.

6. Drop dough by rounded teaspoons onto cookie sheets. Squish dough down with the bottom of a glass that has been dipped in flour. Flatten the dough until it is about 1/4 to 1/3 inch thick.

7. Bake for 8 to 10 minutes.

8. While cookies are baking, make the frosting by combining buttercream frosting with maple syrup.

9. When cookies have cooled, frost them with the mixture. Wait for frosting to set before packing for shipping.

Fingers crossed . . . knock on wood . . . live long and prosper?

A s Buddy's R&R drew closer, I could not help but muse over my superstitious nature. Over the years, I had been worse than any sports star out there with their cherished, unwashed, "lucky" pair of socks. Unfortunately, even though I have never been any sort of a sports star—and I did try to clean all of my socks before they became biohazards—this perfectly described the way I was living with only a few weeks remaining before Buddy was due home for his rest and relaxation.

Every day, I tried to do everything precisely and purposefully to ensure I would not jinx a good day, either mine or Buddy's. In addition, I tried not to daydream at all, because throughout my life, it seemed as though whatever I dreamed, the opposite would happen. Whether it was a chance meeting with the Beatles when I was six or winning prom queen when I was sixteen—or even getting married, having babies, and being a stay-at-home mom and living happily ever after when I was much older—whatever I saw as a possibility playing out in my mind never quite manifested itself in reality. Of course, it might just be that these things were totally unrealistic expectations to begin with, but I am only describing what I felt. Furthermore, it was as if I simply could not accept that good things could happen without having to be balanced by something horrific. I spent my days wanting "pleasant"—but not too pleasant. I feared days that were spectacular because I suspected I would have to pay for them later.

I might claim this was the way I had been living these last few weeks before Buddy was home again for R&R; however, truth be told, the beginning of the deployment was when my superstitions took hold again, with every day bringing a slight escalation in their intensity. Since the day Buddy left for the Surge—and especially at those times when the situation was overly hazardous and unsettled—I attempted to apply all the superstitious standards I had developed throughout my life. I was also praying a hundred times a day, but I felt strongly that every little bit helped. So, in addition to my prayers, I also knocked on wood a lot, never put my left sock on before my right, made sure that I picked up only those pennies found heads up, and refused to make any plans for the future for fear that the future I saw would be changed to something unrecognizable and horrible.

As early as the beginning days of spring, my superstitious idiosyncrasies had become obvious—maybe not to everyone else but definitely to me. It was the first weekend of the year where the weather was pleasant enough to consider a bit of yard work, and I was debating raking up the leftover leaves from the previous fall. While weighing how motivated I was to complete this significant yearly task, my mind drifted to the Thanksgiving break between Buddy's graduation from boot camp and his entry into airborne school. On that Saturday afternoon after Thanksgiving, I was standing in the back corner of my backyard, admiring my work. I was down to the last few piles of leaves and was feeling quite proud that I had almost completed all leaf-raking chores for the year. Given the dozen or so fifty-year-old trees that adorned my yard, this was no small task. My moment of pride, though, was interrupted by Buddy coming through the back gate. I knew in an instant that something was not right. He was rather pale, and his face was twisted with worry or fear.

"What's wrong?" I asked immediately.

"I'm so sorry, Mom! I really screwed up!" he said.

These were certainly not words that a mother expects, nor likes, to hear. I braced myself for whatever he was about to tell me. "What happened?" I asked.

"She pulled me over for speeding," he began. "She said I was doing ninety-seven in a fifty-five!"

She said? Ninety-seven?! I thought. "How fast do *you* say you were going?" I asked.

"I wasn't going over eighty—eighty-four tops!" he replied.

"In a fifty-five-mile-per-hour zone?" I started winding myself up to give him a well-deserved lecture but stopped. I could see on my son's face how sorry and worried he was. I assured him it would all be OK and questioned him about the rest of the incident. The "she" he mentioned was a police officer. Apparently he was trying to get his best friend's attention to show him a Ferrari that was in the fast lane passing all the traffic. As Buddy sped up to catch up to his friend's car, his friend—interpreting Buddy's action as a challenge—sped up as well. It all seemed to me to be youthful exuberance along with a fair bit of stupidity. Unfortunately, from what I was hearing from my friends—some former police, some lawyers—the courts were not going to be as understanding. According to them, there was a mandatory day in jail for every mile an hour in excess of 90—a Class 1 misdemeanor.

As Buddy completed his airborne training, I researched what his options were. It was not that I condoned the speeding or any type of reckless driving, and I was not questioning the officer's conclusions, exactly. But I did find out that my son's car could not go over ninety-five miles per hour because of a governor on the engine. Beyond that fact, I found it appalling that any young man who had not even received so much as a parking ticket would be punished in this fashion, especially one who was due to deploy shortly after he completed his training. This did not apply to just my son but to anyone who fell into this category. The final outcome was that I was able to convince the prosecutor that the punishment did not fit the crime. Instead of a life-altering sentence that would follow Buddy for the rest of his days, Buddy received a speeding ticket with a bite—a bite that included a suspended license and probation.

The incident taught my son a valuable lesson; however, it also made an impression on me. It was a rare occasion when I managed to complete leaf raking before the following spring, but that year I was on top of it all—and that was the last year it happened. In my mind, the fall completion of leaf raking equated to a bad day for Buddy. I had no idea if that was an accurate assumption, but what I did know was that I had no desire to try to debunk the theory, and by the time spring had rolled around, I had begun questioning whether it was the completion of leaf-raking chores, no matter what time of year, that equated to bad days for Buddy.

So what if my grass never recovers? At least Buddy is safe, right?! I thought on that warm spring day at the beginning of the deployment. But that was certainly not the end of it! As the deployment wore on, I was increasingly arguing with myself regarding cause and effect.

Yesterday, nothing bad happened, and I did not get to vacuum. I shouldn't vacuum today! the argument with myself would begin.

Yeah? Well, a week ago, you hadn't vacuumed in four days and horribleness was all over the news!

Well, maybe I should just skip today and then make sure I vacuum tomorrow . . . or maybe the next day . . . but definitely *not the day after!* I would finally conclude.

The word "vacuum" in this argument could be replaced with any other task, chore, or activity that I either wanted or needed to do. There was simply no end to the absolute stagnation I had accomplished by trying not to endanger Buddy by doing something "frivolous" here at home—at least six thousand miles from where he was serving—like cleaning my house. It was not logical; however, as crazy as it sounded, it did help me feel that I was sincerely supporting my son by living this way.

Normally, I would have had the remaining fall leaves cleaned up by early spring, but that obviously did not happen. Whereas regular grass mowing would usually be underway by mid-April, it was well into May—with the grass almost knee high—before my lawn was mowed for the first time of the summer. And, given my inability to commit to vacuuming, and with the Whiskey-Dog in the throes of his shedding season, dust bunnies roughly the size of small animals adorned the corners of my house. But at least I had not inflamed any of my many superstitions regarding cor-relations between absolutely unrelated endeavors.

I had basically become a basket case by attempting to live each and every day exactly as I lived day one of the deployment, when we all were safe, whole, and well. While I worked on *not* envisioning my son's upcoming R&R, I struggled to create some sort of routine for myself that would somehow ensure my son's safety. In fact, with Buddy's homecoming just around the corner, I had decided that the only thing that really mattered was to determine whether it was me changing my socks daily that kept Buddy safe or whether I would need to start rewearing some of those socks that were already in the hamper!

Peanut Butter Pretzel Snaps

2–3 dozen small pretzels (I use
  Snyder's Pretzel Snaps)
1/4 cup peanut butter
1/4 cup margarine
1/4 cup milk
1/4 cup brown sugar

1/2 teaspoon vanilla
1/4 teaspoon salt
1 cup old-fashioned oats
1/2 cup semisweet chocolate chips
  (I use Ghirardelli 60% Cacao
  Bittersweet Chocolate chips)

1. On a sheet of parchment paper, lay out pretzels.
2. In a double boiler, melt together peanut butter, margarine, milk, brown sugar, vanilla, and salt.
3. When thoroughly melted and combined, remove from heat and stir in oats.
4. Drop melted dough by teaspoons onto the pretzels that have been laid out on the parchment.
5. Before the mixture cools, top with a chocolate chip pushed down into the peanut butter mixture so that it is thoroughly connected to the pretzel. Let set until cool.

"The more we get together, the *happier* we'll be!"

For the first time since the deployment began, I was alone. It was just the two dogs, Shesha the cat, and me while Haley and Leo spent the week in Vermont at our timeshare. Though both of my kids and I were born and raised in the Washington, DC, area, Vermont had always felt like home to us. Our time up north had always been relaxing and wonderful, but while Buddy was deployed to Iraq, it just seemed too far away from where I felt I needed to be. Cell phone reception was spotty at best in the Green Mountains, so I was more than happy to let the kids have the week while I spent the time at home, where I was reachable twenty-four hours a day—even if only for a quick chat with my son.

I had been looking forward to this week ever since Haley and Leo announced they were going to Vermont. I had always cherished my alone time, maybe too much. I am not talking about the scary, Norman-Bates-in-*Psycho* type of antisocial behavior; it was more like being someone who simply enjoyed their own company enough to be happy to have alone time, and lots of it. I understood that life was not always kind to individuals with this personality trait, but I had discovered not only that I enjoyed being on my own now and again but also that my alone time tended to energize my creative and innovative spirit.

For the time being, my "energy" was preoccupied on two areas, the first being my living arrangements and second being the current situation. To begin with, the past months had presented some amazing challenges—and not just from the reporting out of Iraq. I was attempting to coexist with not only my grown daughter but her boyfriend as well. Haley was, for the most part, used to my idiosyncrasies; she pandered to them sometimes but also knew when to ignore them and simply leave the room rather than attempt to engage them. It takes years of exposure to reach that level of understanding; it's not something that can be accomplished in the two short months that Leo had lived with us. But to be fair, they each had their own sets of idiosyncrasies that caused living with them to be less than a picnic as well. However, to all of our credit, I believed we all understood this and accepted each other as we were. At least, that's what I chose to tell myself.

As for the current situation, with it being just me and the animals at the house, if only for eight short days, it was somehow easier to anticipate Buddy's closer-than-ever R&R and to begin preparations for it. Despite the minimal easing of stress I felt when I looked to the future, it was still difficult to go against the mindset I had developed since the beginning of the Surge. I still felt that it actually made a difference whether I washed the knives before the forks when doing the dishes—or whether I cleaned the bathrooms twice a week as opposed to once a week or not at all—when it came to the safety of my son. Equally as bedeviling was the aspect of preparing for an event that required the safe return of my son when, according to my current mental deliberations, the preparation itself put my son in danger.

Once again, I debated with myself while trying to strike a satisfactory balance between the anticipation of my son's return and his ultimate safety. I (unsuccessfully) tried to convince myself that a clean house was a welcoming house, which ensured my son's protection. In an attempt at compromise with myself, I endeavored to create harmony between my efforts and my unfounded fears, with only limited results. To counteract any unintended consequences for my son in Iraq, when I finished whatever I was trying to accomplish, I would perform the equivalent of tossing salt over my left shoulder to counter the bad omen caused by spilling it, only I would say an extra prayer as I vacuumed or finished up some preparation for Buddy's homecoming—and toss salt if it happened to be close at hand.

The results of my efforts were minimal at best, but I was at least able to begin the process of preparing for Buddy's return. Cautiously and guardedly, I picked which chores could be accomplished without endangering my son. I fully understood that my actions did not fall under the normal definition of "sane," but oddly enough, they did help me maintain my own personal mental balance. Somehow that made the original insanity acceptable in my mind. In addition, it helped me to go about the business of cleaning, planning, ordering, and purchasing for Buddy's homecoming and birthday party.

With my considerations over Buddy's safety temporarily placated by my mental gymnastics, I went to work on cleaning. As always, housework was a thought-provoking time for me. Since I was already tempting fate by beginning to prepare for his time home, I refused to think more about Buddy. Instead, I focused on the house and my living arrangements. My thoughts wandered to Haley and a conversation we had shortly before she left for Vermont. She was quizzing me on how I was doing—*really* doing—and questioned my feelings on inviting both her and her boyfriend to be a part of my home.

"Are you sure you're not regretting any of this, Mom?" she asked.

That was an interesting question, but I answered it the only way that was appropriate for a loving and caring mom. "Oh, Sweetie! You guys haven't been anything but good for me!"

However, during this unusual period of solitude and scrubbing, I began to analyze my own words. There were Marjorie's potty-training days, which left Marjorie-marks all over my carpet that I was having a devil of a time getting out; Sheesha's hairballs, one of which adorned my cherry dining room chairs with cream-colored seats this very morning; not to mention Leo's drums that now adorned my den or the fact that all the Christmas decorations that used to be stored in Haley's and Leo's closets were now strewn about various areas in the house because the two of them needed space. In and of itself, that was a lot, but then there was the towel incident.

It was shortly after Leo had moved in and we were all in an adjustment period. Leo was adjusting to a new job, a new area, and a new "mom"; Haley was adjusting to having her boyfriend and mom in such close proximity; and I was adjusting to having my house turned upside down! Overall, the move and subsequent adjustments went relatively smoothly, but there was a moment when the stresses of it all peaked.

Leo had been moved in for about a week, and all that was left was the final tweaking of what was going to go where for the foreseeable future. I had already graciously given up part of my den to Leo's drum set and what little extra storage space the house contained to Christmas decorations that could no longer reside in closets—though I love my house, it was woefully short on storage space. I was sure that we were all relatively settled and that there was nothing else that would be required of me. I was in the upstairs hallway evaluating possible locations for hanging some family pictures when Haley confronted me with a stack of bath towels.

"Whatcha got there?" I asked.

"Bath towels. Some are from my old apartment, and some are Leo's," Haley answered. "We figured we would store them in the hall closet with the rest of the towels."

"You what?" I asked.

"I'm just putting these towels with the rest of the towels," she said as she moved towards the hall linen closet.

"You can't!" I said defiantly. "Those are not my towels!"

"What?" Haley asked, a little confused. "There's a problem with co-mingling our towels?"

"There is no *room*!" I exclaimed.

"I'll find room," she assured me. "I'll just squish them in there."

"*Squish* them? You can't! Keep them in your own room!"

A look of concern flashed across Haley's face followed by a brief moment of hurt before she regained her composure and countered me. "Seriously? This is all about my towels hanging out with your towels in the linen closet? Seriously?"

I might have been able to overlook the concern, but that glimpse of hurt that showed on Haley's face pulled me up short. *What are you doing?!* I screamed at myself. *We are talking about towels, for heaven's sake!* But actually, these towels were simply the straw that broke the camel's back. What was being discussed was the slow abdication of any control I might have once held over my own life. I was losing my ability to have any impact on the simplest things, with more being lost every day. Haley's and my current discussion was simply an accumulation of all the helplessness and frustrations of the previous months condensed into seven bath towels that were now going to be squished into a twelve-by-twelve-inch linen closet that was already stuffed full.

I was little chagrined as well as speechless. I stared at my feet for a moment. I wanted to be able to take back the words but did not know how. I raised my gaze to again meet Haley's glare, and I could feel my face starting to flush red as my eyes met hers. She was waiting for me to say something—anything—but words had escaped me. I smiled weakly at Haley, hoping beyond hope that she would now rescue me from the mess I had basically created all by myself.

Haley glared at me a moment, but then paused. She saw in my face that the argument was over. A twinkle sparked in her eyes. "So, what? You're afraid of what will happen if your towels are in close proximity to my towels?" She opened the linen closet and began shoving her towels into any open space she could find. "Maybe too much partying in the hall closet?"

"Absolutely!" I acknowledged, grateful that she had given me a way out of this heretofore painful conversation. "We all know the outcome of unrestrained wild parties in linen closets. Before you know it, we'll be overrun with illegitimate baby towels, and that would be unacceptable, right?"

"Would baby towels, by any chance, be washcloths?" Haley bantered back. "Because I think we could always use more of those, right?"

With her towels now successfully squished in with mine, she shut the linen closet door and turned to face me. She was waiting for my comeback, but I had nothing to add. As far as I was concerned, there was nothing else to say.

I often described my home as being so comfortable and well-suited to me that I felt as though it were giving me a great big, warm, wonderful hug every time I entered. Contemplating the pros and cons of Haley and Leo living with me, I pondered that "hug" and analyzed its energy. When others entered my house to the loud barking of two dogs and a hissing cat, not to mention the general nonstop commotion, did they still feel the warmth of the home that was so often commented on before? I was not sure of the answer, but what I did know was that for the first time in years, I was coming home to something bigger than the four walls of my house and a large, dumb-but-lovable dog. Dysfunctional as it might have felt at times, I was coming home to my family. I could not help but feel that having Haley and Leo living there with me was nothing less than a great big warm wonderful positive hug—even when I didn't want one!

Turtle Cookies

3/4 cup margarine

1/3 cup caramel topping

3/4 cup brown sugar

1 teaspoon vanilla

1 egg

1 teaspoon baking soda

1/2 teaspoon salt

2 cups flour

1–1 1/2 cups mini chocolate chips

120 pecan halves (for 2 dozen cookies)

1/4–1/2 cup chocolate chips

1. Preheat oven to 350 degrees.

2. Cream together margarine, caramel, brown sugar, vanilla, and egg with an electric mixer until light and fluffy, about 3 to 5 minutes.

3. Add baking soda and salt. Continue to beat with electric mixer for about a minute.

4. With a spoon, mix in flour, then fold in mini chocolate chips.

5. On a baking sheet, arrange five pecan halves to resemble a star, flat side down. Drop dough by rounded teaspoons onto the center of each star.

6. Bake for 10 to 12 minutes until cookie is flattened and edges are lightly browned. Remove from cookie sheet to cool.

7. For finishing touches, melt chocolate chips and drizzle over "turtles." Allow to cool and harden.

Heaven only knows!

T he time was at hand, but I just was not sure *where* that hand was! I knew that Buddy was due home sometime soon, but as with all things army, he would arrive when he arrived. We did have the general time frame, and basic preparations for the homecoming had been planned, if not completed. Now all that was left was to be patient—still not one of my strengths—and wait for the phone call that would let us know he was on the way. The problem was that, beyond my lack of patience, I was just *really* tired of waiting. I had tried to fill every second of every day with some activity to help me feel as though I were not really waiting, but it wasn't really working. Somewhere not-so-deep inside, I understood that I *was* waiting, and I did not appreciate the concept nor had I ever quite mastered it.

It was no secret that the fuse on my temper had become amazingly short. Even though I was aware of this, it just seemed that I could not help myself. I had become that obnoxious fool flashing my lights at the car ahead of me because they had the unmitigated gall to do thirty-four miles per hour in a thirty-five zone. I was also that irritatingly impatient dolt sighing loudly and exasperatedly in the "ten items or less" line at the grocery store because the person in front of me had *eleven* items—I had counted! I had even become that idiot stepping off the curb onto a crosswalk and staring down the oncoming eighteen-wheeler trying to make a turn. I knew the rules, and the crosswalk light was flashing the little walking man indicating that *I* had the right of way—no matter that the truck's light was green as well. I was not necessarily proud of my behavior—even when I was in the midst of acting it out—but it also seemed I had little ability to stop it.

The shift in my personality seemed to be directly connected to the previous eight months. It had been such a long and arduous journey to get to where I was. Despite Nana's cautions, with each passing week, it seemed as though I had lost a little more of myself to the situation overseas. With Buddy's R&R so close—yet still feeling like it was an eternity away—the effort to simply get through each day with my disposition intact was becoming more difficult by the hour. And poor Haley and Leo! Even when they did and said the *right* things, I could not seem to rein in my lashing out.

I had asked Leo to rake up and bag some backyard leaves and debris—probably left over from the previous fall—while I mowed and edged the front yard. Leo collected the "debris" into a rather spread-out pile so that I could simply suck it all up into the lawnmower when I mowed the backyard after I completed the front. Honestly, it was solid reasoning that led him to believe that this was an acceptable response to my request—if not *exactly* what I had asked. However, when the swarm of ground hornets—not particularly happy with me mowing directly over their home—decided to attack the intruder, in this case me, all sense of soundness to his overall judgment was erased!

Several hours later, still smarting from the dozen or so stings I had received from the irate hornets, I was "loaded for bear" when Haley arrived home from work. I made sure I was subtly noticeable in the kitchen, making as much noise as possible while emptying the dishwasher, when she walked through the front door. Haley heard me in the kitchen and came in to say hello.

"Hey, Mom!" she began cheerfully. "What's going on?"

"We need to talk!" was my unyielding response.

The tone of my voice was unmistakable, and Haley was not unfamiliar with its implications. "What's going on?" she asked while attempting to nonchalantly make her way to the refrigerator to retrieve some libations—mostly to galvanize her against anything I might be saying in response to her innocent question.

"I can't take this anymore!" I began. I drew in a deep breath in preparation to blast my daughter, who was looking confused by my outburst. I had every intention of informing Haley of the injustices of the day brought about by her boyfriend's inability to follow a simple request when Leo showed up in the doorway of the kitchen.

"Hey, Baby!" he said, walking over to Haley and giving her a little kiss. "How was your day?"—a question *I* should have asked the moment I saw my daughter. Haley gave a little shrug of her shoulders and then hesitantly glanced back at me for what I might add to the conversation, but before I had the chance to say anything, Leo began explaining the events of the day that reached a crescendo during my confrontation with the ground hornets.

"Oh my God! Are you OK, Mom?!" Haley asked. I could not help but be moved by the real concern in her voice and on her face. I nodded to her that I was fine, but in reality I was falling headfirst into an abyss of self-reproach and regret.

What the hell is wrong with me? I could make up a dozen valid excuses for my behavior, even some that would sway others to excuse it, but I was having real problems with my recent lack of emotional restraint. My life was filled with uncertainty because my son was serving in the Surge—fine! But my son was my daughter's only brother. I could not imagine that anything I was feeling was not equally shared by her.

I needed Haley and Leo to know that I realized they were an incredible blessing to me, even if I was not able to articulate my gratitude. I also knew that my volatile temperament was certainly not a very effective way to go about achieving this. It was as if I had become a slave to my emotions—the world and my understandings regarding the current state of affairs ruling my life—and I seemed unable to do anything about it. The funny thing was that when I reflected on the past eight months, the only one who had been able to set me back on my heels had been my sister-in-law's mom, Alice, and I am not sure that she was even aware of the soul-searching effect her simple statements had on me.

The family had gathered at my brother Albert's house for a family barbecue a few weekends before, and my sister-in-law's mom and dad were there as well. Though I had taken to mostly sitting quietly, one might say "brooding," at any gatherings, family or otherwise, at least I was making the effort to get out and socialize when I was invited. I guess Alice noticed my aversion to joining in and was simply trying to engage me in conversation by her question.

"So, what do you think of all the attention given to Cindy Sheehan these days?" she asked.

This was not a good conversation starter for me *anytime*, let alone since the beginning of the Surge. Cindy Sheehan lost her son in Iraq a few years before, so my heart went out to her in her pain. But she took that pain and used it as a foil against the Surge, the army, the president, and anything else she held responsible. She and her protests were what was playing in the news, not the good work our soldiers were doing. However, Alice simply had a question and I had always been taught to respect my elders, no matter what the situation. This was family, so I chose my words carefully.

"To begin with," I explained quite seriously, "I can tell you I *never* want to know the woman's pain! My heart absolutely goes out to her. But that being said, my son and I actually talked about all this."

The conversation I was referring to took place well before Buddy deployed to the Surge—in fact, it was before Buddy's first deployment. To me, it had always seemed easier to handle difficult issues when you remove their edge with a touch of humor, so Buddy tackled the dangers of his job during that chat with me in much the same manner as most of our other conversations regarding serious subjects—lightheartedly and with humor. Buddy's words regarding my behavior should something happen to him seemed as good as any to convey my feelings on the matter at hand without having to address the very serious underlying implications.

"He told me that I was never to follow in her footsteps should anything happen to him," I continued, changing the tone of my voice to reflect the playful nature of Buddy and my conversation. "He further explained that if he looked down from heaven and saw me acting inappropriately, when I got to heaven, he would ignore me and never speak to me again!"

I then smiled at Alice, partly to show I was done talking and partly to further emphasize my desire to not delve into the serious side of what I had just shared with her. I am not sure of the reality of what happened next. I was, after all, tainted by the effects of the slowly increasing stress level of my world. But in my mind, she did not return my smile but instead spent a few seconds just looking at me as if she were actually looking through me.

She then responded, "Oh! So you think you're going to heaven, do you?" Only then did she return my smile.

I could feel my insides slowly tie into a dozen knots as Alice's words sunk in. Her response confused me. *Why did she say that? Do I seem like someone who couldn't get into heaven? Was she kidding?* I was having trouble deciding because she still seemed to be staring right through me to the depths of my soul. *Was she waiting for an answer? How does someone answer that question? "Yes, maybe!"?* I decided to treat it all as a bit of a joke, gave a half-hearted laugh, and then excused myself from the room to find some other place to sit quietly and brood.

I could still feel the effects of Alice's piercing stare as I stood in my kitchen with Haley and Leo. I simply could not figure out why I had allowed myself to get so wound up over something so stupid. Leo had also grabbed himself a libation and sat down at the kitchen table with Haley while they continued to chat about their days. Periodically, I would notice Haley glancing up at me, most likely waiting for the rest of the lambasting that she was certain she was getting. However, I had quietly returned to emptying the dishwasher—and brooding.

"Did you want to talk to me, Mama?" she finally asked.

"No, we're good," I replied and then gave her a smile to try to emphasize that everything was OK.

I had no desire to finish our original conversation. Instead, while the two of them talked, I wondered whether Alice said what she said because my inner turmoil had become so obvious that she could not help but notice it. I needed to know if people still saw me as who I was rather than what I felt I had become—that, and whether my "new" emotional, bad-tempered personality was a permanent feature or something that would hopefully reverse itself . . . eventually!

Cookie Crumb Cookies

1/2 cup shortening

1/2 cup margarine

1 cup brown sugar

1/2 cup powdered sugar

1/2 tablespoon corn syrup

1/2 tablespoon cornstarch

1 teaspoon vanilla

1 egg

1 tablespoon powdered cocoa

1 teaspoon baking soda

1/2 teaspoon salt

2 1/4 cups flour

1/2 cup chocolate chips

1 cup cookie crumbs (I used chocolate chip cookie crumbs)

1. Preheat oven to 350 degrees.

2. Cream together shortening, margarine, brown sugar, powdered sugar, corn syrup, cornstarch, vanilla, and egg with an electric mixer until light and fluffy, about 3 to 5 minutes.

3. Beat in powdered cocoa on low speed.

4. Add baking soda and salt. Continue to beat with electric mixer for about a minute.

5. With a spoon, mix in flour until well blended. Stir in chocolate chips and cookie crumbs.

6. Drop dough by rounded tablespoons onto cookie sheets.

7. Bake for 10 to 12 minutes.

The waiting really is the hardest part.

We knew that Buddy's R&R was just around the corner because we knew that he wanted to be home for his twenty-first birthday, which was fast approaching; we were just not sure which day he would be arriving. It seemed I spent every waking moment hanging out by the phone, impatiently waiting for it to ring. When it would, my heart would skip a beat as I rushed to the phone to answer it, only to hear "Hello, Ms. McCreath, would this be a good time to talk to you about . . . ?" Normally, I would take the time to be polite to whomever was on the other end of the line, phone solicitor or not. However, it did not take many of these types of calls before my ability to be polite was completely depleted.

The problem was that Buddy's phone call could be coming from *any* number at *any* time, so *all* phone calls needed to be answered. Worse than answering the phone to some obnoxious telemarketer was missing a phone call altogether. It was the cruelest form of torture that could be inflicted. Late one night while I was "indisposed" in the bathroom, I heard the phone ring. It was so late that I knew it could not be a telemarketer and, in fact, had to be Buddy. I finished my "business" as fast as humanly possible and ran downstairs to find out from the kids what the phone call was all about. I was sorely disappointed to discover that both Haley and Leo had fallen asleep, so no one answered the phone.

"Really? Neither of you could have answered the phone?" I asked.

"I'm sorry, Mama. We are just so tired, and we knew we couldn't have gotten to the phone in time. If it was Buddy, he'll call back," Haley answered drowsily.

"But *when?*" I shot back.

Since there was nothing else I could do about it, I headed for bed to try to get some sleep. On the way, I checked the phone. The call was from an unknown number, and no message was left. I thought I was going to go crazy. I was on pins and needles. I needed to know *where* Buddy was and *when* he was going to be home! How could my children, including Buddy, have done this to me?! The only thing left for me was to be patient—a feat that obviously escaped me!

Blueberry Cream Cheese Cookies

1/2 cup cream cheese
1/2 cup margarine
1/4 cup brown sugar
1 1/2 tablespoons lemon juice
1/2 teaspoon lemon zest
1/2 tablespoon cornstarch
1 egg
1/4 teaspoon cream of tartar

1/2 teaspoon salt
1 cup flour
2 cups blueberry muffin mix with
   freeze-dried berries
1/2–1 cup walnuts, coarsely
   chopped
Cream cheese frosting

1. Preheat oven to 350 degrees.

2. Cream together cream cheese, margarine, brown sugar, lemon juice, lemon zest, cornstarch, and egg with an electric mixer until light and fluffy, about 3 to 5 minutes.

3. Add cream of tartar and salt. Continue to beat with electric mixer for about a minute.

4. With a spoon, mix in flour until well blended. Stir in muffin mix and walnuts.

5. Drop dough by rounded tablespoons onto cookie sheets.

6. Bake for 10 to 12 minutes.

7. After cookies have cooled, frost generously with cream cheese frosting.

Buddy's R&R

Homecoming
24 August 2007

The eagle is landing—if only for eighteen days.

L ike everything else about the deployment, no matter how much something was expected or prepared for, when the "something" finally came about, it felt like a spur-of-the-moment, impromptu event. I had been waiting for days for a phone call from Buddy—not to mention randomly lecturing telemarketers for their thoughtless and inconsiderate intrusions. People at work had learned to keep their distance unless it was really important, and a few had threatened to set out flares around my desk to warn others to stay away. I was tired—tired of work and tired of waiting. I slogged my way to the Metro and took the escalator deep below ground to board the subway and make my way home. I was beginning to think that Buddy's phone call was never going to come.

I had left work early enough that the subway train was relatively uncrowded, despite the fact that it was summer. I took a seat close to the train doors and shut my eyes, shutting out the world as I wallowed in a touch of self-pity. The train chugged down the tracks—sometimes for long periods, sometimes for short periods—but every time the doors opened, it was a stop. I was counting those stops; I was counting to know where we were on the Metro map that was positioned just above the seats closest to the train door and counting to know when the train would be above ground again, signaling that I was just one stop from home—well, one stop from my car that would take me home!

The train was heading to that first stop above ground. I was waiting for the flash of light that let me know we had left the underground, but moments before it hit my eyes, my cell phone started ringing. Since there was no cell service below ground, I had no idea how long the call had been active. I frantically rummaged through my purse, grabbed my phone, flipped it open, and put it to my ear. "Hello, hello!" Breathlessly, I waited for a response. "Hello?"

"Hi, Maggie! I was just calling to find out all the details," Keith said.

"Details? Details about what?" I asked.

"Haley called me and left a message. I figured you knew and could fill me in," he replied.

"Fill you in? About what?"

"Buddy!" Keith exclaimed. "He lands tonight, right?"

"He lands? I'll call you right back!" I hung up on my nephew and immediately phoned my daughter.

From what I heard on my end, Haley's phone barely rang once. "Mom! Where have you been?! I have been trying to call you! Buddy arrives tonight!"

"Tonight? When? I'm still on the Metro! Where is he?"

"He's in Atlanta, but you have time," Haley replied. "His plane has already been delayed. He originally called about twenty minutes ago and then called back to let me know about the delay. But I have been in newsroom-crisis-management mode ever since. I tried to call you first at work and then on your cell, but you didn't answer."

"I'm sorry Sweetie; I left work a little early today. I was—"

"I then started calling everyone else to let them all know," Haley interrupted. "I have everyone meeting us here at the house around 6:30 to go to the airport. When will you be home?"

"I'm still ten minutes away from my car, then another thirty minutes till I get there if I head straight home, but I'm thinking I should pick up balloons on the way, you know? Maybe a dozen red, white, and blue ones. What do you think?" I asked.

"You have time," she answered. "He doesn't even land until 7:30 now. Just get home soon!"

Buddy was all but home—just about two hours and counting until I would see my boy again! All I needed to do was to get home, and at the moment, I had no control over how long that was going to take. I could hardly contain myself as I tried to will the Metro train to move faster. Despite my efforts, I do not believe that the train had ever moved slower nor spent longer at the Metro stop before mine. By the time the doors opened at my stop, I felt as though I would burst at the seams.

I arrived home shortly before the welcome-home party started gathering. The final number of participants ended up being five: Haley, Leo, Keith, his girlfriend Sasha, and me. The party might have been smaller than I anticipated, but what we lacked in size, we made up for in enthusiasm. Besides, I do not believe I could have handled any more people. I was so tightly strung with anticipation that when Haley informed me that the plane had been delayed *again*, I almost screamed—one of those bloodcurdling, primal screams that shatters eardrums and windowpanes for miles!

As the family of a soldier returning from a war zone, we were allowed to greet

Buddy at the gate as he disembarked at the airport. Like all other passengers, we needed "tickets," which were more like airport passes, and had to pass through all the appropriate security checkpoints. Though it was still a bit early, we headed to the airport to give ourselves time to get our passes from the ticket counter and get to the gate with plenty of time to spare—mostly to prevent me from having a nervous breakdown along the way. Despite a lifetime of being late for everything—hence the term "Maggie time," which is on time plus fifteen minutes—airports are the one place that this does not hold true. Whether catching a plane or greeting a traveler, if I am not extremely early, I am late. Make that traveler my soldier son returning from war, and I would have had to arrive at the airport yesterday to feel I had given myself enough time.

"We're going to be late!" I exclaimed as I tried to hurry everyone to the cars. We were taking two cars because although there were only five of us leaving for the airport, there would be six of us on the way home! Besides, the back of my SUV was filled to the brim with a dozen red, white, and blue helium balloons plus a mylar red, white, and blue shooting star.

"We're going to be late and miss meeting Buddy at the gate!" I lamented while impatiently sitting at a red light.

"We've got time," Haley tried to assure me.

"Keith better keep up, because I'm not waiting for him once we get to the airport!" I proclaimed when I looked in my rearview mirror and could not see Keith's car behind mine.

"Relax, Mom. It's going to be fine," Haley said rather impatiently. "I really should have insisted on driving!" she mumbled to herself, sparking a rather enthusiastic non-verbal agreement from Leo.

It was a good thing that the airport was so close to home. Even with the heavy traffic of rush hour, it was a relatively short time before we were parked and making our way to the ticket counter.

"We're here to meet my son's plane," I began explaining to the airline representative behind the counter. "I was told that as the family of a soldier, we could go to the gate to greet him."

"You're all family?" she asked, eyeing us above the rims of her half-frame glasses.

I had no idea whether she was simply making conversation or doubting my statement, but I answered like it did not matter either way. "Yep! We are his family, and I am the mom!" I exclaimed, causing the others behind me—including my family—to giggle a little. "His name is Benjamin Rogers; he's flying in from Atlanta. The plane was supposed to be here around 7:30, but it got delayed," I added so that she could look him up and see that we were legitimate.

Though I am basically a shy person, when I am nervous or excited, I tend to talk—a lot. At this point, I was both nervous and excited. I could not stand still, and I could not stop talking. As the lady behind the counter typed away on her computer, I rambled on.

"He's coming home on his R&R from Iraq. He has been fighting in the Surge and has been gone for eight months; he's coming home for his birthday. I am so excited he is finally going to be home; I can't wait to see him! We can actually go to the gate, right? The plane hasn't landed yet, has it?"

The woman stopped typing and again eyed me above the top edge of her glasses. "The plane has been delayed again," she informed me with a smile. "May I see your IDs, please?"

Delayed?! I thought. *Ugh! Am I ever going to see my son again?!*

"See? I told you it would all be OK!" Haley said to me as she stepped up to the counter with her driver's license. "When does the plane land now?" she asked the representative.

While the ticket lady filled out our passes, she explained, "You have about a two-hour wait. The plane hasn't departed yet, but it is on the runway and should be leaving any minute now. It should not be delayed again." With that, she handed back our IDs and our airline passes and sent us on our way. "Good luck!" she called out to us as we left the counter. "And God bless! Thank your son for his service for us, too."

I turned around, gave her a smile, and waved good-bye. "I will," I called out to her, and with that, we were off to airport security.

Originally, Keith took charge of the balloons. Shortly after he did, though, one with a shorter ribbon than the rest worked its way loose from the knot which tied them all together and floated wistfully to the ceiling of the airport terminal, several dozen feet above us. Keith, who never wanted to be in charge of them to begin with, immediately decided that holding balloons was a job better handled by a mother. "Besides," he added. "These still need to get through security, and what better way than in the loving hands of a soldier's mom?"

Really? I thought. *Balloons are a problem?*

But moments later, we were standing in front of security with a TSA agent telling us, "You're going to have to untie that bunch of balloons and send them through the X-ray machine one at a time!"

"Ah, come on!" I pleaded with the man. "They're just balloons! Can't we just walk through the metal detector with them?"

"No, ma'am," he said. "They need to be sent through that X-ray machine somehow. If you can figure out how to do it without untying them, have at it, but no matter what, they need to pass through that machine!"

Immediately, the five of us began discussing just how we could feed a large bouquet of balloons about the size of a small car through that *little* X-ray machine. The problem was that even if we spread them out to send them through one at a time without untying them, sooner or later the majority of the bouquet would be trying to pass through the machine at the same time. All I could think was, *It's gonna take us the next two hours just to get through security!*

We had just about resigned ourselves to the fact that we were going to be untying that very tight knot when a TSA supervisor came along to find out what was going on. She examined the situation for a moment then asked for my airline pass. After reviewing the pass, she requested that I bring the balloons to her. She took one of the balloons in her hand, held it up to the light, and shook it vigorously for a second or two. She then took the balloons from me and handed them to the agents behind the X-ray machine. "Check the rest of them just like that," she told the agents. "Have a nice day," she said to us. "Tell your son 'Welcome home' from us," she added, and then walked off. Thank goodness for common sense! In a matter of minutes, we were on our way to the designated gate with an hour and a half to spare.

It was not all that difficult to figure out what to do with our wait time. After all, I had been the one drinking beer from a sippy-cup when Buddy and his battalion redeployed home a year and a half before! Alcohol was not allowed in the military hangars where families waited for their soldiers, but I was *way* too high strung to face the emotional stress without it—well, I could have if the people around me did not mind me hyperventilating and passing out on the flight line. However, my beloved nephew Keith figured anything that could calm me down enough to enjoy the moment was well worth it. Besides, I was not guzzling six-packs; I was simply sipping on beer as an alternative to blowing into paper bags when I felt the dizziness of hyperventilation due to the excitement of the moment setting in.

The current choices were between allowing me to pace the terminal while unrestrainedly accosting anyone we met with "What time is it?" (or, alternatively, "Do you know if the plane from Atlanta has landed yet?") or to attempt to relax for the next couple hours in the bar that was almost directly across from the gate through which Buddy would arrive. The choice was surprisingly easy. We sat at the bar discussing innocuous things, everything from current politics to extraterrestrial infestations, all the while sipping on our drinks. We passed the time without feeling like time was passing at all, as the minutes seemed to drag on as slowly as all the minutes of the last eight months put together. But eventually, we heard on the intercom that Buddy's plane had landed.

Having done what we could to calm my nerves with two glasses of wine—with limited results, I might add—we made our way to the gate. Since the general public was no longer allowed past security without being a ticket holder, there was not a huge group gathered there, but there were more people than I expected. I noticed a woman standing to the side. She seemed to be a kindred spirit who did not have the advantage of a "posse" standing behind her for support.

"Are you waiting for your son, too?" I asked her.

"Yes," she answered, and then flashed an anxious smile.

"It really has been a difficult wait, hasn't it?" I offered.

"Oh, yes!" she exclaimed.

"Has your son been deployed since the beginning of the Surge, like my son?" I asked.

"What?" she responded, looking a little confused. "My son is seven years old. He has been with his father for the last week," she said, and then added, "Thank your son for his service for me."

I smiled at her as I nodded. We were not exactly on the same page, but I did understand her emotions as well, since I had been there myself when Buddy was younger. And now I was waiting for my son again.

It is difficult to articulate the emotions I felt standing there with my balloons, fidgeting like a child waiting her turn to see Santa. We watched through the window as the plane pulled up to the gate. We watched as a ramp extended out toward the plane to provide a walkway to the terminal, and we waited for what seemed like an eternity for the door to the plane's Jetway to open.

I had slowly moved forward until I was now standing in front of everyone else, as close as I could get to the gate door without actually blocking it. I shifted from side to side, clinging to the balloons as if they were my lifeline, waiting . . . waiting . . . waiting for Buddy. And then it happened: the doors were opened. It took several moments, but eventually the travelers started exiting. I expected that Buddy would be one of the first out of the plane, but I was wrong.

As the past eight months had slowly dragged on, I had become acutely aware of how quickly Buddy had been deployed. There was hardly enough time to get his barrack room packed and his equipment squared away, let alone to say the things a parent feels the need to say in these types of situations. Several months ago, when the reports of soldiers wounded and killed in action started rolling in, I started praying as hard as I could that God would just allow me this one last chance to see my son. And now the time was at hand . . . and still more people were exiting the plane . . . and still there was no sign of Buddy.

I stood there, impatient to get my first glimpse of Buddy's face in the sea of faces walking down the ramp from the plane. The past eight months had brought an individual stress that I do not believe can be explained to someone else. It is very personal how each and every one of us handles the news we hear—both good and bad, but especially bad—that comes when a piece of our heart is so far away and in so precarious a situation. As the days slowly passed, life seemed to quickly shift from living to coping and from coping to just getting by. Every day ended with the same uncertainty with which it began and with no clear indications of what to expect from the days to come. And now Buddy was home again—but still nowhere to be seen.

Behind me, I could hear Haley's phone ring. "Hello?" I heard her answer. "Where are you?!" I heard her ask. "Sedated? Well, about as much as two glasses of wine can accomplish." She hung up the phone, laughing. "That was Buddy, Mama," she called out from behind me. "He borrowed someone's phone to make sure you were 'properly sedated'!" she explained, to the amusement of everyone standing within earshot.

About a minute later, I saw my son walking down the ramp.

To say I was overcome with emotion would be an understatement. As soon as he was close enough, I grabbed my boy and hugged him with all my might, partially blocking the sea of people still exiting the plane. As I hugged my son, I felt eight months of carefully guarded emotion, and stress, and tension, and fear drain from my soul. I remember my son hugging me back. I remember hearing the people there at the gate saying "Aww" in unison. I remember not being able to stop crying. And, after a minute or so, I remember my son turning to his sister and saying, "Hey! I thought you told me she was sedated!"

On the drive back home from the airport, I got the balloons and Keith got Buddy—but it was only a fifteen-minute ride. Beyond the actual homecoming event, it was a very low-key evening. Truthfully, all Buddy wanted to do was to get home, see his Whiskey-Dog, and get into some civilian clothes. He was not hungry and had no desire to be anything but home. The homecoming party chatted a bit in the living room after we arrived, but it was not long before Keith and his girlfriend left. It was late, and it had been a long day—let alone a long eight months. I took a moment to hug my son again and tell him that I was glad he was home. I then left him in the living room playing video games with the Whiskey-Dog and headed to bed for what I expected to be the first good night's sleep I'd had since the beginning of the year.

The next morning, while everyone else was still asleep, I took a few minutes to jot down a couple of notes to myself. I realized that this was probably the first time since Buddy deployed that I actually felt capable of spending a few minutes to just sit and think and *relax*. Yeah, there were still things to be done around the house: a yard that needed mowing, bathrooms that needed tending, a birthday party to plan, and vacuuming—*always* vacuuming. But for the moment, there was time to just sit and enjoy the peace, for it was the first time in eight months that I had truly felt peace! The anxious days and sleepless nights, bottles of wine and weekends of cookie baking had all been put on hold. Sitting there on my couch writing down my thoughts, I could not know what the next eight months of the deployment would bring, but what I did know was that for the next eighteen days, Buddy was home—and I could *breathe* once again.

Rest and Relaxation, Part 1
25 August 2007–31 August 2007

So what's your favorite drinking song?

B uddy's R&R was only a couple days old, but there was very little resting and relaxing going on. It was Sunday, and after spending the day at several different family functions, including church with Nana and dinner at my brother's house, it was around 11:15 p.m. when we returned home. Buddy let the Whiskey-Dog and Marjorie out and upon returning upstairs announced, "Well, in just over thirty minutes, I will be twenty-one years old!"

Buddy's birthday celebration was coming up the following weekend, but Buddy's actual birthday was on Monday, "just over thirty minutes" away. As I contemplated all possible implications of having my youngest turn twenty-one, Haley had a whole different set of ideas running through her head.

"You know, Buddy, at one minute past midnight on *my* twenty-first birthday, I started drinking, and by the time last call was sounded less than two hours later, I had managed to drink my age in mixed drinks and shooters. So, what do you think?" Haley asked her brother, her eyes flashing with her mischievous intent.

As a mom, it is sometimes better not knowing! Actually, I did know this story, and the number of drinks Haley managed to ingest that night was nowhere near twenty-one but was definitely still excessive. However, at that moment, I knew she would have said just about anything to instigate the sibling rivalry. And now the challenge was out there, the gauntlet thrown, and it seemed there was no turning back. However, Buddy did not seem to be feeling the challenge—yet.

"I don't know," Buddy began. "I'm kinda tired. I think—"

"Come *on*, Bud!" Haley said, stoking that brother/sister one-upmanship with which I was all too familiar. "Are you gonna give up without even the smallest hint of a fight? Are you gonna let your sister do better than you?!"

Buddy was obviously torn between what he wanted to do and what he felt he should do—let alone what he felt he *could* do. He hesitated, and that was all Haley needed to drive home her point.

"Come on, Buddy! Don't be a girl; be like *me*!" Considering Haley *is* a girl, this argument made no sense to me, but it worked on Buddy.

As the three of them left the house in search of an open bar to officially begin the celebration of Buddy's birthday, the most I managed to do was to ensure that Leo was going to be the designated driver. Since there was no talking Buddy out of anything at this point, and Haley was primed to egg Buddy on in whatever way she could, the only thing I could think of to do was to call after Leo as they were piling into his car.

"Remember, you promised to be designated driver! Try to keep them from getting too stupid!" And with that, it was out of my hands and I shut the door. After spending a few minutes catching up on the news, which I found much easier to watch since Buddy was home, I headed for bed.

It felt as though I had only been asleep for a minute when I heard my kids fall back into the house through the front door. The Whiskey-Dog and Marjorie barely even made a sound, but they did not need to, because the ruckus at the front door sounded like a herd of elephants charging through my house! I lay there a moment listening to the commotion, trying to decide whether to get up and greet them or to simply ignore them until morning. It was difficult to decipher any intelligible—or intelligent—conversation among all the hushing and giggling.

"Shh!" I heard Buddy admonish Haley. "Shush! You're gonna wake Mom!" he loudly declared.

"You shush," was Haley's brilliant and equally loud comeback, "or *you'll* wake Mom!"

Clearly, there would be no sleeping for anyone as each of my two offspring tried to silence the other. I looked at the clock on my dresser; it was almost 3:00 a.m. as I rolled out of bed to see how the evening went—and to see if Buddy managed to at least keep up with his sister.

I walked up to the "conversation" as Buddy—giving his sister one last, loud hush—turned to stumble down the hall to his bedroom. Immediately he was face-to-face with me. "I *told* you that you were going to wake Mom!" Buddy shot at Haley, who was now on the landing of the stairs engaged in what looked like a staring contest with the dogs. Having successfully delivered the "last word" to his sister, he then turned back to me. "Hi, Mama!" he said with a big grin. "I'm *drunk!*"

"How did it go?" I asked Leo, who was in the process of locking up the house. I realized that at this point, he was most likely the only one who could give me a coherent answer. But they all started talking at once.

Buddy held up a collection of fingers that changed constantly as he announced, "I had *this* many drinks . . . and a Duck Fart!"

"Huh?" I asked, looking to Leo for an explanation. But before he could answer, Haley was already filling in the details.

"He couldn't do it!" Haley announced. "He just couldn't keep up with me—couldn't break my record!"

"Yeah, but I've been at war for the past eight months!" Buddy countered in an attempt to defend himself.

Haley taunted him with "'Scuses! You're just making excuses!"

"You had a *Duck Fart*? What the heck is that?" I once again directed my question to Leo, knowing that at this point, the other two were absolutely useless.

As Leo gave me a Reader's-Digest version of the evening, Buddy made his way to the bathroom that guests use for all our social events and Haley proceeded to proclaim that she *used* to be able to stand on her head but she did not know if she was still able. As Leo described a layered shot of Bailey's, whiskey, and Kahlúa called a "Duck Fart," I eyed the bathroom that Buddy was now holed up in, doing who knows what—and I had *just* cleaned that bathroom for his upcoming birthday party, too! At the same time, Haley—still on the landing of the steps—was attempting to ascertain if she was still capable of doing headstands! I interrupted Leo's retelling of the evening's events to call out to my son.

"Are you doing OK, Bud?" I asked.

The reply was undecipherable but definitely had that telltale sound of someone speaking directly into the Porcelain Goddess. Being the caring, compassionate mother that I am, I began laughing even as I continued to inquire as to his well-being. His response also tickled Haley, who was rather contorted with her head on the ground, her feet over her head but also on the ground, so that I was looking at her face, her butt, and the soles of her feet all at the same time. And now she was laughing uncontrollably at her brother, like she was the pillar of sobriety at this point. After a quick evaluation of the level to which my little family had deteriorated, I realized it was time to call it an evening for everyone.

As I walked by the bathroom that Buddy was still occupying, I felt the need to call out, "I just cleaned that bathroom, Buddy! You just make sure that it's spotless when you're through!" I then headed to my bedroom and shut the door behind me—just like any caring, compassionate mother would do.

The Party

1 September 2007

Let the celebrations begin! Well, maybe just continue?

I t was a beautiful late summer's evening. The skies were clear and the temperature was not too hot and not too cold—perfect for a birthday bash. The house was clean, the yard was mowed, and everything that was required for a birthday party was present and accounted for. There were appropriate decorations in red, white, and blue: party poppers, balloons, and, specifically for Buddy, brandy, cigars, and a fully functional, fully sanitized—at least as far as we knew—hot tub.

In the weeks leading up to his R&R, I heard quite a bit from Buddy about how excited he was to spend a soothing moment soaking in a delightfully not-too-hot, bubbling tub with a cognac in one hand and a cigar in the other. Up until the party, however, he had not been able to do so. The one problem that plagued me was the proper care and feeding of the newly installed hot tub—with an ozonator instead of bromine—especially considering all the horror stories conveyed by the hot tub people about the septic disaster that awaited all who failed to properly sanitize their tubs.

I wanted to make sure I had it right—especially since I knew that the tub was going to get some use over the course of the evening. I was unsure of the accuracy of the instructions I had been given by the hot tub people, mainly because of the apprehensive manner in which they were delivered, and the supplied hot tub documentation and various internet searches proved to be unhelpful, if not useless. Eventually I decided to just wing it, figuring that if I believed the hot tub was sepsis-free, it was almost equivalent to it actually being sepsis-free—sort of a mind-over-matter type of thing.

So, with the house readied, the hot tub finally prepped, and the weather perfect, I was excited for the celebrations to begin. As always, Nana was the first to arrive—fifteen minutes before anyone else would even think of showing up. I watched as she hugged Haley and Leo hello then gave Buddy an extra-long hug as she wished him a happy birthday. I watched her face and understood the emotions that flashed across it as she embraced her grandson. I could not imagine the past eight months had been any easier on her than they were on me. She released her hug and turned away from Buddy, patting him on the arm, almost as if to dismiss him, and made her way to say hello to me. I could see she was fighting back tears. I did her the favor of pretending that I didn't notice, but it touched me.

As the guests arrived over the next hour or so, that scene repeated itself several times as people greeted Buddy and wished him a happy birthday. There were essentially four groups of people invited: Buddy's friends, Haley's friends, my friends, and our family, but each group knew Buddy well. I saw young ladies wrap their arms around Buddy's neck and give him a big kiss on the cheek and guys give Buddy their signature three-slaps-on-the-back hug, all just to let him know that he was missed. More than once, I was almost moved to tears, so I decided to leave the greetings to Buddy and focus my energies elsewhere, concentrating on the other aspects of being a good hostess. I mingled when mingling was required, entertained where appropriate, and generally worked to keep the party on schedule—even though, as a birthday party, the schedule was rather loose, to say the least. I tried to introduce various individuals from one group to individuals of another to keep the party appropriately interblended, but my efforts might not have been needed. Though the different groups represented different social circles, ages, and ideas of what was considered "fun," the guests seemed to integrate quite nicely on their own. Mostly, when nothing else was required of me, I just stood back and watched.

The hot tub was most definitely the exciting new toy and the center of activity for the younger folk. As the older crowd lounged in chairs on the upper and lower levels of the deck waiting for the dinner bell to ring, the younger crowd congregated at the hot tub on the middle level. There was a steady stream of bathers filing in and out of the tub, the only seemingly permanent occupant being Buddy. When one group got waterlogged and pruney, they would give up their seats to the next group to soak for a while. Though the hot tub was billed as a six-person tub, there were times when I witnessed that number almost doubled, essentially a standing room–only affair.

The revelry taking place in and around the hot tub was providing the night's entertainment to the less adventurous guests as well. Even though everyone was invited and welcomed to participate, there were those who had no desire to partake in the bubbly goodness of the tub. Instead, they were gathering on the upper level of the deck to observe the antics taking place there. However, their eagerness to stay dry did not stop them from injecting themselves into the tomfoolery of the younger crowd.

Buddy had taken a bathroom break and temporarily relinquished his "permanent" seat in the back corner of the tub. The moment he returned, he playfully demanded that his spot be returned to him. As one bather was stepping over the edge of the tub to exit, Buddy was stepping over the edge onto the seat to head back to his spot. The seat, however, was slippery, and Buddy lost his balance and fell butt-first into the center of tub, much to everyone's amusement.

"Is that how they taught you to do it in the army, Bud?!" my friend who retired from the air force after twenty-four years of service called out from the upper deck as Buddy attempted to regain his footing.

"What was that?" Buddy called back, now standing in the center of the hot tub shaking off his half-smoked cigar, which he managed to salvage during the spill.

"That was so graceful!" my friend answered. "Of course, the air force taught us not to fall in the first place."

Ah! There it was; the old service rivalry, especially prominent between the army and the air force—not to mention the navy and the marines, or the army and the navy, or any branch, really. "I dare you to come down here and say that to me face to face," Buddy joked back.

"Nah, I think I'm good up here," my friend replied.

"Really?" Buddy asked. "Well, the army taught *us* not to take crap from the air force!" And with that, Buddy splashed his hand across the surface of the water toward the upper level of the deck. I watched as the half-dozen people standing at the rail scrambled to get out of the way of an airborne wave of water on a trajectory to splash them all!

The party was in full swing by the time the caterer arrived. Haley had managed to convince me early on to cater Buddy's party, though it left me feeling marginally guilty for shirking my "motherly" duties. Haley advised me that it would, first of all, save me time and, second, make the party that much more enjoyable because of the lack of things that were required of me, leaving me free to mingle and fully participate in the party rather than be tied to the kitchen for the evening.

I allowed Haley to convince me, but it took actually being able to participate in the party and fully experience the events of the evening to thoroughly appreciate accepting her suggestion. I was on the deck when the doorbell rang, and the chorus of "Someone's at the door!" coming from the living room alerted me to it. I ran to the door to let the gentleman in, and before he even stepped inside the house, he asked me, "Where's the birthday boy?"

Buddy was just walking through the foyer to the back deck after a bathroom break.

"Buddy! Get your butt over here!" I called to him.

He walked up beside me and asked, "What's up, Mom?"

"This is the birthday boy, fresh out of the Surge," I told the caterer as Buddy reached out to shake the caterer's had.

The caterer took Buddy's hand in both of his as he shook it. "God bless you, son!" he said. "Happy birthday to you, and thank you so much for your service."

Once again, I could feel my throat tighten and my eyes threaten to well up. "The dinner will go in here on the dining room table," I interrupted. I did not know if "the moment" was finished, but I needed it to be before I broke down. I showed the caterer the dining room table and left him to set it all up. In the meantime, I retrieved the check, and after he had set up his fare, I handed it to him and gave him a great big hug. I did not know if he felt that I was ungrateful for his gratitude for my son's service, but I did want him to know that I appreciated his efforts. With that, the caterer left, and the dinner bell was rung.

After everyone had their fill of the catered spread of barbecue and side dishes, there was a raucous chorus of "Happy Birthday Dear Buddy" as he blew out the twenty-one candles on his birthday cake. While the party celebrators enjoyed the cake and optional ice cream, Buddy opened his gifts. Some were intended for immediate enjoyment, like a bottle of flavored vodka; some for the remainder of his tour of duty in Iraq, like a half-dozen or so fine cigars; and some were the types of gifts that people give other people to hang onto until the end of their days, like a hard-bound book on the history of the army.

About an hour after Buddy opened his presents, the older crowd started heading home—beginning with Nana, who left fifteen minutes before anyone else even thought of leaving. When she hugged Buddy good-bye and wished him a happy birthday one more time, she knew she would be seeing him again before his R&R was over, but that was not necessarily true for the others leaving. Once again, I decided to busy myself elsewhere rather than witness the emotions of those saying good-bye and wishing Buddy luck—urging him to be careful once he got back to Iraq. It was simply too much of a reminder of how fast the time was flying by.

Despite all the work of being a good hostess and the general stress of putting on a successful celebration, I really did enjoy myself. Once the last of the older crowd left, I instantly became a member of the younger crowd, donning my bathing suit and taking my turn getting soaked and shriveled in the hot tub. As the night wore on, the various couches, chairs, and floors of my house became littered with partygoers who finally tuckered out. The party ended with just me and my nephew George sitting in the hot tub, discussing politics and solving the world's problems. It was after 4:00 a.m. when we finally called it quits, thus officially ending Buddy's twenty-first birthday party.

It was a wonderful evening and an amazingly good time, but there were moments when the experience smacked of the surreal as the joy of the occasion bumped up against the reality of the waning days of Buddy's R&R, like that moment just before a pleasant dream turns inexplicably into the darkness of a nightmare; Buddy was home, but that was not a permanent arrangement. At least I had a whole new collection of memories to cherish and to get me through whatever the future would bring, though my memories remained a bit fuzzy. It was not an artificial, alcohol-induced "fuzzy" but a sort of haze caused by a combination of the excitement of the party and an underlying disquiet brought on by the fact that my son would soon be heading back to Iraq. But, like everything else since the beginning of Buddy's R&R—let alone the beginning of the deployment—the best moments of the evening were not the obvious ones; the smaller, seemingly more insignificant moments were the ones etched upon my heart and my soul.

I remember how good it felt watching Buddy enjoying his "dream" of sitting in the corner of the bubbling hot tub with a cigar in one hand and a cognac in the other—even though he decided he was not that fond of cognac—or hearing Buddy and Haley bantering back and forth like all brothers and sisters do, just like old times. It warmed my heart to see Buddy resting on the living room floor using Whiskey (the dog, not the bottle) as a pillow, just as he always has, as he watched the other partygoers duke it out playing video games. And when my son hugged me to thank me for a great party, I almost cried again.

It seemed a bit strange and counterintuitive, but I began to realize that I was actually relaxing a little more with each passing day, even though the passing days meant that Buddy's return to combat was drawing ever closer. Buddy's birthday party only added to my peace of mind. It was more than the basic fact that the situation was now safer in Iraq—"safer," of course, being altogether relative. No, it had more to do with the fact that each passing day brought more confirmation that Buddy truly was OK—physically, mentally, spiritually, and emotionally. As the days passed, it became more obvious that not only was Buddy OK, but we—the Bear Cave—were OK as well. Above all, this was the answer to my prayers.

Rest and Relaxation, Part 2
2 September 2007–5 September 2007

Passing the time with Buddy, my soldier son!

Despite all the learned opinions I have encountered regarding the error of parents trying to be their children's "friends," I have to say that my kids are two of my closest friends. And, though I have always encouraged them to stand on their own and find some grand adventures to live (I guess like being a soldier at war?), I have also encouraged them to keep me in their lives as well.

Beyond the obvious burdens of having a son deployed to a war zone, I think the most difficult thing I faced during the previous eight months of the deployment was my lack of communication with Buddy. Sure, I wrote him at least once a week, sending him cookies and other goodies from home, but Buddy did not always have the time or the energy to write back. I knew he called me whenever he could, but it certainly was not as often as he did when he was here in the States. With that being said, one of the nicest things about having Buddy home was simply being able to sit and talk with him and to hear firsthand exactly how he was doing.

I discovered that the years I spent working at the Pentagon with all those Vietnam veterans—and the hours I spent listening to the tales of their own experiences with war—made the biggest difference in the simplest ways. I do not want to rehash the different political views of their day; that has been done by all sides, repeatedly, since the days of their service overseas decades ago. However, the simple fact was that there was a common thread throughout all of their stories—there seemed to be a feeling of isolation once they redeployed to the States. Whether it was because they were unsure of how their stories would be received or whether their stories were just too raw to recollect, let alone to retell—even, if not especially, to those they were closest to—they all felt a similar pressure to keep their stories bottled up inside. The culmination of all my discussions with these guys taught me to be patient when it came to my son—let him talk when he needed and when he wanted to—not to pressure and, above all, not to judge—certainly not what he said and, even more importantly, not what he kept hidden away.

For Buddy, this was not as dramatic as it might sound. I think my son is a stand-up comic at heart. No matter how a given story began, most of time, there was a punch line at the end that left you laughing. Needless to say, with all of us as a willing audience, my son was full of reminiscences and anecdotes regarding the FHOTA and others during his time in Iraq.

Generally speaking, news regarding the FHOTA had been relatively scarce since the beginning of the deployment. The different members of the group ended up on separate teams, and maybe even in separate platoons, though I am not sure—my lack of understanding regarding the basic structure of a military division is legendary in the "Wait a minute, how many platoons in a company?" category, despite Buddy's numerous attempts to educate me over breakfast at the Fayetteville IHOP. The bottom line was, however, that they were all housed in the same building and they all got their share of the care packages, no matter which team or platoon they were with.

Because Buddy knew that we wanted to know, he began his storytelling with a summary of incidents regarding the FHOTA. Toby was the first to get wounded, and apparently it was "just a scratch." Christian was the next, and though his wound was not life threatening, it was worse than Toby's. Shelby's incident decidedly stood apart from the rest.

"Shelby *absolutely* earned his Purple Heart," Buddy began his story. "Compared to the other two, his wound was definitely the worst so far."

So far?! I thought, but I let Buddy continue.

"Shelby took shrapnel to his head."

"Oh no!" Haley exclaimed.

"Is he OK?" I asked at almost the same time.

"Yeah," Buddy said with a smile. "His head is pretty hard, you know."

Clearly, it was all a little humorous to Buddy, but I was not convinced. "What happened?" I asked. "Did they send him home?"

"Nah," Buddy answered. "He's still there. It really isn't as bad as it sounds. Here, watch this; it's from one of the guys' helmet cams."

Buddy opened his laptop and maneuvered to the video while he continued to explain the incident. "To make a long story short, Shelby's team was on patrol when they were ambushed. While engaged in the firefight, something went boom and a piece of shrapnel hit Shelby in the head! He stayed at his post, though, and continued to fight until the attack was neutralized. He received a bronze star for his actions that day, too. Anyway, it was the aftermath of the firefight that was recorded." Buddy started the video.

It began with Shelby sitting in the front seat of a vehicle, smoking a cigarette and bleeding rather profusely from a wound on his forehead. The video showed another soldier running up to Shelby asking excitedly, "Are you OK? Shelby! Are you OK?!"

Shelby's response was typical Shelby. With the cigarette dangling from his lips and in a deadpan voice, Shelby responded, "Do I look [expletive] OK to you?!" at which point, the other soldier started excitedly calling for a medic.

Despite everything inside of me that told me not to, I could not help but laugh. It was no different for Haley. Notwithstanding the humor we were finding in the current story, we also could not help but think back to the day the FHOTA deployed. When Shelby showed us the brand-new, very large Superman "S" tattooed on his chest, we could not resist teasing him mercilessly. We both thought the tattoo was such a huge mistake, but that was then.

"Well," I said, "I guess Shelby has most definitely earned the right to wear that 'S' with pride. Don't you think, Haley?"

"I don't know, Mom," Haley responded. "I think he might really *be* Superman!"

"By the way, Buddy, what did you mean when you said 'worst injury *so far*'?" I asked him pointedly.

Buddy smiled at me, looking a tad sheepish. "Think about it, Mom," he said. "Each one of the FHOTA except me has gotten injured, and each injury is a magnitude worse than the injury before; I'm the only one still unscathed. It just left us all wondering just what might happen to me!" He then proceeded to describe the very disturbing scenarios involving himself and various levels of death and dismemberment that the FHOTA had graciously developed.

I thought about it a moment before I decided to make all those scenarios null and void. "You do realize that you were actually the *first* to be injured, right?" I asked. Buddy did not seem to know what I was talking about, so I continued. "You know, that damned spider bite you got during your first deployment to Iraq? Which led to MRSA? Which, by the way, *is* life threatening, so yours was the first and yours was the worst! No more scenarios—you've had your injury!"

Buddy was not necessarily convinced by my logic, but he was willing to let it go. In an effort to change the subject, I asked about the one care package that I had doubted would ever reach him. "Hey, Buddy, did Haley's and my masterpiece of duct-taped glory that we sent at the beginning of summer ever actually get to you?"

"You mean that shoe box thing you sent?" he asked. "Yeah! It got to me. It was the most frustrating package I ever received—had to use my KA-BAR knife to get into it." Buddy paused a moment before adding, "Don't ever do that again!"

I laughed at his comment but could not help but feel pride in Haley's and my accomplishment.

Buddy continued to talk about the previous eight months and what the Surge had been like for him. In addition to the stories regarding the original FHOTA, Buddy also spoke of the new members to the group. By my count, the FHOTA was now doubled in size—I guess making it the EHOTA? I am not sure how that works, unless the singular "horseman" becomes a "horse-pair." Even so, they were all still reluctant to claim Pestilence. The new members definitely sounded a great deal like the old members if what we were hearing was any indication. I think my favorite stories were the ones that involved Bobby MacGregor. He seemed to be the one that had the least trouble "playing" to let off steam—a quality essential for maintaining sanity in less-than-sane situations.

There had still been no Wiffle ball games between B-Company and C-Company, but Buddy still told some great stories. I think my favorite involved four Lego Power Racer cars that I had sent Buddy in one of the care packages. Buddy was always a fan of Legos, and these self-propelled cars were my attempt to give him a chance to play and to remember life beyond Iraq. Apparently, Bobby was one of the lucky guys who got to "play" the day the cars arrived. As I had intended, after the cars were assembled, Buddy, Bobby, and the others began racing them. From what I gathered, Bobby's car was having trouble keeping up with the others; in fact, it was losing every race. In frustration—and pretty much responding like a petulant child—Bobby took his car and slammed it up against the wall, smashing it into its original seventy-plus pieces. The others, seeing this as a *much* better game, did the same. Immediately, my intended stress-relieving Lego races degenerated into nothing more than a demolition derby.

This obviously was not what I intended nor what I had envisioned. However, having learned my lesson well from the Wiffle ball incident, I refrained from judging. Instead, I acknowledged to myself that they did laugh, they did play, and they did have fun. I could not have expected more from my efforts. In addition, I was actually comforted by the fact that as long as Buddy had friends like the FHOTA—both old and new members—he had the best chance of being OK in the long run.

Rest and Relaxation, Part 3
6 September 2007–11 September 2007

Hey! It's my birthday too!

I am not sure how much sons normally share with their moms, but both my kids have always tended to share a great deal with me—whether it was something a mother normally wanted to hear or not. For my son's stories out of Iraq, I tended to want to hear everything he wanted tell, but I knew there was more. In spite of the lighthearted nature of most of Buddy's narrations, I knew that underneath the bravado and humor, there were untold experiences that he needed to recount. I was ready to listen, but I did not know how to get the conversation started. I tried to hint at this without really asking any questions, but mostly Buddy just ignored my attempts to start a dialogue in these uncharted territories. The time I spent with other veterans who had faced combat let me know that these experiences did need to be discussed, whether Buddy wanted to or not. However, I also understood that, to a large extent, it needed to be on his time and with whomever he chose.

With the end of Buddy's R&R so close, I was grateful to Keith for requesting Buddy's help with some home improvement projects. Keith had been to Iraq and Afghanistan; I figured if there was anyone that Buddy might open up to, it was him. So while Buddy assisted in the various tasks at whatever stage the renovations were at, I happily puttered about the house, reassured in the knowledge that Buddy was safe, my family was whole again—at least for the time being—and all felt right with the world. However, it was here that things began to go stupid.

My birthday falls just over a week after Buddy's. I decided that since Buddy was home, the best present my kids could give me would be a traditional Bear Cave family dinner. Generally, this meant a gathering of my kids and a random selection of their friends at one of the local family restaurants. For me, there was just no better way to spend an evening, so the plans were made and the date set.

The day of my birthday began like any of the others since Buddy's return, and since I had taken leave for the whole time he was home, when Buddy was off doing other things, I was free to do whatever.

Buddy had, once again, spent the night with Keith so they could tackle a couple more items on the renovation to-do list, so I had the day to myself. I took the Whiskey-Dog for a long walk, watched some news, did some light cleaning, vacuumed, and, around 3:00, took a shower and prepared myself for my birthday dinner with my kids.

Haley was not due home from work until 8:00, so it was going to be a late dinner. But I figured that would simply give Buddy a little extra time to finish up whatever he was doing with Keith and still make it home for the festivities. However, when 7:00 rolled around and I had still not heard anything from him, I called Buddy to find out what his estimated time of arrival would be. To my surprise, they had been drinking—enough so that neither he nor Keith was able to drive. I was disappointed, to say the least. However, this was Buddy's time for resting and relaxing, so I did not mention my birthday, the plans for dinner which we had just discussed the evening before, or, for that matter, my disappointment.

With my idea for a Bear Cave family dinner canceled out, I saw no reason to bother with going out at all; in fact, I was no longer hungry. Instead, I decided I needed a soak in the hot tub. I put on my bathing suit, poured myself a glass of wine, and headed outside. Leo arrived home from work first. When he heard that dinner was canceled, he grabbed a beer and joined me, as did Haley when she finally arrived home. We ended up tubbing it for a couple of hours. After we had sufficiently soaked, we headed inside to watch a movie and relax before bed. It was just about midnight when the house phone rang.

Haley answered the phone, said a couple "uh-huh"s, and then handed it to me. I checked the time as I reached for the receiver; it was just five minutes before midnight. I was puzzled because of the lateness of the call and looked to Haley for answers, but all she did was shrug her shoulders and return to her place on the couch. I put the receiver to my ear and timidly asked, "Hello?"

Immediately, I was greeted with a drunken chorus of "Happy Birthday Dear Maggie" followed by my nephew announcing, "See? We remembered your birthday!"

I was stunned into silence. I had no idea how to respond because I was unclear

as to their motivation. Did they know they were disappointing me when they blatantly ignored my plans for a Bear Cave family dinner and yet now were trying to
"make nice"? I'm not stupid! I was aware that there was a great deal of playing being
done among all that work at Keith's house—especially during those overnight stays—
and I was good with that because I knew that Buddy needed to play and to unwind.
However, I was now conflicted as to how much the needs of a young soldier getting
ready to return to war should take precedence over the needs of the mother who has
supported that soldier through thick and thin.

At the beginning of this deployment, the phone calls were few and far between
as Buddy created a necessary separation from home and turned his focus to the tasks
at hand. As the time grew closer for his R&R, the phone calls came more frequently
as Buddy began to connect again in anticipation of his homecoming. But over the
previous few days, I had watched as Buddy pulled away from home once again as he
prepared to shift gears back into soldier mode. I understood that this needed to happen, that this was an unavoidable transition, but I didn't think it gave Buddy the right
to dismiss me or the few requests I had for the remaining time of his R&R.

I have mentioned before that anger is at least a second emotion, and this incident
did nothing to disprove it. At first, the uncertainty of my feelings gave way to hurt.
Even though I knew I was wrong, my gut reaction was to blame Keith for everything.
Yet whether Keith was an instigator or simply an enabler, Buddy had a large part in
the heartache I was feeling as well, because it felt like I had been summarily dismissed
by the both of them. The hurt then gave way to a sort of indignation. I was insulted
that either of them, after ignoring me for the day, would think that a drunken phone
call just minutes before the official end of my birthday was acceptable. I could not
stop myself from wondering if that was all I was worth to them. And then I was just
plain ticked off!

I knew that Keith was waiting for some response, but at that moment I had nothing to say to either of them. "Real nice," I managed rather dryly, and with that, the
phone call was pretty much over. From the tone of Keith's voice as he said good-bye,
I assumed that he had not the smallest clue of how upset I was. I stared at the receiver,
pondering whether this was because of the alcohol or because he just did not care.
Either reason seemed only to feed my anger. I looked to Haley and Leo, who were still
on the couch trying to watch the end of the movie. "Am I wrong here?" I asked. "Am I
wrong to have expected Buddy to be home for my birthday instead of drunk dialing at
midnight?" But I didn't wait for an answer. Instead, I announced, "I'm going to bed!"
and retired to my room for the rest of the night, though I did not sleep. The bottom

line was that not only did the evening upset me a great deal, but this was not exactly the way I wanted things to be as I sent my son back to war.

All night long, I wrestled with whether I had a right to feel the way I was feeling, whether Buddy should have to worry about anything other than just resting and relaxing—wherever that took him. *Is it right for me to rain on his parade, so to speak, and burden him with my hurt feelings?* I asked myself. *What if my previous evaluations were wrong and this was the first sign of him losing himself?* Normally, Buddy never would have so blatantly ignored his family. *Was this a mistake or a trend? And, even more than that, what do I do about it, either way?*

I was still a bit miffed the next day when Buddy stopped by the house for some clean clothes—and that is putting it mildly. Though I had solved nothing regarding how I should respond to the events of the previous evening during my sleepless night, it made no difference; when Buddy walked through the front door, my feelings just boiled over and spilled out—there was no stopping it. He might not have been fully aware of the situation before he walked into the room, but it became crystal clear when he saw the look on my face. "Hey, Mom. What's wrong?" he asked, even though I suspected that he had a fairly good idea of what the answer was.

"I don't appreciate your behavior from these past few days," I began, "and I certainly don't appreciate being blown off on my birthday!"

I did not get much further than that when Buddy started apologizing. "I know, Mom. I'm sorry; I'm sorry," he said. "I don't know what I was thinking. I'm sorry."

I took a moment to evaluate. I examined Buddy's face—more importantly, his eyes—for any sign of what might be in his heart at that moment. What I saw was sadness. It could have been because I was upset with him—my kids have never liked it when I was upset with them—but it seemed to me the sadness was more because of remorse. It most certainly took the edge off my sour mood. Immediately, anything I might have added to my original statement dissipated. The anger was disappearing and all that was left was a desire to put the whole unpleasant affair behind us. Like I said before, this was *not* the way I wanted my son's R&R to end.

"It's OK, Buddy," I began in an attempt to release him from his guilt. "I was just hurt when you ignored my only birthday wish." *Well, that was stupid!* I thought as I watched my son grimace at my words. *I just never seem to know when to shut up!*

"I am so sorry, Mom." Buddy walked over and gave me one of his big old bear hugs. And with that, everything felt normal again. All the negative feelings of the past evening were gone. However, they seemed to be replaced by a gut-wrenching awareness that Buddy's R&R was almost over. I was not ready.

I knew that Buddy was going to have to transition back into soldier mode before he actually left the Bear Cave, if for no other reason but to carry him through those first hours back in Iraq. However, it just seemed to me that he was pulling away too much and too soon. We still had a little bit of time left—just a little, but certainly enough to give me at least one more mother-and-son or, better yet, family activity to etch upon my memories. I knew I needed that; just like the memories of those five days of helping Buddy prepare to leave for the Surge back at the beginning of it all helped me survive the previous eight months, I needed good memories of his R&R to see me through the next. I already had some wonderful ones, but I felt I needed more.

Over the final few days of Buddy's R&R, I did get some cherished memories to hold in my heart for the remaining months of the Surge. Interspersed among hours at Keith's helping with the renovations and random outings with his friends, Buddy and I found time to share our love of cars by spending a few hours riding through the mountains, enjoying the wind in our hair and the freedom of the road. In addition, we finally held my birthday dinner at a local fondue restaurant. This one included Nana, Albert and George, Keith and Sasha, and, of course, the members of the Bear Cave. Who doesn't enjoy playing with their food for a night of fun and fellowship? And, less than two days before Buddy was due to leave, there was a Guitar Hero contest at the local family sports bar. It all filled my heart, but before we knew it, the eighteen days had drawn to an end and all that was left was to say good-bye—again.

Good-byes

12 September 2007

All good things must come to an end, and it's a cursed shame!

It was just over nine months ago that Haley and I were down at Fort Bragg, hanging out with Buddy and the rest of the FHOTA as they waited to be assigned their equipment and board the buses which would take them to their waiting military transport at the beginning of this deployment. Once again, Haley and I were sitting with Buddy as he waited for his plane to take him back to Iraq, only now the wait was at Dulles Airport and the plane was from Delta Airlines. It felt decidedly different this time, even taking into consideration the change in venue. Though the familiar pangs of apprehension and uncertainty tugged at my heart, the excitement (for lack of a better word) of the unknown experience ahead of us was now spent. Marginally comforted by the knowledge that things were better in Iraq, even if not perfect, the glaring danger of complacency was not lost on me.

I realized that Buddy needed to do this. More than a few times over the past eighteen days, Buddy had been overwhelmed with anxiety as he agonized over the well-being of the FHOTA, his team, and his platoon back in Iraq. He commented more than once on his need to finish what he and the rest of the 504th had started, even if it seemed that their accomplishments were not recognized by everyone. I reminded myself more than once that this day, the day Buddy would return to Iraq, would come and I would face it with a positive attitude, a smile on my face, and absolutely no tears in my eyes. And once again, as the family of a soldier, Haley and I were allowed to accompany Buddy to the gate as he waited for his flight.

For all the mischief we could have immersed ourselves in during the time we had to kill before Buddy's plane was ready to board—and we have a great deal of experience in getting into mischief—after visiting the various kiosks for the obligatory collection of snacks, we found the designated gate, settled into some chairs, and, for the most part, were uncharacteristically quiet for what seemed like an amazingly short hour-long wait. Except for an occasional outburst of stupidity which would leave us all laughing for a few moments, it seemed we had very little to say to each other. However, I realized that simply being able to sit together, even quietly, was a blessing. Lost in our own thoughts, I believe we were caught up in the contradictions between the relative peace of the last eighteen days and the upheaval of the previous eight months—even as we avoided any substantial thoughts of the unpredictable future.

The time for Buddy's departure was drawing near when a flight attendant came to offer him a seat in first class to honor his service. I was once again assured that my son had not been irreversibly changed by what he had faced in Iraq as I listened to him, in all humility, try to refuse the offer. However, being the good family that we are, Haley and I would not let him.

Sitting there in those final minutes before boarding began, I could not pretend to know what Buddy's or Haley's thoughts and feelings were, but mine were clear and unambiguous. For the past eight months, I had been praying that God would give me a chance to see Buddy, my only son, one more time. In these last moments of Buddy's R&R, I was grateful to God for giving me the opportunity to let Buddy know that I loved him dearly and could not be more proud of him.

Buddy's homecoming was vibrant and full, and I knew the memories would last a lifetime. In contrast, waiting for him to board the plane back to Iraq and the Surge felt dull and empty. Because he was a soldier returning to war, not to mention a newly assigned first-class passenger, he was invited to board the plane first.

"Take your time," the flight attendant said to us, and then walked away to begin the boarding process for everyone else.

My stomach was doing summersaults and my throat was tight. I did not know what to say. There was an odd moment of the three of us exchanging glances before Buddy sighed loudly, leaned over, grabbed his assault pack, and stood up. Haley and I stood up slowly as Buddy put his pack on his back. He turned to Haley first.

"I love you, Haley," I heard Buddy say, followed by a muffled "I love you, too," as Haley hugged her brother with all her might. Buddy then turned to me.

"No tears!" Buddy said and then smiled before adding, "I love you, Mom."

As I reached out to give Buddy a hug, I affirmed, "I know, no tears." I hugged my son tightly, trying to imprint the moment on my heart. "I love you, Bud. Be *safe*," I added before releasing my embrace.

Buddy turned and headed to the gate. Right before he entered the Jetway, he turned to give a quick wave. I gave him the "I love you" sign for the deaf, which we have used as a way to wave good-bye since the kids were very young. With that, he disappeared through the gate.

Haley and I stood in silence a minute and watched random people enter the gate behind Buddy. I had no way of knowing if this was my last opportunity to be with my son. It definitely was one of those "only time will tell" moments, but what was clear to me was that any scenario that would take him from me was simply not acceptable. In the end, I was left with my all-too-familiar (and this time silent) mantra, *I simply cannot do this again!*

Cookie Weeks: Part II

Sometimes you just need a change of scenery.

I was feeling undeniably melancholy. It was wonderful having Buddy home again, but now, heading into that time of year my family has always liked the best—autumn to winter—he was back in Iraq. Baghdad was a much safer place, but "safe" is definitely a relative term and I had no idea how to judge its relativeness. There still seemed to be a multitude of people jamming the airways willing to "accept" our defeat over there; in a *Meet the Press* segment on September 9, just days before Buddy headed back to Iraq, Joe Biden analyzed the Surge this way: "I mean, the truth of the matter is that [this administration's policy and the Surge] are a failure . . . there is, in fact, no real security in Baghdad and/or in Anbar province."

These certainly were not the words I wanted to hear from the senator from Delaware, though from everything I was seeing, he was just plain wrong—we were making progress, if not winning. The calls for retreat in defeat did not seem to jive with the boredom subtly (or not-so-subtly) reflected in what I was hearing from Buddy and his fellow soldiers. What I did know—and told Buddy often—was that they *all* needed to stay vigilant, because "safe" *is* a relative term.

The good news was we were now past the halfway mark of the deployment—as long as it stayed at the current extended time and did not grow further. The bad news, however, was that I was still struggling to not think too far ahead and, in some ways, struggling just to get by. Cookie dough and vacuuming simply were no replacement for having my son home safe and sound—hence the assemblage of Whiskey hair gathering in various corners of my house again. I needed and wanted to clean, but I just did not have the energy. Even my cookie inventing had become a struggle. I realized I had to do something, so I took a forty-five-day temporary assignment away from home. The way I figured it, I had Haley and Leo to watch over things, especially the Whiskey-Dog. *So why not take a little break from the "norm"?* I thought. *Maybe it will do me some good.*

The assignment took me to Fayetteville, North Carolina, which put me in close proximity to the home base of the 82nd Airborne Division. Not only did that somehow help me feel closer to Buddy, but after the five years it had been since I worked for the Pentagon, in a strange way, heading down the road to my new, temporary life almost felt like "going home"; I would once again be working shoulder to shoulder with our troops, and the change felt good. I had reserved a room at an Extended Stay hotel that included an oven to allow me to maintain my cookie-baking efforts, both for sanity's sake and to continue my care packages to Buddy and the rest of the guys. Haley and Leo were psyched about playing Suzie and Sam Homemaker during my absence, so all that was left was to let the adventure begin.

The only downside I could see to my new assignment was its southerly location. Even my own home was a good deal south of where I longed to be; in my heart, I was a northern girl who saw New England as one of the best places to live in the world. Believe it or not, one of the reasons was the weather—especially all that snow. I had been watching the weather in Fayetteville and was not exactly pleased, though I know others might have been. Where my soul was crying for crisp autumn mornings and trees ablaze with color, I was heading to downright sultry evenings and thirsty trees with dry, brown leaves. Jack Frost was definitely on a hiatus there, but for the previous several days, Mr. Frost had been on a hiatus up north as well. As petty as it seems, somehow this did help me feel a little better, and it made it easier to turn my car in that southerly direction rather than give in to my desires and run away to the north.

Even with the warm weather, this adventure felt exactly like what I expected autumn to feel like. Despite the fact that this was the time of year when all the summer blooms and blossoms began to wilt and die, autumn had always felt like a new beginning to me. As a child, no matter how much I had wanted the previous school year to end, when I received that three-by-five postcard with teacher and classroom information sometime during the first week of August, heralding the new school year, I was excited. No matter what had transpired the previous school year, I had a clean slate and the possibilities were endless. Never mind the probability that teachers from the same school most likely spoke to each other and shared information about various students; I was as much of an unknown to my new teacher as my new teacher was to me.

I remember how invincible I felt as I headed to school that first Tuesday of September with my new pencils, paper, crayons, and lunch box. Not only was I invincible, but I felt like my potential was immeasurable . . . if only for that year.

Now, Buddy had returned to Iraq and I was beginning a new assignment. To me, it felt like Labor Day, and I was once again waiting for my first day of school the next morning. I wondered what the next six weeks would bring, both for me and for my son. As Buddy and the rest of the 504th continued their fight in advancing the tentative peace they had achieved, I wondered what issues I would be required to face and hopefully conquer. When I compared our different circumstances, it seemed as if it were just another year of high school for Buddy but that I was just starting first grade. The funny thing was, I felt very similar to the way I remember feeling as I stood in a line on the blacktop of my elementary school, waiting to be led to my classroom for the very first time—excited, with a huge helping of apprehension.

Sitting on the couch in my temporary living room, dining room, and kitchen combination, it occurred to me that this was the first time in forever that I had been alone; no kids and no Whiskey-Dog, just me and the stark bareness of a hotel room. Though the room was nicely appointed as far as hotel rooms go, I could not help but notice that it had not a pinch of my personality reflected in it in any way. I flipped through the different TV channels looking for something to distract me without success. My stomach was in knots, just as it had been so many times since the beginning of the year. Amazingly enough, though, for the first time since January, I was more concerned with how I was going to do in my new adventure than I was about Buddy and Baghdad—at least for the time being!

Apple Spice Cookies

1/3 cup shortening
1/2 cup margarine
1 1/4 cups brown sugar
1/3 cup applesauce
1 teaspoon vanilla
1 egg
3/4 teaspoon baking soda

1/2 teaspoon salt
2 cups flour
1 cup old-fashioned oats, finely
   chopped
1 cup white chocolate chips
1/2 cup dried cranberries

1. Preheat oven to 350 degrees.
2. Cream together shortening, margarine, brown sugar, applesauce, vanilla, and egg with an electric mixer until light and fluffy, about 3 to 5 minutes.
3. Add baking soda and salt. Continue to beat with electric mixer for about a minute.
4. With a spoon, mix in flour and oats until well blended. Stir in chocolate chips and dried cranberries.
5. Drop dough by rounded teaspoons onto cookie sheets.
6. Bake for 10 to 12 minutes.

I know how to spell "Mommy"; how do you spell "support"?

It was the first Friday of the first work week of my little adventure. Having survived the week, it occurred to me that besides the disagreeable weather—warmth, sunshine, and such—being down in Fayetteville was a welcome distraction. In addition to my days spent learning what was expected from me during the assignment, the evenings were spent wandering the little shops around town looking for ways to turn a hotel suite into a home. The nights were spent watching movies (I still shied away from the news), reading books, writing letters, or baking, and, even better, I did this all with no external demands on me like mowing lawns, cleaning bathrooms, vacuuming, or house repairs—all of which had become a bit of a burden in the past several months and all of which were now handled by hotel staff. Before the Surge, these external demands had always been welcome pastimes that I had thoroughly enjoyed. Since January, however, the demands of these necessary activities only seemed to beat me down.

I was looking forward to my first weekend as well. I was excited for the opportunity to explore the outer reaches of the countryside—always good for an adventure or two. Though I had yet to find evidence of a local corn maze or a suitable pumpkin patch (essential for October weekends), I had seen roadside signs for a local vineyard or two that I definitely wanted to visit. There were also a few local museums and a botanical garden vying for my attention. Considering the limited number of weeks I had, it seemed as though my weekends in Fayetteville would be full. All in all, this appeared to be adding up to forty-five days of ignorant "bliss" for me, though I did realize that by working so close to the military, it would be difficult to hide from any bad news emanating from Iraq. Despite that, it felt as though I were a million miles away from the insanity of the past nine months without being too far away from Buddy. I was ready for whatever life was going to bring me—but first, I had to get to work.

As I had done every day since January 2nd, the last thing I did before I left for work was hang Buddy's dog tag and the pair of silver crossed rifles around my neck. Though they often sparked interest and words of encouragement, I had never experienced the deep respect that I felt that afternoon when I was introduced to a colonel who had stopped by to see how everyone was doing. Though one or two of the individuals I worked with already knew that I was the mother of a soldier, it was only after the colonel inquired after Buddy's dog tag that it became general knowledge to the rest of the office.

"Your son is fighting in the Surge?" the colonel asked in a typical booming military voice.

"Yes, sir," I responded. "He is an E-4 with the 504th."

Most officers are aware that, no matter what the official pecking order is, the army and the rest of the military run on the backs of the enlisted—from the lowly private (E-1) to the senior enlisted (E-7 or E-8)—and this fact was not lost on the colonel. After years of "sir"ing and "ma'am"ing the officers I worked with at the Pentagon, all of a sudden, it seemed as though the tables were turned.

"Well, God bless you, ma'am," the Colonel said. "And tell your son that I said 'Hooah!'"

I smiled and promised to pass the battle cry on to my son—"Hooah" being the army's version of "Go get 'em," "Good on ya," "Attaboy," "Roger that"; basically anything but a negative response.

With that, the colonel left, but for the next several minutes, it seemed as though everyone in the room found a reason to come over and express their unwavering support for me and for Buddy. It was an endless stream of "God bless you and your son" and "I will be praying for your son" that touched my heart deeply. Considering these types of emotional support were still very much connected to my tear ducts, it was not long before the whole experience became quite overwhelming—though not necessarily an unpleasant overwhelming. . . except for the whole totally-breaking-down-in-an-office-full-of-people-that-you-just-met thing.

It felt like the whole room was giving me one of those great, big, warm, wonderful hugs of appreciation that people sometimes desire but are not always able to get. It was exactly what I was trying to convey to Buddy and all the guys he served with; it was why I baked every weekend and spent all that time shopping for necessities like trail mix, cigars, baby wipes, movies, toothpaste, glow-in-the-dark footballs, Axe body wash, Lego race cars (that really worked until slammed into walls), and whatever else struck me as a necessity at the time. However, I was the one who was now receiving what I was so desperately trying to convey to our soldiers: support.

Many times since the beginning of the Surge, I would tell my mom, "I feel so alone, Mama. Not *lonely*—I have plenty of people to spend my time with—but *alone!*"

Nana responded with incredible wisdom, which was somehow always a bit surprising to me. "Maggie," she began, "no one could ever understand exactly what you are feeling these days. They can empathize and even offer encouragement, but without having a son serving on the front lines, they could never know or even imagine what you are going through."

Nana's words comforted me but never quite consoled me. I knew my mother understood, but she left me doubting that anyone else would ever be able to. Nonetheless, I always seemed to succumb to my sense that it was necessary to at least *try* to explain the way I felt and why. It was a never-ending struggle—mostly internal—to say the exact words to help others understand the plight of the mother of a soldier without going too far or stopping short of making my point. And yet, that day, I felt I was understood, if only momentarily.

I left work that evening and went straight to the grocery store to pick up something for dinner and to purchase the needed supplies for my first Saturday morning cookie-baking session in my home-away-from-home. I quickly walked through the aisles, trying to develop an original idea to turn into care package cookies for Buddy. What I ended up with was an old idea, straight out of Buddy's childhood. My kids would often participate in my creative cookie-baking bouts when they were young. Walking down the cereal aisle, my memories crystallized on one that involved oatmeal, peanut butter, and Buddy's strong dislike of both—even though he had an active part in this cookie's creation. I hurried down the different aisles collecting the various ingredients, all the while wondering if, when he first tasted the cookies, Buddy would remember it all like I had.

I carefully counted all my groceries and realized that I had just under the magical amount of fifteen items, which allowed me to check out in the express lane. As always, the word "express" was subject to interpretation. There were several people ahead of me, and the queue seemed to grow exponentially behind me with every passing minute. As the line inched forward, my mind drifted back to the day that Buddy and I first created the cookies, which were eventually named "Mursmub Cookies."

Buddy was only about five years old at the time, and as that first sheet of cookies baked, I asked him what he thought we should name them.

"These are Mommy's cookies, *all* Mommy's cookies!" Buddy said. "We should call them 'Mommy Cookies' so *everyone* will know!"

I was tickled by his choice of names, especially considering the cookies contained ingredients that he was not very fond of at the time. Even so, he thought the cookie *dough* was decent—probably because everyone in the Bear Cave seemed to have a weakness for cookie dough. "Mommy Cookies, huh?" I commented. "But just how should I spell that?"

What I was referring to was whether we were going to call the cookies *Mommy's* Cookies, as Buddy had first stated, or *Mommy* Cookies, which was his final answer. I was just thinking aloud, but my son took me quite literally. "Mommy Cookies!" he insisted to my rhetorical question. "M-U-R-S-M-U-B. That spells 'Mommy'!" With that, a cookie was born.

I was almost to the conveyor belt that carried the groceries to the checkout clerk— it all depended on how the people ahead of me placed their items on the intermit- tently moving surface. My mind was still a decade or so away as I reveled in memories of my kids when they were young. The woman in front of me placed her groceries on the belt, squished them all together to make room for mine, and placed the obligatory plastic bar at the end of her pile. She then motioned to me that there was now enough room for my groceries. I did the same and motioned to the woman behind me, my mind rather preoccupied with my memories all the while.

"Husband?" the woman ahead of me asked. Her question jolted me to the present, but I had no clue what she had just said. I looked up and noticed she was tapping her upper chest and nodding to what I had placed on the conveyor belt: oatmeal, shorten- ing, brown sugar, flour, peanut butter, vanilla, and a chicken TV dinner. Seeing what must have been a blank expression on my face, she re-asked her question. "Is it your husband who is deployed?"

It took a moment, but it finally sunk in that she was referring to Buddy's dog tag and my eclectic collection of groceries. "Nah!" I answered casually. "It's my son who is over. And you?" I inquired back, noticing her own eclectic collection on the conveyor belt.

"Oh my, no!" she answered. "I just bake cookies every now and again to send to my husband's old unit to show our support. He is retired now."

The woman behind me in line joined the conversation. "My husband is with the 325th. Is that where your son is?"

"No," I answered. "He's with the 504th. Where is your husband located?" I asked, totally forgetting about my usual concerns regarding how my words might be con- strued or deemed inappropriate. And with that, the three of us were chatting away as if we had known each other forever. During our remaining time in line, we discussed our soldiers, our lives, and how we had coped since January 2nd.

Driving back to my hotel room from the grocery store, I became keenly aware that Fayetteville just felt different. This close community just outside Fort Bragg was apparently providing a relief that I hadn't realized I needed. For the first time in what seemed like forever, I did not feel that I was required to defend myself, my son, the Surge, the war, the president, or this country. But even more than that, I felt that most in Fayetteville understood why a majority of those things were not even a part of the equation when considering what was really important.

More than once during Buddy's R&R, I witnessed the effects of a basic lack of understanding of soldiers and their sense of duty and honor. I saw his face flash with a tinge of exasperation when a stranger came up to Buddy to thank him for his service and then felt the need to add, "I just don't support the war!"

Buddy thanked the man for his gratitude but added under his breath to me as we walked away, "Just what the hell does that man think my job is?!"

I had also seen my son's face go from "happy to see an old friend" to a rather pained grimace when a high school acquaintance of his who we ran into at the local Best Buy inquired if my son had ever killed anyone. Haley had shared with me just how sensitive Buddy was to that question by relating her own experience of simply asking her brother, "Hey Bud, can I ask you a question?"

Haley was taken aback by Buddy's response: "As long as you don't ask if I have ever shot or killed anyone."

"That's not what I was going to ask!" Haley scolded her brother. However, when she told me this story, she added, "Mom! I would never have asked that! In fact, I don't think I would ever want to hear the answer."

And therein lies the rub.

It was during our stop for some refreshments and a bite to eat on our mountain drive at the end of his R&R that Buddy asked a question of his own. "Mama," he began, "I feel like I'm going to go to hell. Do you think that there's any hope for me otherwise?"

I do not think I had ever felt so alone, both for me and for my boy. My heart ached as I grappled for an answer to his inquiry beyond the knee-jerk "Of course you aren't going to hell!" that fell out of my mouth almost instantaneously. I did not ask him where the question came from or why he felt the need to explore it. I knew my son, and I was hugely aware of what career path he chose. Even more, I understood the ultimate objective of the Surge, including what it required of our soldiers. And, like Haley, I did not necessarily want or need to hear the details. I would have listened if he wanted to talk, but I did not get the impression that was what he was after. Buddy was waiting for an answer of substance, and I was at a loss for words.

I picked at my food for a minute, trying to come up with some substantive answer to his earnest inquiry. I could feel him watching me, waiting for me to say something. I looked up and met his gaze. "Why do you ask? What's bothering you?" I asked, even though I realized that I might not necessarily want to hear the answer.

"I don't know Mom; it's just the way I feel sometimes," he answered before changing the subject. I guess I could have insisted, but the truth was that I was a little relieved to leave that discussion behind.

I knew from my own experiences that when hostilities heated up in Iraq, what Buddy did was more for the FHOTA and the soldiers he served with than for the altruistic (or, some might say, mistaken) goals of the war. At the moment of impact, it was simply about survival—for all of them. However, I also knew that believing in the ultimate goal of the mission helped make the cost of survival a little more palatable. Others did not need to compel our soldiers to question the reasoning for their presence in Iraq or their actions, because these guys did that all by themselves—and so did their families.

Neither my son as a soldier nor I as the mother of a soldier needed any help in conceptualizing the big picture or breaking down the value of the effort. It was a never-ending internal struggle to maintain that delicate balance between cost and worth, belief and doubt, right and wrong, survival and the alternative. I hesitated to speak with friends, family, and strangers alike when it came to any of my concerns regarding my son or the Surge. I did not want to be responsible for perpetuating any lack of understanding or respect for what my son did because of my disquiet in moments of weakness, nor did I want anyone else fueling my own ambiguity.

I was exhausted and felt like I had nowhere to turn, so I simply isolated myself instead. However, Fayetteville was changing all that. I no longer felt so alone; in fact, I believed I had shared more with those two total strangers in the five minutes we stood in line together than I had with anyone else since the beginning of the Surge. Even when talking to Nana or Haley, I tended to hold back—not because I was afraid of their reaction but more to keep them from worrying. I wished I had introduced myself to those women, asked for their phone numbers or to meet for a drink or something; I just wanted to be able to continue our conversation. But I also felt sure that, statistically speaking, it was an improbability that I managed to strike up a conversation with the only two women in Fayetteville who felt like I did. I was sure that more random conversations were just around the corner and that my feeling of isolation would not be returning any time soon—or at least for the next forty days.

Mursmub Cookies

Cookie:

1/2 cup shortening
1/3 cup margarine
1/4 cup peanut butter
2 tablespoons brown sugar

3/4 cup powdered sugar
1/4 teaspoon salt
1 1/4 cups flour
1 cup quick oats

Filling:

1/4 cup margarine
1/4 cup peanut butter
1 1/2 cups powdered sugar

2–3 tablespoons water (enough to make a spreadable but firm consistency)

1. Preheat oven to 350 degrees.
2. Cream together shortening, margarine, peanut butter, brown sugar, and powdered sugar with an electric mixer until light and fluffy, about 3 to 5 minutes.
3. Add salt. Continue to beat with electric mixer for about a minute.
4. With a spoon, mix in flour and oats.
5. Split dough into quarters. Roll out a quarter of the dough between two floured sheets of wax paper until approximately 1/8 inch thick. Use cookie cutters to cut dough into rounds. Transfer onto cookie sheets with a pancake turner. (Alternately, drop dough by rounded teaspoons onto cookie sheets and use a floured cookie stamp or a floured bottom of a glass to flatten the dough to the appropriate thickness.)
6. Bake for 8 to 10 minutes until the edges are lightly browned.
7. To make the filling, mix margarine, peanut butter, powdered sugar, and water in a bowl.
8. After cookies are cooled, squish a heaping teaspoonful of filling mixture between two cookies.

"Put on your boots, boots, boots / And parachutes, chutes, chutes!" —"The 82nd Airborne Song"

I guess most areas surrounding military bases have some sort of museum celebrating their local troops, and my temporary home in Fayetteville was not an exception. I have always loved history and museums, so I could think of no better way to spend a lazy Sunday afternoon than wandering through the different exhibits of the Airborne and Special Operations Museum. Among other things, devoting the effort to learning more about the 82nd and Fort Bragg's history felt like a nice way to honor the service of Buddy, the FHOTA, the 504th, and all the rest of the troops.

When I first walked in the front door, I saw what I thought was a mannequin standing at parade rest and dressed in a WWII army uniform, which I recognized from pictures I have seen of my dad from the same period. I was startled when this "mannequin" greeted me with a "Good morning, young lady," which led me to the discovery that this was *actually* a WWII veteran—airborne to boot. He was the museum's greeter and did his job admirably by engaging in appropriate casual conversation about me, Buddy, my current visit, and acceptable methods of contributions to the museum. He reminded me so much of my own father that I found it hard to move along to the actual museum part of my visit. A few minutes into my conversation with this gentleman, however, another man joined the discussion. It turned out that he was a Vietnam veteran, also airborne. As the WWII airborne vet began to engage the Vietnam airborne vet in a comparison of war stories, I felt it was time to move on.

The museum was set up as a winding timeline of different exhibits that took visitors from the 82nd's beginnings before World War II through to today and their current mission. Wherever possible, the museum depicted all the significant events and defining moments of the paratrooper, both past and present, in walk-through scenes that helped you feel as though you were actually there. I began my journey through the museum at the scene of the very first test jump of the very first paratrooper on

August 16, 1940, as posted on the plaque that introduced the exhibit. From that display, there was more than a single option for the flow of the timeline. There was a
museum map available, but I believe it had to be purchased through the gift shop
which was on the opposite side of the lobby from where I was. I did, however, try
to maintain the chronological order of things through exhibit comments and direc-
tional arrows, at least at the beginning.

After the first test jump, I started my transition into World War II. I was entering
into the part of the museum where there were many dark nooks and crannies as a
part of the exhibits. In addition, most of them contained lifelike mannequins dressed
as soldiers training their weapons on the museum's visitors as they wandered by. It
was very exciting, but also a little creepy . . . but maybe that was because I was alone.
It didn't matter though because I was on a mission.

The exhibit that I really hoped to find was something on the Anzio beachhead of
Italy where the soldiers of the 504th received their nickname "The Devils in Baggy
Pants" from the enemy. When Buddy was accepted into airborne school and the 82nd
Division, I think he was more proud that he was becoming one of those "devils" than
anything else. I was excited to experience where it all began but was not sure what
time period I was looking for. I tried to take a logical path to lead me to the 504th
and its beginnings in 1942, but I was not having much success. Each door I stepped
through seemed to present two or more different timelines with none clearly identified as to where they would end—not to mention that there always seemed to be
one that lead back to the beginning and that first test jump. At times, it was a little
frustrating.

I started paying more attention to how I would next alter the timeline rather than
fully experiencing my incredible surroundings and the amazing displays, but that
changed when I stepped through a door somewhere around 1943 that greatly resembled the hatch of a plane. I had stepped into a smallish room painted sky blue with
sporadic white clouds splashed across it. When I looked up, I was under the canopy of
an opened parachute with its risers falling freely about my shoulders. It was an awesome experience, after which I totally forgot to care whether or not I was following
the correct timeline to the 504th.

I slowed my pace a bit to really digest the exhibits of this museum. It was not long
before I was in Normandy in June 1944—D-Day. This was one of the walk-through
scenes, and it was amazing. Against the painted backdrops of war-torn Europe, there
were different structures that jutted out toward the timeline path, even as sounds of
the invasion played in the background. On one side of the path, there were huge full

hedges that almost came up to the path. Armed Nazi soldiers were hiding behind the hedges as well as a few of the structures. On the other side of the path were depictions of paratroopers landing and trying to advance. I stood on the path between the two, by myself but not really feeling alone. According to the exhibit's comments, the hedges were one of the unforeseen problems that the paratroopers faced after being dropped behind enemy lines that day.

It was at the very moment I was acknowledging that it was quite disturbing standing there with all those soldiers behind the hedges—even if they were only mannequins—that the lights went out! So there I was, standing in 1944 Normandy, with the only illumination coming from a few distant skylights and one emergency light. I was not able to see enough to know which direction to head in order to make my way back to 2007 and the front door, but I certainly saw enough to feel the creepiness of all those hidden soldiers staring at me. I was actually missing the sounds of battle that had also died with the absence of electricity. I decided my only option was to remain still and wait for the lights to come back on. Unfortunately, that did not happen.

For as many people as I had seen in the museum that morning, I was all alone there in Normandy. Waiting in the semidarkness and silence, I looked around and tried to determine, among other things, if I could actually decipher between man and mannequin; I was unsure. I began to feel very vulnerable. I then wondered who was just around the edge wall to the exhibit. Was there a family, maybe a dad with a mom and their kids, who would be willing to rescue a damsel in distress in Normandy if the need arose? I waited uneasily for whatever was to come next.

After what seemed like forever but was probably only about five minutes, a museum worker with a flashlight wandered back to escort all of us who were trapped somewhere between 1943 and 1944 to the emergency exit. Once back in the light, I pondered my options. Do I wait for the museum to open back up, or do I find some other way to spend my Sunday? It was more of a difficult decision than one might imagine. After all, I never did find Anzio, Italy, and the battle that named the Devils in Baggy Pants.

Meandering through the various scenes, exhibits, and years, I was moved not only by what my eyes saw but also by what my heart saw as a connection between those young men of the 1940s and the young men who were currently serving in Iraq. At the time of the blackout, I had not reached anything beyond World War II, but my short time in the museum did give me insight into my son's current situation. Even more, when I looked into the faces of the airborne soldiers in the museum's pictures, I saw what I observed in the FHOTA's faces. As the museum depicted the various scenes of World War II through pictures and walk-through panoramas, it was not difficult to see Toby, Shelby, Christian, and my son somehow involved. Most certainly, the 504th's dedication, determination, diligence, and heart had not diminished in the sixty-plus years between World War II and the Surge of 2007. Though the times were different and the equipment improved, the uncertainties and danger really were the same. What had been only stories that Buddy shared with me a few weeks back had now somehow taken on a tangible feel.

I regretted not being able to finish my tour of the museum—it took another three hours for the lights to return—but I am glad I saw what I did. Even though my visit was short, I left that museum with even greater pride in my son, the FHOTA, and the rest of the 504th.

On-a-Dare Cookies

1/2 cup shortening
1/2 cup margarine
1 1/2 cups powdered sugar
1/2 cup brown sugar
3/4 cup crumbled bleu cheese
1 teaspoon vanilla
1 egg

1 teaspoon baking soda
1/2 teaspoon salt
3 cups flour
3/4 cup chopped pecans
1/2 cup dried cranberries
Blue sprinkles

1. Preheat oven to 350 degrees.
2. Cream together shortening, margarine, powdered sugar, brown sugar, bleu cheese, vanilla, and egg with an electric mixer until light and fluffy, about 3 to 5 minutes.
3. Add baking soda and salt. Continue to beat with electric mixer for about a minute.
4. With a spoon, mix in flour until well blended. Stir in pecans and dried cranberries.
5. Drop dough by rounded teaspoons onto cookie sheets. Squish the dough flat with the bottom of a glass dipped in flour until dough is 1/8 inch thick.
6. Decorate the tops of the cookies with blue sprinkles.
7. Bake for 10 to 12 minutes or until the edges are just beginning to brown.

Double, double, toil and trouble!

I was neck deep in my temporary, substitute life, but I was not insulated from incidents happening in Iraq. I awoke one morning and showered and dressed, just like all the other mornings. I headed to my kitchenette to grab a mug of tea before I left for work, and on my way, I switched on the news for a bit of catching up. I was greeted with a story straight from the streets of Baghdad reporting on the deaths of some soldiers in another firefight. I had just spoken to Buddy the night before, so I was confident that my son was still safe; however, that knowledge did not alleviate my feelings of sorrow and regret for the affected soldiers and their families, nor did it stop my stomach from doing flip-flops. Months ago, I had discovered that trouble in Iraq disturbed me greatly no matter what Buddy's team, platoon, or company involvement was. As if I could ever forget, the news report let me know that Iraq was still a dangerous place. It also reminded me to keep praying—and to stop watching the news.

I was determined not to let my support for Buddy and the rest of the guys be diminished despite my current assignment, especially after the morning's news. Being that it was October, it was definitely time to get the Halloween edition of care packages off to "my boys." I liked to get any holiday boxes off early enough that the troops had the opportunity to enjoy the celebration. This was even more important when talking about fake pumpkins to carve and foam-sheet haunted houses to build.

I already had most of the shopping for the care packages completed. I had collected various Halloween crafts, candy masks, skeleton PEZ dispensers, and gummy worms in assorted sizes and colors. During one of my shopping excursions, I had found a Halloween cookie cutter and press set, which I would use to make some Cake Mix Cutouts, a recipe I created while noticing all the different autumn-type flavors in the cake mix section. I would bake them up right before I closed up the care package boxes, but what I still needed was some unanticipated distraction to bring it all together. I needed something like what I sent to Keith during his second deployment to Baghdad in 2004. Along with the standard candies, decorations, PEZ dispensers (there *always* has to be at least one PEZ dispenser), and crafts, in his Halloween care package that year I included the pièce de résistance: a scarecrow flashlight with a pumpkin head that when turned on would shine a light through the pumpkin head's open mouth as it cried out "Ga-ERrrrrrrrrr!"

Keith loved it and kept it on his desk throughout the rest of his deployment, and it turned out to be quite useful. He tells the story of how one evening, the compound lost electricity, which was not an uncommon occurrence. In the dark, no one else could find any form of light, let alone their flashlights, but Keith's trusty scarecrow flashlight was right there in front of him. He tells of how all over the compound, first there was darkness, then the tell-tale "Ga-ERrrrrrrrrr," and then light. Keith was the hero that day—he and his trusty scarecrow flashlight, thanks to his Aunt Maggie.

In the following years of care packages, I had never been able to match the greatness of that scarecrow flashlight—until now. While hunting through the local shops for trinkets and treasures to include in the upcoming Halloween care packages, I stumbled across what I considered to be a rare find. It was the perfect distraction: a little plastic black cat wearing a purple witch hat, standing on a patch of plastic green grass. Sitting on the grass under the raised black tail of the cat was a small plastic brown bag. Now, what made this cat so special was that when its back was pushed, the cat would meow and hiss as it pooped out a brown jelly bean into the brown bag. *What* could possibly be more perfect for a group of soldiers fighting on the front lines? I actually felt I had equaled the magnificence of the scarecrow flashlight—although most likely not its usefulness.

It was not hard to imagine that something as brilliant as my little black cat was scooped up immediately by all who saw its profoundness, especially in a town like Fayetteville where everyone was looking for care package treats. There were not more than a couple left on the shelves of any given store that carried this little treasure. I scoured all the local shops and bought up every pooping plastic black cat that I could find, even the ones whose little plastic tab (to prevent the meowing and hissing of the cat until it reached its final destination) had been removed. Even so, I only found a half dozen or so cats to split between the two care packages that I was sending to the 1-504th.

Normally, the premature removal of the little plastic tabs would not have been an issue, but these cats were being shipped to Iraq. I figured that it would not be too much of a problem to rig up the untabbed few to prevent them from sounding off from the confines of their packaging as they were being shipped; it was simply a matter of interrupting the battery's connection inside the cat without breaking the stupid thing open to accomplish it. I honestly believed that I had achieved that goal. After carefully packing all the goodies into two large boxes, one for C-Company and one for B-Company, I put them into the car so I could mail them during lunch the next day, which had become my standard operating procedure for Mondays.

Generally, the post office on base was a quiet little place with hardly ever more than one customer in line when I was there, if that. I had no idea why, but this time when I arrived at the post office, it was full. There were four people in front of me, and almost immediately after I got in line, another two arrived behind me. It was a little frustrating, especially because the line was moving so slowly! I only had a limited amount of time for lunch, and I had yet to get something to eat. Feeling the frustration of the slow-moving line, I set the care packages onto the floor in front of me.

I guess the shock of the packages hitting the floor was a little more abrupt than I had anticipated, because the moment the boxes touched the ground, *Meow, meow, FSSST, FSSST, meow!* rung out in that little mail room. Everyone looked around for the source of the noise. I debated pretending that I had no idea where it was coming from and looking around as well, but it occurred to me that I had a bigger problem. If a package a mom is sending to a war zone hisses, will it arrive at that war zone without being blown up by the bomb squad? I was not sure, so I had to confess that I was the cause of the hissing.

Every time I inched the packages along in line, the plastic cats would sound off from inside the care packages and everyone around me would giggle. No matter how gently I tried to move the boxes, those stupid plastic cats meowed away, and I was not sure what to do about it. The postmaster did not seem to think that there would be a problem, but I was not convinced. In a last-ditch effort to make sure my son could enjoy his Halloween goodies, I borrowed a black Magic Marker and spent the rest of my wait in line writing a big, bold warning that I hoped would be enough:

HISSING NOISES ARE COMING FROM FAKE PLASTIC CATS

Cake Mix Cutouts

2/3 cup shortening	1 egg
1/3 cup margarine	1/4 teaspoon salt
1/3 cup brown sugar	1 1/3 cups flour
1/3 cup powdered sugar	2 cups cake mix

1. Preheat oven to 375 degrees.
2. Cream together shortening, margarine, brown sugar, powdered sugar, and egg with an electric mixer until light and fluffy, about 3 to 5 minutes.
3. Add salt. Continue to beat with electric mixer for about a minute.
4. With a spoon, mix in flour and cake mix.
5. Split dough into quarters. Roll out a quarter of the dough between two floured sheets of wax paper until approximately 1/4 inch thick. Use cookie cutters to cut dough into various shapes. Transfer cookies onto cookie sheets with a pancake turner. (Alternately, drop cookies by rounded teaspoons onto cookie sheets and use a floured cookie stamp or a floured bottom of a glass to flatten the dough to the appropriate thickness.)
6. Bake for 10 to 12 minutes.

"How much is that doggie in the window?"

The week began like any of the others since temporarily relocating to Fayetteville, yet things were not feeling exactly right. The work was steady and, by all accounts, going well; the weather, on the other hand, was remaining quite un-fall-like, not to mention that I was slowly coming to the realization that there was no escaping the anxiety and anguish of being the mother of a soldier serving in a war zone. There was nothing catastrophic or earth-shattering that I could point to that would account for my diminishing good spirits. I reasoned that it could be nothing more than an evaporation of the natural high I had been on because Buddy had been home, or it could simply be a growing case of homesickness because I missed my daughter, her boyfriend, and my big, dumb dog! But whatever the reasoning—and despite the positive aspects of my life—I was just feeling a little blah.

It was about 9:00 on a Thursday evening when one of the women I had been working with called me with a problem. Kristine and I had gotten to know each other on a personal level on an ill-fated wine tasting tour in the mountains to the west of Fayetteville. The wine tasting was a good time and went quite well; however, it was our decision to stop at a seafood place in the mountains before heading back to Fayetteville that tainted our otherwise lovely excursion. That stop added a bit of "indigestion" to the trip back to our hotels. We learned something that Saturday—mainly to never eat seafood if you are not near a sea. Through that experience, however, we discovered that we seemed to be kindred spirits, if only in the poor choices we have made throughout our lives.

Kristine had called to ask if I could keep a puppy for her. I knew she had brought her dog along with her for her stint in Fayetteville, but she was not talking about him. Earlier that evening, Kristine was walking her dog along the busiest section of a six-lane road that separates two shopping centers near where she was staying. She noticed a small dog dodging traffic at one of the intersections. Worried about the safety of what appeared to be a puppy, she called to it. To her surprise, the little dog came to her immediately. He had no collar nor any other type of ID. Even so, Kristine spent the next couple hours trying to find the puppy's rightful owners by knocking on doors in the area surrounding that intersection.

When her attempts failed, she took the puppy home. Unfortunately, her roughly sixty-pound dog was not comfortable cohabiting with a roughly ten-pound puppy, especially when it came to sharing Kristine's affections. She had nowhere else to turn, so she asked me if I would keep the puppy overnight and take him to a shelter the next morning. I told her to bring him on over to my hotel room, but I had reservations. I was a little hesitant to take on this little dog—as well as the responsibility that went along with him—even if it was only for one night. I was all too aware of my weakness for small fluffy things, and I knew I was already vulnerable due to my bout of homesickness.

About a half hour later, Kristine knocked on my door. I opened it to let them in and saw my coworker standing there with her arms full of a long-haired, fluffy, black-and-brown dog—black on the longer outer hair and brown on the fluff underneath. At first glance, anyone would have guessed the dog was a Pomeranian given his upright, pointy ears, his foxlike face, and his poofy hair. But this was obviously not a purebred. Kristine put him on the floor and walked in herself. The puppy immediately went to work exploring his surroundings while Kristine and I chatted about the options and possible outcomes of this situation.

I watched the dog as he went bounding across the room after wadded-up pieces of paper we were throwing for him to fetch. Though he was small, he was obviously no longer a puppy by the strictest definition of the word. He certainly was a cute little thing, though. Buddy and I had always talked about getting an STD (that would be Stupid Tiny Dog) to go along with our own BDD (Big Dumb Dog, the Whiskey-Dog), but the details of our planned acquisition were completely different. We wanted a black-and-tan Cavalier King Charles Spaniel, which tended to have similar features to a Bernese, only on a micro scale. In fact, we had already picked the planned STD's name—"Reese's," as in the peanut butter cup. As I watched the dog sniffing around the room, my heart went soft. And as I tripped over the coffee table trying to get to the dog who was now lifting his leg to pee on the couch, I realized that I am one of those people who could never turn my back on anyone or anything in need. It was highly unlikely that I was going to start now, so I agreed to take the dog for the night.

Once the sleeping arrangements of the puppy were confirmed, Kristine left. I shut the door behind her and locked it. When I turned around, this fluffy, adorable little dog was sitting on the floor behind me, staring up at me with his big brown eyes and happily wagging his tail in a loving but rather disturbing way, considering he was just plucked out of a six-lane highway. What I knew about him so far was very limited. He loved attention, playing fetch, and peeing on things he had no business peeing on. All that being said, I was falling in love with the little guy. But, as a lifetime of experience had taught me, falling in love was one thing; protecting oneself was something else entirely!

In an attempt to be "safe" considering my little guest's unknown origins, I barricaded an area near the bathroom for the puppy. I put out some water and food that Kristine had left, put the dog in the barricaded area, and turned out the lights for sleep. However, my little guest would have nothing to do with any of it. No matter how I configured the barricade, nor how high I made it, the puppy would simply not stay behind it. He was not aggressive and not disagreeable, but for that little dog, the only place was on the bed with me. And, despite all my concerns regarding "where he had been," the night passed uneventfully—mostly with this puppy just sitting there at the foot of my bed staring at me; at least, he was every time I opened my eyes to look.

The only organization willing to accept the dog, who I had not yet named because I did not want to get too attached to him—like that helped at all—was animal control. After our one night together, I was a little concerned regarding the implications of this arrangement, but I also had no choice. If I was to have any success in finding where this puppy belonged, I needed him to be put in the care of people who had more experience in finding wayward pets' owners than I did. So, after informing work that I would be late, I took the dog to the local pound.

With no collar and no leash, when I reached animal control, I simply carried the dog in. If looks could kill, I would be dead right now. Erroneously thinking that I was simply trying to "dispose" of a dog that was no longer "convenient," the workers behind the counter looked at me with such disdain that it made me extremely uncomfortable. It was not until they realized that the dog was not mine and that I was simply trying to find his rightful owner that their attitudes softened. They verified that he was not electronically tagged to forever connect owner to pet and then took him to the back. Visions of Mugsy's last walk from Disney's *Lady and the Tramp* flashed through my head as I watched this little dog that I had become so attached to so quickly disappear behind the double doors. My last words to the clerks behind the counter were, "If his owner doesn't claim him, I'll take him home!" And, after leaving every possible means to contact me, I left.

In the following days, I was consumed with thoughts of this little puppy. I had not shared his existence with anyone, because I did not know how the whole experience would unfold. In the meantime, as I prayed for Buddy, the FHOTA, the 504th, and our troops, I also prayed for a small, fluffy, precocious dog that sat by himself in a cage at animal control, waiting for someone to bring him home.

Mini Reese's Cups Cookies

1/2 cup shortening
2/3 cup margarine
1 tablespoon light corn syrup
1/2 tablespoon vanilla
1 cup dark brown sugar
1/3 cup powdered sugar
1 egg

1 1/2 teaspoons cinnamon
1 1/2 teaspoons baking soda
3/4 teaspoon salt
2 1/3 cups flour
18 Mini Reese's Peanut Butter
    Cups, frozen and coarsely
    chopped

1. Preheat oven to 350 degrees.
2. Cream together shortening, margarine, corn syrup, vanilla, brown sugar, powdered sugar, and egg with an electric mixer until light and fluffy, about 3 to 5 minutes.
3. Add cinnamon, baking soda, and salt. Continue to beat with electric mixer for about a minute.
4. With a spoon, mix in flour until well blended. Stir in the frozen Reese's cups.
5. Drop dough by rounded teaspoons onto cookie sheets.
6. Bake for 12 to 15 minutes or until lightly browned.

Something lost, but something gained

I was down to my last couple weeks in Fayetteville, and the pangs of homesickness were becoming a constant companion. Even though I was enjoying my assignment and ultimately glad that I had accepted it, the bottom line was that I had left all that I loved to be here. In addition to my longings for home—or possibly because of them—sleep had become a bit elusive as well. Laying in my bed in the dark, waiting for slumber to overtake me, I was haunted by uneasy feelings that somehow things were not right. More than feelings, they almost seemed like premonitions of something horrible waiting to happen. What I was unable to figure out was whether my lack of sleep was a result of the premonitions or the cause. I was a mess, but I still had a couple weeks to go.

The day after I learned that we were going to be able to adopt the puppy, now named Sergeant in honor of where he was found, my spirits were a little more upbeat than they had been of late. The morning began as usual with a bit of world news from the TV in my hotel room and then a cup of tea on my short drive into work. Despite being homesick for the better portion of my stay in Fayetteville, I had settled into a comfortable routine in my temporary life. This routine included being pestered for cookies within five minutes of walking through the door to my office area, as my coworkers always received leftovers of whatever creation I had sent to Buddy and the rest of the troops.

"Any culinary masterpieces last night, Maggie?" one of my coworkers asked.

"Not last night," I replied. "You know I only bake on the weekends."

"Couldn't you make an exception for us?" I heard from across the room. "Just this once?"

I turned around to see exactly who this last request had come from but was greeted by my supervisor walking up to me from his office. He had an unusual look on his face, but I could not determine whether it was concern, frustration at the ruckus I caused by simply walking through the door, or something else.

"You have a phone call," he said in a tone that scared me. "It's Haley. Take it in my office."

Because those of us who were only there temporarily did not have our own desks, let alone phones or computers, any "emergency" calls, including a phone call from Buddy just to say hi, came in through our supervisor's office. So when he came to me and said my daughter was on the line, I swear my heart stopped for a moment. The way I saw it, there were several possibilities as to why my daughter would be calling me at work so early in the morning, and none of them seemed good. Trying to stay as calm as possible, I walked into his office and picked up the phone. As I did so, my supervisor left the room and shut the door behind him to give me privacy. I sat down at his desk, took a deep breath, and then spoke into the receiver.

"Hello?" My voice quivered as I simultaneously tried not to hear while bracing myself for anything Haley might say.

"Mom?" Haley said, and then she paused for a moment. I was getting ready to speak again when Haley continued. "Mom," she said again, "I have some bad news."

My heart was pounding so hard that I could feel it in my ears. I quickly tried to figure out the definition of "bad." I had heard nothing on the news out of Iraq, and I had spoken with Nana the night before to tell her about Sergeant. What else was there? I tried to control the tone and tenor of my voice when I asked, "What's going on, Haley? What's happened?"

There was another pause and then Haley said, "Whiskey is gone, Mama. Whiskey ran away!"

My head spun as I tried to wrap my brain around what my daughter had just said. *Run away? The Whiskey-Dog, run away from home?! Not just highly unlikely, but impossible!* As I started to ask for clarification, Haley began speaking again.

"Well, he really didn't *run* away; he just kind of strolled off, slow-like!"

"What are you talking about?" I asked, probably with more of an edge in my voice than I had intended.

"When we went to the farm this weekend, we decided to take Whiskey with us," Haley answered.

Leo's parents, Greg and Ellen, lived on several acres about an hour outside of Richmond, Virginia. When Haley and Leo went to visit, they often took the Marjorie-Dog with them for a few days of running "free" out in the country. When they told me about this trip, they mentioned that they were planning on taking the Whiskey-Dog as well. "The good news is," she said, "up until he disappeared, he was having a great time! But when it came time to leave, he did not come when we called. I mean, he was only outside for a couple of minutes without someone there with him. You know he doesn't *run*, Mama, so he couldn't have gone far, right? Yet we called and called for him and he didn't come. I figured he was just being stubborn, you know? Like when he decides he's not going to listen to you anymore and just pretends that you're not there."

I knew that the Whiskey-Dog could be stubborn, and I know from personal experience that, though he did not do it often, if he did not want to listen, he just did not listen. I knew how much the thought of this conversation must have tormented Haley, let alone the conversation itself. I tried to muster up a few words to let her know that I was not angry at her, though I was definitely sad that Whiskey was gone.

"Yeah, I know!" was all I managed.

"I figured he was just out in the fields with the cows so we couldn't see him, and he just wasn't ready to come home yet," she added.

Haley had a point. Whiskey was a big black dog, and the cows were big black cows. It was no wonder that Whiskey would just blend in until he ended up so far away he was lost. But now what? Haley went on to explain that they all took the Monday off in hopes that someone would stumble across him if they spread out in the daylight, but it was to no avail. By this point, they were alerting surrounding counties to be on the lookout for Whiskey, and they were putting up "Lost dog" fliers all over the neighborhood. The prospect of ever finding him again was not looking too good. And then came my next thought: *What about Buddy?!*

I let my supervisor back into his office and explained what had happened. As Nana often said, Whiskey was a great, big, lumbering, gentle giant. He had never been microchipped, so if someone just decided to keep him, there would be nothing we could do. I was so excited about being able to adopt Sergeant and had figured I would be sailing through my last few days in Fayetteville on my newly acquired high note, but life had another agenda.

"I didn't want the puppy to *replace* the Whiskey-Dog!" I explained to my supervisor. "And I certainly don't want to cause someone else this pain, but since nobody claimed the puppy, what other choice did I have? And *how* on earth am I supposed to tell Buddy about Whiskey?"

This was the dog that had seen Buddy through some incredibly rough days; it was not going to be easy to tell him that Whiskey had disappeared. I was beginning to wonder if I should even try, given where he was, but my supervisor was adamant that Buddy needed to be told. I was not relishing that thought. I did not like the idea that I might be creating danger for Buddy by upsetting him with bad news, and I certainly did not believe that I should just put it all in a letter. Eventually, I decided that I would have to tell Buddy the next time he called.

The evening after I took Haley's call at work, I had a very difficult phone conversation with Leo's dad, Greg. He had called me to convey the absolute anguish he felt over Whiskey's disappearance and his determination to do everything possible to get him back.

"Ellen and I really enjoyed having Whiskey here," Greg said. "He is such a great dog! When we were having dinner on Saturday evening, he came right over to the table and sat at its corner between Ellen and me. Whiskey looked longingly around the table at everyone sitting there having their dinner, and when no one would give him any food, he rested his head right there on the corner and sighed as loud as he could!" Greg started to laugh as he added, "I told him that we didn't allow that behavior at our house, that dogs were not allowed to rest their heads on the table!"

Though I knew that Greg was trying to comfort me, the things he said only reminded me of the uniqueness of Whiskey and the hurt that he was gone. Still, I could tell that Greg really cared.

He was honest about his concerns as well. "We are very worried about Whiskey's well-being, because the temperature is dropping below freezing at night," Greg said, "and there would be no food available to him."

Those thoughts were bad enough to consider, but Greg had more. "We also worry about the dognappers that are known to be active in our area, not to mention that there are also several packs of coyotes roaming around. Whiskey is a very large dog, but an entire pack of coyotes would be more than a match for him."

Once again, my stomach was twisted into knots. The prospects for Whiskey's return seemed slim at best. No matter what the outcome, though, I knew we would do everything we could to get the Whiskey-Dog back—the problem was that it just might not be enough.

I learned a new lesson this week—I learned that not every bad thing that could happen during this deployment would be out of Iraq. It was one of those emotionally draining times that left me feeling unquestionably that I simply could not do it—any of it—anymore. I just wanted everything to be over and back to normal—immediately—but I was afraid that was never going to be the case again!

Half-and-Half Cookies

3/4 cup shortening

1/2 cup margarine

1 1/2 cups powdered sugar

1/4 cup light corn syrup

1/2 teaspoon vanilla

1/2 teaspoon butternut flavoring

1 egg

1/2 teaspoon baking soda

1/4 teaspoon cream of tartar

1/2 teaspoon salt

2 1/2 cups flour

Chocolate half:

1/4 cup powdered cocoa

1/2 cup powdered sugar

1/2 cup mini chocolate chips

Walnut half:

1/4 cup flour

1/2 cup chopped walnuts

1. Preheat oven to 350 degrees.
2. Cream together shortening, margarine, powdered sugar, corn syrup, vanilla, butternut flavoring, and egg with an electric mixer until light and fluffy, about 3 to 5 minutes.
3. Add baking soda, cream of tartar, and salt. Continue to beat with electric mixer for about a minute.
4. With a spoon, mix in flour until well blended.
5. Split the dough equally between two bowls.
6. For the chocolate half, mix the powdered cocoa, powdered sugar, and mini chocolate chips into one of the bowls.
7. For the walnut half, mix the additional flour into the second bowl until well blended. Stir in the walnuts.
8. Drop half a rounded teaspoon of each onto cookie sheets, making sure that both halves are touching (so that when baked, the halves will become a whole cookie). Fill the cookie sheet in this manner, leaving an inch or so between each cookie.
9. Bake for 10 to 12 minutes or until the light half of the cookie is lightly browned.

One man's STD is another man's treasure . . . ? (Or something like that!)

The scariest component of the previous few days was experiencing firsthand how life can, and does, turn on a dime—not something I ever relished being reminded of, let alone with Buddy serving overseas. The thought that Whiskey was possibly—and, in all likelihood, probably—gone forever stung my heart, but it did not take a far stretch of the imagination to understand that things could definitely be worse. It was a difficult balancing act to feel the pain of my loss but thank God for its limited extent. In fact, I was afraid of my own sorrow for fear the Fates would up the ante. It was befuddling, and my heart spun relentlessly between regret and gratitude. Worse yet, I loved to hear from my son, but I was practically avoiding any communication from him because I did not want to have to tell Buddy that the Whiskey-Dog, *his* dog, was gone.

My life became a series of phone calls with Haley, Leo, and Leo's parents, discussing what course of action was being taken and what our next plan of attack would be in making sure all viable options—and some long shots—were exercised in our attempts to find and bring the Whiskey-Dog home. Pictures of Whiskey decorated telephone poles with contact information and pleas for help. Local radio stations were issuing alerts and requests for information. Neighboring county officials and animal rescue had all been notified to be on the lookout, and Greg and Ellen and their neighbors continued to keep their eyes peeled. Leo's parents were even offering a $100 reward for any information leading to Whiskey's return. Down in Fayetteville, I was getting updates on all efforts every few hours, but it was killing me that there was nothing I could do to help. All that was left for me was prayer and the endless wait for news—any news.

And then—once again—my life turned on a dime.

Three days after Haley's first call that let me know the Whiskey-Dog was gone, I took another phone call at work from my daughter. "Hey Mom," she began. "I'm sorry to be calling you at work again, but I just had to give you the news—Whiskey showed up back at the farm! Almost exactly three days to the minute, he decided to come back home again!"

"He's back?!" I exclaimed. "Where was he? Who found him? Where has he been?"

"Hold on a second!" Haley scolded. "Give me a chance to tell you! Leo just got off the phone with his dad. We were awoken this morning by Greg sending us a picture of Whiskey that he took with his cell phone and we had to know what was going on, so we called him back right away and then I called you right away!"

I knew that Leo must have been relieved. Even though I had mostly talked with Haley over the past three days regarding the whole ordeal, she had said some things indicating that Leo felt terribly responsible. It was he who had let Whiskey out that morning before stepping back inside only for a moment, leaving Whiskey to wander off. He did not expect that from Whiskey—none of us would have—but he ultimately felt the stress of the guilt. I was almost as happy for him as I was knowing that Whiskey was coming back home again.

I realized that my mind was wandering, yet Haley was trying to tell me how this all came about. It was rather rude of me, but I interrupted her midsentence and asked her to start the story all over again.

"It is a great story, Mom! You need to listen to it," she reprimanded me before beginning again. "Apparently Greg felt he was running out of ideas and options on how to find Whiskey. He just couldn't figure out—well, none of us could—how such a large dog could so completely disappear, even in a rural area like where the farm is. He said he decided to grab a little thinking time in the woods. He took his tractor and his dog, Speckles, and began his trek down the trail that led to the woods. He said he kept on trying to think like a very large dog to figure out where he would go and what he would do if he got separated from his people. Greg just wasn't convinced that Whiskey would try to find his way home again, like Leo and I thought—but, if not that, he just couldn't figure out what happened."

"So what *did* happen?" I interrupted.

"I'm getting there," Haley said. "Greg was continuing to head up the path through the woods when he noticed Speckles starting to act a little strange, as if she sensed or smelled something. She would leave his side and trot ahead a couple hundred feet toward a neighbor's pasture and then return back to his side. She did this several times, which was really unusual. Greg was afraid she might have detected some coyotes or something. He shut the tractor down and stood up on it to get a better idea of what was upsetting his dog. He listened closely for any tell-tale rustles and studied the direction Speckles kept on taking. That was when he spotted this huge animal ambling through the high grass of the pasture between his and his neighbor's property."

"Was it Whiskey?" I asked. "Wait a minute; is the Whiskey-Dog OK?" I demanded, a little concerned as to the direction the story was taking.

"At first Greg thought it was a bear—it certainly was big enough," Haley answered, ignoring my questions. "He became concerned for Speckles and sat back down on his tractor to start it back up again. But before he had a chance to, the animal had approached the pasture fence. He said he noticed the Whiskey-Dog's white muzzle and then the two long floppy ears. Greg yelled for him and was actually a little surprised that Whiskey came right up to him. It was so sweet, Mama. Greg told Leo that he was unable to hold back his tears of joy as he gave Whiskey a 'good head and chest scratch.'"

"So Whiskey is OK then?" I interrupted again.

"Yeah. Greg told Leo that Whiskey was hungry and very thirsty, but other than that, he seemed to be fine," Haley answered. "But it was also a little funny how he got Whiskey back to the cabin. Greg said he was a little concerned that Whiskey might wander off again during the half-mile or so walk back to the house, so he left the tractor where it was. He had to use his belt as a leash, which he fastened under Whiskey's collar," Haley said with a laugh. "Greg said that he had to hold his trousers up with one hand and his belt with the other as he hoofed it back up the path to the cabin."

I chuckled at the mental image. "I am so glad it's all over and *all* OK!" I told Haley, feeling both relieved and a little choked up. "But is there no indication as to where he went or what he was doing these past few days?"

"Nope, none!" Haley answered.

The lack of information available about the Whiskey-Dog's three-day hiatus did not repress the generation of quite a few speculations. Leo wondered whether Whiskey found himself a girl and just wanted to spend a little extra time with her. Personally, I surmised that Whiskey was in some way having a sort of mid-life crisis and decided he wanted to try his hand at being a cow. Haley just figured the dog was off in a field somewhere saying "I'm not listening! I'm not listening!" every time she called, because Whiskey *was* a stubborn dog!

For all of our speculation, there was one thing I knew for sure. In less than a week, I would be heading back up the highway to home, and from what I was hearing, Whiskey would be there to greet me. It was at that moment, just like that—the flip of a switch, the turn of a dime—that my world felt normal again. I just could not imagine my home without that big, gentle, stubborn dog! In addition, I was now looking forward to a phone call from Buddy so I could fill him in on all the exciting details of the last couple of weeks, especially now that we knew everything had a happy ending.

Lately, however, phone calls from Buddy had been few and far between. I felt strongly it was time to get the whole story to him, even if it was only in a letter. That night when I got back to my hotel room, I began my letter-writing process in the standard fashion: I put on my sweats, grabbed my cell phone, and headed for the exercise room to gather my thoughts. The room was not an extensive one, but it had enough equipment for six people. Most of the time when I had been there, I was alone, which made it nice for "creative thinking," especially when I tended to "creative think" out loud, but that night, I shared the room with two other people.

I was not even a full mile into my elliptical workout when my cell phone rang. It was Buddy.

"Hey, Mom! What's up?" Buddy asked when I answered the phone.

"Buddy!" I responded. "Guess what? I've got our STD now!" I exclaimed with absolute glee.

I was focused on telling Buddy the exciting news about our new family member, but Buddy did not seem to be on the same page as I was.

"What?!" Buddy responded.

"STD!" I replied with pride. "I found an STD for us. I have him now, and I can't wait for you to meet him! I know you're gonna *love* him!"

Of course, I do realize that there was another definition to the acronym STD that did not include stupid tiny dogs, and I was not paying attention to the other exercisers in the room who might be overhearing my conversation. It just seemed to me that the actual meaning of my statements should have been obvious. That being said, when the runner on the treadmill next to me called it quits after what must have been only a couple of miles and left the room, I thought nothing of it. However, at this point, Buddy began to understand what I was saying.

"You got Reese's?" Buddy asked.

"Well, yes, but no," I said. "I have named our STD Sergeant!" At this point, the second exerciser abruptly left the room, but I barely even noticed as I continued my conversation with my son.

"And this STD is not a spaniel but a little mixed dog that Kristine and I rescued from traffic," I explained. "But trust me! This dog *is* tiny, and *is* undeniably stupid, in a very intelligent sort of way, so he definitely fits the definition of STD!"

Buddy did not seem as excited about Sergeant as I was, and that was a little disappointing. I just contributed his reaction to being where he was, but somehow his lack of enthusiasm for our new family member made it that much more difficult to tell him about Whiskey.

"OK," I began. "I have something to tell you, but first you need to understand that everything is OK."

"OK . . . ?" Buddy answered apprehensively.

I proceeded to tell the story of Whiskey's big adventure, making sure to keep the story upbeat—despite its content—to emphasize that everything really was *OK*. I ended the story by explaining to Buddy that Leo was heading down to the farm to bring Whiskey home the same day I was bringing Sergeant home. "So you see," I added at the very end of the story, "everything is back to normal—except now we have an STD, too."

"Whiskey is OK, though?" Buddy asked.

"Yes! According to Greg, he was tired and hungry, but he was just fine."

Buddy was quiet for a moment before he spoke again. "OK." He paused before adding angrily, "Nothing better happen to my dog before I get home! You all need to be more careful!"

I was a little stunned by his response but also understood. "It's OK, Bud! Everything is *OK* now. I promise we will take more care to watch out for Whiskey. You just need to make sure you take care of *yourself*, you hear?"

With that, we said our good-byes. My letter-writing session was now a moot point for the time being, so I grabbed my towel and cell phone and headed back to my room. My Fayetteville adventure was almost over and I still had packing to do; however, that was not what was on my mind. Despite all that had happened, one thing was clear to me—all was as it had always been, normal—and it felt great.

Lavender Lemon Cookies

Cookie:

3/4 cup margarine

1/3 cup brown sugar

1/3 cup granulated sugar

1 tablespoon lemon juice

1/2 tablespoon light corn syrup

1/2 teaspoon vanilla

1/2 teaspoon lemon flavoring

1 egg

1/4 teaspoon cream of tartar

1/2 teaspoon baking soda

1/2 teaspoon salt

1 3/4 cups flour

Frosting:

1 tub of buttercream frosting, preferably not whipped

1 tablespoon of lavender leaves

1. Preheat oven to 350 degrees.
2. Cream together margarine, brown sugar, granulated sugar, lemon juice, corn syrup, vanilla, lemon flavoring, and egg with an electric mixer until light and fluffy, about 3 to 5 minutes.
3. Add cream of tartar, baking soda, and salt. Continue to beat with electric mixer for about a minute.
4. With a spoon, mix in flour.
5. Grease a 9x11–inch baking dish and spread the dough into it.
6. Bake for 20 to 25 minutes or until lightly browned on edges.
7. To make the frosting, combine buttercream frosting and lavender leaves with an electric mixer.
8. Allow cookies to cool. When cool, spread with lavender frosting mixture. Allow frosting to set before cutting into bars.

Just click your heels together three times and think to yourself, *There's no place like home . . . there's no place like home . . .*

On the first of November, as scheduled, the STD (a.k.a. Sergeant) and I headed back up the road toward home. Earlier in the morning, I had retrieved Sergeant from the veterinarian he was sent to directly from animal control. There he was checked over, neutered, given a rabies shot, and chipped in preparation for his trip north. I had no idea how this little dog was going to react to me and the five-hour road trip ahead of us nor how he was going to adjust to his new life. After all, the only time I had actually spent with Sergeant was the one night before I unceremoniously dumped him at the animal shelter. But upon seeing Sergeant again, he seemed happy to be a part of this new adventure, and I was happy to have him along.

As always, the trip home seemed unending. As we made our way up the highway, I felt that a good use of my time would be to get to know my little passenger. Before I had even picked Sergeant up, I had already bought him a collar and ID tag that stated his new name, address, and phone number, which, with his newly implanted chip, tied him to our house forever. Whether he realized it or not, Sergeant was now a full-fledged member of the Bear Cave, and I was intent on filling him in on what exactly that entailed.

I began talking to him and telling him all about his new life. I guess I did not necessarily believe that he understood a word I said, but I could not think of a better way to pass the time in a car (or anywhere, for that matter) than by talking! I told him about my kids, the dogs, and my life. I also told him about my last few days in Fayetteville since he and I spent our one night together, including my marvelous stroll through the local botanical garden and what I was going to miss most about my stay there. As the miles passed, Sergeant sat quietly in the passenger seat with his little head cocked to one side, appearing to listen attentively to all I had to say. For the next few dozen miles, I talked and Sergeant listened until, eventually, I ran out of things to say.

Though I had enjoyed talking nonstop to my captive audience, I found I was equally enjoying not talking and simply listening to the hum of the car tires as they rolled along the road. Sergeant was still sitting quietly, and even though I was no longer talking, he was still intently watching me. Every once in a while, I would reach over and rub his head or scratch his back, but other than that, I drove and he watched. We had probably gone another fifty or sixty miles when Sergeant let out one quick, loud bark, which startled me so badly I almost ran off the road, and then crawled in my lap and stayed there the rest of the way home. I believed our bonding was not only complete but successful.

We had left an area where the weather was just beginning to cool and small patches of color were only just starting to appear on the trees. However, the closer we got to home, the cooler the outside temperatures became, and the cooler the outside temperatures, the more brilliant the leaves on the trees. By the time we pulled into my driveway, the outside temperature was hovering around forty-five degrees and the neighborhood trees were ablaze with the colors of autumn. It was a breathtaking sight as the leaves floated lazily to the ground in splashes of yellow, orange, and red, shaken from their branches by a slight, crisp breeze. It was a beautiful autumn day that made me feel as though God were giving me a warm, wonderfully reassuring hug!

I had a strong desire to extend that hug as long as I could, so after I emptied the car and introduced Sergeant to his new home, I decided that it was the perfect day for a long walk. I knew that the Whiskey-Dog would have loved a walk through the turning leaves in the chilled air as well—though maybe not so much at that moment, considering he spent those three days "lost" in the woods—but he was not home; Leo had not yet returned from his trip to his parents' to retrieve him. However, rather than pass up the opportunity to enjoy the day, I decided it would be a great time to introduce Sergeant to the neighborhood, in addition to seeing how well he behaved (or misbehaved) on a walk.

With Sergeant securely hooked to his new leash, we started down the driveway. It was too early in the season for raking—at least that is what I told myself—and I purposely kicked up the ankle-deep leaves with every step I took. When the stirred leaves got caught in the afternoon breeze, they swirled around me in a blur of color that reminded me of early morning walks to school through the woods at the end of the street I grew up on. Even as Sergeant tugged at the leash, enticing me to walk faster, I found myself slowing to take in the moment. There were three different paths that Whiskey and I would take depending on which type of walk we were in need of; one was for when we were in a hurry, one was for when we did not have a lot of time but needed exercise and wanted the scenery, and the third, by far our favorite, was over the river and through the woods—well, maybe just a creek, and only that after a heavy rain. Still, with the brilliance of autumn surrounding us and my soul crying for release, I decided it was most certainly a day for a walk through the woods.

I followed the familiar path down the steps and into the woods while my mind meandered down a path of its own, consisting of a myriad of mostly disconnected thoughts. At times, I remembered my youth and walking through the woods to and from my elementary school, but I also remembered my walks with Buddy when he was just a boy through the very same woods I was currently enjoying—not to mention hundreds of walks with the Whiskey-Dog exploring every nook, cranny, and tributary-type creek that flowed throughout the neighborhood and the surrounding wooded areas of the nearby lake. As disjointed as the memories seemed, they somehow felt related and current. For every random thought from my childhood, there was a current pang that ached for that simpler time. For every memory of Buddy as a boy, there was some haunting visual from the last several months to counter it. And as for Whiskey . . . well, I was just happy that he was on his way home again.

Surrounded by the comfort of the woods I was so familiar with, I felt isolated from the emotional turmoil of not only the past couple weeks but the past ten months as well. Sergeant and I wandered down a path into a small gully that led to one of the little tributaries. I was still kicking through the leaves every chance I got, marveling at the contrast of colors that enveloped us. The red, orange, and yellow leaves still on the trees set against the backdrop of an azure sky blended almost seamlessly into the brown, yellow, orange, and red that were now swirling around my feet. It was truly a cathartic experience to breathe in the crisp air while my eyes drank in the spectacular scenery.

I took a path that followed one of the creeks back to my neighborhood. I shuffled my feet through the leaves, enjoying the smells of autumn from both the leaves and the smoke wafting through the air from the chimneys of the surrounding neighborhoods. My mind continued to drift from recollections of the past to thoughts of the present and then to images from the start of our walk. Abruptly, my thoughts crystallized on a paper flier that was tacked to a wood post at the top of the steps that led to the woods.

COPPERHEAD ALERT! it said, followed by an explanation. "There has been an unusually high occurrence of copperheads reported here this year . . ."

Once again, I focused on the leaves that engulfed my feet and the path. "What color are copperhead snakes, anyway?" I wondered out loud to Sergeant. "You realize that you would be the first to encounter any unwelcome surprises on the path, right?"

Sergeant was unmoved by my revelation. Even as he continued to tug at the leash in an attempt to get me to move faster, I was starting to see snakes in every twig and small branch that had fallen onto our path. For me, the walk was over, but unfortunately, we were not out of the woods yet, so to speak! To the dog's delight, I decided it was time to quicken my pace. Skillfully—but certainly not gracefully—I made my way through the last quarter mile of our wooded walk stepping from log to rock to cleared path in an attempt to avoid all snake-colored, leaf-covered areas.

By the time I was heading down our street to home, it was just past dusk and well on its way to dark. Immediately after we turned onto the street, Leo also turned the corner and headed toward our driveway and home. Leo did not see us, but I saw Whiskey sitting in the car, happily staring out the window and watching the world speed by. I was of the opinion that seeing Whiskey again even without his "big adventure" would have been an emotional moment for me; for six years, he had been my sole constant companion. However, considering the recent events, just catching that glimpse of him riding down the road choked me up a bit. Once again, I quickened Sergeant's and my pace for the last couple hundred feet of our walk.

We were just heading up the driveway from the street when Whiskey hopped out of the car. Upon seeing us, he came lumbering down the driveway to greet me and his new "little brother." His tail was wagging, and his huge mouth was slightly opened with his tongue hanging out to the side. As always, the corners of his mouth were turned up at the edges so that it looked like he was smiling. I squatted down onto my heels so that I was eye level with Whiskey, and when he was close enough, I grabbed him around his oversized neck and hugged him with all my might. Though I tried, I could not stop the tears from falling.

For his part, the Whiskey-Dog pushed into me until he knocked me over onto my backside. I was pinned to the driveway by a 150-pound Big Dumb Dog, now sitting on my lap. Not to be ignored, the Stupid Tiny Dog also tried to climb into my lap, ignoring the fact that there was no room. Much to Sergeant's dismay, he was accosted by Whiskey with a loving but thorough cleaning for his efforts. Originally, the Marjorie-Dog was being held at bay by Haley and Leo near the front door of the house. Upon witnessing the pandemonium taking place at the foot of the driveway, they let Marjorie loose to join in the fray. Inundated with doggy drool and doggy kisses, all I could think was, *My goodness, it's so good to be home again!*

Pumpkin Cheesecake Buttons

Cookie:

1/2 cup shortening
1/2 cup margarine
1/4 cup brown sugar
2/3 cup granulated sugar
1 tablespoon maple syrup
1/2 teaspoon vanilla

1 egg
1/2 teaspoon pumpkin pie spice
1/2 teaspoon cream of tartar
1/2 teaspoon salt
2 1/2 cups flour

Filling:

4 ounces cream cheese
1/4 cup canned pumpkin
2/3 cup granulated sugar
1/2 teaspoon vanilla

1 teaspoon pumpkin pie spice
1 egg
2 tablespoons flour

Optional toppings:

Decorative sugars
Finely chopped nuts

Crushed graham crackers

1. Preheat oven to 350 degrees.
2. Cream together shortening, margarine, brown sugar, granulated sugar, maple syrup, vanilla, and egg with an electric mixer until light and fluffy, about 3 to 5 minutes.
3. Add pumpkin pie spice, cream of tartar, and salt. Continue to beat with electric mixer for about a minute.
4. With a spoon, mix in flour.
5. Drop dough by rounded tablespoons onto cookie sheets. With the bottom of a small glass (or the bottom of a standard spice container),

flatten the dough to about 1/4 inch in the center. The edges of the dough should be slightly higher, creating a shallow bowl.

6.   Bake for about 5 or 6 minutes or until the cookies are just set.

7.   While the cookies bake, make the filling by combining cream cheese, pumpkin, sugar, vanilla, pumpkin pie spice, egg, and flour in a bowl with an electric mixer.

8.   While the cookies are still warm, drop a dollop of the cream cheese mixture into the "bowl" of the partially baked cookies. Bake another 5 to 6 minutes until the edges of the cookie are slightly browned and the cream cheese center is set. Before completely cooled, dust the tops of the cookies with either decorative sugars, finely ground nuts, or finely crushed graham crackers.

A random act of kindness!

T he day after Sergeant and I returned home, I made an appointment for him with Whiskey's veterinarian. Even though I knew Sergeant was put through the wringer by animal control and the veterinarian down south, they always suggest that you get your adopted pet checked out by your local vet. I knew that Sergeant was now a permanent member of the Bear Cave, so I could think of nothing my local vet could tell me that would cause me to abandon him, but nonetheless, I felt obligated to do all that was required of me to verify that my new STD was good to go.

Whiskey's veterinarian hospital was quite the pet spa. It was definitely what one might refer to as "upscale," which included being marginally pricey as well. However, they had always taken amazing care of the Whiskey-Dog in the past, so I refused to go elsewhere. More than that, they never seemed to be crowded or overbooked when I had been there. In fact, there were times when I felt that I was their only appointment. The night of Sergeant's initial checkup, however, was not one of those times. There were a few more people than usual in the waiting room that evening, but it was not so crowded as to be stressful. In a reasonable amount of time, we saw the vet, received an estimated puppy age of nine to twelve months old, were informed that, price-wise, it had been smart to get Sergeant's major medical expenses taken care of in North Carolina (like I had a choice), received a clean bill of health for Sergeant, and headed to the front desk to pay our bill.

When Sergeant and I got to the counter, we took our place in line to await our turn at the cashier. There was only one woman ahead of us, and she was in the process of paying her bill. The receptionist behind the counter seemed involved with some sort of issue in preparing the final cost of this woman's visit, so we were in the queue a bit longer than normal. Even so, there was no acrimony or agitation because of the delay. Instead, the women behind the desk, as well as all of us waiting in line, chatted away like old friends about everything in our lives, including our pets and families. Somewhere in this conversation, the woman in front of me noticed the sweatshirt I was wearing, specifically the patch it bore on its upper left-hand side.

"Is that a lion?" she asked. "What organization is that seal from?"

Confused, mainly because I could not remember what I had thrown on after work, I looked down and realized that I was wearing the sweatshirt that Keith sent me a couple of years earlier when he was deployed. The emblem the woman was referring to was simply a Baghdad Green Zone patch.

"My nephew sent me this sweatshirt from Iraq," I explained. "This is just a patch from Baghdad."

"Oh!" she responded. "Is he over there now? Is he a part of the Surge?"

"No, ma'am," I answered. "My nephew came back in 2005, but my son is serving in the Surge now." It has never taken much to get me to talk about Buddy and to sing the praises of our troops; this time was no exception. As I pulled Buddy's dog tag out from behind my sweatshirt, I explained all about Buddy, the FHOTA, and the rest of the guys. I talked about how much they had accomplished since January and what the year had been like for me and my family. I told her all about the cookies and the care packages and how much fun it was to ensure the soldiers got the opportunity to play. I ended my soliloquy by explaining how we were, at long last, closing in on the final stretch of the deployment and excited to get the date of their homecoming, without trying to look too far ahead. As I chatted away, the people behind the counter even got involved, sharing their stories of family members who also served. It was a very touching moment for me.

After she finished her business with the receptionist, the woman in front of me took a moment to thank me and my son for his service. As always, the words she spoke tugged at my heartstrings and left me without an audible reply. The most I managed was to nod at her in appreciation of her support right before she walked out of the office. So when she walked back through the doors to the animal hospital, holding out her credit card and asking me, "Do you mind?" I thought she was simply addressing some issue with her bill. I motioned to her to be my guest and stepped back a bit to give her free access to the cashier. She gave her credit card to the woman, said something to her that I could not decipher, and then turned to face me.

Having regained my ability to talk—specifically small talk—I immediately began chatting with the woman again; I wanted to let her know that needing to come back in and address an issue was no big deal. However, the woman was much more pointed in her conversation upon her return. "I just couldn't leave it with a 'Thank you,'" she began. I smiled and nodded, a little confused, as she continued. "What you must go through day in and day out. We—I—am indebted to your son and to you for your support of him and the rest of the soldiers!" She paused a moment, like she was waiting for a response from me, but I was still a little unsure of what she was trying to say. Once again, I smiled and nodded, and she continued. "I was getting into my car when it occurred to me that I could do more. I could put an action behind my words to make clear that your son is appreciated, to demonstrate that your family's service has not gone unnoticed." She then followed up with the question, "Is that little guy your son's dog?"

Having been asked a specific question, I felt less confused and more capable of providing input to the conversation. "Well, yes and no," I began. "He is the ST—er, Stupid Tiny Dog that my son and I always talked about getting, but Buddy hasn't met the puppy yet. His arrival to our family was a bit unexpected!"

"Well, I hope that your family and the puppy have many long years together," she replied. "Please tell your son I was happy to contribute!"

Slowly, it all began to sink in; she had come back in to pay *my* bill. I was at a complete loss for words—which, I am sure, is why I began babbling like a mindless boob! I think it had something to do with trying to fill a void where I knew that appropriate words should be spoken, but at that particular moment, I had no idea what those words should be. Where a simple "Thank you" probably would have sufficed, somehow it just did not seem like enough. This woman, whose name I did not even know, continued to chat as she paid my bill, thanked me again for my son's service, and then left.

I stood there dumbfounded, with tears filling my eyes and flowing down my cheeks, without a clue as to what I was supposed to do next. As the mother of a soldier, I had at times felt isolated, especially during the Surge, but every so often, I had the pleasure of speaking with someone who unmistakably let me know that I was not alone. At no time had I felt more support than during my encounter with that woman at the vet. I was so grateful for her encouragement, not just for me but for my son and all the other troops who served our country. After the woman had left, it was a few minutes before I could speak again. However, I did eventually manage to ask the receptionist for the woman's name and address so that I could properly thank her. I was not surprised that the receptionist had already written down the information to give me.

At the height of the Surge during the past spring, I had asked Haley how she managed to get through the day having to face all the reports that were coming out of Iraq. Her response was simple logic—sort of. "I told you, Mom," she said. "My brother is Superman, as are the rest of the FHOTA! Because of that, he is *faster* than a speeding bullet—and if not, they will just bounce off of him! Right? At least that's what I keep telling myself—*don't* tell me differently!"

I guess we all needed *something* to get us through the deployment. It was the kindness of others that helped see me through the endless days of anguish and uncertainty. Nothing was more moving to me than the appreciation I received from random strangers during chance encounters—and *nothing* since the beginning of the Surge had been more uplifting to me than the unabashed appreciation and generosity of the woman from the veterinarian's office.

Almond Joy Macaroons

14 ounces shredded coconut

2 tablespoons flour

1/4 teaspoon salt

3/4 cup mini chocolate chips

3/4 cup sliced or slivered almonds

3 large egg whites

1 teaspoon vanilla

1/3 cup granulated sugar

1. Preheat oven to 350 degrees.
2. Use a wooden spoon to combine coconut, flour, salt, chocolate chips, and almonds in a bowl.
3. In a separate bowl, mix egg whites and vanilla with an electric mixer until soft peaks form. Gradually add sugar, continuing to beat. After all sugar has been added, beat until soft peaks become stiff.
4. Fold egg white mixture into dry ingredients. Mix until just combined.
5. With either a cookie scoop or your hands, form mixture into golf ball–size balls and arrange on cookie sheets.
6. Bake 15 minutes. Macaroons should turn a lovely golden brown.

I have good news and bad news; which do you want first?

I had just finished a phone call from Buddy and felt overrun with emotions. Now, "overrun" should not be confused with "overcome," though the one could lead to the other. It was just that after finishing my talk with my son, I had an overabundance of sentiments all colliding within me, each one competing to be the prominent feeling, and they all were just about equal in strength if not in intensity. It felt a little like having multiple personalities.

Buddy was coming to the end of his enlistment and trying to decide what to do about it. He had broached the subject with me off and on over the past few weeks, but mostly in passing comments or rhetorical questions. However, Buddy had just made E-5—sergeant—and that promotion came with some expectations from the army and from Buddy as well. And, as if the whole "Well! Whatcha gonna do now?!" aspect of the decision was not enough pressure, he was also getting pressure from his chain of command to "re-up," or re-enlist.

When Buddy first started talking about his re-enlistment prospects, I emailed 1st Sgt. Ramirez looking for guidance—not on how to stop Buddy from re-enlisting but more to help me help my son navigate through this decision-making process. First Sgt. Ramirez informed me that my son had already come to speak with him. According to him, Buddy was a fine soldier and an asset to the 82nd—the All-Americans. He also acknowledged that my son could do just about anything he wanted and be successful. However, 1st Sgt. Ramirez pointed out that this was the reason he and Buddy's chain of command were "encouraging" him to follow in the footsteps of the other soldiers, past and present, who elevated the All-Americans to legendary status. He further explained that it was one thing to get soldiers straight from boot camp and something else entirely to keep a seasoned, first-rate soldier like Buddy in the ranks. The first sergeant apologized to me for putting the pressure on my son, but he pointed out that it was part of *his* job to identify and keep good soldiers. He then apologized for not being of more help to me, thanked me for my recent care package to him, wished me the best, and said good-bye.

First Sgt. Ramirez let me know that my son was appreciated and wanted. For a mother, that was always nice to hear; however, it was not a great deal of help for the current situation. So when Buddy called for a bit of a discussion regarding the matter at hand, I felt a little unprepared. Buddy truly did seem at a loss for what he should do. He spent a good deal of our conversation relating what others had said to him and reiterating all his reservations to their "encouragement" but not a lot of time telling me what he wanted. I knew my son well; I knew that he had an opinion on this and was trying to convey it to me, but I was having a hard time figuring out what exactly it was. He seemed to like and dislike the army at the same time—par for the course for an infantry soldier. He liked the structure and discipline of the army, but its rigidness was apparently irritating to him. The re-up bonus the army was offering seemed to make a difference, but I could not tell how much. And the FHOTA was just plain ticking him off—apparently becoming more of a band of annoyers rather than brothers.

For the most part, I felt that Buddy just wanted me to be a sounding board. I was good with that, especially considering that I was trying hard not to actually have an opinion on what my son wanted to do with *his* life. He had already demonstrated that he was capable of sound decisions, and I had already decided that no matter what he chose—including infantry, airborne, and more deployments—I would be OK with it all. With his brains and background, I felt that he would succeed at whatever he chose—he just had to choose.

"Mom," Buddy said, "if I stay in the army, I could retire after twenty years at thirty-seven."

"That's true!" I said.

"But then what?" he asked. "What do I do with the rest of my life? How do I get another job? I mean *honestly*, what skills would I have?"

"Buddy!" I exclaimed. "You would have your service. Honor, integrity, honesty—"

But before I had the chance to continue, Buddy provided his own thoughts on the subject. "'And, sir, what is your skill set?' the interviewer would ask. And what would be my answer? 'Well, sir, I can kill people, and in twenty-seven ways, at that!' That just doesn't seem like good résumé material—"

"Buddy!" I interrupted him. "Don't be ridiculous! Your skill set would begin with your ability to lead. Your successful career of twenty years would be the proof of that."

"I just feel like I need to be able to do more."

I spent several minutes trying to draw out of him what *he* wanted to do, what would constitute "doing more." But after several minutes of giving "outstanding" advice to my son regarding him following his dreams, I was a bit surprised by his request.

"Mom!" Buddy interrupted me in the middle of my "only you know what is best for you" oration. "Just treat me like I'm twelve years old and tell me what to do!"

I was shocked at his words. *You're kidding me, right? Heck, I wouldn't even have done that when you were twelve!* But I could think of nothing to say to my son in response to his appeal. The silence was deafening. I waited for Buddy to say something else, but apparently he had spoken his mind and now was waiting for an answer from me.

"Oh Buddy, you don't really mean that," I finally said to break the silence.

"Yes! I *really* do!" he insisted.

With our conversation at an impasse, we decided to call it a day. Before we hung up, Buddy urged me, "Think about it, Mom, and tell me what you decide next time we talk!"

Haley had explained to me on more than one occasion how I can and *do* control her and her brother's lives through subtle manipulation. However, I think they both like to accuse me of this because it gives them someone to blame when things do not turn out well. This was different, though, because Buddy was *asking* for overt manipulation to point to and blame as the reason for his decision. Through our conversation, I perceived that he was receiving pressure from both sides of the argument, for as much as the army was "encouraging" Buddy to re-enlist, some of the guys Buddy was closest to, the FHOTA and such, were "encouraging" him to get out. Both groups were still very important to my son, and I could see that he did not want to disappoint either. I might have recognized this, and even understood it, but there was no way on God's green earth that I was going to be the deciding factor!

Something told me that my son meant what he said and that sooner or later he would be expecting an answer, which caused me a great deal of concern. As I hung up the phone with Buddy, I reiterated to myself that the choice had to be his and only his. However, I also understood that Buddy's decision might require guidance, but I was confused as to how exactly I was supposed to help him address his concerns without actually influencing the outcome. It was always at times like these that I regretted being a single parent; not only did I not have anyone to bounce ideas off of, I also had no one to pass the phone to and say, "Here! You handle it!" Though Haley's support had always given me the courage to be strong for Buddy over months of the Surge, it did nothing to help me treat Buddy like he was twelve!

Buddy's phone call did remind me that I needed to get this week's care package in the mail. Since Thanksgiving was just around the corner, that was the theme of the care package—and what is Thanksgiving without a turkey? Haley and I came up with the idea to make turkeys out of the fake pumpkins that you can find at any craft shop in the fall. The pumpkin was the turkey's body. Twirled autumn-colored pipe cleaners and cigars made up the turkey's back feathers, and autumn-colored foam leaves made up its wings. We used a cigar for the neck and a Styrofoam ball covered in autumn-colored mini pompoms for its head. It had a pistachio-shell beak and bobble eyes. To top it off, the turkey wore a pilgrim's hat made out of an inverted clay pot and some black felt. The final touch was to fill the pumpkin body with chocolate candies and to tape a wishbone to the inside of the pumpkin's lid.

The finished product looked quite animated. When we placed the turkey in its eighteen-square-inch box for shipping, Haley could not help but comment, "Kinda seems like we should be including some food and water for its journey, doesn't it?"

"Yep! It certainly does!" I laughed.

We made two turkeys, one for B-Company and one for C-Company. There was not much room left after the turkeys were put in the boxes, but I managed to make room for some cookies. I was ready for some kitchen time after my phone call with Buddy, and I already knew what I was going to create. To me, cinnamon and cloves are synonymous with fall colors, crisp air, and fires in the fireplace, so my goal was to create a spiced cookie that would taste like fall. I called them "Autumn Spice" cookies. After the cookies went into the boxes, we filled them with packing peanuts in an attempt to keep our turkeys still during shipping, then taped the boxes shut.

On the way to the post office, my thoughts shifted back to Buddy. Overall, I guess our conversation gave me a great sense of relief. In the course of just one phone call, a question that had burned deep within my heart over the past year had been answered. Early on in the Surge, I realized that there was more than one way to lose my son during the deployment. There was, of course, the danger of physical harm, but there was also an insidious threat that was much subtler: his emotional health. At the beginning of the year, my son could have been described as a fine man with a huge heart and an infinite capacity for giving. I was concerned that a year at the front lines of war might have changed him in such a way that that would no longer be true. Had that happened, I could honestly say it would have broken my heart almost as much as if he were taken from me. But after this conversation, I was able to acknowledge with confidence that my son was *still* my son! However, that relief came at a cost. Somewhere before Buddy's next phone call, I had to come up with an answer for Buddy's request that *I* could live with—and somehow, I did not think that was going to be easy.

Autumn Spice Cookies

1/2 cup shortening
1/2 cup margarine
1/3 cup brown sugar
1 cup powdered sugar
1 tablespoon cornstarch
1 teaspoon vanilla
1 egg
1/4 teaspoon baking powder
1/4 teaspoon baking soda

1/4 teaspoon cream of tartar
1/2 teaspoon salt
1/2 teaspoon ground allspice
3/4 teaspoon ground cinnamon
1/8 teaspoon ground nutmeg
2 2/3 cups flour
Cream cheese frosting (preferably
   not whipped)
Decorative sprinkles

1. Preheat oven to 350 degrees.
2. Cream together shortening, margarine, brown sugar, powdered sugar, cornstarch, vanilla, and egg with an electric mixer until light and fluffy, about 3 to 5 minutes.
3. Add baking powder, baking soda, cream of tartar, salt, allspice, cinnamon, and nutmeg. Continue to beat with electric mixer for about a minute.
4. With a spoon, mix in flour.
5. Cover the bowl with aluminum foil and refrigerate for about an hour until dough is firm.
6. Drop dough by rounded tablespoons onto a cookie sheet. Flour the bottom of a flat-bottomed glass and use it to push the dough down until it is about 1/4 inch thick.
7. Bake for 10 minutes until cookie edges are lightly browned.
8. Remove the cookies from the cookie sheet using a pancake turner and place them onto a cooling rack.
9. After the cookies have cooled, frost with cream cheese frosting and sprinkle liberally with decorative sprinkles.

We gather together to ask the Lord's blessing, and his protection, and his grace, and his forgiveness.

Thanksgiving is inarguably one of our favorite holidays here at the Bear Cave. Haley, however, will tell you it is the best. Considering how we overdo everything at our house, from New Year's to Christmas, it is hard to imagine how Thanksgiving rates number one. However, Haley is always at the ready to explain that whereas all the other holidays are fun because of all the "stuff" we do, Thanksgiving is fun simply because it is all about family—and her birthday, but mostly about family. Although I have not necessarily always agreed with Haley's ranking of Thanksgiving, I have always agreed with her reasoning. With that in mind, I was more determined than ever to make our Thanksgiving this year as family-centric as possible, even with such a significant part of our lives and hearts so far away and still in danger.

Long before the Surge, Thanksgiving had become "my thing." I always wanted to have it at my house and invite all my family and extended family, as well as all who had nowhere else to go. Not only did I love to cook, but I had acquired all the appropriate accoutrements over the years. These included plates, serving dishes, and linens decorated with red, yellow, and orange autumn leaves as well as autumn leaf garlands to hang around the doorways, scented candles, autumn bears, and various other autumn paraphernalia. In addition, thanks to Buddy's birthday request, we had a hot tub as well! My brother Roy and his family were coming in from California, and my other brother Albert was bringing his wife, Virginia, and a smattering of her family from New York. Added to the various other local family members, such as Nana and George and Keith, one or two Thanksgiving "orphans" were going to join us as well. All that was left was to let the festivities begin—and the cooking, of course.

I sensed that this Thanksgiving had the potential of being another Bear Cave event steeped in bedlam. To begin with, our little house was not expansive. In order to seat all who were invited to our Thanksgiving celebration, I had to artificially extend my dining room table with a concoction of card tables and plywood. The finished

product spanned halfway through my living room from the outer wall of my dining room. Despite the limited clearance between the extended table and the archway
between the two rooms, I assumed this would not be an untenable arrangement with
good planning and a sufficient amount of hot plates. Secondly, our animal menagerie
was now increased by one. Though all the beasts appeared to be getting along sufficiently, there were still the all-too-frequent moments of indiscriminate humping and
impromptu dog-led games of Poke the Kitty. I had no idea if Nana was planning on
bringing her dog Annie, the first canine to stir Whiskey's soul, but if she did—and I
would never suggest that she not—I saw all hell breaking loose.

As always, our Thanksgiving Day began with the Macy's Thanksgiving Day
parade followed by the 1994 *Miracle on 34th Street*—at least until the football games
began. The turkey was dressed before the parade even started and sat on the counter
waiting for that predetermined moment when it was to be put into the oven. During
the commercials, I worked on the fixings for the turkey dinner. It was a great way to
spend the morning. Despite the hustle and bustle of preparing a Thanksgiving feast,
there was a certain level of peace about it all. It was a time to get lost in the memories
of Thanksgivings past and to reflect on the present. It was a time to appreciate the life
I had built for myself. In fact, these morning hours had always been a "quiet" time for
me—a sort of calm before the storm of people showing up ready to eat when dinner
was still not quite ready due to my personal timing miscalculations.

It was just a little past noon when Keith showed up. Dinner was planned for 5:30
or so, and that was what he was told. However, because I knew that he lived alone, I
added a heartfelt "But feel free to show up when you want." Keith had just finished a
Thanksgiving run with his Hash Club and, with nothing else planned, came straight
to the Bear Cave. A Hash Club, as succinctly put by Keith once upon a time, was
"either a running club with a drinking problem or a drinking club with a running
problem!" Needless to say, Keith was at *least* two sheets to the wind when he arrived
and definitely looking for that third sheet.

Keith was somehow under the impression that Thanksgiving dinner was being
served early in the afternoon. I assured him that was not the case and suggested that
he find ways to entertain himself while I completed preparations. Unfortunately for
me, Keith chose not to follow the traditional and accepted Thanksgiving Day activity
of drinking and watching the football games on TV. Instead, he wanted to "help" me
with my endeavors in the kitchen. Not surprisingly, his ideas of helping had nothing to do with peeling potatoes, cutting up carrots, or anything else that might have
been even marginally useful—in fact, Keith's puttering about the kitchen, repeatedly

opening the oven to check the turkey, opening the refrigerator to look for snacks, and continually trying to poke his fingers into the bread dough that was set aside to rise was the antithesis of helpful. It appeared that this Thanksgiving was getting off to an unusually rocky start.

I was starting to stress over the fact that I was already falling behind, and I did not see the situation improving any time soon. The way it was looking, I would be lucky to have everything ready by 6:30. With Keith "helping" me, that time frame was slipping by the minute. To be honest, there was a certain entertainment value to Keith's behavior that kept me going for a short time. However, when he decided that he wanted to listen to the seventeen messages I had saved on my answering machine, things got a little tense.

There was an overabundance of messages saved because every time Buddy would call and I was not home, he would leave a message. Whether he was in an upbeat mood or he was solemn, I did not have the heart to delete any of them. Keith listened to the first few messages in which Buddy was lighthearted and silly. Though I could tell Keith did not understand why I was saving the messages, he simply let it go. However, the next message was one of Buddy's more sober moments; his voice was tight and his words were strained. It was actually a little painful to listen to, but it was my boy's voice and I was determined to save it. Keith, on the other hand, felt differently.

"Oh, that has got to go," he stated decidedly, looking for the 'delete' button.

"Don't you dare!" I interrupted him. I turned from the counter where I was in the process of shredding brussels sprouts for a new recipe and glared at Keith, daring him to defy me.

"Oh, come on," he countered. "You can't mean to save *that!*"

"Don't!" I said emphatically. "Just leave it!"

I have no idea whether it was the tone of my voice or the look of resolute insanity in my eyes, but Keith backed away—and I was a little surprised that he did. However, I had no time to marvel at my minuscule victory because I was still behind in all that I had to do and losing hope that we would be eating any time before midnight. Thank God for Haley and Leo! I have no idea whether Haley was hearing my voice begin to tense or whether she just knows me that well, but as soon as they finished the few pre-dinner cleaning and setting up chores I had asked them to do, Haley grabbed Leo and showed up at the kitchen door, ready to be tasked with whatever needed to be done next.

The other issue for our modest little home was the limited expanse of the kitchen.

With its insufficient counter space and humble size, it was barely big enough for one cook, let alone four—well, three cooks and an inebriated runner. However, the confined space did allow for Leo to keep his eye on Keith and minimize the trouble he was endlessly attempting to get into. With all of us focused on the preparation of the celebratory meal, I found that we were recovering lost time at an amazing pace—but unfortunately not amazing enough to have dinner prepared for our guests when they arrived.

Surprisingly enough, my big concern when everyone began arriving was not the fact that I was behind schedule but rather the Stupid Tiny Dog. Since I had brought Sergeant home, the fact that we had found him as we did in Fayetteville had become a bit less of a mystery considering the number of times I had been required to chase after him in the few short weeks he had been living at the Bear Cave. The biggest reason for Sergeant's escapes was simply someone leaving the front door open for longer than two seconds, and the biggest problem with our little STD and his escaping out the front door was the fact that if someone started running after him, the little idiot apparently thought, "Oh, awesome! GAME ON!" and proceeded to run faster.

So it was no surprise when Sergeant slipped out as the first contingent of celebrators were trying to enter the Bear Cave. I was not surprised, but I was a little annoyed. Every able-bodied person who was not otherwise engaged—which at this point consisted of my sister-in-law Virginia, her nieces and nephews, and Keith—took off after the dog. I was bogged down with the final push for dinner, so I did not want to concern myself with what was going on outside the confines of my kitchen, but I was starting to panic just a tad. Sergeant was proving to be elusive, and if I had to go running after the little twit, I felt that dinner would never get served. I was in the process of weighing my options—cooking dinner or chasing a puppy that had taken off into an unknown direction—when word came back from one of the neighbors that Keith had caught up with Sergeant. Apparently, Keith managed to chase the miniature moron until he no longer realized he was being chased. Of course, by this point, our little STD was dodging traffic on our local four-lane highway.

No matter how I was feeling before, I was grateful that Keith, a bona fide member of a running—or drinking—club, was there. But you know the old saying: one "Oh, poop!" erases a thousand "Attaboys!" Keith erased his attaboy almost immediately after bringing Sergeant back. I had taken the turkey out of the oven just after Sergeant made his escape. While the puppy was running wild and being chased by half of my dinner guests, I started baking the remaining side dishes in the oven. While the side dishes baked, the carving of the turkey began. My kitchen sous chefs (Haley and Leo) began the process of moving everything to the table by starting with the condiments. Normally, it was about forty-five minutes from the removal of the turkey to the sounding of the dinner bell.

Keith returned with Sergeant just halfway through the process. He showed up at the kitchen door to present the puppy and receive his praise. I was just starting to convey my appreciation when he noticed the half-carved turkey on the counter. "We're ready to eat!" he stated.

"No, Keith!" I began. "We still have to—"

"Has everyone arrived?" Keith interrupted.

"Well, yes—"

"Then we're ready to eat!"

I was too busy with the last of my dinner preparations to take the time to argue. "No, Keith!" I stated firmly—like I used to talk to my own kids when they were about five and starting to get on my nerves. "Just go sit down and wait with everyone else. It will only be about fifteen minutes, OK?" I then turned my focus, once again, to the tasks at hand.

I was no longer paying attention to Keith or whether he was doing what I asked of him. I assumed that he had gone into the living room to watch a bit of football with everyone else, but I was wrong. Instead, he decided it was time to call everyone to the table.

I walked through the swinging kitchen doors to lay out hotplates for the vegetable casseroles, which were almost ready to be removed from the oven, only to find that half the guests were already seated while the other half were looking for guidance as to where they should sit. Consequently, the *only* space I had to maneuver in was the space between the kitchen door and my chair just in front of it. The hot plates I was seeking were still in the china cabinet, which was now blocked in by three people sitting in front of it, as were the serving utensils.

"*What* are you doing?" I asked, rather shocked that anyone would sit at a table before they were invited to do so by the host.

"He said dinner was ready," Albert claimed as he pointed at Keith.

"What did you do, Keith?!" I demanded. "I *said* it would be another fifteen minutes!"

"But—but I was hungry!" Keith replied, sounding more like the five-year-old his behavior resembled than the almost-forty-year-old he was.

"Where's all the food?" Virginia's sister asked.

"You all need to go back to the living room!" I declared, defiantly ignoring the question. "Dinner is not ready yet!"

"But you said 5:30 and it is now almost 6:30!" I heard someone say, but I was unable to determine who.

I was beginning to feel a tad overwhelmed by it all—especially considering that my guests, now seated, refused to move. Ever helpful, Nana offered what she considered a solution. "Well, why don't we just start with what we have?" she asked.

Yeah, that would be half a platter of turkey, olives, and pickles. Heck, the cranberry sauce had not even made it to the table yet, not to mention that the rolls still needed to bake. Of course, these last preparations could have taken place simultaneously and relatively quickly if I had free range of my dining room, but that was no longer the case since everyone, even my sous chefs, had taken their place at the table and let me know in no uncertain terms that they were not going anywhere!

While my guests played a game of Telephone around the table, I did my best to get dinner out to them. To tell the truth, it felt a little like when I was young and had been sent to my room for some unnamed indiscretion. I could hear everyone else laughing and having a good time, yet I was not able to be a part of it. The game of Telephone, of course, requires a message to be whispered from ear to ear of the players until it reaches the player who originated the message. With the group that was gathered together in my dining room, the messages needed only to reach my slightly-hard-of-hearing mom who was sitting next to Virginia's dad (who apparently was having trouble with the concept of "whispering") for the whole game to break down quite humorously. But I had chores to do that did not include having fun, at least for the moment.

With no other choice, I tasked my recalcitrant guests with all that I was no longer able to accomplish myself because of them. My efforts produced limited results. My brother Roy was closest to the drawer with the hot plates and retrieved them for me. While I was in the kitchen fetching the first casserole, the hot plates were set about the table. Even though I tried, my reach was just not sufficient to place the casserole safely on any of them. Considering that what I was taking from the oven was presumably 350 degrees, I could not see passing the casseroles to one of the plates, either.

The solution to this was to pass all the hot plates back to within arm's reach of my seat at the table. Though this allowed me to successfully move items from the oven to the dining room, it also created a bottleneck in the process of serving the food. Where normally the duty of dishing up food that was too hot to pass was distributed fairly equally among the dinner guests, I was now left as the sole server for half a dozen casseroles. Generally, I would not have seen this as a big deal, but considering the impudence of my guests up until now—and the basic insanity of passing the food around the table, even during the best of situations—I felt that this had the potential of being a bit of a problem. Still, I felt that I had no choice.

I was almost ready to take my seat at the dinner table with my dinner guests. All I needed was to move the first batch of rolls from the oven to a bread basket and get the serving utensils. While I worked in the kitchen, I asked Roy's wife Ginny to grab the appropriate utensils from the china cabinet drawer behind her. Unfortunately, she did not realize that it was a short drawer. I was reaching into the oven to pull out the first pan of rolls when I heard a hellacious crash from the dining room. "What the heck was that?" I called from the kitchen.

"Nothing," I heard from the dining room among a smattering of laughter.

I put the pan of rolls on the cooling rack and pushed open the doors into the dining room. My sister-in-law twisted awkwardly as she tried to reach underneath the table, though she had no room to do so. "What's going on?" I asked.

"I thought the drawer was longer—you know, normal sized," Ginny answered sheepishly. "All the serving pieces fell under the table when the drawer came out of the cabinet."

"Oh, never mind!" I replied with a rather short-tempered edge. I was simply amazed that I seemed to be the only "adult" in the room—that almost never happened. "Just leave them be," I continued. "I will simply get what we need from in the kitchen."

I was annoyed. Normally, I am the one with the ridiculous childish behavior at any given family event; however, despite my childish behavior, I always appreciated when things had order and, even more than that, when things were coordinated. My serving utensils needed to match the flatware, but those serving utensils were now strewn about underneath the table with the dogs, so it seemed reasonable that other arrangements needed to be made. It was reasonable, but also a little disappointing.

I grabbed a handful of serving spoons from my everyday stainless steel flatware, which definitely were not as pretty as my imitation gold–plated, "fancy" flatware, and the basket of rolls just retrieved from the oven and headed for the dining room. Normally, this was when I called everyone to the table—except, of course, they were already there. I placed the rolls on the table, the serving spoons in the casseroles and on the serving dishes, and sat in my chair. "It's time for grace," I began. "As always, our grace will be going around the table and taking turns naming one thing we are grateful for."

As mentioned before, this was a family tradition. It started shortly after my dad passed away. For most of my siblings' and my lives, Dad would give the blessing at all family gatherings. For a short while after he passed away in 2001, that task fell to my oldest brother, Albert. It was not that my brother did not want that honor; however, we all loved our dad so much that the simple act of saying grace became an emotional reminder that Dad was no longer physically there. It was difficult for all of us, but especially for Albert who was expected to talk through this emotional upheaval. After a suggestion from Haley, I decided to give Albert the option to share that upheaval with all of us, and he jumped at the opportunity.

From that point forward, it had become tradition, but it was not the tradition of everyone there at the dinner table. Nana, who always sits to my left, began the blessing by being thankful for family and friends. From there, the "blessings" began to break down, possibly because everyone felt that whatever they were grateful for needed to be unique and possibly because some there just did not understand the concept of blessings. But by the time it was my turn to say what was in my heart, I was overcome with the emotion of the evening and of the year. What I wanted to be able to convey was my gratitude for the continued safety of my son and the rest of our military as well as the continued love and support from family and friends. However, at that moment, it all seemed rather muddled. Instead, when I tried to speak, no words came out. All that I managed was a rather hoarse "Amen" to end the prayer.

Despite the mischief and mayhem of the day, for the most part, the actual dinner was quite successful—once we were able to move beyond my tumultuous attempt at being the single server for all the vegetable casseroles, that is. The conversation (basically) was amiable and pleasant, with (almost) everyone steering clear of the age-old social taboos of religion, politics, and sex. Haley's friend from work, Jake—one of our Thanksgiving "orphans"—turned out to be a sort of Keith II, which inadvertently caused a bit of one-upmanship between the two of them. Every time Keith would say something unsuitable for the gathering, which was most of what he had to say that evening, Jake felt obligated to go one better—essentially, a duel of the inappropriate. But all in all, everyone seemed to enjoy the cuisine, camaraderie, and holiday cheer.

Once dinner was over, we retired to the family room for a bit of dessert. In front of the roaring fireplace, we all sang "Happy Birthday" to Haley. Afterward, while we contentedly indulged in some of Nana's homemade pumpkin pie, we watched as Haley opened her birthday presents. It was not long after Haley's last gift that our guests began to leave for home. Eighteen minutes later, it was once again just Haley, Leo, and me.

I had work the following day but was not yet ready for sleep. Instead, we all grabbed one more drink and headed back to the family room. The fire was still going strong when I sat down on the hearth in front of it. Leo was trying to find something suitable on TV while Haley went to put her pajamas on. The heat from the fire warmed more than just my back; it warmed my soul. I took a sip of my wine and sighed loudly.

Haley was just walking back into the room. "What's wrong, Mama?" she asked.

"I don't know," I said. "I just feel kinda funny, you know?"

Haley walked over and took a seat next to me on the hearth. She put her arm around me and hugged me close. "It was a great evening," she said.

"You're right; it was," I replied in a tone that would suggest that I had just lost something near and dear to my heart. Haley did not say anything to my response, but I could tell that she did not understand—and neither did I, necessarily. The day was brimming with laughter and joy, and my heart was full of family. But somehow, with Buddy still in Iraq, it just did not feel right that we should have had so much fun. No matter how well the evening went, I could not chase away or ignore the nagging feeling of guilt that accompanied the day. The bottom line was that the day was perfect—except for one thing: the day was missing Buddy, from beginning to end.

Pumpkin Pie Cookies

Cookie:

2/3 cup shortening   1 egg
2/3 cup margarine   1/2 teaspoon cream of tartar
1 3/4 cups powdered sugar   3/4 teaspoon salt
1/2 teaspoon vanilla   3 cups flour
1/2 teaspoon butternut flavoring

Filling:

2/3 cup cream cheese   1 1/2 cups powdered sugar
1/3 cup canned pumpkin   1 teaspoon pumpkin pie spice

1. Preheat oven to 350 degrees.
2. Cream together shortening, margarine, powdered sugar, vanilla, butternut flavoring, and egg with an electric mixer until light and fluffy, about 3 to 5 minutes.
3. Add cream of tartar and salt. Continue to beat with electric mixer for about a minute.
4. With a spoon, mix in flour.
5. Split dough into quarters. Roll out a quarter of the dough between two floured sheets of wax paper until approximately 1/8 inch thick. Use cookie cutters to cut dough into rounds. Transfer cookies onto cookie sheets with a pancake turner. (Alternately, drop cookies by rounded teaspoons onto cookie sheets and use a floured cookie stamp or a floured bottom of a glass to flatten the dough to the appropriate thickness.)
6. Bake for 8 to 10 minutes or until the edges are lightly browned.
7. To make the filling, mix cream cheese, canned pumpkin, powdered sugar, and pumpkin pie spice in a bowl with an electric mixer.
8. After cookies are cooled, squish a heaping teaspoonful of cookie filling between two cookies.

When good superstitions go bad

M any, many years ago, somewhere between "no longer a child" and "have children of my own," someone told me that if the first word out of my mouth on the first day of the month was "Rabbit" (which was more recently corrected to "Rabbit, Rabbit"), I would have a financially successful month. It was a pretty exciting concept—one or two simple words twelve times a year and I could be *rich*—if only I could remember! However, though I had been trying for decades to access this seemingly untapped wealth, I'd had only limited results. It was sometime before Haley was born that I heard about this—and she had just turned twenty-four last week—yet the times I had remembered to actually say "Rabbit" or "Rabbit, Rabbit" as my first words of a new month could be counted on one hand with fingers left over.

In an attempt to capitalize on this golden egg, I would often share my "secret" to financial success with others—trusted coworkers, neighbors, and such—so that as they went about securing their own financial stability in remembering "Rabbit, Rabbit," they would, by default, help me secure mine. But it all was to no avail! Sometimes, I would even mention "Rabbit, Rabbit" to total strangers like store clerks and gas station attendants in an attempt to simply remind myself to say the words on the following morning—but, as always, it would not work. Words like "Morning already?" or "Is this trash day?" or "Ooof! Get off me!" (said to a 150-pound Bernese Mountain Dog on a stormy morning) would always be falling out of my mouth first. Inevitably, my elusive chance at financial success would, once again, be spent for another month!

Maybe it was the fact that the news out of Iraq had been uncharacteristically quiet that eased my stress level a bit, or maybe it was the extra calls I had been getting from Buddy in recent weeks that allowed my mind to venture into thoughts other than my son and the Surge. But whatever the case, December 1, 2007, seemed to change all that came before. It was Friday and the last first-day-of-the-month of the year. I was awake but still laying quietly in bed. My mind raced with everything I had to do that weekend. *Let's see,* I thought. *Of course I need to get a care package off to Buddy, but what else? I guess since it is now the official Christmas season, I should also start thinking about Christmas lists and shopping sprees. How many days is it till Christmas, anyway?* And then it hit me. I realized that it was the first of December.

I opened my eyes and saw my two dogs staring at me, waiting patiently (or, in the case of Sergeant, not so patiently) to be let outside. The dogs cocked their heads first to one side and then to the other, looking for some coherent response from me. Instead, I sat up in bed, looked them both in the eyes, and triumphantly announced, "Rabbit, Rabbit!"

Bursting with pride at my achievement, I proceeded to lead the dogs to their downstairs doggy door, securing it in the open position so that they might tend to their business.

Now things will be different, I silently proclaimed. I was sure that my accomplishment had set a new path for my life. I continued through my morning routine with unusual vim and vigor for a workday, all the while contemplating all those things I would purchase with my newfound wealth. *New appliances, professional landscaping, my coveted raised roof; maybe I can even open that bed and breakfast I have always dreamed about! Oh, this is going to be great!* By now, the dogs had finished their business and were staring at me, waiting for their morning meal. "This is great," I explained to my dogs, who were still cocking their heads from one side to the other, waiting for me to say anything that resembled words like "breakfast" or "eat"—or "cookie"! I was elated. I started the kettle for my tea and dished up the dogs' bowls of food. As they ate their food, my mind still raced with possibilities. "This is going to be a *good* day," I announced to the dogs. "I can't wait!"

After making sure the dogs were secured in their beds while I was at work, I hopped into my car and began my morning commute. Yes, I did realize that the "Rabbit, Rabbit" thing was just an old superstition, but while backing down my driveway, I began wondering what dollar amount would satisfy the term "financial success," especially if it was qualified with "for the month." In addition, I wondered where that success would come from. Was Publisher's Clearing House going to be knocking on my door? A highly unlikely scenario, considering I almost never responded to their urgings that I "might be a winner!" Was I supposed to start playing the lottery or maybe some high-stakes poker? It seemed to me those things would jeopardize my financial security. So where was the money going to come from?

I sat at a red light pondering the situation. Out of the blue, a new possible scenario came to mind. "Maybe a long-lost uncle has left me his fortune, and his lawyers will finally track me down this month!" I thought out loud. Never mind that I had three siblings who would be sharing in the wealth, and, once again, I understood it was all just make-believe, but I could not stop daydreaming about it. Besides that, the long-lost uncle plot intrigued me; it somehow seemed plausible. The only problem with it was that I knew of no long-lost anyones—however, that *was* the definition of "long-lost," was it not?

"So!" I said to the universe, "*Who* is willing me money?"

And then it hit me like a ton of bricks—my eighty-seven-year-old mom, Nana! I recoiled from the idea as I tried to think of another scenario that did not include Nana's will, only to be struck with an equally abhorrent thought. "Buddy!" I said out loud. "Oh no, I'm Buddy's beneficiary!"

My glorious day had just turned to dust. I wanted to take it all back. I wanted to go back to my first waking moments of the day and unsay my "Rabbit, Rabbit." I wanted to replace it with a prayer for my mom and my son. It did not matter that I knew it was a make-believe superstition; that did not stop my stomach from churning like it had been doing almost constantly since the Surge began. And with that, the weight of the world fell back onto my shoulders with a crushing force.

I had arrived at the train station but did not have the energy to get out of the car. The boundless vitality I had felt earlier was gone. In its place was the all-too-familiar trepidation that had so persistently drained my soul since January 2nd. If I had had the strength, I would have cried. It was just plain exhausting being the mother of a soldier, especially this year. I sighed loudly, trying to generate the fortitude to continue my day. Slowly, I opened the car door and dragged myself to my feet. "I'm sooo tired!" I said out loud as I walked toward the train platform. "Why can't it all just be over?"

I prayed all the rest of the way to work. I knew it was irrational, but I felt that I just could not take the chance. When I first arrived at my desk, I paused for a moment to collect my thoughts and to remind myself that it was only a silly superstition before logging onto my computer. The computer went through its normal gyrations, flashing various pieces of information on the monitor, the last being the current date: November 30, 2007.

November 30?! My heart skipped a beat as I quickly checked the calendar on the wall behind me. Yep—it was Friday, but it was only the thirtieth of November! What a relief that I had my dates wrong. Apparently, I still had not achieved the seemingly unattainable "Rabbit, Rabbit," and I could not have been happier. I felt as though I had been given a second chance. Miraculously, I was suddenly and totally content with my financial stagnation and modest lifestyle. Somewhere in my exultation, it also occurred to me that for the next several months—if not years—it would probably be best to give that old superstition a rest!

Carrot Cake Cookies

1/2 cup shortening

1/2 cup margarine

3/4 cup brown sugar

2/3 cup granulated sugar

2 tablespoons maple syrup

1 teaspoon vanilla

1 egg

1 teaspoon baking powder

1/4 teaspoon cream of tartar

1/2 teaspoon salt

1 1/2 teaspoons ground cinnamon

1/4 teaspoon ground cloves

1/4 teaspoon ground nutmeg

3 large carrots, shredded (approximately 2 cups)

2 1/2 cups flour

1 cup chopped walnuts

Cream cheese frosting

1. Preheat oven to 350 degrees.
2. Cream together shortening, margarine, brown sugar, granulated sugar, maple syrup, vanilla, and egg with an electric mixer until light and fluffy, about 3 to 5 minutes.
3. Add baking powder, cream of tartar, salt, cinnamon, cloves, and nutmeg. Continue to beat with electric mixer for about a minute.
4. With a spoon, mix in carrots, then flour, then walnuts.
5. Drop dough by rounded teaspoons onto cookie sheets.
6. Bake for 12 to 14 minutes.
7. Let cool, then ice with cream cheese frosting.

Say it with flowers—or,
better yet, BEARS!

W hen I was very young, Nana once told me that when I became an adult, I would enjoy the taste of coffee. Well, despite all my passing years, I have yet to achieve adulthood! To this day, I still cannot stand the taste of coffee. I am, however, an avid tea drinker. As such, for Christmas 2006, my sister Evey signed me up for a tea-a-month club. My first installment came sometime during December 2006, and each following installment was delivered during the first week of the following months. So, upon returning home from work last week and finding a box outside my front door, I was not really surprised. Well, not until I realized that if they were sending me a December tea, either they must have been employing the concept of a baker's dozen or Evey had signed me up for another year. Both scenarios were more than acceptable to me, so I simply placed the box on the floor next to my front hall bench and forgot about it.

This morning, I was in the process of preparing for my day. I had already showered and dressed and was feeding the dogs when I remembered that I had run out of my supply of tea at work. I was calculating whether I had the time before my commute to stop at the local grocery store to pick up some more when I spotted the box still sitting next to the hall bench where I had left it earlier. Rather than deal with slow checkout clerks—which most of the time, because of self-checkout lanes, was me—I thought, *No biggie. I will just use what I have here.* I grabbed the box from the front hall and took it to the kitchen. I cut through the outer layers of packaging only to find a second box, not the paper stuffing I normally would have to dig through. Confused, I dug the box out and placed it on the kitchen table to see what I was dealing with.

Generally speaking, I am not ever a "bright light" person, but especially not in the morning. In the dimmed light of the kitchen, I noticed there was a pattern on the outside of the box that I recognized, but only somewhere in the recesses of my memory. I turned up the light to get a closer look. Squinting through that harsh light, I could discern no other identifying marks on the box. I grabbed up the outer box and checked it; the only label it bore was the one with my name and address on it. It seemed a little strange to me, but I decided, *What the heck?* and cut into the second box to discover its contents.

I opened the flaps, reached in, and pulled out a soft, fluffy brown bear in a camouflage uniform, wearing the black beret of the army with the blue flash of the infantry. Around the bear's neck was a dog tag engraved with the initials B.A.B.W. for Build-A-Bear Workshop. On the right paw of the bear was a note that said, "Thanks for the cookies, Mom. We will take care of Princess for you."

My throat tightened a bit. Through the blurred vision of tear-filled eyes, I lovingly examined every inch of that bear. I remembered that once upon a time, I had built my own bear at the Build-A-Bear Workshop. When the workers went to stuff the bear I chose, they gave me a little plastic heart and told me to make a wish on it before they placed it in the bear and sewed it up. I could not help but wonder if a wish was made on my bear's heart. I reasoned that given its creators were a group of soldiers on the front lines, there probably was no wish, but if there was, what could it possibly have been?

I stood there in my kitchen, hugging the bear as if that hug could transfer to those who sent it to me. Even though the note was unsigned, it was obvious where it had come from. Though all who knew me knew that I was nuts for bears, there were a couple telltale clues in the package. To begin with, there was the note itself; many people had been treated to my cookie inventions since the beginning of the year, but only a few (or maybe just one) ever referred to my son as "Princess." I still had no idea where that nickname came from, or why it existed—I had asked but was told to just leave it alone. However, what I did know was that it was used to torment Buddy, as only friends can do.

In addition, there was the birth certificate for the bear. On it, the bear was named "Sgt. Huggles" and his date of birth was listed as January 3, 2007. This was the day after Haley and I saw Buddy off from Fayetteville, but it would have been the first day the 504th was considered deployed. Immediately, I knew this bear was if not from the FHOTA, at least initiated by them—and, more specifically, by Christian. The fact that these guys would take the time to go online to create and dress the bear and leave me a note really tugged at my heart. It was so sweet but made me miss my son and the rest of them that much more.

It was just after 5:00 a.m. when I went downstairs to knock on Haley's door. I should have been on my way to work by then, but my heart was so full it felt like it was on the verge of exploding. Besides that, tears were still falling down my cheeks rather uncontrollably. I needed to share, and my daughter was the one who was there—poor child! I knocked on her door and called out with a quavering voice.

"Haley? Are you awake?" A rather stupid question considering how early it was.

"Mom?" Haley responded immediately, and amazingly coherently. "What's wrong?!"

Before I had the chance to utter another word, Haley was out of her bed and opening her bedroom door. "What's wrong?" Haley asked again. She saw my tearstained face, and a look of alarm came across hers. "What happened?"

"Look!" I said as I held up Sgt. Huggles for her to see. "The FHOTA sent him to me. They wanted me to know that they appreciated my support. See?" At that, I held up his little paw so that Haley could read the note.

In an instant, I watched Haley's face go from worry to agitation to appreciation and then to slight confusion. "Where did this come from?" she asked.

I felt a little embarrassed that I had caused my daughter such anguish, even if it was only momentary. I explained to her how the box showed up the week before but that I thought it was just more tea. I then let her know that I just wanted her to see the bear before I took it to work. Somehow I wanted, and even needed, to have that bear with me, always.

"I am so sorry that I upset you, Sweetie," I said remorsefully. I then kissed her, told her to go back to bed, and left for work, bear in hand.

It was only that evening as I looked in the box for who I might send a thank-you note to that I found an invoice. It did not list the purchaser's name, but that did not matter—I felt I already knew who sent the bear. It did, however, list an email address, though it did not exactly indicate who was responsible for Sgt. Huggles. Because personal email addresses do not necessarily reflect someone's name, the fact that I had the name of "Thadeous" (maybe like J. Thaddeus Toad from *Wind in the Willows*, but misspelled?) on a Hotmail account told me nothing. I just accepted the fact that I was able to deduce who to write the thank-you note to without needing absolute "proof." In addition to the email address, I learned that my bear had the appropriate mechanics to moo like a cow, which I had not realized before because, for all the tousling the bear took on the way into work, he did not make a sound. If I did not suspect it before, the "moo" mechanics definitely screamed Christian's involvement.

When I wrote my thank-you email, I made sure to address it to all who might have been involved, which encompassed all of the FHOTA. I explained that they had touched my heart and that I was awestruck by their desire to thank *me* for my support! I then told them that it was I who was grateful to *them* for their service and sacrifice and that I would always cherish my Sgt. Huggles.

Mocha Chocolate Chip Cookies

1 tablespoon water

3 1/2 teaspoons instant coffee

2 1/2 blocks semisweet chocolate

1/3 cup shortening

2/3 cup margarine

3/4 cup brown sugar

1/3 cup powdered sugar

1 tablespoon cornstarch

1 teaspoon vanilla

1 egg

1 teaspoon baking soda

1/2 teaspoon salt

2 cups flour

1 cup semisweet chocolate chips

1. Preheat oven to 350 degrees.

2. Heat water and instant coffee in microwave until coffee is dissolved. Add blocks of chocolate and continue to microwave until melted.

3. Cream together shortening, margarine, brown sugar, powdered sugar, cornstarch, vanilla, and egg with an electric mixer until light and fluffy, about 3 to 5 minutes.

4. Add coffee mixture to bowl and beat with electric mixer until well mixed.

5. Add baking soda and salt. Continue to beat with electric mixer for about a minute.

6. With a spoon, mix in flour until well blended. Stir in chocolate chips.

7. Drop dough by rounded teaspoons onto cookie sheets.

8. Bake for 10 to 12 minutes.

Yes, Virginia—er, Maggie— there *is* a Santa Claus!

For as long as I can remember, when someone would ask me what I wanted to be when I grew up, no matter what I said out loud, in my heart I would say, *I want to be one of Santa's elves and live at the North Pole forever!* I know it is not very mature—or sane; however, that would be the perfect life for me. I could imagine nothing better than living in a permanent winter wonderland, drinking hot cocoa and eating or baking cookies all day as I spent my time creating the perfect toy—or cookie. Even more than that, I think it would be amazing to have the wherewithal and means to live a life of perpetual giving.

Just to clarify, my adult side is aware of the realities of life and the possibilities— or impossibilities—of living at the North Pole. The child in me, however, throws a little tantrum when I am pressed on the issue. For me, life was better when I was free to ignore sense and sensibility and to simply believe—especially during the rough parts. I believed in the spirit of Christmas born out of God's great love for his people, and I believed that Santa Claus was the personification of that spirit. Using that as the premise, logic told me that if the spirit of Christmas was real and lived in my heart all through the year, then not only was Santa real, but Santa lived all year long as well— so he needed elves. That was my perfect job, and I was excited to take it on.

My kids have always understood that I saw life this way, and even more than that, they embraced it. That was why Christmas was such a spectacle at the Bear Cave and most likely why most who knew this wanted to be a part of it. So, with just over two weeks until Christmas and Buddy so far away with no chance of getting home, I once again set my sights on bringing a Bear Cave Christmas to him. This time, however, I was not planning for just Buddy but for the FHOTA and others he served with as well.

It's funny, but you can always recognize the families of deployed troops who will not be home for the holiday season. Those are the ones who are not complaining about Christmas showing up on the store shelves right after Halloween—or even better, before! Instead, they are scooping up everything that looks Christmas-y and shippable. They are not thinking about unrestrained commercialism or debating whether it is offensive or not; they are imagining how it is going to make someone near and dear to their hearts—and a long way from home—smile. They know that even if the smile is only fleeting, it will be well worth it. There is never a thought of playing down the holidays with the idea that there would "always be next year," because there is never the inclination to pass up the chance to not just say but to demonstrate "I love you!"

I had begun the actual planning for a Bear Cave Christmas to-go weeks before. It commenced with the strategic compilation of all the paraphernalia required to have a great Christmas experience: a book to read on Christmas Eve, *The Night Before Christmas, In Iraq*; the obligatory Christmas movie, something innocent, probably a smidge stupid, and most likely starring Muppets; Christmas music, the old-fashioned kind; Christmas crackers, the English type for Christmas morning; a gingerbread house to build, for an amusing holiday craft; and a small fiber-optic Christmas tree, with appropriate tree and room decorations. I was a little disappointed that I was not allowed to include our standard Bacardi eggnog or the mimosas—though I probably would have if I could have figured out how to finagle it.

Once that was accomplished, sometime during the beginning days of November, I set to work on shopping for Buddy's presents from Santa to open Christmas morning. I managed to find a small collection of functional, but not necessarily practical, gifts. I kept in mind his sparse living arrangements and the fact that he would be attempting to bring home most of what I sent. But even considering these details, I just could not resist the most illogical present of all: a slightly smaller (only by an inch) but fully operational electric guitar with the amp and speaker built into the body of it that functioned on a nine-volt battery and was totally awesome. I could not picture anything being more useless in a war zone, and I could not wait to hear what Buddy had to say about it!

With Buddy's Christmas taken care of, I turned my thoughts and attention to the FHOTA and the other troops that served with my son. These were the guys who had been Buddy's family since January and in a very real sense were the guys who helped keep my son safe from harm. Some I had met while others I had not, but in my heart, they were all my boys. For almost the full year, I had been touting my gratitude for their service in addition to wishing I could do more to show them my appreciation. I saw Christmas as a chance to put action to my words, so I wrote both Buddy and 1st Sgt. Ramirez for the names of all the "good little soldiers" who needed a stocking from Santa.

For me, the wannabe Christmas elf, the most fun was in filling the Christmas stockings. It was the one place where I felt I could successfully mix the immature and useless with the practical and needed. I spent weeks collecting copious amounts of stocking stuffers, including such delectables as cigars, small electronics, Silly Putty, Slinkys, and a miniature book called *Find Bin Laden* like the old *Where's Waldo* books—only the hunt was for Bin Laden and the scenes were from the Middle East. I also amassed a conglomeration of toiletries as well as various seasonal candies like candy canes, PEZ dispensers, and plastic, pooping reindeer, polar bears, and other arctic animals. It was my hope that the recipients of my stockings would get the chance to experience the "magic" of Christmas morning that, in my humble opinion, everyone longed for, no matter what their age or where they were. For what these guys had been through during the year, I felt it was the least they deserved.

It took over two hours for Haley and me to stuff all the stockings, mostly because cramming all the goodies I had accumulated into the limited amount of stockings took some manipulating. With more goodies going into the stockings than there was room for, we ended up covering the tops of each of the stockings with cellophane so that if anything fell out, it would still be obvious to which stocking it belonged. Afterwards, the stockings went into either the C-Company box or the B-Company box. Both boxes contained mostly identical items; the only difference between the two was the fact that I felt since most of these soldiers had families of their own, I only needed to augment what they were already receiving. As such, I did not try to supply trees and decorations or additional presents for anyone but Buddy. I did, however, make sure that each box contained some of my homemade cookies, a DVD of a fire in a fireplace to create an atmosphere of home, and a Santa hat for whomever was lucky enough to get to pretend to be my dream boss, Santa Claus.

The cookies for this care package were my attempt to send a very impractical Bear Cave Christmas tradition to Buddy. For all of Buddy's life, Christmas Eve was a time for baking chocolate chip cookies—Santa's favorites—and eating copious amounts of dough as the cookies baked. I decided I should be able to make a cookie-dough-flavored filling without eggs or anything else that would spoil and put the filling between two chocolate chip cookies—kind of the whole tradition wrapped up in a sandwich cookie. I was pleased with the results, even if the cookies were a bit thick. I called these cookies "Christmas Eve Cookies."

I was running out of time on the last possible day to send anything to Iraq and have it arrive there before Christmas. There was no more time for gift buying, stocking stuffing, or cookie baking. I was done writing individual notes to the soldiers and attaching them to the stockings, and it was finally time to begin closing all the boxes to be mailed. Standing over the box bound for 1st Sgt. Ramirez and B-Company, I paused a moment before taping it up. I reflected on the last email he sent me in which he requested a stocking for one of his young soldiers. He explained that it was the soldier's first time away from home, and though the soldier was doing "really great," 1st. Sgt. Ramirez felt that the young man "could really use your touch."

My heart began to ache for this soldier. I could not imagine having my first big "trip" away from home be an all-expenses-paid tour to a war zone. I wondered what it was like being that young and living through even one firefight, let alone a year's worth. I wondered if, even once, the young man questioned whether he would actually make it to his next birthday or if he ever felt isolated by his circumstances. I understood that young or not, he was a well-trained soldier; however, like 1st Sgt. Ramirez said, I also knew that everyone needed a mother's touch sometimes. I wondered why this young man needed mine. I started regretting my decision to confine my contributions for Buddy's compatriots to only Christmas stockings.

My stomach started to twist into a bit of a knot. I did not know what this soldier's home life was, or whether he was going to be receiving any other care packages. What I did know, however, was that this young man needed something more than just a Christmas stocking, but there really was no more time for shopping. As a last-ditch effort, I went to my stash of crafting supplies to see if I could at least provide the soldier some festive decorations. I went to my craft corner and dug through the different drawers of my cabinets there. I pulled out a small artificial pine tree, tree garland, and a matching star for the top of the tree. I found a set of battery-operated lights and small ornaments to hang from the tree. I even found a small tree skirt to send along to the soldier. In the course of five minutes, I had collected all the trappings to fully decorate a Christmas tree, and it felt just like magic.

Elated, I ran back upstairs and began packing all the newfound goodies into the B-Company box. It warmed my heart to think that I had a small part in comforting anyone, but especially a soldier who might have been missing home just a little more because of the holidays. I smiled as I imagined the look on the soldier's face as he decorated his little tree. It gave me amazing gratification to envision the soldier with his buddies in front of a TV screen showing a silly Christmas movie or a fire in a fireplace as they sorted through their Christmas stockings and compared the contents. It was so satisfying to put the final strips of tape on the box knowing the joy it would bring at the other end. Then it hit me—*Of course! I am one of Santa's elves!*

Cookie Dough Cookies
(a.k.a. Christmas Eve Cookies)

Cookie:

2/3 cup shortening

2/3 cup margarine

1/3 cup brown sugar

1 1/2 cups powdered sugar

1 teaspoon vanilla

1 egg

1/2 teaspoon cream of tartar

3/4 teaspoon salt

3 cups flour

1/2 cup mini chocolate chips

Filling:

"Fluffy" white frosting

Chocolate chip cookie mix with mini chips or chocolate flakes (I used

Betty Crocker Chocolate Chip Cookie Mix, but any cookie mix will do.)

1. Preheat oven to 350 degrees.
2. Cream together shortening, margarine, brown sugar, powdered sugar, vanilla, and egg with an electric mixer until light and fluffy, about 3 to 5 minutes.
3. Add cream of tartar and salt. Continue to beat with electric mixer for about a minute.
4. With a spoon, mix in flour and chocolate chips.
5. Refrigerate the dough until thoroughly chilled. Split dough into quarters. Roll out a quarter of the dough between two floured sheets of wax paper to the thickness of the mini chips. Use cookie cutters to cut dough into rounds. Transfer cookies onto cookie sheets with a pancake turner. (Alternately, drop dough by rounded teaspoons onto cookie sheets and use a floured cookie stamp or a floured bottom of a glass to flatten the dough to the appropriate thickness.)
6. Bake for 8 to 10 minutes.
7. To make the filling, mix 2 parts frosting with 1 part cookie mix (no other ingredients). Test for taste and adjust if necessary.
8. After cookies are cooled, squish a heaping teaspoonful of frosting mixture between two cookies.

Let it snow, let it snow, oh *please* let it snow . . . I think!

T he weather report had predicted snow—a fifty percent chance of precipitation after midnight! Now, I was aware that no one in my little family had a firm grasp on maturity—though Buddy fighting in a war had to have added something to his ability to be a grown-up—but basically, a prediction of snow transformed me into a small child whose face was pressed up against a windowpane, waiting for that first snowflake and praying for that coveted "snow day." The problem was that I lived in the outlying area surrounding Washington, DC, and predictions from the meteorologist had about as much weight as predictions from a woolly bear caterpillar. Sometimes it felt as though they could not have given an accurate forecast if they were looking at its results right outside their window, but as always, hope sprang eternal!

It was no secret to anyone who knew me that I loved snow; I always had, and I surmised that I always would. However, I was not sure why. Normally, by the time someone reached my age, snow had become a burden and sometimes even a fear. I, however, never seemed to have matured beyond the magic of the event—and to me, snow *was* magical.

I remember the first report I ever wrote for school in the second grade. Not surprisingly, the report was on snow. I do not remember what the actual assignment was, but because I wrote that report late in the fall, I think my motivation was simply wishful thinking—or maybe hopeful wishing! I remembered how excited I was about the "research" aspect of my report, and I also remembered that I received a C for my efforts. Obviously, I was more enthralled with the subject than I was able to portray in my writings.

Back then, I used our family's World Book Encyclopedia to do my research—such that it was for a seven-year-old. But ever since the World Wide Web came into being, there has been so much more to research and report on. A quick search across the Internet still touted the marvel that is snow. And even though a couple in Wisconsin swore they had found two identical snow "crystals" while the snow was still in the clouds, most scientists carried the opinion that *every* snowflake that fell to earth was unique. If one considered the innumerable snowflakes that had fallen or ever would fall, their uniqueness in and of itself was miraculous! Add that uniqueness to the wonderland that was created when an area was covered with just a couple inches of snow, and the miracle of snowflakes became an extraordinarily wondrous affair.

So who cared about the wonders of snowflakes? Besides me, Buddy cared about snowflakes and missed them as well. Because of this, I was a little conflicted. I could not help but crave snow—after all, it was winter. However, I also recognized that any snow *here* only increased Buddy's desire not to be *there* anymore. In fact, even when it snowed in Baghdad, which was happening more often than it snowed in Northern Virginia this winter, it simply intensified Buddy's longing to be home again. Though I was happy that Buddy had a little snow to enjoy, the fact that it was snowing there when we had not yet had snow here was a little irritating.

Yet, in these waning weeks of the deployment, my predicament regarding the whole snow thing highlighted some of the amazing difficulties of the past year. Striking a balance between continuing as usual when *nothing* was "as usual," even though I was pretending that it was, proved to be an unwieldy venture. What was in question was my ability to maintain the façade that everything in my life was hunky-dory in honor and support of my son's service without giving the impression, both to Buddy and to the public at large, that Buddy's deployment had not fazed me in the least. I had yet to strike that balance.

The problem was that I liked having stories and adventures to tell my son when I wrote him and when he called but I hated the idea of him thinking that we did not feel his absence because we were continuing our normal exploits. I did not wish for him to be burdened with the thought that we were not able to "soldier on" with him overseas, but I also hated the idea of giving him the impression that life had remained the same. Then again, I was also not too fond of the idea that Buddy might have felt his deployment had caused the rest of us some sort of life-altering, unbearable pain—though in a way, it had, if only temporarily.

So I sat there silently wishing for that first flake to fall, even though that wish came with a dash of self-reproach. I could not help it. While my mind worked to reconcile my guilt-riddled desire for snow against the pressures I felt as the mother of a soldier, the child in me simply refused to give in. *Buddy has already had snow!* I thought. *I just want a dusting. OK, I want a few inches . . . well, maybe several inches . . . or a foot!* I concluded. *Yeah, just one foot of snow; that would do!* I shifted the curtains to one side to see if the meteorologist had gotten it right for once. The contrition I might have felt at the sight of falling snow gave way to excitement in anticipation of possibly getting the first snowstorm of the winter. However, even as I tempered my own expectations for the snow outside my window, I prayed with all my heart for a glorious bout of snow in Baghdad, Iraq.

Butter Scotchies

1/2 cup shortening

10 tablespoons margarine

1 cup brown sugar

1/2 cup powdered sugar

1/2 teaspoon vanilla

1/2 teaspoon butternut flavoring

1 teaspoon water

1 egg

1 teaspoon ground cinnamon

1 teaspoon baking soda

1/2 teaspoon salt

1 3/4 cups flour

1 1/2 cups old-fashioned oats

1/2 cup finely chopped walnuts

1 cup butterscotch chips

1. Preheat oven to 350 degrees.
2. Cream together shortening, margarine, brown sugar, powdered sugar, vanilla, butternut flavoring, water, and egg with an electric mixer until light and fluffy, about 3 to 5 minutes.
3. Add cinnamon, baking soda, and salt. Continue to beat with electric mixer for about a minute.
4. With a spoon, mix in flour until well blended. Stir in the oats, walnuts, and butterscotch chips.
5. Drop dough by rounded tablespoons onto cookie sheets.
6. Bake for 10 to 12 minutes or until lightly browned.

"And so, as Tiny Tim observed, God bless Us, Every One!"
—A Christmas Carol

I t was Christmas once again, and not just Christmastime, which I had managed to wrap myself up in since Thanksgiving by embracing my inner Christmas elf. No, it was Christmas Eve and the beginning of the actual celebration which culminated in the opening of presents on Christmas Day—the time all children (literally and mentally speaking) lived for! My son might have been in Iraq, but I also had a daughter and her boyfriend who cared enough about me to make sure that I was not alone for this wonderful day, even though Leo had never spent a Christmas away from his own family. They were there to share with me the all-important Christmas morning and the thorough enjoyment of Santa's visit!

As it had been since before my little family began, the celebration of Christmas started on Christmas Eve with church services. My job did not always allow for me to make time for such diversions, but this year it seemed more important than ever that I at least try. I always wanted to attend church as a family, but with Haley and Leo both working late into the evening, we decided that it would probably be best if I attended the service alone. The plan was that after we finished our evening obligations, we would meet up in the family room for our traditional early festivities. Before I left for church, I brought in some wood for a fire, made sure the champagne for mimosas was chilling, and put the three packages from the PJ Fairy underneath the Christmas tree. In previous years, the evening was always ushered in with a family cookie-baking session; however, with Haley and Leo not expected home until after 10:00, my better judgment said it would be too much for the late-night celebration. I reluctantly let the activity go, but even without it, I figured it was going to be a late night—and an early morning.

This was Leo's first Christmas at the Bear Cave. I already knew that he could release himself from the shackles of maturity, a prerequisite for thoroughly enjoying one of our Christmases both for him and for us; there was nothing worse than trying to return to the joys of childhood and childish behavior and having someone *tsk-tsk* you the whole time. Leo had already proven his ability to adapt during our Easter egg hunt earlier in the year, before he had even moved in. If Leo could giddily prance about the house with an Easter basket in one hand and a drink in the other, he could certainly appreciate the magic of a Bear Cave Christmas.

Having attended one of the earlier services, I was the first to arrive back home. I did not want to change out of my church clothes; tradition stated that this was only done after opening the gifts from the PJ Fairy. Instead, I started a fire and set the mood with appropriate Christmas music. I poured myself a glass of wine, pulled the rocking chair up to the edge of the hearth, put my feet right up close to the fire screen to warm my thoroughly frozen toes, and waited for Haley and Leo to join me.

It was not a long wait before Leo arrived home. Since business at his store had slowed to a crawl, management decided to call it a night and close up shop earlier than planned. He grabbed himself a beer and headed down to the family room and me.

"Hey, Maggie. Nice fire!" Leo said as he walked down the stairs to join me.

I had already pushed my chair back to make room for him at the fire. I expected him to sit down on the hearth to warm himself as we chatted like he and Haley always did, but he chose not to. Instead, he stood in front of the fire, beer in one hand and taking turns petting the dogs with the other. He seemed a little anxious.

"You're home earlier than I expected," I began. I was getting ready to ask him if everything was OK when he exploded with an unbridled enthusiasm that I was not expecting.

"Where are the presents?" he asked. "You guys said we open presents on Christmas Eve! Where are they?!"

I was a little surprised—and a lot amused—by his question. "We said we open one present on Christmas Eve, and they are there under the tree," I explained.

"Oh!" Leo sounded a little disappointed. "When do we get to do that?"

"Well, not until Haley gets here, right?" I said, sounding more like an adult than I had intended.

"Oh," Leo said again, sounding even more disappointed. Before he sat down by the fire, he walked over to the tree and examined the smattering of presents around its base. Most of what was there was from them to me, but there were a few others— mostly from out of town family—that seemed to intrigue him. "How about a couple of these?" he asked, pointing to the packages neatly stored to the back of the tree. I met his sheepish grin with as stern a look as I could muster, but that only held Leo back until Haley got home.

My daughter had barely walked through the front door when Leo began demanding her presence in the family room. "Hold on!" she called out from the kitchen. I could detect a tinge of amusement along with the impatience in her voice. It was only a few minutes until she was walking down the stairs to join us in front of the fire, but it was obviously too long for Leo. "Hi, Mama!" Haley began cheerfully as she walked over to the fireplace. She gave me a hug and a kiss on my cheek and sat next to Leo on the hearth, giving him a kiss. "What movie are we going to watch tonight?"

Leo could not take it any longer. "Presents first!"

The rest of the evening was pretty much like all other Christmas Eves. Much to Leo's delight, we did finally open our presents from the PJ Fairy. Afterward, we all put on our new Christmas pajamas and spent several minutes taking pictures of ourselves in them. We watched our Christmas movie—one of the Muppet movies, of course—but we talked and joked so much through it that by the end, I do not believe any of us could have told you its plot, such that a Muppet movie might have. As the evening wore on, the anticipation of the next morning grew, and as the anticipation grew, so did Leo's desire to open "just *one* more present?" We finally called it an evening—mostly to save Leo from some sort of breakdown because of his overwhelming yet unfulfilled desire to unwrap gifts. It's funny, but I believe that was the first time since my kids were small that I actually felt the need to instruct them that if it was not getting light outside, it was not time for getting up—Christmas morning or not.

Before the sun had fully risen above the horizon the next morning, all three of us were out of bed. The dogs had already had their morning constitutional and breakfast and were now adorned in their Christmas finest, compliments of Haley and Leo: antlers for Whiskey, bells for Marjorie, and a Christmas jester's cap for Sergeant. The cinnamon buns were baking, the fire was stoked, the mimosas were poured, and we had gathered in the family room for the great unveiling. The smattering of gifts around the Christmas tree the previous evening had now magically—after about an hour's effort by me—swelled to encompass the whole corner of the room where the tree stood. More importantly, hanging from the mantle above the fireplace were three Christmas stockings stuffed to overflowing.

I have indicated before that I believe the Christmas stocking is where adult utility meets childish whimsy. Many hours are spent picking out the exact combination that will achieve those results, and it has always proven to be worthwhile on Christmas morning. The unveiling of the contents of the Bear Cave Christmas stocking normally takes a half hour or more. There are little puzzles, brain teasers, and games that need to be played with. Beyond that, there are gizmos and gadgets that need to be explored and examined to determine how they work, let alone their usefulness. At the bottom of each stocking, there is a collection of Christmas candies (mostly chocolate), and best of all, there are the English Christmas crackers with chintzy trinkets, ridiculous paper crowns, and bad jokes that have somehow become one of the more noteworthy components of a Bear Cave Christmas stocking. To the delight of us all, this Christmas was no exception.

Comfortably seated on the floor around the coffee table, our mimosas resting securely on their coasters, we each began the descent to the bottom of our stocking— and the chocolate! The first items retrieved—as always, by tradition and by the sheer come-hither nature of them—were the Christmas crackers. The efforts of making them "pop" with an acceptable noise was an engaging enterprise that occupied our attention for several minutes. Then there were the paper crowns and the bad jokes, after which we moved on to the trinkets. Haley received a plastic pacifier key chain as she has done for what seems like decades, and Leo received a tacky plastic necklace, traditionally a burden for Buddy. I, on the other hand, was surprised by a tangram puzzle, which promised at least a few minutes of fun and was a decidedly great toy for work!

The Christmas crackers popped and emptied, we turned our attention to the remaining contents of our stockings. Not surprisingly, Leo was the first to reach his stash of chocolate, while Haley and I had barely made it past our first layer of stocking stuffers. I was thumbing through the pages of a *Find Bin Laden* book that was stuffed in the top of my stocking, and Haley was examining a book of mazes from hers. Leo attempted to amuse himself with a brain teaser puzzle that he retrieved from his stocking to give us some time, but it was no use. Leo tossed another chocolate into his mouth and, as casually as possible, asked, "Is it time to open presents?"

It was almost a form of torture for Leo to have to wait for us to finish before the morning could progress. We were content to slowly peruse the contents of our stockings while Leo longingly eyed the gifts that surrounded the base of the Christmas tree. He indulged himself in a couple more pieces of chocolate while he examined some of his stocking stuffer gadgets, but what he wanted to do was to dig into the menagerie of packages calling to him from underneath our tree.

In the days leading up to Christmas morning, Haley and I had decided that Leo should be "Santa" when it came time to hand out the gifts—a privilege that Haley and Buddy have fought over for years. It is hard to accredit an exact reason for this particular sibling rivalry other than the honor of wearing the Santa hat—handmade by me! When it finally came time for Leo to transition from his paper crown to the "official" Santa hat, he simply could not contain his excitement. As he reached across the coffee table for it, he knocked over my drink. When he pulled the hat back across the coffee table, his elbow caught his own drink and knocked it to the floor. Haley and I quickly grabbed everything that could be damaged by the champagne and orange juice slowly spreading across the tabletop and dripping to the floor while Leo ran to the kitchen for some paper towels. The dogs, however, were downright gleeful at the current circumstances and readily lapped at the puddle of drink before it could be contained otherwise.

Haley yelled to Leo to hurry with the paper towels, but I had used the last couple while preparing the cinnamon buns and had not replaced the roll. Leo was left having to rummage through the storage closet for more while the dogs got stupid lapping up the remnants of the spilled mimosas.

"Got 'em!" Leo called from the upstairs hallway, but by that point, it was essentially too late.

Whiskey and Marjorie were large enough to not be greatly affected by the alcohol in the drinks, but it was a bit different for twelve-pound Sergeant, who was first to the spill and refused to give ground to the other two. Leo ran down the stairs with a handful of damp paper towels in one hand and the newly retrieved roll in the other. After the excitement of the initial spill had worn off, Whiskey and Marjorie had returned to their Christmas bones. Sergeant, on the other hand, had to be shooed away as Leo cleaned up the few remaining drops from the coffee table and the floor.

Sergeant looked a bit woozy as he stumbled away and plopped down in front of the fireplace. I eyed him suspiciously; he swayed ever so slightly as he watched Leo wipe up the last of the mess. *Great!* I thought. *All I need is for this little putz to puke! That would be a splendid addition to my already-unkempt house.* I shifted my attention to Leo—in my current frame of mind, the cause of everything messy around me. The fact that I had slowly lost most of my desire and energy for cleaning over the past twelve months aside, it seemed to me that there had to be a reason my house was now in a constant disheveled state, and at this point, it was Leo. He glanced up from wiping down the coffee table and met my gaze. "Oops!" he said nonchalantly, flashing me a huge smile.

As God is my witness, it was hard to stay mad at that boy! I smiled back at him. "You really are an idiot, you know!" I said jokingly. "A Christmas idiot, I would say, but an idiot nonetheless!"

The rest of the morning was a blur of festive bows, bright-colored paper, and an endless stream of "What did you get?" followed by the appropriate *Oohs* and *Ahhs* for the newly revealed surprise. After each round of gifts, Leo was sent back to the tree for more while we all chatted happily about our presents, different memories, and the day in general. A round of gifts equaled a single gift for every person in the room. A long standing rule for the Bear Cave is that only one present gets opened at a time. This way, all participants get to enjoy the gift from all aspects: the giver, the receiver, and the enjoyer—the one who gets to experience the moment as an uninvolved but engaged bystander.

Needless to say, when Christmas is relished in this way, a handful of presents can last hours, let alone the multitude of gifts that surrounded our tree. We were barely halfway through them when the phone rang.

"Where are you?" Albert asked. "When are you going to get here?"

"Soon," I replied. "But we're still opening presents!"

"What?" he asked incredulously. "But it's 11:00!"

I was amazed that my brother seemed to have forgotten how we could make the events of Christmas morning last until noon when we were growing up. In my house, we had learned to extend our celebrations even further. To be fair, however, our extended family—which for this Christmas included all my siblings and their families—were waiting for us to begin the next round of festivities. It was tough, but we managed to quicken our pace and arrived at Albert's house by 2:00. From the beginning, the plan was for Haley, Leo, and Marjorie to spend the morning with me then head down to Leo's parents' house to have Christmas with them. They popped in at my brother's to say hi, but with the long ride ahead of them, they did not stay.

It was always nice to hang out with my extended family; however, I felt a bit out of place amid all the Christmas cheer and frivolity. Almost immediately after Haley and Leo left, I began to notice a sense of loneliness growing deep within me. Even though I was surrounded by my amazing and loving family, I felt isolated. It was not the fact that my kids were not there; not all of my sister's kids were there either. It seemed to be more because of the uniqueness of why *my* son was absent. There is a somewhat embarrassing and childish undertone to the phrase "no one understands," whether spoken aloud or not; however, that is what it was. Shortly after Christmas dinner, and rather early for the evening, I left for home and the growing comfort of solitude.

I changed back into my Christmas pajamas and headed to the family room and the fireplace. I put a log on the smoldering embers from the morning's fire and coaxed the flames to return. I tuned the radio to a station still playing Christmas music, pulled the rocking chair to the edge of hearth, and sat down to reflect on the day. Sergeant, long since recovered from the mimosas, was perched happily on the back of the couch, closely watching my every move. The Whiskey-Dog lay quietly next to the rocking chair in his familiar repose, with his front paws crossed in front of him and his head resting gently on them. Every so often, he would raise his head and look at me. It was as if he were asking, "Are you OK?"

I watched the fire dance across the logs, listening to its soothing pops and crackles, and allowed a flood of memories to invade my thoughts. It was difficult to conceptualize that one year earlier, we were all in Fayetteville celebrating Christmas with Buddy. At that time, we did not understand the significance of our little family get-together. We did not realize that before the New Year was rung in, we would be told that Buddy was being deployed, and that before the year was even forty-eight hours old, he would be on his way. We did not comprehend the emotional drain or the volatile events of the many days that would follow. In many aspects, it had been a staggering year of unbelievable circumstances. I felt older than I ever wanted to be, especially over the Christmas holiday; however, I was also aware that there were many families whose emptiness that Christmas would never be completely healed. I felt my throat tighten in that all-too-familiar way as my eyes began to fill with tears.

Oh, come on, I scolded myself. *You're not going to cry again!* But it was no use. All the Christmas festivities were still fresh in my memory, yet the hint of emptiness that I had been fighting all day long finally overtook me. A huge tear that had been blurring my vision for several seconds rolled down my cheek. Immediately, Whiskey sat up and put his head in my lap. I reached down and scratched him behind his ear without looking away from the fire. "I'm OK, big boy," I reassured him. "I'll be all right, just give me a minute."

Whiskey kept his head on my lap for several minutes and I continued to scratch his ear. Even if I had stopped scratching, I knew he would not move until I had recovered from my moment of weakness. That was my Whiskey-Dog; he was my Lassie or my Rin Tin Tin without the smarts to "Go find Timmy!"—but that was OK, because I didn't need Timmy found; I just needed my son home safe and sound. When I looked down into Whiskey's normally bright and happy eyes, I could see that I was not the only one.

Not-So-Thins

Cookie:

1/2 cup shortening

1/2 cup margarine

2 2/3 cups powdered sugar

1/3 cup powdered cocoa

1/2 teaspoon vanilla

1/2 teaspoon peppermint flavoring

1 egg

1/2 teaspoon baking soda

1/2 teaspoon salt

2 1/4 cups flour

Filling:

1 1/4 cups 60% cacao semisweet chocolate chips

1/2 cup margarine

1 1/3 cups powdered sugar

1 teaspoon peppermint flavoring

1. Preheat oven to 350 degrees.

2. Cream together shortening, margarine, powdered sugar, cocoa, vanilla, peppermint flavoring, and egg with an electric mixer until light and fluffy, about 3 to 5 minutes.

3. Add baking soda and salt. Continue to beat with electric mixer for about a minute.

4. With a spoon, mix in flour.

5. Drop dough by rounded tablespoons onto cookie sheets. With the bottom of a small glass (or the bottom of a standard spice container), flatten the dough to about 1/4 inch in the center. The edges of the dough should be slightly higher, creating a shallow bowl.

6. Bake for about 10 minutes or until the cookies are set.

7. Remove from the cookie sheet to cool.

8. To make the filling, heat chocolate chips, margarine, powdered sugar, and peppermint flavoring in a double boiler. Stir until melted and well mixed.

9. While still warm, drop a dollop of the chocolate mixture into the bowl of the baked cookies. Allow to set for several minutes; an hour or two would not be unusual.

New year, same reflections

I t was just barely 2008, but for all intents and purposes, we were in overtime. January 2nd marked the end of Buddy's twelfth month of deployment. This should have been the time that he was returning home, but instead, Buddy and his battalion were some of the "lucky" ones who were extended to sixteen months. Though we had found out about the extension early on, it now felt like an unwelcome surprise. And it was not just me; conversations with my son let me know that they, too, were tired and ready to be home.

Any talk of re-enlistment had been put on hold because of the impact of that one-year mark. Though we did try, Buddy was not really interested in listening to anything I had to say on the subject. I am not quite sure whether it was because he was not agreeing with what I said or because he was not agreeing with army life. Either way, it was a blessing for me; I still had no desire to treat him like he was twelve and tell him what to do—and, truth be told, I had no idea what to tell him, even if it was only advice and not a command.

With the re-enlistment uncertainties out of the way, I was able to refocus on my own self-absorbed views as the mother of a soldier. Even as I contemplated Buddy's extra four months of deployment with frustration, my thoughts once again gravitated toward the soldiers of World War II. Many of those soldiers, like my dad, served from the beginning. Once they were conscripted, they were obligated until the end of the war, and once trained, most were deployed for the duration. That was almost four years, but that was also a different time.

Over the previous twelve months, I had often thought about Dad and his service during World War II. As I mentioned before, he had been conscripted into the army approximately eleven months before December 7, 1941. He was home on a weekend pass when it happened. He told of how his family was gathered in the living room listening to the radio when the news of Pearl Harbor broke. Dad remembered how over the next few hours, every several minutes or so, programming would be inter-rupted as another battalion was called back to base. Dad said that when his battalion was finally called, his whole family walked him to the bus stop. At the time, he did not give it a second thought; it was only later that it struck him that he could not remember that ever happening before—it would always be one or two family members but never all of them. Dad explained how it occurred to him only then that his future was one big question mark. Neither he nor his family had any idea as to when or even if he would return. I could absolutely relate to that story now—and I could also assure anyone who asked that knowing the "when" did not make the "if" any easier.

Nana and I had also periodically discussed the differences between then and now. Nana often told of how Pearl Harbor was a wake-up call for America that pushed our country into the war in Europe. She spoke of how dissent over involving ourselves in a war that "did not really concern us" melted away after we were attacked. She recalled how the churches were full with all those affected by the war, which was basically everyone. In her memories, the church was where the community worked their way through the turmoil of the long war years. Nana regularly talked of collective belt-tightening, personal sacrifice, and the rationing of various items so they would be available for the troops and the war effort. She would explain that the war was not left to the military but fought by the entire country as everyone did their part for victory.

I could not help but wonder if that type of national support and community involvement made the uncertainties for the families of those fighting any easier to bear. What my parents described felt foreign to anything I had known or experienced with this conflict, at least on a grand scale. Maybe Nana and Dad remembered things differently than they really were, but I doubted it—there were too many corroborating witnesses. Maybe it was simply a matter of "out of sight (or out of family), out of mind," but that did not necessarily seem right, either. I was fairly young during the Vietnam War, and even though my family was not directly involved in the conflict, I remember baking cookies on the weekends with my sister to send in care packages to the troops.

I felt like I was comparing the difference between yin and yang, up and down, black and white. It seemed as though back then, the troops had so much more support to see them through. There was more of a common experience between neighbors and in the community as well as a collective effort by all segments of the country. Even Hollywood openly offered its support, if only through some movie that portrayed our guys as heroes. Still, I did not know whether that type of national support would make the whole experience any easier to take.

A full year after the beginning of the Surge, I felt like I did the previous January, with more anxiety than assurance—but this time I had a clear understanding of all possible outcomes and a palatable desire for it all just to be *over*. I was very proud of my son and all the rest of the guys with whom he served—what they had accomplished was nothing short of amazing. They took a country that was volatile and on the edge of civil war and turned it around. Some of this accomplishment was through a show of force, but much of it, unlike the soldiers of World War II, was through a sort of front-line diplomacy that required our troops to make themselves approachable and available to the local peoples. It was a dangerous endeavor, but the results had been absolutely outstanding.

Even given their accomplishments, Buddy seemed unconvinced of their success. First, it was difficult to assess whether their accomplishments were worth the cost— and we all understood with great clarity that the cost was dear. Second, he was unsure how long the tentative peace they had established would even last after they left the country. These things were totally out of his hands and did not affect the magnitude of his successes, but that did not alleviate his desire to leave that country nor my desire to have him leave!

I understood and even shared his concerns. What I could not figure out was how much my concerns and unsettled feelings had to do with support. I could not decipher whether that subtle concept had any connection to the ability to endure being the mother of a soldier. But, things being the way they were, what I did know was that the past year had been so completely draining that I could hardly imagine four more months, let alone the three extra years it would have been if this were World War II—support or not.

Cranberry-Macadamia Nut Oatmeal Cookies

1/2 cup shortening

1/2 cup margarine

3/4 cup brown sugar

1/3 cup granulated sugar

1 teaspoon butternut flavoring

1 egg

1 teaspoon baking soda

1/2 teaspoon salt

1/2 teaspoon ground nutmeg

2 3/4 cups flour

1 cup old-fashioned oats

1/2 cup chopped macadamia nuts

1. Preheat oven to 350 degrees.
2. Cream together shortening, margarine, brown sugar, granulated sugar, butternut flavoring, and egg with an electric mixer until light and fluffy, about 3 to 5 minutes.
3. Add baking soda, salt, and nutmeg. Continue to beat with electric mixer for about a minute.
4. With a spoon, mix in flour and oats until well blended. Stir in macadamia nuts.
5. Drop dough by rounded teaspoons onto cookie sheets.
6. Bake for 12 minutes.

Cookie Week 48

7 January 2008-13 January 2008

Aren't we there yet?!

To "hit the wall" is a runner's phrase that refers to the moment in a marathon when a runner's energy gives out. Once "the wall" is hit, even running downhill feels like climbing straight up the side of a mountain. The runner's feet will feel like two huge blocks of cement that grow a little with each step, their arms will feel like two weights that are being unwillingly dragged along for the rest of the run, and their concentration gives way to every random thought possible. Eventually, though, a runner becomes overwhelmed with a single thought, a thought that had become very familiar to me:

"I just can't do this anymore! I am *done!*"

I must say, using the concept of a marathon as a metaphor for the deployment was an excellent way to describe the previous year and one week. Even though during the preceding week, I had placidly noted the passing of that one-year mark with only a dash of complaint, at the one-year-and-one-week point, I "hit the wall." It took every ounce of energy I could summon—and then some—to drag myself out of bed every morning. Then there was the overwhelming task of brushing my teeth, followed by the equally crushing effort of taking a shower. I could not even begin to describe the staggering burden of choosing what to wear and getting dressed, and my day did not get any better from there. Each morning was followed by a long ride into work then a painful eight hours of trying to think. All the while, there was but a single thought on my mind. It was the ever-present, ever-familiar thought that would not subside: *I just can't do this anymore!*

More often than not, I would spend the first few minutes of the day just sitting on the edge of my bed, my feet dangling over its edge, slightly swinging back and forth, as I collected my thoughts. The time spent there every morning summoning the energy to begin my day had been increasing since the beginning of the Surge, but over the past couple of weeks, it had grown exponentially. It seemed that most days, I would have to fight back the tears because I was just so emotionally exhausted. I felt a bit like a child toward the end of the school year who was tired of classrooms and homework and just wanted the school year to be over, to get the chance to relax for a while and give their mind a rest.

Like all children in this situation, I did the only logical thing: I told my mommy that I was tired, did not feel well, and wanted to stay home for a day or two—or ten. And Nana gave me the answer all mothers give in this situation: "It's time to get up! Get out of that bed and get dressed!"

Actually, given the circumstances, Nana had a little more to say. She encouraged me to get out of my self-imposed rut and shake up my life a bit. "Like how?" I asked her. "Just what am I supposed to do?"

"I'm not talking anything extreme," Nana answered. "Try to do something new and different every once in a while, like the pottery class you took with Keith; just do a little something to break up your days to make them feel less like endless waiting."

The pottery class had been kind of fun, and it certainly was a distraction. But by the end, even that had felt more like an obligatory burden than the release of inner tension it was supposed to be. The classes had ended in May, but it had taken me until the end of July to get back to the school to finish up my remaining projects and pick up the finished pieces, a collection of randomly shaped and colored bowls, two of which could be roughly classified as soup bowls. Enjoyable though it was, I had no taste for beginning another obligation like that for the time being, even if it was supposed to be for my benefit. In fact, by this point, I did not have a taste for any activity; not cleaning, not vacuuming, not cookie baking—not anything.

I figured I should at least try what Nana proposed, but I was at a loss as to where to start. I had no intention of starting something big or involved; I just wanted to do something simple to break up my days. Haley and Leo were involved with their own distractions, so I decided to give Keith a call. I figured if nothing else, we could at least go out and grab a bite to eat. Not only would it be good to see Keith again and hear what he had been up to, it would also fit the bill for Nana's proposal.

"Ah, you've met the monkey!" was Keith's response when I explained to him how I was feeling.

"Huh?" I asked. Having never heard that term before, at first I thought he might have been saying something naughty to me—maybe even rude and inappropriate.

"You know," Keith began to explain. "You're fine, and then you meet the monkey."

"Oh . . . what?!"

"When you're running long distances, after you meet the metaphorical monkey, he is with you for the rest of your run. He rides your back, beating you about the head and shoulders every step of the way until you either give up or finish the race!"

"Yes!" I exclaimed. That I understood, and that was exactly how I felt—only instead of running, I had reached the end of my limit to cope. When most runners "hit the wall," "meet the monkey," or whatever analogy suits, they adopt the attitude of "just one more step . . . just one more step . . ." and try to run through the experience. I was not quite sure what attitude to assume as the mother of a soldier who had reached the point where she felt she was unable to continue. Furthermore, for a runner, there can generally be only two outcomes—they either reach the finish line standing, most likely after gaining some sort of second wind, or they end up in the emergency room on a stretcher, having failed at the whole second-wind thing! Yet, as the mother of a soldier, I was not even sure that a second wind was a possibility.

I felt that I was only capable of facing not even one day or hour at a time but more like a single moment at a time. Like a runner in the final stretches of a marathon, I tried to concentrate on simply putting one foot in front of the other as I focused on making my way through the final few months of the deployment. I figured that in the end, I would either end up at the finish line waving a "Welcome Home" sign for my son, having finished the race . . . or find myself in some sort of restrictive garment in a room with padded walls because the race had finished me.

Oreo Cookie Cookies

1/2 cup shortening
1/2 cup margarine
1 cup brown sugar
1/3 cup powdered sugar
1 teaspoon light corn syrup
1 teaspoon vanilla
1 tablespoon cornstarch

1 egg
1 teaspoon baking soda
1/2 teaspoon salt
2 cups flour
8 Double Stuf Oreo cookies,
    chopped
1/2 cup finely chopped walnuts

1. Preheat oven to 350 degrees.
2. Cream together shortening, margarine, brown sugar, powdered sugar, corn syrup, vanilla, cornstarch, and egg with an electric mixer until light and fluffy, about 3 to 5 minutes.
3. Add baking soda and salt. Continue to beat with electric mixer for about a minute.
4. With a spoon, mix in flour until well blended. Stir in chopped Oreo cookies and walnuts.
5. Drop dough by rounded tablespoons onto cookie sheets.
6. Bake for 12 to 15 minutes or until lightly browned.

It's kind of hard to explain . . .

Buddy finally made the decision to "re-up," and he made it on his own, without me offering my opinion or telling him what to do as he had demanded—thank God. He agreed upon an additional four years of enlistment, and the army agreed to train him in computers. He was satisfied with his choice, and so was I. However, the amount of phone calls I received from him trailed off as he, once again, turned his full focus to the tasks at hand. There was very little information coming out of Iraq from the news media, and we were left to what little we were hearing from our soldiers, the FRG, and the monthly newsletters from Command. So close to the end of the deployment, it was difficult not to look forward, but I hesitated to do so—Iraq could still be a dangerous place. Instead, I chose to look backward and inward.

At the front of my parents' house is a very large horse chestnut tree—beautiful flowers in the spring, lovely leaves and shade in the summer, but hideous in the fall. The leaves go from glorious green to brown and dead with no brilliant autumn colors in between. In addition, that time of year also means lots of thorny nut shells and horse chestnuts falling to the ground and normally taking weeks to get cleaned up. I once stopped in to see my parents on a cold winter evening. In front of the roaring fire was a coal bin filled with a portion of the fall's "harvest" of horse chestnuts.

"Hey, Dad! What's going on?" I asked. "Why do you have the bin of horse chestnuts there?"

"I had to get rid of them somehow, so I'm roasting them." he replied. "Every time I add wood, I add a handful of chestnuts to the fire as well."

"Dad!" I exclaimed. "Aren't horse chestnuts supposed to be poisonous? Why on earth are you roasting them?"

"Well," he replied, "you know the song 'Chestnuts Roasting on an Open Fire'? I thought it would be nice to hear them pop as the fire burns!" He paused a moment and then added, "Besides, I would never eat the things, even if they were edible. I've had roasted chestnuts before and they taste like mushy lima beans!"

That was the very essence of who my Dad was; he never ceased to find the magic in life. Despite everything that had happened to him along the way, he was always positive, always saw the good in people, and always found time to appreciate God's work. He and Nana made sure every occasion was special, even if it was just a random fire in the fireplace on some random evening.

I supposed that was why I also had a love of life and a childlike marvel for the world. I tended not to be burdened by the outward appearance of something, but rather looked beyond what my eyes saw and listened to my heart. I was not always successful in that endeavor—not to mention that that simple act led me to trouble more often than I would like to admit; however, I was inclined to see beauty and selflessness in things others found ordinary and familiar. In recent days, I had been seeing the extraordinary in the past fifty-five weeks.

It was not that I thought that war should be romanticized in any way or was extraordinary in and of itself. However, I could not help but feel that the idea that there were people in this country who still believed there were things worth pre-serving—things worth fighting for, even if it meant giving their last full measure—smacked of something amazing. For all the stress the past year had piled on me, the fact that my son was one of those willing to fight for this country stirred my heart. The fact that Buddy would re-enlist, given all that went before, was extraordinary to me—especially considering his motivation.

By September 11, 2001, I had spent over fifteen years working both at and for the Pentagon. At that time, Haley had just begun her freshman year of college and Buddy had just started his sophomore year of high school. It should not be difficult to imag-ine how hard that day was for me and my family, as it was for all Americans, but as Buddy waited for the phone call that assured him that I was all right, he became deter-mined to protect not just me but his sister and his Nana as well. His future was shaped by that one awful event beyond the leanings of public opinion. He saw dangers that day that threatened his way of life and directly threatened his family. No spin on those events or the events that followed would ever change that.

I knew better, and it was very much unlike anything my dad would think or say, but it seemed that since the beginning of Buddy's service, one negative com-ment could erase a thousand random acts of support. It was even more so since the beginning of the Surge. And though I would never have shared any of my negative experiences with Buddy, there was no need, because he, too, had felt the sting of inappropriate comments regarding his choice of profession. However, I also knew that he would be the first to tell any who attempted to defend him that he was willing to make the sacrifice for everyone's right to speak whatever way they choose, even if it was against him.

A question I was often asked was "What's it like?" Explaining what it was like to have a son serving in the Surge, peppered with all its idiosyncrasies regarding public support or lack thereof, was to share the pride that a mother of a soldier felt for her son. The bottom line was that my son made the conscious decision that he was willing to lay down his life for his family and his country's protection. It would have been one thing to have done what the majority of every other consenting adult male was doing, like in World War II. However, those who served in the Surge were in the minority. As the mother of a soldier, I could not help but feel deeply moved by my son's gesture, nor could I help but feel almost sad for those who could not claim, "I am the *proud* mother of one of our troops!"

Bacon Drop Cookies

8 slices of bacon
3/4 cup shortening
1/2 cup margarine
1 1/2 cups brown sugar
1/3 cup powdered sugar
2 tablespoons corn syrup
1/2 teaspoon vanilla

1/2 teaspoon butternut flavoring
1 egg
1 1/2 teaspoons baking soda
1/2 teaspoon salt
3 cups flour
1/2 cup toffee bits
1/2 cup finely chopped walnuts

1. Preheat oven to 350 degrees.
2. Dice bacon and cook until crispy. Remove from heat and drain well. Set aside.
3. Cream together shortening, margarine, brown sugar, powdered sugar, corn syrup, vanilla, butternut flavoring, and egg with an electric mixer until light and fluffy, about 3 to 5 minutes.
4. Add baking soda and salt. Continue to beat with electric mixer for about a minute.
5. With a spoon, mix in flour until well blended. Stir in bacon, toffee bits, and walnuts.
6. Drop dough by rounded teaspoons onto cookie sheets.
7. Bake for 10 to 12 minutes.

The good, the bad, and the ridiculous!

I just knew it was going to be a bad day. I walked out of the bathroom with my skirt tucked into my pantyhose, dropped my plate of eggs in the elevator, and, after getting back to my desk, watched my computer "eat" the document I had been working on for the past few days. There was no doubt about it: the die had been cast. For the rest of that day, my stomach churned, my nerves were on edge, and my temper was short, anticipating just what else might go wrong.

A day like this one was annoying, to say the very least. I knew the only course of action was to brace myself and proceed; however, I also knew this was not a worst-case scenario. Whereas bad days when everything goes wrong were exasperating, days that were bad for no obvious reason were downright scary. Sometimes it was just that the causes of why things felt amiss were subtle: a missed phone call, a less-than-stellar—but not horrible—news report, or a forgotten bad dream. But at other times, there was nothing to point to and nothing to explain why things just did not feel right or maybe even felt horrible. Those days were my worst nightmares.

For years, I had tried to explain to others that I have this sort of metaphysical connection to my kids. There were numerous occasions that the kids and I had seemed aligned on some ethereal level that did not appear to have any relation to our proximity to each other. It did not matter if we were in the same house, across the state from one another, or across the world; when one was distressed, chances were we all were distressed, and it all began years before.

I remember when I was pregnant with Haley; it was late November and well after she was due, but there was still no sign that I was going into labor anytime soon. She was my first, and as all first-time mothers will tell you, it is a bit unsettling. To know that there is this six- to nine-pound thing growing inside you that you know needs to come out sooner or later—but you have no idea what it is going to be like when it happens—is enough to make anyone a little crazy. In addition, I had been having dreams that I was in the hospital with my baby in my arms, but for the life of me, I could not remember the experience of childbirth. I would try so hard to recall the actual event of the birth because I wanted to know what I was up against, but to no avail. It was impossible to remember something that had never happened.

I was anxious and on edge and decided a walk would help ease my concerns and maybe even bring on labor. I circled the neighborhood, allowing my musings to wander the universe looking for any thought that would satisfy an apprehensive mind. I recalled Nana telling me, "Don't worry, women have been having babies since the beginning of time!" I knew she was right, but I was unconvinced. I remember walking down the street and talking to myself. "What the heck was I thinking?" I asked out loud. "In fact, what the heck am I doing!? I don't want to do this anymore; I want to back out! I don't want to do labor! Who in their right mind would do this to themselves on purpose?"

The answer came as a crystal-clear thought that did not seem to be mine. It was faint at first but continued to grow as I headed towards my front door. "What was I thinking?" it said. "I don't want to go out there. I am warm in here, fed regularly; I don't want to be born! Who in their right mind would ever want to be born?" And that was just the beginning.

Since then, there had been many random occurrences where the kids and I still seemed that connected, and almost at that level. More than that, it had happened regularly enough that it no longer felt like an enigma, a fluke, or a coincidence—not to me and not to my kids.

Whenever I spoke of how my kids and I shared our emotions, most people thought I was talking about a conversation where one of us would say, "Oh, was my day ever [bad, good, exceptional, pathetic, whatever]!" and someone else would respond with, "Please, tell us about it!" But what I referred to was an instance where one of the kids would say to me, "Mom! I am having the *worst* day!" and as they continued to describe their day, I would think, *Oh! No wonder I was feeling so crummy!* Alternately, I would get a phone call that said, "Are you OK, Mom? I have just been feeling so weird, like I am having a bad day, but nothing is going wrong!" Or it would be me sitting around trying to figure out why I was feeling so agitated, even though I was alone and had not left the house all day. I would call either of my kids just to hear their voice and instead hear about their horrible day where everything was going wrong.

We realized it was rather an unusual affiliation for a mother and her kids—both from their standpoint as well as from mine. Nonetheless, it was what it was, and we accepted it. When the kids and I all shared the same house, especially when they were young, people would often attribute our connection to simply the kids playing off my emotions, or me playing off theirs; any parent can attest to the fact that if something is wrong with your kids, be it physical, emotional or mental, you do not feel "right" either. But our connection continued well past my kids moving away from home. Even with Haley in Richmond, Buddy in Fayetteville, and me in northern Virginia, we could not keep our emotional states from affecting one other. It was not that we picked up the other's mood after we spoke; it was the fact that we felt the impact of what was going on somewhere else without knowing exactly what we were feeling.

The kids and I realized that this emotional bond between us was an unusual one that made us and it rather special, and for the most part, we sort of liked it. However, since the beginning of the Surge, it presented some serious drawbacks as well. For one thing, there was an inability to check on Buddy if we were having an unfounded bad day. Before the Surge, it was not uncommon for Haley to call me to ask about my day because she feeling a bit off, and my response would be, "I haven't heard from Buddy in a few days. Let me give him a call."

But since the beginning of the Surge, these types of conversations had not been so easily solved, and the various mental images of exactly what might have been going wrong with Buddy's day could be absolutely beastly. In addition, as unlikely as this all might have seemed, I wondered if, because Haley and I were being affected by Buddy's bad days, he was being affected by ours. It was a bit of a frightening thought for me that my eggs on the floor of an elevator could cause my son difficulty.

I had always figured that this atypical association went beyond simply bad days, but it seemed that only the bad days stood out. I could certainly remember days where I felt exceptionally good—maybe even great—for no apparent reason other than I woke up. Maybe those good days were as attributable to my kids as the bad ones. And, that being said, I could not help but wonder if I projected positive good moods all day, every day, no matter what, would it have forced good moods and good days on my kids—especially Buddy? I really had no idea, but it did not matter. As long as I felt that what went on in my life had an effect on what was happening on the other side of the world in Buddy's life, I felt I had no choice but to silently tame my annoyingly bad days to prevent them from becoming terrible days for my son.

No-Oats

1/2 cup shortening

1/2 cup margarine

1 1/3 cups brown sugar

1 tablespoon light corn syrup

1/2 teaspoon vanilla

1/2 teaspoon butternut flavoring

1/2 tablespoon cornstarch

1 egg

1 teaspoon ground cinnamon

1 teaspoon baking soda

1/2 teaspoon salt

2 1/4 cups flour

2/3 cup coarsely chopped walnut
   pieces

2/3 cup butterscotch chips

1. Preheat oven to 350 degrees.
2. Cream together shortening, margarine, brown sugar, corn syrup, vanilla, butternut flavoring, cornstarch, and egg with an electric mixer until light and fluffy, about 3 to 5 minutes.
3. Add cinnamon, baking soda, and salt. Continue to beat with electric mixer for about a minute.
4. With a spoon, mix in flour until well blended. Stir in the walnuts and butterscotch chips.
5. Drop dough by rounded teaspoons onto cookie sheets.
6. Bake for 10 to 12 minutes.

The light at the end of the tunnel

I t was Sunday morning, and it started like all the others. After getting out of bed, I grabbed a mug of tea and headed for my laptop and the TV for a little early morning email and news as I put off taking my shower and heading for church. I sat on the couch, flipped on the television, and opened my laptop. The Whiskey-Dog took one of his favorite places of repose, lying on his belly across my feet between the couch and the coffee table, his big old head resting gently on his crossed front paws. Sergeant took his place laying on a blanket on the back of the couch.

Sipping my tea with one eye on the news and one eye on the laptop screen, I eyed my recent email subject lines. Along with the standard advertising spam that I loved to peruse for good deals, there were a few emails from my friends and family and one email from the FRG leader with the subject line "Fwd: Red Devil Mail." Since the 1-504th were known as the Red Devils and I was looking for news on my son, I went to that email first.

For the moment, I only wanted to glance at it to make sure it was not something I needed to know right away. I figured I could spend more time reading its contents when I was not supposed to be getting ready for church and had a little more time. However, almost immediately my eyes caught sight of something different; the format was unusual, the words a little stiffer than what I was used to. I set down my mug of tea, squared the laptop in front of me, and read the email carefully. It read:

Please disseminate this information to all family members and parents:

1-504 . . . will begin redeployment activities in March. It is recommended that mail and packages are not sent after 15 FEB 08. Adherence to this deadline will ensure all mail and packages are received before redeployment activities begin.

I was sure that if a heart monitor had been attached to me at that moment, it would have registered my heart skipping a beat! Immediately after I read those words, I wanted to share them; I wanted to go to the front door and shout them to the world.

However, considering it was still fairly early on a Sunday morning, I figured that it might not be appreciated. Haley and Leo were unavailable because they had already left for work, and I could not tell Nana because I knew she would already be at church. *I guess it won't be that long before I will be able to share the happy news*, I thought.

"It's almost over," I said out loud to the Whiskey-Dog and Sergeant. At the sound of my voice, Whiskey looked up at me, wagged his tail a few times, and smiled. I reached down and scratched him behind his ears, prompting Sergeant to leave the back of the couch and lie beside me, resting his head on my leg, waiting for his head scratch.

"You understand, don't you, boys?" I said, still contemplating the joyful news. But before even five minutes had passed, my euphoria had begun morphing into just another worry!

My first thoughts reveled in the fact that the deployment was almost over. Rather than knowing that Buddy would be coming home sometime in 2008, I finally had a month to focus on. I then spent a few moments reflecting on the past thirteen months. It seemed as though it had been an eternity since the beginning of the Surge. The months had been long and, at times, much more eventful than I would have ever expected or wanted. However, the Bear Cave had managed to make it through intact.

But immediately from there, my mind wandered to those soldiers who had already "made it home." Every loss during the deployment had been deeply felt and took a little bit more out of all of us, and with every report, whether officially through the FRG or just over the news, there came a bizarre combination of a sorrowful, "Oh my God, no!" followed by a guilt-riddled wave of relief that began with the words, "Oh, thank God it wasn't Buddy!" However, any relief I felt was always overshadowed. Military families of both deployed and returned troops were all painfully aware of how easily the circumstances could have been different. Even more than that, it just felt wrong to experience relief knowing that somewhere a family had been so devastated.

It was understandable that these thoughts had a chilling effect on any desire to celebrate, and I was jolted back into the reality of the situation. March was still almost six weeks away. Word out of Iraq reported that our soldiers' spirits were high and that they were all ecstatic to be in the final weeks of the deployment. We were all ready for them to be on their way back home again, but March was *still* almost six weeks away.

At the beginning of the deployment, I had no idea what to expect—not for me or for Buddy. I was in a sort of numbed haze, gradually forming my own battle plan to help see me through to the bitter end. When it all started, I had to find my courage, solidify my inner strengths, and re-establish my relationship with God. I had to start from scratch to define what it meant for me, my son, and my family to survive and what I needed to do to support that effort. These things did not develop naturally over the endless weeks and months of the Surge, but rather took calculated and focused effort.

As the days wore on, I did fall into the "routine" of the deployment, though I had never thought that would be possible. At any given moment, I anticipated that anything could happen—good, bad, or indifferent. At no time did I expect the worst, but it was always there just out of the range of expectation. It was exhausting, but I learned to navigate the myriad possibilities and continue as if everything were normal. After the Surge hit that one-year mark, that all began to change, despite my efforts to prevent it. It began to feel as if the end was near. I began to relax ever so slightly—and to exclude some of those possibilities.

The soldiers and my son were still performing their military duties, still going out on patrol, and still engaging the enemy. Iraq was safer than when they had arrived thirteen months earlier but definitely remained a dangerous place. The soldiers did not need to be distracted by their closer-than-ever redeployment and neither did I. Worst-case scenarios still existed, and I could not help but feel that any loss at this late date would seem like a bitterly cruel twist of fate.

All of a sudden, it felt a little early to be celebrating. Before I had shared Buddy's upcoming redeployment with a single soul, bar the Whiskey-Dog and Sergeant, the jubilation had already been replaced by renewed concern. I might have finally been able to see the light at the end of the tunnel, but I didn't know whether it was just an oncoming train.

Peanut Butter Blasts

1/2 cup peanut butter

1/3 cup shortening

1/3 cup margarine

1 tablespoon corn syrup

1/2 cup brown sugar

1/2 cup granulated sugar

1 tablespoon cornstarch

1 teaspoon vanilla

1 egg

1 teaspoon baking soda

1/2 teaspoon salt

2 cups flour

3/4 cup Reese's Peanut Butter
 Chips

1. Preheat oven to 350 degrees.

2. Cream together peanut butter, shortening, margarine, corn syrup, brown sugar, granulated sugar, cornstarch, vanilla, and egg with an electric mixer until light and fluffy, about 3 to 5 minutes.

3. Add baking soda and salt. Continue to beat with electric mixer for about a minute.

4. With a spoon, mix in flour until well blended. Stir in the peanut butter chips.

5. Drop dough by rounded teaspoons onto cookie sheets.

6. Bake for 10 to 12 minutes.

Coming full circle

I opened the front door and was immediately greeted by the Whiskey-Dog bounding toward me through the foyer. At the same time, Sergeant began barking excitedly from the kitchen. Early on, I learned that Sergeant needed to be confined while I was out to prevent everything standing upright from becoming his own personal fire hydrant. I released Sergeant from his confinement and began walking them to the laundry room to let them outside. However, they were not interested in that at the moment. The Marjorie-Dog had joined the fray when we reached the bottom step, and they were all more interested in getting a bit of attention, which they sought by impairing my every step with a rather rambunctious game of Ring Around the Rosie—in which I was the Rosie!

"Come on guys, leave me alone!" I said crossly. "GO LIE DOWN!"

Instantly, I was sorry—though the dogs did not seem to be affected by my words in the least. I knew that I was simply distracted. I had gone to the post office and on the way home realized that the trip marked a significant milestone for me. I guess it was significant for B-Company and C-Company as well, but they had not realized it yet and maybe never would.

Valentine's Day 2008 was fast approaching. I had spent the week gathering together all the appropriate components for suitable care packages for "my" soldiers to celebrate the day. I packed up one care package for Buddy, the FHOTA, and the rest of C-Company and one for 1st Sgt. Ramirez and B-Company. Driving home from the post office after mailing the packages, a thought occurred to me. Exactly one year before, I had prepared Buddy's first care package, and Valentine's Day was the theme. It struck me that I had just sent off the last care packages that I would be able to send before the 1-504th's redeployment, and once again, Valentine's Day was the theme. The deployment had come full circle.

It felt like some sort of a celebration was in order, but I was too distracted to even contemplate what that celebration would be. Baking a cake? Going out to dinner with Haley and Leo? Or maybe just a glass or two of wine to numb my thought processes and give my mind a rest? I knew that my thoughts tended to be scattered even at the best of times, but until recently, there was at least a semblance of order to them. I sat down on the couch in the family room. The dogs gathered themselves around me, staring at me intently and waiting to see who I was going to give my attention to. I, on the other hand, stared blankly off into space, thinking about everything and nothing.

When I was young, my flighty thoughts were a burden that my teachers simply referred to as being a "daydreamer" or not "applying myself." As I got older, however, my ability to comprehend several things at once became a blessing that helped me succeed in my professional life. Though I had switched careers, my ability to focus on and handle several things at once had only benefited my endeavors. However, that ability was somehow betraying me now. Though on the outside I was functioning somewhat normally, on the inside, the excitement of having my son home again juxtaposed with random mental images of disastrous outcomes tormented me and kept me from processing any normal thoughts effectively. Throw in various superstitions that I tried to placate, balanced against the already-existing emotional pressures of the Surge, and the situation was fast becoming untenable.

The bottom line was that being able to multiprocess—a term that puts the most positive spin possible on my malady—just did not seem to be much of an advantage in the final weeks of the Surge. I could not hold onto a single thought with both my hands and a vise! My mind jumped from one random musing to another, and I seemed to have little control over any of it. It was bad enough dealing with this in my personal life, but since word of Buddy's upcoming redeployment, it had become an impossible characteristic for my professional life, as well.

While I was on my temporary duty assignment to Fayetteville, my office had been reorganized. My old supervisor was promoted, and my new supervisor, Jeff, happened to be one of the reservists that had returned from Iraq shortly after the beginning of the Surge. He seemed to be a really nice guy, but even so, I mostly tried to avoid him on a day-to-day basis. He seemed to understand this and tended to speak to me only when he had to and mostly only regarding work.

My job was much better with Jeff as my supervisor. Not only did he support me in my work, but he also seemed to understand the ups and downs I was experiencing as the mother of a soldier. That being said, even he recognized that I was no longer functioning at my best. No matter what comment or question Jeff posed, my responses always sounded the same—a jumbled mess of unconnected, incomplete thoughts that conveyed little, if anything. I realized I was slowly melting down but could not seem to pull out of it on my own. And though, generally speaking, Jeff appreciated the natural quirkiness and idiosyncrasies of my personality, it had become apparent to him that I was having some trouble concentrating, to say the very least.

One by one, the dogs got tired of waiting for me to give them attention and made their way through the now-open doggy door in the laundry room. As they did, I recalled the last conversation I had with Jeff. It was toward the end of the previous week, and he had showed up at my desk bright and early one morning. "Hey, Maggie, did you see the email I sent you?" he asked.

I tried to think a moment, but to no avail. "I might have," I began. "If—Hey! Did you see that game last night? Umm . . . I tried to read what you left but—You know, I talked with Buddy yesterday and he said my letters were *very* hard to read because my hand—yeah, my hands have really been shaking recently! I think it's just the stress of waiting for Buddy. You know, I don't hear from him very much these days. Did you want something?"

The email he referred to advertised another temporary assignment which needed some volunteers. Though I was content to muddle through the final weeks of Buddy's deployment (and possibly my career) hiding at my desk while trying desperately to avoid any and all situations where a cohesive, cogent thought might be required, Jeff had a different plan. Maybe it was because of the location of the office where the work was to be performed, and maybe it was the mindless, repetitive nature of the work, but up to that point, there had been no takers for the post. Jeff, however, surmised that the very reasons for the lack of interest in the position made it a perfect fit for me. He had come over to my desk to inform me that I had been volunteered and that I was to start the thirty-day assignment immediately.

I was not happy about the arrangement. Yes, it was closer to home, and yes, it was more suited to my current state of mind, but no one appreciates being volun-told to do anything. This was no exception—at least at the beginning. Halfway through my first week, I was already feeling the reduced pressure. My commute was less than half of what it normally was, and the work required practically no thought at all. My mind was free to wander aimlessly, contemplating all the various aspects of my life without actually focusing on anything specific—and avoiding all thoughts regarding the imminent homecoming. But after mailing the last of the care packages, the imminent homecoming seemed to be the only thing on my mind.

I scrutinized the significance of shipping the last care package, which clearly indicated that the deployment and the Surge were coming to a close. It was clear to me that this by no means made my life any easier. In fact, I figured that in some ways, things would be more difficult because my crucial sanity-maintainer, inventing cookies for Buddy, had suddenly become inconsequential.

Composing cookies from the random thoughts that perpetually flew through my head had become a pleasant respite from the worldly events that had habitually kept me awake at night for the past year. In fact, as the stress of the deployment grew, so did the creativeness I threw into the cookies. I marveled at the fact that the first cookies I sent to Buddy were a batch of plain old chocolate chip cookies, and yet for this last care package, I had invented Red Velvet Cookies dipped in a cream cheese coating. Without that weekly activity to look forward to, I wondered if the days would drag even slower and my attention span would shrink even more.

This final stretch of the Surge had begun to feel a great deal like the first few weeks when I was stumbling through each day not knowing what to expect and looking for something to help me survive—both emotionally and mentally. For all my whining that I did not want the assignment Jeff imposed on me, it was new, it was different, and it was providing a distraction. As for the morning's milestone, I was grateful for the time to celebrate the significance of the day, if only mentally—and for Leo, who, being a bit of a cookie monster, would continue to eat any cookies I felt the need to create.

Red Velvet Cookies

Cookie:

1 cup shortening	1 egg
1/3 cup brown sugar	2 1/2 tablespoons powdered cocoa
1 cup granulated sugar	1 teaspoon baking soda
1 bottle (2 ounces) red food coloring	1/4 teaspoon cream of tartar
1/4 cup buttermilk	1/2 teaspoon salt
1 teaspoon vinegar	2 1/3 cups flour

Coating:

12 ounces white chocolate	1/4 cup margarine
3 ounces cream cheese	1/4 cup powdered sugar

1. Preheat oven to 350 degrees.
2. Cream together shortening, brown sugar, granulated sugar, food coloring, buttermilk, vinegar, and egg with an electric mixer until light and fluffy, about 3 to 5 minutes.
3. Beat in powdered cocoa on low speed.
4. Add baking soda, cream of tartar, and salt. Continue to beat with electric mixer for about a minute.
5. With a spoon, mix in flour.
6. Refrigerate dough until firm.
7. Split dough into quarters. Roll out a quarter of the dough between two floured sheets of wax paper until approximately 1/4 inch thick. Use cookie cutters to cut dough into various shapes. Transfer cookies onto cookie sheets with a pancake turner.
8. Bake for 10 to 12 minutes. Place on a cooling rack to cool.
9. To make the coating, melt white chocolate, cream cheese, and margarine in a double boiler. Stir in powdered sugar until well mixed.
10. Dip the cooled cookies into the white chocolate mixture (at least half of each cookie) and place the cookies onto a sheet of wax paper to cool and harden.

Post-Cookie Weeks

My kids, my heart, my heroes!

T hey say the sense of smell is the most powerful trigger for memories. From my own experiences, I could attest to the fact that on occasion, smell did bring about memories. There were many times when I took my daily Whiskey walk (the dog, not the bottle) and passed through a waft of aromas that prompted a ton of memories, starting with my pre-K remembrances and rolling right on through to Buddy and pre-Iraq. For me, however, it was music that sparked the most amazing memories.

There are several songs that awaken various memories and emotions in me. I cannot hear bagpipes, specifically "Scotland the Brave," and not fondly think of my dad and years of going to see the Black Watch Regiment when they came to Washington, DC, as I was growing up. Several sixties songs remind me of being very small and sharing a room with my sister. Elton John's "Don't Let the Sun Go Down On Me" somehow makes me think of high school, staying out past curfew and skipping classes. One of my more powerful memories, evoked by the hymn "How Great Thou Art," still brings tears to my eyes as my thoughts wander back to sitting between my parents for a church service at one of my parents' reunions many, many years before. However, the song that can mess me up no matter how many years have passed by is Bette Midler's "The Wind Beneath My Wings."

It was almost two decades before; Haley was in third grade, Buddy was in kindergarten, and I was working at the Pentagon. I was in my office one afternoon when the phone rang. It was the counselor at my kids' grade school. This counselor also happened to have been one of my favorite former high school teachers, so she knew me on a personal level. When I first heard her voice, a chill went through me. "What's wrong?" I asked immediately.

Mrs. Watson explained that Haley had been brought to her office during lunch. "It seems that Haley was right in the middle of her peanut butter and honey sandwich when she was overwhelmed with a desire to talk to you. Her teacher brought her to me, and I knew that if you were not too busy, it would be OK if Haley took a moment of your time."

"Is she all right?" I asked.

"Oh, yes," the counselor answered. "She just felt a little sad and thought that talking to you would help." Mrs. Watson then let Haley have the phone.

"Hi, Mama," Haley said in a rather subdued tone.

"Hey Sweetie!" I responded. "Are you doing OK?"

"Yeah, I'm OK. I was just thinking of a song that I heard on the radio this morning, and it just made me want to talk to you and to tell you that I love you," she replied.

At this, my heart melted and I was barely able to choke out, "Well, I love you too, Sweetie! Bunches!" And that was pretty much the end of the conversation.

I thanked the counselor for calling me and tried to make it through the rest of the day without bursting into tears as the conversation played itself over and over again in my mind. By the time I got home, my emotions had given way to curiosity and I wanted to know what song Haley had heard that had reminded her so much of me. While the kids jumped up and down on my bed, I changed out of my work clothes, still searching for an appropriate moment to broach the subject. When Buddy left the room to torment the cat for a while, I decided that this was my chance.

"Hey, Haley," I began. "What was that song you heard that affected you so?"

"You know," she answered. "It's the one we heard this morning. It sounds like this . . ." Haley hummed a conglomeration of notes that, though she was quite proud of them, pretty much sounded like nothing I could identify.

"Oh!" I said. "I'm not sure I know that song. Do you remember any of the words?"

"You are my hero!" she said. "Do you know the song I'm talking about, Mama? It's the one that asks if you ever knew that you're my hero, 'cause *you* are my hero!"

It was an amazingly powerful moment in my parenting journey, and I was blown away by her words. Not in a million years would I have ever thought that of myself. As Haley continued to explain to me how I was the one that always stood in the background and lifted her and her brother up so that they could succeed, I almost broke down in tears. Throughout the many years that followed, this has remained one of my outstanding memories, not only of being a parent but of my life.

In these last few weeks of the Surge, with my job set to autopilot and my home life in neutral, I was left in the undesirable position of not wanting to look forward and not wanting to focus too intently on the past. In the future, there was uncertainty, but in the past, there were memories that I was afraid would be all I had left. With nowhere else to turn, I found that I was spending more and more time musing over the simple truths of my life. For instance, as I looked back over the deployment, I could not help but feel that I had been truly blessed by my kids. Yes, Buddy was right there out front and had spent his time fighting for our country and the rights of others. But I also had a daughter, and she was absolutely amazing.

It might have been easy for some people to overlook the contributions of my daughter during the seemingly endless weeks of the Surge, but it wasn't for me. Somehow over the past twenty-four years, Haley had become the one person who knew me best, maybe even better than Nana or Buddy. Because of this, over the past fourteen months, Haley knew what to do to support me and to see me through it all. I looked back to January 2, 2007, and Haley was the one who found a way to bring her and her "family" to me. She was the one who opened the emails and answered the phone when I felt like I was not strong enough. She was the one who would cook dinner or suggest we eat out "as a family" when she realized that I was starting to ignore my own health. She was the one who would bring home a bottle of wine to share with me after a bad day, the one who would get up early even though she was working nights to watch soap operas in other languages so that we could distract ourselves by making up what they were saying, and the one who spent hours helping me write notes to soldiers and filling care packages to send to Buddy, the FHOTA, and the rest of the troops. Looking back over the deployment, I do not believe I could have made it without my daughter's support.

Even though both my kids have let me know that they still think the world of me despite the numerous times that I have screwed up, I had to wonder if they realized not just how much they meant to me, but also how much they have done for me. For many years, they have lifted me up. They have been my friends, my confidants, and my entertainers. They have helped me to laugh when I wanted to cry and have been my encouragement when I simply wanted to give up. They were the inspiration behind my strength to continue to "fight the good fight" and have been the secret to every one of my successes. My kids own my heart, and even more than that, they are my heroes, because beyond a shadow of a doubt, my kids have been, and always will be, the "wind beneath my wings."

No, seriously! Aren't we there yet?!

I felt like I was in limbo. I could no longer support Buddy, and therefore myself, with care packages, and I still did not have the slightest clue as to when exactly— or even approximately—he would be home. It was a heck of a place to be, given that I still could not claim patience and calm as personality traits.

I was a little edgy and was snapping at everything and everyone. It did not help that my temporary assignment was not the distraction I had hoped it would be. In fact, it only added to my agitation. Because of its location, the time I spent in my car for my commute was cut in half and it no longer involved a train ride. However, that did not prevent me from disparaging my fellow commuters who simply had the audacity to be ahead of me on the road. In addition, parking produced another bout of irritation, as did the monotonous nature of the job. Even worse, arriving back home in the evening did not reduce my ire.

To begin with, the Bear Cave was no longer the pristine retreat I was once able to keep. Though the word "pristine" might be a bit superfluous, my home was where I escaped to for rest and rejuvenation—as long as it was tidy. Beyond the fact that for several months I had lost my zeal for cleaning, I had managed to acquire Sergeant, who seemed to be compelled to mark his territory on every corner (or furniture leg) in the house. In addition, being that it was winter, there always seemed to be mud outside that the other two dogs happily tracked everywhere, completely oblivious to the mess they were making. Then there were Haley and Leo, who simply had a different definition of "lived in without being dirty." The only occupant that seemed to be able to maintain a level of cleanliness within the house was Shesha the cat, and even then I had to deal with her occasional hairballs. Something had to give, and most of the time, it was my composure.

In an attempt to prevent myself from turning into a constantly nagging shrew, I turned my focus inward and tried to ignore the chaos that engulfed my life. For someone like me who double- and triple-thought even the simplest decisions, to become even more reflective was saying something. An uncomplicated action like checking the time left me practically catatonic as I weighed the infinite number of intricate facets that surrounded the question of whether to check the time before I walked downstairs or after. Nonetheless, in that relatively suspended state, I was not able to bring my attention to the other less perplexing, but more aggravating, circumstances that surrounded me.

In addition to the various daily efforts that left me somewhat debilitated with indecisiveness, there were other musings that occupied my thoughts—mostly of my son. Since communication with Buddy was rare, if not nonexistent, I could not help but think back over the past several months of the deployment. Surprisingly, what I reflected on most were not the peaks and valleys of the deployment or the big events that all would recognize as significant. Instead, it was more like the ebb and flow of the daily grind of being the mother of a soldier. As a mother, there were many things about the previous several months that I knew my heart would always remember and would forever reduce me to tears, even if they were not carefully preserved in a journal.

Other memories, though, seemed to be more fleeting. I remembered times when my thoughts of Buddy as a boy would merge with those of Buddy as a man and soldier. Sometimes during our phone calls, when he was telling me a story regarding some event over there, it was difficult and a little distressing to see him in my mind's eye as anything but a six-year-old with a plastic squirt gun playing with his friends out in the backyard. Though periodically, these types of reflections would brazenly stomp through my consciousness, for the majority of the Surge, they lived in the shadows of my mind. And the funny thing was, it was these memories that seemed to have the greatest emotional impact during these final weeks as I waited for word of *exactly* when my boy would be heading home—though they did nothing to help my deteriorating disposition.

The beginning of the end

Nothing was ever easy in my life. It seemed as though nothing good could ever be anticipated or enjoyed without something bad to counterbalance it. I think that was why it had been so difficult in the weeks following the announcement of Buddy's upcoming redeployment.

Even though I had not heard anything officially—or unofficially, for that matter—I had heard enough through the rumor mill that I fully expected Buddy's arrival within the next couple of weeks. I knew that I needed to start preparing for my trip to Fort Bragg to greet his plane when it landed, but I was a little apprehensive about possibly jinxing the event. I did not want to begin collecting the required paraphernalia, such as champagne and cigars, and I still refused to pack a bag, but I did have rather lengthy discussions regarding tentative plans with the approximately dozen family and friends who were planning on showing up for Buddy's long-awaited return.

We batted around ideas for commemorative T-shirts and balloons and attempted to solidify extremely flexible suggestions for accommodations once we all arrived, depending on just how many were able to make the quest when the time came. Because of the number of people and the different directions that everyone would be coming from, we were all planning our own transportation to the event. Since Haley and Leo were spending some time in Florida, their plans were to stop at Fort Bragg on their way home, so I only had to worry about getting Nana and myself to the Green Ramp at the allotted time. It was going to be a great homecoming and I was psyched, but like I said before, nothing was ever easy in my life!

Heading into the week, it was quite clear that the Whiskey-Dog was just not feeling himself. We all first noticed that something was up several weeks back. We were in the family room watching TV and the big boy decided to come down and join us. Midway down the steps, Whiskey stopped and just stood there for a few moments, literally swaying back and forth. He then continued on down the stairs, but very slowly and gingerly as if he were in great pain.

"What was that?" Leo asked.

"I have no idea!" I replied. "He hasn't locked himself in the bathroom lately, has he?"

For all of his "talents," the one that got Whiskey into the most trouble was his ability to use his great big mouth to turn door knobs and open doors. The main reason this caused him grief was because his favorite door to open was that of the guest bathroom. The problem was that once he pushed the door open, he always felt the need to enter the room, and it was too small for such a big dog. The results were generally that as he tried to turn and exit the bathroom, he would accidentally shut the door. At that point, he would be trapped because he did not have the room to pull the door back open, so he would simply settle down and wait for someone to discover him. But because the room was so small, he inevitably ended up with a crick in his neck if he was not discovered in short order.

Once he reached the bottom of the steps, I called Whiskey over, and he bounded to me with such enthusiasm that we all quickly forgot his moment on the steps. But there was a second incident as well, equally uncharacteristic of the big boy and equally ignored. I was vacuuming, though not as enthusiastically as normal. Whiskey had taken one of his regular spots on the stone tile in the foyer. Normally, when I would turn the vacuum on, Whiskey would vacate the area; however, this time he refused to move. I figured he was just being stubborn, so I teased him a bit with the vacuum head as I moved it across the floor around and about him. Though the Whiskey-Dog would never, ever be aggressive, he let me know in no uncertain terms that he was not happy with being pestered. I was shocked and confused, but I let it go because I realized that I was the one out of line.

These episodes were brought back to mind during what should have been nothing more than a trivial, unimportant event. It was such a lovely day, I decided to take Whiskey and Sergeant for a walk. We had barely reached the end of the cul-de-sac when Whiskey decided he needed a rest. This was highly unusual, considering that this was normally the part of the walk where I needed to practically run to keep up with him. We tried to continue on, but after a few minutes it seemed like a hopeless cause. It was obvious that though Whiskey's heart was willing, his body just couldn't manage. I called the veterinarian the minute we arrived back home.

Normally, Whiskey loved to be in the car. On many occasions, if the car door was left open long enough for Whiskey to jump up into a seat, he would stay there until he got a ride, and after the ride, there was a fifty-fifty chance that he would refuse to leave the car. More than once, after a stern talking-to, I had left the Whiskey-Dog "to rot" after unsuccessfully coaxing him from the seat. If a 150-pound dog refuses to move voluntarily, it is quite possible that he will not be moved by force either. With my big boy feeling so poorly, I doubted he would be able to manage the step up into my SUV, and even if I got him into the car, I doubted I would be able to get him back out again, so I had the veterinarian come to my house instead.

I sat in the foyer on the tile floor with my beautiful Whiskey-Dog, his head resting on my knee. While we waited for the veterinarian to arrive, I scratched Whiskey behind his ears just like he liked. I looked down at Whiskey, and my heart sank a little. It finally seemed so apparent to me that something was seriously wrong. I could not help but wonder why I hadn't managed to see it before.

As all doctors do, the vet asked a bunch of questions as she examined Whiskey. In the course of the conversation, Whiskey's grand adventure came up. I explained that after spending three days in the fields with the cows, Whiskey was covered in ticks. Haley, Leo, and I removed about twenty-five of them before I decided it was a job for professionals. When I picked the dog back up, the groomers said that they probably removed an additional seventy-five ticks before they were through. When the vet heard all that, a light bulb went on above her head and she gave her diagnosis: Lyme disease. I was not even aware that dogs could get Lyme disease, but it all finally made sense. The veterinarian took a blood sample, prescribed a ton of antibiotics, and went on her way.

Though I knew that the disease could be horrible, I was glad to know what it was and that we were fighting it. Even so, I was a little dismayed that Whiskey was not responding faster to the medication. According to the vet, I just needed to be patient—*still* not something I could claim as one of my virtues. I was trying, but it was tough. I had hoped that by the time Buddy was on his way, Whiskey would be his old self again. However, looking at Whiskey, I found it hard to believe that was going to happen.

This was not the first time during the Surge that things in my life were not where I wanted them to be. I wanted only to be excited that Buddy would soon be home; I wanted to be happy and carefree and fully experience the exuberance of the times. Instead, I was feeling sadness and concern as well, and it was not just my worry for Whiskey. Over the past week, the FRG leader had been sending out information regarding the dangers of PTSD and the different symptoms to watch out for. I knew about the disorder and knew that it was something that needed to be closely monitored; however, I was hoping those types of serious subjects could have been put off for just a bit. I simply was not feeling what I thought I would be feeling by this point in time.

What I needed was a good dose of unbridled energy. I had plans to devise and preparations to gather. I was still trying to figure out what our "Welcome Home" sign should look like. For Buddy's first deployment, there were five of us on the Green Ramp, the hangar used for returning troops. Each of us had a poster board that we had decorated with markers and glitter paint. Each poster board had one of the letters in Buddy's name on one side and "Welcome Home Spc. Rogers" split between them on the other. As we waited for Buddy on the Green Ramp, we practiced holding up our signs and flipping between his name and the phrase. Of course, when the time came for us to "perform," Keith was all too happy to purposely screw up so that his sign was either upside-down or on the wrong side (such as "Wel U Home Spc. Rogers"). However, the effort was fun, occupied my energies sufficiently to help me stay sane as we waited, and definitely got Buddy's attention as he stood in formation before the troops were released.

For this deployment, I was drawing a complete blank. I tried to focus my creativity to come up with an idea—any idea—but then I would look at my Whiskey-Dog lying so sadly on the floor beside me and my heart would ache. Instantly, any thought that might have been forming simply vanished. I tried to think positive, to convince myself that it all was going to be OK so that I could get things done, but somehow there was a growing darkness in my heart that left me feeling very uneasy, and I could not tell whether it was because of Whiskey or some underlying premonition regarding Buddy.

No, I was sure it was just my nerves. I was sure that given just a little time, Whiskey would perk up, Buddy would be fine, and my lethargy would lift. No matter what else, I was sure it was going to be a great homecoming; I just needed to alleviate my apprehension and foreboding. If my life experiences were any indication, I knew this was probably going to take more time than I had before Buddy redeployed. However, I had always known that nothing in my life was ever easy!

Finally! The fat lady sang!

I t was a long time coming. Actually, it felt like an eternity, but the day was finally at hand: Buddy was coming home! I was beginning to feel some real excitement; Whiskey had just begun to perk up ever so slightly, and I had managed to devise and finalize a set of plans to appropriately celebrate Buddy's homecoming. In addition, the FRG leader had sent out word that our troops, specifically C-Company of 1-504th, were on standby for redeployment. She advised that we should sit tight and be patient. (It was almost irritating how many times that word and all its derivatives were being thrown in my face.)

After much discussion between Haley, Leo, Keith, and me, we had decided that each of the participants attending the redeployment festivities on the Green Ramp should carry enough balloons to spell out something along the lines of "Welcome Home Buddy." We had also determined that, since the balloons would have to be inflated at the last minute, the balloon-buying should be completed closer to the actual redeployment and maybe even once we arrived in Fayetteville. I had picked up a couple bottles of some real French champagne and a box of fine cigars for Victory Dances for Buddy and the rest of the FHOTA. And last, but certainly not least, I had completed a collection of celebratory T-shirts for all who would be in attendance, plus a few extras.

The T-shirts were a stroke of genius, if I do say so myself. On the front of the plain white T-shirts, I put the 504th's emblem surrounded by the words "WELCOME HOME." On the back, each shirt had one of a couple dozen "Buddy Facts." Buddy Facts were what Haley, Leo, various friends and family, and I came up with to describe Buddy. There were two parts to the Buddy Fact: the fact itself and the designation of the fact. For instance, my T-shirt said, "Buddy Fact #1: Mama's Boy." Nana's said, "Buddy Fact #XOXO: Our HERO." Haley's said, "Buddy Fact #150: Whiskey's Best Friend." There was also "Buddy Fact #82: Airborne," and "Buddy Fact #LII: Cookie Dough Aficionado."

Clearly, not everyone would be able to understand every Buddy Fact without an explanation, but we certainly would and, even more importantly, Buddy would. Our idea was that everyone in the welcome home party would choose a T-shirt and be wearing it on the Green Ramp. Any remaining T-shirts would be handed out to anyone else in the hangar who wanted one, since the fronts of the shirts applied to most everyone there. The hope was that as Buddy looked around the room, he would be confronted with Buddy Facts at every turn. Since it was only his family that knew him as "Buddy," I figured it was a great way to tease him a little without embarrassing him.

Everything was ready, although I had still not packed a bag. I knew that the chances of everything going exactly as planned were slim to none—but I had no idea how "off" the plans would actually be. The trickle of unofficial information that we had been receiving up to that point indicated our boys would be arriving sometime during the upcoming weekend. The size of our little armada to Fort Bragg all depended on which day Buddy landed, with the greatest number in attendance if Buddy redeployed on Saturday the fifteenth. It was Monday afternoon when Buddy called. "Hey, Mom! We're on our way!"

It had seemed like forever since I had heard my son's voice. "Buddy!" I exclaimed. "You've already left? Where are you? When are you due to be home?"

"We should be there Wednesday, sometime around 9:45 p.m.!" he answered.

"Wednesday? 9:45? Are you sure?!" I asked. "I haven't heard anything from the FRG leader. You're sure about this?"

"Mom!" Buddy declared. "Trust me! I know what I'm talking about!"

I was sure he did, but just the same, I tried to verify everything through the FRG leader. Her only comment was, "We have not heard anything official; however, you are not the first to have heard this from the soldiers."

This was just *not* supposed to happen this way—not even considering that we were dealing with the army. Then again, who cared? My son had just told me he was coming home, and nothing else mattered. But there were logistics to consider, not to mention that nothing was "official." If what Buddy said was true, and I certainly did not doubt him, our little welcoming committee had just been reduced from roughly a dozen to two. Obviously, there were not enough participants to pull off the balloon thing, so new plans needed to be made.

I discussed the situation with Nana, and we decided that it would be better to be down at Fort Bragg waiting than be up here, five hours away, and hear that the boys were due to land in two hours. Nana and I decided to leave early Wednesday morning to allow for all possible "contingencies," which left me just one day to get everything ready. I called down to Fayetteville to arrange for a room only to discover that I should have made those arrangements *much* earlier. I wanted a suite to accommodate as many as possible; what I ended up getting was a single room barely big enough for two. After room arrangements were made, I finally decided it was time to throw together a bag of clothes and toiletries. Through it all, the only thing I could think was, *What am I going to do to replace the balloons?*

There would only be two of us, and I had no idea what we could possibly do to make a statement on the Green Ramp. It did not have to be something big, but it needed to stand out enough so that Buddy could see it as he waited in formation. I considered my options and pondered various designs. Right in the middle of my contemplations, I was struck with inspiration! All I required were two poles, some black foam crafting sheets, some camouflage fabric, and glue.

On Tuesday morning, I called into both my temporary assignment and my regular office and let them know that I was out for the duration. I then set to work collecting everything I needed to make sure I was packed and ready to go by the time Nana showed up at my house the following morning. The Whiskey-Dog was not doing any better, but he was holding his own. Thank goodness my neighbors were willing—even happy—to care for him, even though it entailed all the additional attention to medicating. The only thing left to worry about was getting Nana and me to the Green Ramp for the now-10:30 p.m. arrival of the troops.

The minute Nana arrived on Wednesday morning, I piled all of our things into my car and we headed down the road. Our talk was rather limited for the long ride. I presumed that was because my mind was otherwise occupied with thoughts of the past—specifically those of the past year—and of the future. Though I contemplated both the immediate and the distant future, mostly I was concerned with the events of the day. To begin with, there was our ability to meet Buddy's plane on time. Nana and I left Northern Virginia by 9:00 in the morning. It was only, at the worst, a five-hour drive to Fayetteville and the Green Ramp, maybe five and a half. It would take something catastrophic to make us late, so for that I was at ease, even as I knocked on wood for good measure. What was less sure, but more immediate, was the matter of our "Welcome Home" sign that still needed to be constructed once we arrived at our hotel room.

The new concept for our sign was a relatively simple one. It had an arts and crafts edge that was reminiscent of our poster board sign from Buddy's first redeployment. As such, it kept me sufficiently busy and relatively sane for the six hours Nana and I had to kill before it was time to head to the base. We used the black foam sheets for lettering that said "Welcome Home Sgt. Rogers." Because the camouflage material we used was about six feet long, there was plenty of room for big bold lettering that would be readable from a distance. The letters were glued and stapled to the material, with pockets stapled along the left and right edges for the poles I had brought. I figured this would allow Nana and me to hold our sign up high enough that Buddy could see it, even if we had to stand at the back of the hangar behind hundreds of people!

Up until this point, all was going as planned—at least for the current plan. It was around 9:30 p.m. and Nana and I still had not heard any news, official or otherwise. Since there was no other information coming in, Nana and I decided it would be best to head to Fort Bragg and look for more information there. The base was only ten minutes away from where we were staying, but in a relatively uncharacteristic move by me, I decided that, if nothing else, it would be good to get to the Green Ramp a little early, just in case. We donned our "Welcome Home" T-shirts, packed the extra T-shirts and our sign into the car, and headed down the road.

In no time at all, we were pulling up to the Green Ramp. It was not even 10:00 yet, so I was expecting the parking lot to be relatively empty. Instead, there were soldiers all over the place, definitely more than I would have expected from the military's welcoming committee that is always present at these affairs. In addition, these soldiers were in full armor and carrying weapons—also not commonplace. I parked the car, opened the door, and gazed around at the commotion surrounding us. As my eyes adjusted to the dark, I began to pick out dozens of civilians meandering around the parking lot as well, children and adults alike. I stood up beside the car, my mind racing, trying to interpret what I was seeing. Unexpectedly, the moment overtook me. "Oh, Mama!" I cried. "We're too late! How could we be too late?" My agitation began to rise. "I did it all right! We got here early! We shouldn't be late! How can we be late?!"

My mom did not like it when I lost control. She had not seen it very often, but she had seen it enough to know that it was almost a Dr.-Jekyll-and-Mr.-Hyde event. "Just stay calm!" I remember her saying.

It was just about then that we heard "Taps" beginning to play over the Green Ramp loudspeaker. "Oh, Mama!" I said again, only this time much more subdued and tinged with pain.

"What's going on?" Nana asked.

"It's 'Taps,' Mama." I answered. "They're playing it to honor those who have not returned." My heart gave way to a combination of sorrow and gratitude. I bowed my head, but mostly to hide the tears welling up in my eyes. *Where is Buddy?* I silently cried out to the universe. *What's going on?*

Nana and I stood silently until "Taps" had finished. Immediately after the last note, though, we headed toward the hangar to find anyone who could tell us *anything* about C-Company and their whereabouts. Apparently, they were still somewhere over the Atlantic. They got held up in Germany, or England, or Iceland, or somewhere not here, and had yet to land back in the States. According to the sergeant we talked to, first they had to land in New York, and then they would be heading for Fort Bragg.

As far as all the combat-laden soldiers we were seeing, the tens of thousands of troops that made up the Surge could not return home on a single flight. What had never occurred to me before was that there was going to be a constant stream of flights all week, all carrying the soldiers returning from Iraq. We had a bit of a wait ahead of us because they were telling us that it would most likely be midnight before Buddy landed.

Reassured that we had not missed Buddy's flight and that we had at least a couple hours' wait ahead of us, Nana and I took a jaunt around the base looking for any place where we could pick up some snacks to amuse us during our long wait, only to discover that *nothing* was open past 9:00 on a Wednesday night at Fort Bragg. Failing in our quest for snacks, we returned to the Green Ramp. We found a suitable place in the hangar—not too close, and not too far away—and settled in for our long wait for Buddy.

It was not even 10:30, and if past experiences were anything to go by, the estimated midnight arrival of our boys was a long shot, at best. Nana and I passed the time with little chats and rounds of "I Spy," but mostly we just people-watched, though the pickings were rather slim for the activity. There were no other planes expected for the rest of the evening except for Buddy's. Most of the families that lived on base were staying at home and waiting there for word of the plane's arrival.

There was a steady trickle of people wandering in and finding a place on the hangar benches for the long wait for the arrival of our boys. A small group of young ladies took a seat next to Nana and me on our bench. We chatted with them a little to pass the time. They were meeting their boyfriends. I tried to coax them into wearing one of our extra Buddy Fact T-shirts, but apparently, some of troops returning were not from 504th but were from the 325th. The emblem on the front of the T-shirt did not represent the 325th, and the young ladies thought that wearing the emblem of the 504th would be insulting to their boyfriends.

My eyes were drawn toward a gentleman at the front entrance to the hangar. He was a little more well-groomed than the rest of us hanging out on the Green Ramp, but what gave him away as a newsman was his microphone with the ABC logo on it. At one point over the previous few weeks, I had joked with Haley that she should bring her news team with her to welcome her brother home. She gave me an emphatic "No!" but I already knew that it would have been a bad idea. I could imagine it would have been a bit unsettling for her to have to worry about professionalism when her brother was finally returning after serving almost fifteen months on the front lines. Nonetheless, I could not resist commenting on it.

"See, Mama?" I said to Nana as I pointed to the newsman. "Haley should have brought her news team here. She sure wouldn't have had much competition for the story, huh?"

"Maybe it's because Buddy's group is coming in so late," Nana offered as a possible reason for the lack of media present. "Maybe there are more news people here for the daytime returns."

"I guess," I said, but I really did not think so. I watched the news on a regular basis, and there was a distinct absence of reporting on the subject. Considering the amazing success of the Surge—and these boys *were* the Surge—I could not figure out why there would not have been representatives from every major news organization to record the event for generations to come. I was a little disappointed but not really surprised.

"We should go over and talk to him!" I asserted.

"*You* do it!" Nana teased back at me.

At first, I was hesitant to take Nana up on her challenge. After all, beyond what anyone saw in me at first glance—or even second glance—I was quite shy. However, once the young ladies next to us joined in, I felt almost compelled to at least give it a try.

I reached into the bag that Nana and I had brought and grabbed one of the extra T-shirts: "Buddy Fact #55: Speed Racer!" I walked over to the newscaster, introduced myself to him, and showed him first the "WELCOME HOME" front of the shirt and then the "Buddy Fact" back. I handed him the T-shirt and I asked, "Are you willing to wear this T-shirt to help me tease my son when he lands? If nothing else, the front shows your support of the troops!"

At the beginning, he was simply curious about the T-shirt. After I explained to him the significance of it, specifically the meaning of the Buddy Fact, referencing Buddy's infamous speeding ticket, he accepted the T-shirt but continued to ask questions. During the course of our conversation, he became enchanted with my mom.

"Do you mind if I ask how old she is?" he inquired.

"Eighty-six—no, eighty-seven years old now!" I exclaimed.

"Is she doing OK?" he asked. "I mean, how long have you two been sitting here?"

"Not that long," I replied. "The problem is that since we don't live around here, if we don't stick close to the Green Ramp, we might miss information and then miss my son's plane. But she's a trooper and is doing quite well."

"How is she to talk to?" he inquired.

"Huh?" I responded.

"I mean, does she understand what people are saying?"

"What?" I shot back. "She was born in America; she speaks English!"

"No!" he exclaimed. "I meant, does she comprehend her surroundings?"

I could not help but laugh. *Oh, this is rich*, I thought. *He's asking if Nana is coherent!* "You'd be surprised," I answered. "She's quite sharp!"

"Do you think she would mind talking with us?"

"Probably not; I can ask her, if you'd like."

I returned to Nana and told her about the newsman's request. "He wants to interview you, Mama!"

"Really?" she asked. "Why would he want to talk to me?"

"I don't know, Mama." I paused for a moment before adding, "At first, he just wanted to know if you were lucid!"

We both watched him a minute or two as he made his way around the hangar, a microphone in hand and his cameraman in tow behind him. He seemed to be making his way toward us, but in a very roundabout fashion. He talked to a few people before he stopped a young mother who was pushing a toddler in a stroller. We watched him first talk to the mom and then kneel down to talk to the toddler.

"But he was certainly enthralled by your presence here," I recounted. "Maybe he is going after an interview with the youngest in attendance and the oldest—I guess that would be you," I teased.

Eventually, the newsman did make his way over to us. I was more or less pushed aside as the camera started rolling and the interview began. It was OK, though; I was happy to watch Nana as she expertly handled the situation. The newsman asked Nana her name, asked if she minded giving her age, and asked how she was doing. Nana answered all questions confidently and without even a hint of shyness. He then spoke of our T-shirts and our sign, which was laid out on the benches between us because of the still-drying glue. Nana held up the corner of the sign and then glanced over to me. It was right then that my cell phone rang. I turned my back to the interview and answered the call.

"Mom, it's me!"

"Buddy!" I exclaimed. "Where are you? What's going on?"

"We just landed in New York!" he answered. "We still have to go through customs, so we are still a couple hours out. Who all is with you?"

"Well," I began, "if this was Friday night, there would have been about a dozen people here, but you're early. Keith, Haley, and Leo are still going to stop by over the weekend, but Nana is with me here, and right now she is being interviewed."

"Interviewed? By whom?" he asked.

I took a minute to explain it all. "If you have access to the Internet, try to find her on ABC news in Fayetteville while you wait to go through customs!" I kidded. But then I told him I needed to get back to the interview—at least watching it, anyway. I told him I loved him, and we said our good-byes.

The last words Buddy spoke to me were, "Remember, Mom, no tears!"

Yeah, right! If you asked any soldier what they asked of their moms in the same situation, they would say "No tears!" Now, if you asked the moms what their response was, they would blow a raspberry. I turned back to the interview just in time to hear what ended up being the last question.

"So," the newsman began, "what has it been like having your grandson serving in Iraq?"

"We just waited!" Nana smiled and shrugged her shoulders. Her answer was almost coy, but in that simple answer, I saw the amazing complexity of the last fifteen months. Perhaps the newsman did as well, because he thanked Nana for her time and the camera went dark.

Immediately, Nana began scolding me for not holding up the other side of the sign as she had indicated with her look. I defended myself by telling her about my phone call with Buddy. "It looks like it's going to be a longer evening than we had planned," I said. "I think Buddy's arrival by midnight is a long shot now."

Even though we knew we were looking at more than a couple hours of waiting, Nana and I continued to remain at the hangar for the duration. Though we were not getting many updates on when the boys were due to land, we knew that the time was getting close when the place began to fill up with people. We watched as a steady stream of friends and families of the troops filed into the huge room. The excitement and anticipation was plastered all over everyone's faces. Even the youngest among them—two-, three-, and four-year-olds—were caught up in the moment. They were not cranky or rambunctious, even though it was late. In fact, most were as quiet as little church mice as they waited patiently with the rest of us for their daddies to arrive.

A few of the people gathering actually recognized Nana from the 11:00 news. They came up to her and asked, "Didn't I see you on the news tonight?" They would then turn to me and exclaim, "Your mom is such a doll, a real star!" or something along those lines. They were not wrong.

The more crowded the hangar got, the more the excitement grew. Even though Nana and I had been there for hours, we found that butterflies were beginning to form in the pits of our stomachs. We were no longer isolated at our place on the benches. The young ladies that had taken a place to the right of us were still there, though they chatted among themselves as to whether they should try to get a little closer to the hangar door where the troops would be entering. In addition, along with the dozens who took a place on the benches in front of us and the dozens gathered behind us, a couple of young mothers with their kids took a place on the bench to the left of us. One of the women glanced at our sign and asked, "'Sgt. Rogers?' Would that be Sergeant Benjamin Rogers?" I nodded my head yes and she added, "I know that name; he's one of my husband's soldiers."

I could not read her face to determine if that was a good or bad thing, but I asked, "And your husband is . . . ?"

She told me he was Buddy's platoon sergeant. "Oh!" I replied. "That would be the one who demanded a second batch of my Lemon Zingers, right?" She looked a little confused, so I continued. "I'm Benjamin Rogers' mom. I sent a different recipe of cookies every week, and apparently your husband's favorite were the lemon cookies I sent over."

She and the other woman nodded their heads in acknowledgment as the second woman added, "That definitely sounds like him!"

In those final minutes while we waited for the soldiers, we pretty much kept to ourselves, as most everyone there did. It is an unusual experience to feel so connected to all the people around you—almost like a huge extended family—and yet feel so isolated in your own personal involvement. But finally, the announcement that our boys had landed came over the loudspeaker. The room erupted into cheers and applause. Everyone who was sitting, including Nana, rose to their feet and waited for the boys to come marching in.

It felt like an eternity, waiting those last few minutes to see our soldiers again. An army band had been playing in the corner of the hangar for the past several minutes, but we could no longer hear them over the din of excitement that had erupted on the Green Ramp. Many began to migrate to the area where the troops would be gathering in formation, but Nana and I stayed put, practicing holding our sign up as high as we could using our six-foot poles.

I stood eagerly waiting for my son, mostly lost in my own thoughts. I recall looking at that young mother standing beside me—Buddy's platoon sergeant's wife. She was waiting calmly, at least on the outside, maintaining the appropriate decorum for the wife of an army leader. I watched her as she held her young daughter, swaying back and forth ever so slightly; her son quietly stood on the bench in front of her, gently waving a small American flag. I was reflecting on that little family's composure when I heard someone yell out, "Here they come!"

Before I was totally distracted by the moment, I remember how alone I felt standing there by myself, separated from Nana by the six feet of our Welcome Home sign. I remember envying that young mother just a little because she had someone to hold on to after hearing the news that our wait was almost over. Despite the general pandemonium that was building on the Green Ramp, I remember hearing her say quietly into her daughter's ear, "Oh my! Mommy's knees are starting to feel weak!"

You ain't kidding, I thought as my throat began to tighten and my eyes filled with tears.

In the very few seconds that remained, I remember reflecting on the sheer fortitude that was demonstrated in that family's behavior and by almost every family there. I saw a combination of patience, strength, and endurance wrapped in the happiness of the occasion. In fact, the courage and resolve on the Green Ramp that day were as palpable as the anticipation. Though the joy was for the moment, I knew everything else was the culmination of fifteen long months of steadfastness and perseverance, with a dash of faith and a good deal of waiting thrown into the mix—waiting for a moment that was now just an angel's breath away—and then our boys marched through the doors.

A Whiskey Lullaby

For all the initial excitement of the day, it turned out to be a very long night. It was 2:30 a.m. when Buddy's plane finally landed and just about 2:45 by the time he and his company marched into the hangar. The boys stood in formation as the commander said a few words and the chaplain said a prayer. Shortly after that, the troops were released and Buddy made his way to come see us.

Was I thrilled to see him? Yes! Was I overwhelmed? Absolutely! Did I cry? Surprisingly enough, no, and I am not totally sure why.

The whole event somehow felt different to me. Perhaps it was simply Buddy's request that I contain myself. That would have been understandable, considering I realized that if I cried, Buddy would get "moved," and he also was a leader of soldiers who had a reputation to maintain. It was not likely that this was the reason for my lack of tears, considering they were all but flowing a few minutes earlier, but it was worth considering. Perhaps it was simply because I understood that God's strength saw us through it all, and God's strength gave me strength. A really awesome thought, but no—I did not think that was it, either. Perhaps it was the late hour and the amount of time I had to prepare for the moment, or perhaps it was simply an "all of the above" type of thing. But no matter what the reasoning, it did not alter the fact that seeing Buddy again was an emotional moment that encompassed a multitude of subtleties, including the juxtaposition of the homecoming of my son against all those who did not return—not to mention that off in the background, there was a sick Bernese Mountain Dog who was not having a speedy recovery, which I had not yet had the opportunity to tell my son about.

Despite my lack of tears, it was still great to see Buddy again, safe and sound and minus any infections from nasty spider bites, unlike his last redeployment when he came home with MRSA. Directly after Nana and I hugged him with all our might, silently thanking God for his safe return, the moment sank into a rather surreal conversation between the three of us, more like one that might occur if we were greeting my son after a ski weekend in Colorado.

"Hey, Sweetie! Did you have a good flight?" I asked.

"Better than when I was all doped up on Percocet!" he answered.

"Did you get a chance to sleep on the plane?" my mom chimed in.

"Not really, Nana."

"How 'bout food? Did they feed you on the plane? Are you hungry?" I asked, realizing that I could not do anything about it even if he was.

"No, not recently, but I'm not really hungry—"

"Hey, did you see our Welcome Home sign?" I asked.

"Yeah, I saw it. It's pretty good," he said, much to Nana's and my delight, but then proceeded on to another topic of conversation that I was hoping to avoid, at least for the immediate future. "Did you bring the Whiskey-Dog with you?" Buddy asked. "Is he waiting at the hotel room?"

"No, I didn't bring him this time. The room we have is a little small—"

"Yeah, I understand," Buddy said before I had the chance to finish the explanation. "He's probably better off being home for right now."

"Well, yes," I began in reply to his assertion, "but that's not all."

At that, I had Buddy's undivided attention. I took a deep breath and began to explain. I told him about all the ticks that were on Whiskey when he returned from his big adventure. I explained Whiskey's incident on the steps and how there were indications that something was wrong that we all managed to miss, and then I told him about the vet's visit to the house and the diagnosis of Lyme disease. "But he was doing a little better before we left for here," I added in an attempt to ease the moment, without really being convinced that I was telling the absolute truth.

I waited for a response and was rather surprised at Buddy's lack of reaction. *Maybe he didn't hear me right. I mean, it is rather noisy in this hangar*, I thought. *Maybe he didn't grasp the severity of what I just said.* I did not know what was going on in Buddy's head, but I also did not think that it was the time for further explanations. I stopped talking, and Buddy still didn't respond. It was obvious that he had been distracted by something. He was looking across the hangar, but I could not tell at what. "Is everything OK?" I asked, grateful for the diversion.

"I'm just looking for my soldiers," Buddy said. "We don't have that much time, and I don't want to be the last on the bus." When the soldiers depart from Iraq, they are still in possession of every weapon that was assigned to them—maybe not with any ammunition included, but still armed nonetheless. They are only given a short time to visit with family before they are boarded onto buses bound for the armory to turn in their weapons.

Buddy hoisted himself up onto the back of the benches where Nana and I were sitting earlier. From his elevated perch, he gazed around the Green Ramp looking for each of his charges. I watched him as he slowly turned. He was still in his ACUs with his battle knife strapped to one leg and his automatic rifle slung over his shoulder. In my mind, the only thing that was missing was his bulletproof body armor. The boy of my memories and the man that stood before me seemed miles apart but somehow felt perfectly connected as well.

While Buddy saw to his military duties, Nana and I chatted. There were other soldiers, the FHOTA and such, that I wanted to see to give a big hug and welcome them home, but even though it seemed like the perfect event for such an activity, it somehow did not feel like the perfect time. All the soldiers were wrapped in their own families, and given the short time they had to spend with them before they were carted off by the military again, it seemed inappropriate for me to interrupt their reunion. The commander had promised that the soldiers would be released for the weekend after their visit to the armory, but considering the previous sixty-three weeks and the short span of a weekend, it felt as though every moment with our soldiers was too precious to waste—or share.

It was now well after 3:00 a.m. Buddy had reverted to sergeant mode, and I realized that I needed to get Nana to bed, even though she insisted that she was not tired. I was beginning to feel the late hour, so I could not figure out how Nana was not. Buddy had disappeared for a moment to go do his military thing but was now heading back towards us. I met him halfway, out of Nana's earshot. "Hey, Bud," I began. "How long do you think it's going to take for you to finish at the armory?"

"I don't know," he said. "I have to make sure all my soldiers are taken care of, you know? Why do you ask?"

"Well, Nana has been up since early this morning—OK, *yesterday* morning! I'm just a little concerned for her," I explained. "If you try to make her go back to the hotel before everyone else is ready to leave, she'll balk at the idea! I know she'll claim that she's OK, and she probably is—"

"I'll handle this," Buddy interrupted, and then made a beeline for Nana. "Nana," he began. "We are going to be a while here. We all still have to turn in our weapons."

"I'm OK," Nana began, but Buddy would not let her finish.

"Listen," he said to Nana, "I still have to take care of my soldiers, and I know Mom is getting a little tired." He then turned to me and asked, "Did you bring my cell phone with you, Mom?" I nodded yes, and he held his hand out for it as he continued to explain to Nana. "I still have a bunch to do here. You and Mom go back to the hotel and try to get some sleep. I'll call you when I'm done. Mom can pick me up then." He then addressed me. "Is that OK with you?"

I was a bit stunned. This was not the awkward boy that I remembered from grade school years who was always looking for attention. This was a man—a soldier—who had seen more and done more than most of us could ever imagine. I handed Buddy his cell phone and told him to call me when he was finished with his duties. Beyond that, there was nothing else for me to do, so I collected Nana and my things and headed back to the hotel.

For all the time that I had spent at Fort Bragg for Buddy and in Fayetteville for my job, one would have thought I would have a better grasp on my bearings and my ability to find my way, but one would have been wrong. I got lost taking Nana back to our hotel and again driving back onto base to pick Buddy up two hours later. It took about an hour and several phone calls to Buddy to make that ten-minute drive from the hotel to Buddy's company headquarters. I thought I would never get there, but eventually we were all relaxing together in our cramped little hotel room. At last, it felt as though the deployment might finally be over!

As planned, Keith and his dog Gidget showed up on Friday. Haley, Leo, and the Marjorie-Dog did not show up until Saturday. For the most part, it was a quiet week-end of all six of us camping out in a room meant for two—at the very most four, and that doesn't include dogs—watching movies and just spending time together. It may have been cramped, but it was wonderful to have my family together again. But all too soon, the weekend was over and it was time to head home.

In a change from what I remembered from Buddy's first deployment, my son was not allowed to return with us when we left Fort Bragg for home after the redeploy-ment weekend. Then again, the 1-504th was gone only six months during Buddy's first deployment, and they were not in a combat situation. This time, the army intended to do what they could to keep a close eye on Buddy and the rest of the troops to make sure they were adjusting appropriately.

The army's primary concern was, of course, PTSD. The most comforting thing I had read about the condition was the assessment that support during the deployment and at the homecoming made a great deal of difference in the occurrence of the mal-ady. That was one area in which I felt confident that I had done everything I could for my son and the rest of the troops. And even though Buddy was not necessarily thrilled with the arrangement, I was comfortable with the army taking a little extra time to monitor our boys and provide the required social and psychological support in the aftermath of the deployment.

In the meantime, with Buddy being closely watched by the army and Haley, Leo, and Marjorie taking the long route home to visit Leo's parents on the way, Nana and I headed back to Northern Virginia. During our drive to Fort Bragg at the beginning of the week, the excitement and expectation in the car was almost palpable. During the drive home, that emotion was replaced with exhaustion. It had been a long weekend with only a little sleep, so after pulling into my driveway, Nana chose to immediately go home rather than come into the house with me. I put her bags in her car, gave her a big hug, thanked her for being a part of Buddy's homecoming, and told her I loved her. She drove off, and I, also feeling the effects of the weekend, slowly climbed back up my driveway and headed for my front door.

When I opened the door, I was a little surprised to find that Whiskey had joined Sergeant to greet me in the foyer—surprised but pleased. "Well hello, boys!" I greeted them. "How are you guys doing?" I avoided petting Sergeant right away because I had learned early on that if you touched him too soon after you walked through the door, he would get excited and pee on the floor, your foot, or whatever else was underneath him. I did, however, reach out and scratch Whiskey behind his ears, just like he liked. "How are you doing, big boy?" I asked. "Are you feeling any better?"

Whiskey came closer to me for a better scratch and began sniffing my clothes. I watched as his eyes brightened and his tail began to wag even faster. Even the corners of his mouth turned up like he was smiling at me. Immediately, he walked to the door and looked out, but there was no one else out there. Whiskey looked back at me, then out the front door and then back at me again. It was if he were asking, "Where is he? I know he's around somewhere, I can smell him! So where is he?!"

I walked over to the front door and shut it. Whiskey looked up at me with confusion. I scratched him behind his ears again and down his back. "Buddy's not home yet," I explained as if Whiskey understood every word I said. "The army wouldn't let him come home now, but he will be home soon."

Sergeant had also begun sniffing around my feet. I reached down and petted him on his little head only to find out that I did not wait quite long enough before touching him. I walked into the kitchen to get a paper towel to clean up the puddle, both dogs happily trailing behind me. I glanced down at their food bowls; both looked untouched. I looked back at my two boys. Whiskey and Sergeant were now sitting just inside the kitchen door, ears up, eyes bright, and mouths slightly open, panting, with their tongues hanging out to one side. I could not tell if Whiskey was actually doing better or just happy to see me and to smell Buddy, but, at least for the time being, he seemed to be holding his own.

I was sure that Whiskey had smelled Buddy. The biggest indication was that after I arrived back home, Whiskey began parking himself in the front foyer again, leaning up against the front door. This was where Whiskey always waited for my son. Whether he was coming home from school, a trip to the store, a night out, or, I guess, a deployment, whenever Buddy left for a period of time, it was Whiskey's standard operating procedure to wait for my son's return there. When he was not camped out in the foyer, I would find him in the dining room, his nose pressed up against the front-facing window between the slats of the blinds. It seemed obvious to me that he was looking for something—or someone. I would tell him, "Soon, Whiskey. Buddy will be home soon."

In the meantime, Buddy and the rest of his company were confined to the Fayetteville area, working half days that consisted mostly of debriefings, health seminars, and visits with military psychiatrists. The army's main focus was the early identification of any signs of PTSD. Buddy's main focus, however, was to get *all* the way home as soon as possible. Since the redeployment, I had been speaking with Buddy by phone almost daily. He was not satisfied with the army's endeavors and let me know it regularly in no uncertain terms. I was left trying to reason with someone who no longer considered the virtue of reason to be a positive thing. It was either that or the simple fact that once someone is ready to be home, there is no substitute for actually being home.

Two weeks past the redeployment weekend, the army decided that it was time to allow the returned troops a four-day pass. As always, Whiskey sensed Buddy's return before he even turned down our street. Ten minutes before Buddy arrived, Whiskey began standing in the front foyer staring at the front door, waiting for Buddy to walk through. By the time Buddy actually pulled into the driveway, Whiskey had been there long enough to attract the attention of Sergeant and Marjorie. And when Buddy finally opened the front door, he was immediately accosted by the three dogs.

Sergeant was curious as to who had just entered the house. Marjorie seemed happy when she saw it was Buddy but was quickly distracted by a bug that flew in when my son opened the door. Whiskey, though, was downright ecstatic at seeing his Buddy again. His tail was wagging so hard that it was shifting the whole back end of his body back and forth. Before my son was even completely through the front door, Whiskey began nuzzling into Buddy's legs, looking for Buddy to show him some attention. As sick as that dog had been, it was difficult to see any sign of it now. Buddy dropped his backpack there on the floor and fell to his knees. Whiskey immediately buried his big old head in Buddy's lap.

I was standing in the entryway to the foyer and was grateful to be able to witness the moment. The guy who was so adamant about me maintaining a stoic front for his return was a bit overwrought when he saw his Whiskey-Dog. Buddy began scratching Whiskey behind his ears and down his back, saying over and over again, "Hey, guy! How are you doing, boy? How are you doing?" In response, Whiskey tried to make himself small enough to crawl into Buddy's lap.

Buddy's voice slowly trailed off. His hand rubbed up and down Whiskey's side a couple more times and finally rested on his rib cage. He continued looking at Whiskey, whose head was still in his lap, his tail still wagging and his doggy smile clearly visible from where I was standing. Buddy continued to stare at Whiskey for a moment and then looked up at me, his eyes glistening a bit. "He's lost so much weight, Mom!" Buddy said, his voice tight with emotion and concern.

Buddy was right. At first, the weight loss helped Whiskey look healthier because he always was a little heavier than he should have been. But as he continued to refuse to eat normally, I became concerned regarding his overall well-being. The veterinarian told me that the antibiotics we were giving Whiskey were very strong and could affect his desire for food, but somehow I was not convinced that was all. In addition, I was told that the weekend Buddy was home should have been just about the point in the antibiotic regime that Whiskey's condition would start to improve. Though Whiskey did perk up a bit to have Buddy back home again, it did not last.

That moment in the foyer was probably the last good moment that Whiskey had. Buddy eventually stood up and Whiskey went into the kitchen and ate every last bit of kibble in his food bowl. He then spent a few minutes in the backyard with Marjorie and Sergeant, after which he came inside and laid down on the cool tile floor in the laundry room. Buddy was in and out all weekend long meeting up with friends and family, but Whiskey never made it back upstairs to wait for Buddy at the front door. In fact, Whiskey's decline past that day was meteoric.

It was only a few days after Buddy returned to Fort Bragg that I was unable to find Whiskey after I came home from work. He was not in the laundry room where he had been camping out for the past few days nor in any other room of the house. I even checked the guest bathroom, but to no avail. I called for him, even though I did not think he would be able to come even if he heard me. I went into the backyard to see if he was there and saw him lying on the ground just off to the side of the deck. My heart sank. I walked over to him and knelt down beside him. He did not move. I gently touched his head. "Oh, Whiskey!" I said softly.

At the touch of my hand, Whiskey lifted his head. Though he was looking in my direction, he did not seem to see me. "Oh, Whiskey!" I said again as tears filled my eyes. I rested his head on my lap and continued to gently pet him as tears streamed down my face. "Oh, my sweet boy," I quietly begged. "Please don't do this . . . please be OK." But I knew he was *not* OK. In my heart, I knew that whatever it was, it was bad, and I just couldn't face the realities of the situation.

When Haley got home that evening, I asked her help in getting Whiskey to the emergency veterinarian. I had already called them and let them know we would be coming, but because my SUV was too high off the ground for Whiskey to step into, I was counting on using Haley's little Saturn. I was actually hoping she would be OK with taking him alone. I knew I was asking a lot of my daughter, but it was all just too much for me to handle. I put Whiskey's leash on him, and he actually seemed to perk up at the idea he was getting a walk, though he was not able to walk very far. When Whiskey got to Haley's car, he was all too happy to get in. Before I closed the car door, I scratched his ears, kissed the top of his head and told him that I loved him, as if that dog could understand every word I said. My last memory of Whiskey was of him lying on Haley's back seat, head raised, ears up, and the corners of his mouth turned up into his doggy smile.

It was about an hour after they left that I got the phone call. Whiskey was, indeed, most likely blind. What started as Lyme disease ended up as cancer. Haley handed the phone to the veterinarian to let her explain our options. It seemed the most we could do for him was to try to make him "as comfortable as possible" for his remaining, not years, but months or even weeks. I asked the vet to put my daughter back on the phone. "You'll need to give her a moment; she's collecting herself," the vet said.

With Haley at the emergency room on my house phone and Buddy at Fort Bragg on my cell phone, we came to the tear-filled family decision to let Whiskey go. Haley was hesitant at first but stayed with Whiskey to the very end. I was glad she was able to do what I could not, because I simply was not strong enough. She then made all the arrangements to have Whiskey's remains sent back to us after he was cremated. When she finally made it back home, she brought two glasses and a bottle of wine to the family room where I was sitting on the couch. She put the glasses and wine on the coffee table and sat down on the couch next to me. She looked me square in my puffy, bloodshot eyes and said, "This is going to be hard."

Haley then took my hand, opened it, and placed Whiskey's collar and dog tag in it. Whatever composure I had left was gone, as was our big, dumb, beautiful Whiskey-Dog.

It's not over till it's over!

The house seemed intolerable without the Whiskey-Dog lumbering about in it. I thought I would never get used to the unbearable emptiness, but more than that, I felt I had been wronged, gypped. When Buddy and I originally researched the breed, we learned that an owner could generally expect three puppy years, three adulthood years, and three geriatric years—anything past that was a gift. Whiskey was only six and a half years old. We should have had another two and a half years, but disease had stolen that from us.

In the days and weeks following Whiskey's death, I was angry. I was angry at breeders for their arrogant attempts at restricting the gene pool and propagating the cancer. I was angry at the ticks for originally making Whiskey sick. I was angry at myself for not doing more when I possibly could have, let alone not having the courage to be with Whiskey in his final moments. Basically, I was angry at life in general, and so were we all. Even though most people were aware that this was a natural part of the grieving process, they might not have understood that this was also a symptom of PTSD.

As any mother of a soldier will tell you, there are many pitfalls facing someone returning from a war zone, and I would guess that PTSD is at the top of that list. However, PTSD is not just a military thing; it can affect all who have endured tense and grievous situations, including mothers whose sons have served on the front lines of a war.

Anyone with experience regarding PTSD will confirm that anger is one of the prevalent symptoms—the problem being that the anger is not always focused or predictable nor does it further the recovery process. Instead, it tends to be a subtle rage at some times and overwhelming at others, directed at anything or anyone at any time. However, our family's anger had a focus. It was not random, and it was not something that we could not understand; it was the result of Whiskey's untimely death. And even if our anger was the result of PTSD, because it had direction, it was predictable, even expected—and therefore seemed somehow finite and controllable. Somehow, it made it seem like it was possible for it all to be OK again—PTSD or not.

For us at the Bear Cave, life did continue, but I was concerned that life would never be "normal" again. It seemed it was impossible to put all the events of the past sixty-three weeks and their aftermath completely behind us. No matter how normal we were acting on the outside, on the inside, there was an unrelenting emptiness that would not ease. I was especially worried about Buddy, for whom it was that much harder to move past it all, both mentally and emotionally.

Years ago, after Haley and Buddy had gone to bed in the evening and before I headed to bed myself, I would always take a moment to go into their rooms and kiss them goodnight as they slept. About a month or so after Buddy's redeployment, he was managing to get home just about every other weekend, and it had me revisiting those motherly feelings that had me checking on Buddy as he slept, even though most of the time, I was checking on him in the morning before I headed to the kitchen for my tea. One Friday evening, after Buddy had returned home from Fort Bragg for the weekend, he decided not to go out for the evening but instead just headed to his room. A few hours later, I paused at Buddy's room on my way to bed. He was in his bed, sound asleep. A deep gratitude to have him back home safe and sound stirred my heart and I walked over to the edge of his bed and leaned over to kiss him good-night. I do not remember if I actually touched his forehead, or whether he just sensed something close to him as he slept, but he woke up swinging. Before he realized it was me, I had taken a hit to the jaw and the forehead. "Oh, Mom! I am so sorry, but *never* sneak up on me like that!" Buddy said when he saw it was me.

"I didn't think I was sneaking!" I shot back, my jaw stinging a bit from the encounter. But there was a subtle lesson to be learned—Buddy had not totally returned from the Surge, and I could not help but wonder if he ever would.

There are specific recurring dreams and nightmares that a soldier might have after returning from a war zone. To me, these dreams simply exemplify the soldier's internal struggle to assimilate what had been with what will be as the soldier moves forward. In the first few weeks after Buddy redeployed, he did have one or two of those types of dreams, but after Whiskey's death, that all changed. All of a sudden, his dreams were about a big, dumb dog named Whiskey—his dog.

I remember, on one occasion, I took a phone call from Buddy in the middle of the night. He had a dream that had upset him deeply. In the dream, Whiskey was lying near the driveway on the grass in the front yard as he used to do all the time. Buddy had seen him there and called to him to come, but the dog ignored him. Buddy called to Whiskey a few more times as he walked toward him, but as he drew close, he remembered that the dog had died. Whiskey vanished and Buddy woke up crying.

But even Buddy's Whiskey dreams were relatively short lived. It was now June, and it had been just about four months since Buddy's homecoming. The 1-504th was finally granted their block leave. This is when the army lets the major portion of a unit go on leave at the same time and is generally given following deployments and for periods as long as thirty days. Buddy had been home for less than a week when he had another Whiskey dream, but this one was different.

It was early in the morning, much too early for Buddy to have been awake yet, and I was in the family room drinking my morning tea and watching some news—an activity that had become much less stressful since Buddy had returned. I was a little surprised to see Buddy walk down the steps and join me on the couch.

"Well hey, Sweetie. Good morning!" I began. "It's a little early for you; what's going on?"

Buddy looked at me for a few seconds, then down at his feet. "I had another dream," he finally said without looking up.

"Bad dream?" I asked.

"Sort of . . . well, I guess really no . . . oh, I don't know!" he replied. "It was a dream about Whiskey, but this one was different, and I didn't wake up sad."

He fell silent. I waited for a short bit for him to continue, but he seemed to have slipped deep into thought. After a few seconds, I interrupted his contemplation and asked, "Do you want to talk about it? I mean, you know, what was the dream about?"

Still staring down in the direction of his feet, Buddy began describing his dream that not only included the Whiskey-Dog but also my dad and Sgt. Raybon. He told me how he walked into a room and the two were sitting in two big comfy chairs with the Whiskey-Dog lying on the floor at their feet. Buddy would not share the exact conversations that he had with the others in his dream, but he did talk in great detail about the Whiskey-Dog. He described how the dog nuzzled him and buried his big old head in Buddy's lap, just as we had known Whiskey to do throughout his life. Buddy finally looked up at me, a single tear falling down his cheek. "They're all OK, Mom," he said. "I don't have to be sad or angry because they are all doing just fine. They are content where they are, so I should be happy for them!" Almost as an afterthought, he added, "I just need to find a bit of happy for myself now."

For my family, it seemed as though the healing had begun, and not just for our sorrow. It remained rather curious to me that when it came to recovering from the stress and anguish of the Surge, Whiskey's passing seemed to mark the beginning of the process. I could not help but wonder if Whiskey, on some cosmic level, knew that this would be the case. I think Leo put it best when he compared it to watching a movie when you knew that someone was about to get shot. At the very last second, the hero jumps in front of the speeding bullet and loses his life for the benefit of those he loved and left behind. In the last scenes of the movie, it always seemed as though the hero's demise inevitably marked a new beginning for those who continued on— and that was the result of Whiskey's final sacrifice for us.

At the Bear Cave, things were finally beginning to return to normal, but at an ever-so-gradual pace. Life was once again beginning to feel routine and common- place, but it was not until the family trip to Disney World that our lives actually slipped back into being an everyday type of ordinary.

It was during the last month of Buddy's deployment that he decided he wanted to do something for his family, specifically for me. There were a couple of cryptic phone calls during which Buddy tried to decipher what I might want to do for a family vacation, but eventually he decided that nothing would equal a trip to Disney World. It seemed appropriate to me as well—like something you might see in a commercial on TV: "Hey! You've just won the battle and made the world a safer place! What are you going to do now?"

For the response, Buddy would be there in his full battle gear—with a dirt- smudged face and a sweaty brow—saying, "Well, me and my family? We're going to Disney World!"

Buddy had arranged for a week at the Animal Kingdom Resort with unlimited tickets to the various parks. Haley chipped in with the airfare, and it only seemed fair that all other expenses—food, souvenirs, and such—would be mine. All in all, it was a marvelous time.

We played at the various parks from sunup until sundown and beyond. Somehow, the parks that were geared to the young, or at least the young at heart—some might even say the chronically immature—seemed to give us the most joy. In fact, we never made it to the adult-geared Epcot even once, but we did hit a couple of the other parks twice. When we had exhausted ourselves, we headed back to our room where we sat on our balcony and watched the wild animals, mostly from the African plains, roam in their "natural" habitats or amused ourselves with a game of cards or some other family activity. There was lots of talking and lots of laughing, and with every passing hour, I could feel the tension that had been my constant companion for the past year and a half slowly melt away.

As wonderful as all that was, it was something more subtle, even common- place, that caught my attention and settled in my heart. It all began with a family discussion on what activities were a must and in what order they should be enjoyed.

We had only been at Disney World for a couple of days, but in our enthusiasm for being at the resort, we had been trying to cram every activity we could think of into every moment. We were exhausting ourselves, and not unlike other families, once we headed into "meltdown" mode, we were disagreeable, to say the very least. This particular meltdown began with Buddy stating his interests. "There is only one thing that I absolutely want to do while we are here, and that is to see the auto show. The next showing is at 3:40. I think since it is after 3:00 now, we should head over in that direction to get into line."

"But that's still over a half hour away," Haley responded. "I really want to see the 3-D Muppet Movie. It starts in a few minutes and finishes before the start of the auto show. We'll have plenty of time to get there after the movie."

"But that's in the opposite direction of the track!" Buddy objected. "We'll miss the beginning of my show!"

"Oh, come on, Bud. If anything, we'll miss only a few minutes of it. What's the big deal?"

"What's the big deal?!" Buddy demanded. It was obvious the conversation was escalating at a rapid pace. Leo had walked away to smoke a cigarette and remove himself from the line of fire. I tried to defuse the situation but realized that I was only making things worse, so I backed off. The whole thing ended with Haley accusing Buddy of being selfish and Buddy responding by calling Haley a "female dog."

The argument had only lasted a couple of minutes, but it was significant. From the moment Haley and I met up with Buddy at Fort Bragg to see him off at the beginning of the Surge, life had seemed fragile and constantly in the balance. Though Buddy and Haley were a typical brother and sister that could get into it at the drop of a hat, they would also stand between their sibling and the rest of the world to protect the other. For the past year and a half, this altercation would no more have happened than a round trip to the moon. The fact that it did happen meant everything was finally returning to the way things were—the Surge was finally being put behind us. We attempted to compromise—seeing the Muppet movie and then leaving early to catch the auto show—but that just screwed up both activities, so everyone was unhappy. At least it was equal unhappiness!

By midweek, we were ready to go our separate ways for the day. Haley and Leo decided to hit one of the water parks, and Buddy was able to meet up with Toby, who lived reasonably close to the resort, for a trip to the closest beach only an hour or so away. While the kids were off playing with water, I stayed back at the hotel and simply relaxed. I grabbed my journal, which I had not written in for months, found a balcony in the hotel that overlooked the largest collection of wild animals, and pondered life in general.

I spied a couple of giraffes using their freakishly long blue tongues to grab the leaves off of the trees that were just outside the balcony where I was sitting. Fascinated by the spectacle, I watched the giraffes for several minutes before, eventually, my mind began to wander—aimlessly at first but ultimately focusing on how far we had come since January 2, 2007. It struck me how during the deployment, just as Buddy did what he needed to do to survive, so did the rest of us. Every day we steeled ourselves against all possibilities and made sure we were prepared—though not necessarily ready—to face whatever life brought forward. It was as if we were numbed by a surrounding haze that kept our senses slightly dulled in an attempt to keep anything that might happen somehow separated from us. What surprised me was just how long it had taken for that haze to begin to lift.

Even as I contemplated the various possible reasons that a giraffe might have a blue tongue, I could sense that anesthetic fog evaporating from around me, and it was exhilarating. I could feel my emotions reawaken deep from within—emotions that I had almost forgotten existed. Given my newly reacquired awareness, I wanted to use my alone time on that balcony to record my final thoughts regarding my son's deployment, my family, and my life. However, even by that point, the events of the past couple years seemed a bit foreign to me—almost dreamlike.

I could tell that it was going to be a hot day. Even though my seat on the balcony was in the shade, it was starting to feel like a seat in a sauna. I could see a storm brewing way off in the distance, but it was too far away to worry about. In fact, that balcony felt light-years away from any worry—especially the worries of the Surge. I looked down at the blank page, my pen poised to record my final thoughts. *Where to start?*

It occurred to me that a review in the form of a relatively detached look back at the events of the Surge might be a good place to start, but it did not take long for me to realize that I would never be able to unbiasedly scrutinize this period in my life. For even as I fretted over Buddy's well-being—concerning myself with the effects of his intimate involvement with the Surge and PTSD—I had my own healing to attend to. And even though ringing phones or doorbells no longer caused my blood to run cold, even though my emotions were exploding as the worries of the Surge were fading, I was still finding it difficult to separate myself, even partially, from the experiences of the past year and a half. While my son fought on the front lines of war, I sat safely at home, baked cookies, and concerned myself with paratrooping bunnies and Wiffle balls. Somehow, to me, it all just seemed a bit lopsided and unfair. *Where to start?* I thought again. Despite my desire to record my final thoughts of the Surge, no final thoughts ever materialized that day.

It was that evening, compliments of a story told by Toby, that I learned something I did not fully understand before: the full impact of my involvement with the Surge through my care packages to Buddy. After everyone had returned from their adventures, we all headed out for a bite to eat. Gathered around the dinner table at a local seafood place, we each took turns recounting our days. The funny thing was, no matter how the stories started, they all ended with Buddy and Toby sharing a memory from their days in Iraq. All of the memories they shared were lighthearted and carefree and absolutely belied the danger they faced every day, but their ability to see beyond the ugliness of war was greatly appreciated by the rest of us, not to mention that they left us laughing uncontrollably. But there was one story that caught my attention for a relatively subtle reason.

At the prompting of our server, the conversation had taken a detour to desserts, which inevitably lead to a discussion of cookies—specifically, my cookies. Once the subject was broached, I could not resist asking, "So, Toby, which cookie was your favorite?"

"Those filled cookies you sent," Toby answered without hesitation.

"Cake Batter cookies!" Buddy chimed in.

"Yeah! Those were the ones! Not that we ever got very many of them!"

"Huh?" I asked. "I must have sent at least three batches of those things. Surely Buddy shared them?" I said as I turned my gaze to Buddy, trying to make it a glare.

Buddy looked a bit sheepish but said nothing. Toby, however, had another story to relay. "Even from the first batch you sent, your son hoarded those things!" he began. "I had just come in from outside the wire and had stopped by your son's room to say hi. When I got to his door, he was at his locker with his back to me. I asked him, 'Hey, BJ! What's up?' That idiot had the nerve to turn around with his face stuffed full of cookies and say, 'Dathang!'" As Toby said this last word, his face was all puffed out like his mouth was full of cookies as he attempted to say the word "nothing."

Buddy broke his silence. "Hey! I gave you a—well, a half of one of them! But you just couldn't keep your mouth shut, could you?!"

"Your mom had sent one of her care packages!" Toby shot back at my son. "I just couldn't believe that you weren't sharing it! How selfish was that?!"

By now we were all laughing, but the story had resonated with me. Reading a bit between the lines, what I learned was that my care packages made a difference. I learned that even though our individual efforts might have been lopsided, the pursuit of paratrooping bunnies and Wiffle balls was a worthwhile endeavor. I had already read that support for our soldiers was paramount to a soldier's successful reacclimation into society, but I learned that it was true. What I found in Toby's story was a dash of pride in my modest efforts to show the troops that I care, and what I heard in his story was "Thank you."

Basically, Toby's story had given me a sort of peace that was reinforced by a string of Buddy's comrades-in-arms. After returning from Disney World, several of the soldiers with whom Buddy had shared his care packages stopped by the house on the way to and from Fort Bragg. Buddy would always call me to the foyer to meet them. After the introduction, instead of the standard "Hey! How's it going?" or a handshake, I would get these warm, wonderful hugs—most of the time with the words, "Thank you so much for everything!" At times, it was overwhelming. However, I was always left with the unmistakable feeling that though it might not have seemed like much to me, I was able to do something for these guys that somehow made a difference, and that gave me peace.

Over the course of the Surge and beyond, I had heard the War on Terror compared to World War II as well as Vietnam. In fact, I had done so myself on occasion. But the reality seemed to be that they were as different as they were the same. Two began with an attack on US soil, but past that, those two conflicts began to diverge. Two lost public support along the way, but past that, those two conflicts began to diverge. I would submit that the constant between them all was the troops and their families. These were the ones who bore the brunt of it all, most of them honorably and with courage. In World War II, this included virtually all Americans, whereas during the War on Terror, that group had been reduced to around one percent of the population; Vietnam was somewhere in between.

The point is that it was a little harder to allow your opinion to be swayed by the nightly news, a movie, or a celebrity when it was your son or daughter, father or mother, or brother or sister who was trying to survive in a hellhole halfway around the world. In fact, if you were someone in that one percent, you might have found yourself willing to throw down over your opinions regarding even the smallest nuances of the conflict. However, over the past several months of the Surge, I had discovered that not everyone in the ninety-nine percent was swayed by public opinion, and that gave me hope.

I sat in solitude, accompanied only by my slightly hyper Sergeant-Dog, reflecting on the almost two years since our Christmas at Fort Bragg in 2006. It was difficult to articulate what was in my heart. It seemed all too easy to become overly reflective, but I needed to at least try to be succinct—for once in my life. I was grateful that my son had made it back safely and remained the "boy" I had always known. I knew that this was not the case for far too many families, and for those families, my heart broke. I continued to remain grateful to all who served, and continued to pray for them every day, especially for all those still in harm's way. And I was grateful for my family who, in my opinion, was the greatest family in the world! But here, at what finally felt like the end of Buddy's deployment, I knew just one thing for certain: no matter what the politicians, Hollywood, CNN, NBC, or even Fox News had to say, I would always view the Surge—and any other conflict in which our troops were committed—through the eyes of those who served with honor, and I was happy to admit that I could never see that changing.

Afterword

Buddy is now a warrant officer in the army. He lives with his wife and two children and continues to serve and protect.

Haley and Leo eventually moved out and spent a few years having an adventure or two of their own. They are now married and live in a small town in central Virginia. Haley continues to work with the news, but she would rather tend bar.

Nana is now in her nineties and is still going strong.

Keith still lives in the area and is also married. He and his wife have just welcomed their second child.

And Maggie?

She still enjoys baking cookies and vacuuming . . . and continues to chase after Sergeant every time he manages to jump the fence or escape the confines of the house.

Acknowledgments

This book could never have been written without the dedication and courage of those who serve. Despite the hardships and sacrifices of our troops and their families, they continue to write that "blank check" that can be cashed up to and including their lives. It is a mind-boggling concept that always humbles me.

I would like to thank my family and friends whom I have leaned on tremendously, not only during my son's deployments but also during my efforts to pull this book together. I thank my first-draft readers for their tough but honest feedback, without which this book would not have its heart and soul—instead, it would be a collection of dry facts and hollow stories. It is not easy to bare your soul and lay your feelings wide open for the world to judge, but given your help, I believe this story is now worth reading.

I am also grateful to Familius Publishing for not only taking the risk of publishing this first-time author but also in publishing the other side of the story when it comes to our troops, their families, and the Surge. I especially thank my editor, Katie, for her tireless dedication to the story and her endless patience with my questions and concerns.

Finally, I want to thank Nana and my kids. You are my support, my stability, and my sanctuary. You are my inspiration and my encouragement, and I am so blessed to have you in my life. Without you, this book would not exist.

About the Author

MAGGIE McCREATH is a single mom with two grown kids. She received a degree in Computer Science from George Mason University, and has worked in the field for over thirty years. Her life has always revolved around her family. Her kids began as her pride and joy, and have grown into her best friends and confidants.

Though Maggie's interest in the military strengthened with her son's enlistment, her fondness for the military and those who serve began years earlier. Her father served during World War II, and she has spent a large portion of her adult life in direct support of the military. This includes the fifteen years she worked for the Joint Staff at the Pentagon, with an additional five years working for the Pentagon at an off-site facility. On September 11, 2001, though Maggie was not at the Pentagon, she was at an off-site location working in direct support of its mission. The events of 9/11 not only catapulted her to the position she holds now, but have undoubtedly shaped her family's lives as well.

About Familius

Visit Our Website: www.familius.com

Join Our Family: There are lots of ways to connect with us! Subscribe to our newsletters at www.familius.com to receive uplifting daily inspiration, essays from our Pater Familius, a free ebook every month, and the first word on special discounts and Familius news.

Get Bulk Discounts: If you feel a few friends and family might benefit from what you've read, let us know and we'll be happy to provide you with quantity discounts. Simply email us at orders@familius.com.

CONNECT:
   www.facebook.com/paterfamilius
   @familiustalk, @paterfamilius1
   www.pinterest.com/familius

FAMILIUS

The most important work you ever do will be within the walls of your own home.

Lightning Source UK Ltd.
Milton Keynes UK
UKOW01f0014300416

273265UK00002B/24/P

9 781942 934363